This Book
belongs to the Proprietors
Of the Town of Lunenburgh, for
the Gift of Mr. William Clark
Of Boston, Mercht. March 24.
Anno Domini 1730

The Proprietors' Records
of the
Town of Lunenburg
Massachusetts

INCLUDING
FITCHBURG AND
A PORTION OF ASHBY

1729-1833

Being a Complete Transcript of the Proprietors' Records as Preserved in a Volume Owned by the Town of Lunenburg, and Given by William Clark, Esq., of Boston, Merchant, March 24, 1730

Compiled by
Walter A. Davis
City Clerk

HERITAGE BOOKS
2008

HERITAGE BOOKS
AN IMPRINT OF HERITAGE BOOKS, INC.

Books, CDs, and more—Worldwide

For our listing of thousands of titles see our website
at
www.HeritageBooks.com

A Facsimile Reprint
Published 2008 by
HERITAGE BOOKS, INC.
Publishing Division
100 Railroad Ave. #104
Westminster, Maryland 21157

Originally published by authority of the city council:
Sentinel Printing Company
Fitchburg
1897

— Publisher's Notice —
In reprints such as this, it is often not possible to remove blemishes from the original. We feel the contents of this book warrant its reissue despite these blemishes and hope you will agree and read it with pleasure.

International Standard Book Numbers
Paperbound: 978-0-7884-1456-5
Clothbound: 978-0-7884-7458-3

CITY OF FITCHBURG, MASS.

IN CITY COUNCIL, Feb. 18, 1896.

The joint standing committee on printing, to whom was referred so much of the recommendations contained in the Mayor's inaugural as relates to the appropriation of eight hundred dollars ($800) for completing the old town records, have attended to the business committed to them, and present the following report, and would recommend that eight hundred dollars ($800) be appropriated for the same, said sum to include the expense of copying and of printing and binding two hundred copies, and the expense of the same to be charged to incidentals.

HENRY F. ROCKWELL, *Committee*
CHARLES H. BLOOD, *on*
FRANK C. HOYT, *Printing.*

IN BOARD OF ALDERMEN, Feb. 18, 1896.
Report read and accepted. Sent down for concurrence.
WALTER A. DAVIS, *Clerk.*

IN COMMON COUNCIL, Feb. 18, 1896.
Read and accepted. In concurrence.
FRANCIS MCMURRAY, *Clerk.*

MAYOR'S OFFICE, FITCHBURG, MASS., Feb. 19, 1896.
Approved.
HENRY F. ROCKWELL, *Mayor.*

A true copy. Attest:
WALTER A. DAVIS, *City Clerk.*

CITY CLERK'S OFFICE,
FITCHBURG, MASS., April, 1897.

Previous to the incorporation of this town, under the name of Fitchburg, in 1764, it formed a part of Lunenburg.

To begin, then, at the beginning, and acquire a knowledge of our origin, it is necessary to search into the early records of Lunenburg, in the transactions and events of which town the people who inhabited what is now Fitchburg had an equal interest and an equal share.

In Whitney's "History of Worcester County," the account of Lunenburg commences as follows:

"On the 4th of November, 1719, the General Court, at the request of a number of gentlemen, made a grant to them of this territory for a valuable consideration," etc. Who these "gentlemen" were is not known, but it is presumed they were among those whose names are preserved in the proprietors' books as the earliest settlers. The "valuable consideration" above mentioned will be made known by the terms of the grant.

Furthermore, this order, or grant of the General Court, is of great importance, for it is not only the foundation of our municipal rights, but it is the basis upon which rest all the titles to real estate in this town and Lunenburg. An exact copy of the original grant here referred to is to be found on page 7 of "The Early Records of the Town of Lunenburg," a book previously published by this city.

These two townships were designated by the committee appointed to allot and grant them out as the north and south townships. The former was afterwards incorporated by the name of Townsend, in the county of Middlesex. The south township included the present towns of Lunenburg, Fitchburg and a portion of Ashby.

The work of copying these "Proprietors' Records"

has been performed by Miss Lucy A. Hayward, assisted by Miss Edith L. Davis.

The work was necessarily somewhat delayed on account of the difficulty in translating the writing, some of which is very nearly obliterated.

In this connection I desire to extend my sincere thanks to Mrs. George W. Stone of Boston, Mass., for having rendered the cause much assistance by copying and forwarding to me the petition and bill to confirm the titles of land in Lunenburg and Fitchburg. I give these in full for the benefit of all who may be interested.

What this volume may lack in interest will be atoned for by bearing in mind that the names here recorded and the lots described are those of the original settlers of Lunenburg and Fitchburg. As such it will be a valuable companion book for "The Early Records of the Town of Lunenburg."

Among the names of the original settlers we find the name of Walter Beath, which in the other book, "The Early Records," was given as Walter Bees. The last letter was without doubt meant for an "f," being mistaken for an old-fashioned "s," and the Beef was meant for Beath, written as it sounded to the clerk.

The use of both kinds of the letter "s" in the same book and at the same time is liable to be confusing unless great care is exercised.

We believe that this book will be found to be of much service as a reference book to all persons interested in ancient records, and as showing the great amount of labor required of the early settlers in opening up this territory for civilization.

I think that all who take the trouble to read it will realize in a small degree the careful work required to copy it.

Walter A. Davis.

City Clerk.

Province of the } To his Excellency Thomas Hutch-
Massachusetts Bay inson Esq. Captain General and
Governor in chief The Honble his
Majesty's Council and Honble
House of Representatives of the
Province aforesaid in General
Court assembled.

John Taylor Representative of Lunenbourg and Fitchbourg, for and in the behalf of said Towns Humbly Sheweth,

That the Great and General Court or Assembly of said Province did on the fourth day of November 1719, Grant a Township called Turkey Hills lying South of North Town.

That the said Great and General Court did on the Seventh day of December 1719 appoint and fully Impower William Tayor, Samuel Thaxter, Francis Fullam Esqr. Capt. John Sheple, and Mr. Benjamin Whittemore a Committee to allot and grant out the Lands in said New Township called Turkey hills —— and to make return of their proceedings.

That said Com^tee did afterwards agreable to the order of said Court allot and grant out said New Township called Turkey hills —— The said Com^tee also transfered Sixty three House lotts in said Township now called Lunenburg and Fitchburg, and made return of their proceedings into the Secretary's office as appears from the Proprietors Book under the Committees own hand.

That the Return of some part of said Com^tees proceedings are not now to be found in said Secretary's office, and are Supposed to have been consumed by Fire when the Court house was burnt, whereby the property of some Hundreds of the good People of this Province is rendered in some measure precarious, as they have Improved, Sold, and wholly conducted themselves by the

Copy of said Com^{tees} proceedings as they left the same in the hands of said Proprietors Clerk and unless something further is done by this Great and General Court, to Confirm & establish the proceedings of the Com^{tee} aforesaid agreable to their return it is greatly feared that in some future time not only the Inhabitants of said Towns but many others more remotely concerned may be led into very great difficulties & expences.

Your pet^r therefore in behalf of said Towns most humbly prays your Excellency and honors would be pleased to take their case into your wise and serious consideration, and that you would be pleased to Confirm and Establish the Transfers made by the General Courts Committee aforesaid and all other their proceedings respecting said Township called Turkey hills, now called Lunenburg & Fitchburg; or otherwise grant relief in such way and manner as your Excellency and honors in your known goodness shall seem meet.

And as in duty bound shall ever pray &c.

     JOHN TAYLOR in the behalf of the
     Towns of Lunenburg & Fitchburg.
Lunenburg 20th of June 1772.

In the House of Representatives June 22nd 1772. Read and ordered that Mr. Phillips, Col. Gerrish, Cap Farley & Cap Searl with such as the Hon^{le} Board shall join be a Committee to take this Petition into Consideration and report

    Sent up for Concurrance
       T. CUSHING *Spk^r*

In Council June 22nd 1772, read and concurred, and James Otis, Saml Dexter & Artemas Ward Esq^s are joined.

     THOS. FLUCKER *Sec^y*

In Council Jan: 27th 1773, Read again and no answer being made to the petition ordered that James Otis, Samuel Dexter, and Artemas Ward Esq^{s.} be a Committee to consider and report what they may judge necessary to be done thereon.

     THOS. FLUCKER *Sec^y*

In Council January 27th 1773.
Resolved, on the Petition of John Taylor
Representing Lunenbourg and Fitchbourg
for and in Behalf of said Towns, that the
Prayer of the Petition be so far granted as
that the Proceedings of the Committee of the General
Court appointed December 7th 1719, respecting
the Alotment of Lands to the original Settlers
and the Subsequent Transfers in Said Town,
then known by the Name of South Town, be
fully confirmed, and that the Petitioner have
leave to bring in a bill for that Purpose.
       Sent down for Concurrence
       THOS. FLUCKER *Sec^y*

In the House of Representatives Jany. 30, 1773.
  Read and Concurred. T. CUSHING *Spkr.*

MASSACHUSETTS ARCHIVES, VOL. 118, PAGES 674 TO 675.

 Anno Regni Regis Georgii Tertii Decimo
 Tertio ——

An Act for Confirming the Titles & Quieting the
Possessions of the Proprietors of the Towns of
Lunenburge and Fitchburge. —— ——

Whereas the Great and General Court or Assembly
of this Province did on the fourth day of December
Seventeen Hundred and Nineteen Grant a New
Township at a Place Called Turkey Hills then
Called South Town, now Lunenburge & Fitchburge
which at that time was a frontier Town of Six
miles Square & Said Court did on the Seventh Day
of December Seventeen Hundred and Nineteen
appoint and fully Impower William Taylor, Sam^{ll}. Thaxter Francis Fullam Esqr^s. Capt. John Shelpe & M^r
Benj^a Whittemore a Committee to Allot & Grant out
the Lands in Said New Town which Committee did
afterwards agreable to the order of Said Court allot
and Grant out said New Township & make Return

Act to Confirm Titles.

of their Proceedings into the Secretarys office as
appears by the Return of the Committee under their
own hands on the Proprietors Book But the Plan
of Each Lot with the then possessors & Proprietors
Names that had the Land Confirmed to them is not
to be now found in the Secretarys office nor
Elsewhere but is supposed to be Burnt among
the files when the Late Court House in Boston was
Consumed by fire by which means the Property of
Some Hundreds of the Good People of this Province
is Rendered Precarious as the Same Lands have been
Brought too out of a State of Nature and been
Improved between forty & fifty years and have
Passed by Sales through a Great Number of hands
So that without the Interposition of this Court the
Present Possessors and others were in Danger of the
Gratest Difficulties, Distresses and Losses Relative
to their Properties in Said Towns.
For the Preventing of which
Be it Enacted by the Governor Council and
House of Representatives that Said Committes
Proceedings in Alloting out and Granting Said
Lands in Said Newtownship now Lunenburge &
Fitchburge with the Records and Transfers of
Lots in Said Towns which were Delivered up to said
Proprietors by order of the General Court be and are
hereby Confirmed with the said Proprietors proceedings
thereon Ever Since and are hereby made valid in Law
to all Intents and Purposes whatsoever.

In the House of Representatives Feb^r 3^d 1773
Read a first time   a second time
Feb^r 4th 1773 Read a Third time & passed to be
Engrossed.   Sent up for Concurance
T. CUSHING *Spk^r*

In Council Feby 8th 1773 Read a first & second
time & passed a Concurrance to be Engrossed
J^{no} COTTON *D. Secry*

ERRATA.

Page 5, fifth line. After "five Degrees and a half" insert "fouth."

Page 9, Meadow Lot No. 2, seventh line. After "making an Angle" insert "and runing North 3 degrees Eaſt 13 rod to a ſtake there making an Angle."

Page 10, Second Division No. 4. The distance on the land of John and Timothy Poole should be 160 rods, instead of 165.

Page 17, third line. After "the Houſe Lott" insert "and ranging on the Houſe Lott."

Page 18, tenth line. For "twenty five rod" read "twenty fix rod."

Page 22. "Jonas Gibson" should be "Jonas Gilson."

Page 32, Meadow Lot No. 2. For "ſaid way" read "ford way."

Page 41, eighth line. For "30 degrees" read "30 minits."

Page 51, Third Division, fourteenth line. For "northweſt corner" read "northeaſt corner."

Page 62. Timothy Gibson's house lot should be No. 33, instead of No. 38.

Page 63, fifteenth line. For "ſouth 18 deg East" read "ſouth 5 deg East." The last word of the next to last line should be "fore" instead of "five."

Page 67. The date of recording Second Division No. 71 should be "1732/3" instead of "1722/3."

Page 76, twenty-sixth line. After "degrees" insert "Eaſt."

Page 80. "Jonas Gibson" should be "Jonas Gilson." In the last line, "24 degrees" should be "21 degrees."

PROPRIETORS' RECORDS

OF THE

TOWN OF LUNENBURG.

[Folio 1]
    The Minister of the Town of Lunenburgh }
      The Reverend Mr Andrew Gardner   }

[Folio 1²] Lunenburg November the 20th 1729.

2^d Divifion   Survayed the fecond Divifion No 80 belong-
No 80.   ing to the Minifters Lott. Begining at a pillar
of Stones Erected for the SowEast Corner and runing
north 17 degree Eaft 125 rod to a ftake there making
an Angle and runing West 11 degrees North 82 rod to
a pillar of Stones there making an Angle and runing fouth
12 degrees Weft 123 rod to a pillar of Stones there making an Angle and runing Eaft 11 degrees fouth 72 rod to
Where it Began

    Survayed by Nathan Haywood and approved of by
the Committee viz Jofiah Willard Edward Hartwell Nathan Heywood and Jonathan Willard recorded may the
7th annoque Domini 1731
                          ℔ Edward Hartwell Clerk.

              Lunenburg May the 6: 1748
Meadow   then furvay for Mr Andrew Gardner mead-
No 3.   ow Lott No three in pearl Hill meadow fo
Called Containing five acres being the moft Wefterly Lott
in faid meadow belonging to the minifters Houfe Lott N^o
one begining at a Certain pitch pine tree marked for the
eaft Corner of faid meadow Lott and runs Weft thirty

two Degs north twenty feven rod on Land of Mr Allen and ten rod on the Land of the Honourable Andrew Oliver Esqr then it runs fouth ten Degs Weft on faid olivers Land twenty Eight rod to a ftak then it runs Eaft thirty Degs fouth on faid Allins Land twenty feven rod then it runs north thirty two Degs Eaft Chifly on the pine ridge twenty five to where it began

℘ Nathan Haywood Survayer

Approved of by the Committee viz Edward Hartwell Nathan Heywood and Jonathan Willard.

Recorded May the 7th 1748

℘ Edward Hartwell proprietors Clerk.

[2]   HILKIAH BOYNTON

House Lot No 2   Granted to Hilkiah Boynton by the Committee appointed by the Greate and General Court to a Lott and Grant out the Lands Within the town of Lunenburg to Granttees Houfe Lott Number two and Meadow Lott Number one in Lower Mulpus

Meadow Lot No 1 in Lower Mulpus.   S^d meadow belongs to House Lott Number thirty fix and all the after grants and Divifions of Land that Shall arife from faid Houfe Lott N° 36 from and after the fecond Divifion N° 31. which 2^d Divifion the General Courts Committee granted to James Jewell.

[3]   EBENEZER SPRAGE of

House Lot No 3   Granted to Ebenezer Sprage by the Committee appointed by the Greate and General Court to aLott and grant out the Land Within the town of Lunenburgh to Granttees fourty one acres and one Hundred and thirty rod within faid town for a houfe Lot bareing Number three to gether with all the rights and Divifions of Land BeLonging thereunto Begining at a ftake fet up for the fouth Corner and Runing Eaft twenty nine Degr north one Hundred and fifty feven Rod on Lott number four there making an Angle and Runing north twenty nine Degr Weft fourty five rod there making an angle and Runing Weft thirty degr thirty minnits fouth one Hundred and fifty feven rod on Lot number two. there making an angle and runing fouth twenty nine Degrees Eaft fourty two rod to where it Began Survayed By Nathan Heywood and Recorded By order of the Committee viz Jofiah Willard Edward Hartwell Jofhua Hutchins Nathan Heywood Recorded March the twenty fifth day In the year of our Lord one thoufand feven Hundred and thirty pr Edward Hartwell Clerk

Lunenburgh March the 25 1730.

2ᵈ Divifion No. 15   Survayed for Ebenezer Sprage a fecond Divifion Number fifteen the Contents of Which is fifty nine Acres. Begining at a ftak and a heap of ftones Erected for the fouth Corner and runing north thirty three Degr Eaft on Jonathan Wheelers Lott No fourteen one hundred and fifty Rod to a heap of ftones there making an Angle and runings Weft thirty one Deg thirty mini north on the north town Line fixty three Rod to a ftake there making an Angle and Runing fouth thirty three deg. thirty minits Weft one hundred and fifty rod on Lott No 16 and fince Laid to Jonathan Dows Esqʳ to a Stake there making an Angle and runing Eaft thirty one Degree thirty minits South 63 rod to where it began. Survayed by Nathan Heywood and approved of by the Committee to Witt Nathan Heywood Edward Hartwell Jonathan Willard and Josiah Willard.

Recorded December the twenty forth Day in the year of our Lord one thoufand feven hundred and thirty ℔
Edwᵈ Hartwell Clerk

[3²]   Lunenburg April the 8ᵗʰ 1731.

Medow Lott No 8   Survayed for Benjamin Hutchens Claimer Meadow Lott No 8 in Lower Mulpus meadows the Contents of Which is four acres and three quarters begining at a ftake which is the Northeafterly Corner of faid Lott ftanding by the brook and runing West one degree north on meadow Lott No: 9: 24 rod and a half to a ftake there making an Angle and runing fouth one degree West on Land of Walter Beeth

17 rod to a ſtake there making an Angle and runing Eaſt on meadow Lott No: 7: 67: rod to a ſtake by the brook there turning and running up the Brook to Where it began ſurveyed by Nathan Heywood and approved of by the Committee Joſiah Willard Edward Hartwell Jonathan Willard and Nathan Heywood.
Recorded June the 14th annoque Domini 1731
 ℔ Edward Hartwell Clerk.

[4]   SAMUEL JOHNSON of
Lunenburg December the 22d 1729.

House Lotts 4 & 5   ſurvayed for Samuell Johnſon two Houſe Lotts Number four and five the Contents of both being ninty one acres and a quarter begining at a Pillar of ſtones and a ſtak ſet up for the ſouth Corner and runs Eaſt twenty nine degrees north one hundred and fifty ſeven rod on Lott Number Six to a Black oak tree there making an Angle and runing north twenty nine degrees Weſt ninty three rod there making an Angle and runing Weſt twenty nine degrees ſouth one hundred and fifty ſeven rods on Lott Number three there making an Angle and runing ſouth twenty nine degrees Eaſt ninty three rod on the Highway to where it began

Survayed by Nathan Heywood and approved of by the Committee Josiah Willard Jonathan Willard Edward Hartwell and Nathan Heywood
Recorded January the 23d 1770.
       pr me Edward Hartwell proprietors Clerk.

[5]   JOHN HEYWOOD of

House Lot No 6.   Granted unto John Heywood By the Committee appointed by the Greate and General Court to aLott and Grant out the Lands Within the Townſhip of Lunenburgh to Grantees   Acres of Land Within ſaid town for a Houſe Lott bearing number ſix together Withall the Rights and Diviſions of Land belonging thereunto or ſhall aRise therefrom — —

Proprietors' Records.

Lunenburg February the 12th 1736/7

Second Divifion No 72

Surveyed for John Heywood 2d Divifion N° 72 Containing 62 acres Begining at a ftake fet up for the foutheaft Corner of faid Lott and runs weft five Degrees and a half on his own Land 61 rod and a half to a Chesnut tree then Runs North four degrees West on land of Nathan Heywood 163 rods to a pillar of ftones then Runs Eaft 5 deg north on the Land of Edward Hartwell Esqr : 60 : rod to a dry white pine tree then runs fouth four Deg and a half Eaft on Land of Benj^a Cory 163 rod to where it began

by Nathan Heywood Surveyer approved of by the Committee viz Jofiah Willard Jonathan Willard Nathan Heywood and Edward Hartwell

Recorded February the 26th 1736/7

℔ Edward Hartwell Clerk

Lunenburg Apriel the 24th 1730

3d Divifion No 6

Laid out by the Committee appointed 92 acres and a half of Land for a third Divifion for John Heywood Arifeing from Houfe Loott No: 6: on the Southerly fide of the River. Begining at A ftake fet up for the Southefterly Corner by the River and Runing West 15 degs fouth 169 rod on Common Land there making an Angle and runing north 15 Degrees Weft 58 rod on Common Land there making an Angle and Runing Eaft 15 Degrees north on Land Laid out to Benjamin Goodridge 152 rods there making an Angle and runing north one Degree Weft on faid Goodridges Lott 63 rod to a pine tree there making an Angle and Runing West 18 Degrees North on S^d Goodridges Land 64 rod to a popler tree there making an Angle and Runing by the River to where it Began

Survayed by Nathan Heywood and approved of by the Committee viz Jofiah Willard Nathan Heywood and Edward Hartwell.

Recorded December ye 5. 1732

p^r Edward Hartwell Clerk.

[5²]   Lunenburg May the 16th 1731.

10 Acres ½ of Land for allowance for Higway

Laid out by the Committee appointed ten acres and a half of Land to John Heywood for Satisfaction for the highways going through His Lott where he now Lives. Scituate and Lying neer the South eaſt Corner of ſaid Townſhip. Begining at a Certain Chesnut tree Marked and runing North 3 degrees 30 min Weſt on Common Land 14 rod there making an Angle and runing north 45, deg Eaſt on Common Land 25 rod there making an Angle and runing Eaſt 3 deg North partly on Gibsons Lott and partly on Common Land 29 rod there making an Angle and runing South on Capt Goulds Lott 32 rod there making an Angle and runing West 25 deg South on Common Land 46 rod there making an angle and runing North 13 deg Weſt on Common Land 18 rod to Where it Began Survayed by Nathan Heywood and approved of by the Committee viz Edward Hartwell Joſiah Willard

Recorded April the 16th Anno Domini 1731.

℔ Edward Hartwell Clerk

Lunenburg May ye 27th 1731

Meadow Lott No 5.

Survayed for John Heywood Meadow Lott No 5 Below Cattaconamoug pond in ſaid town Ship the Contents of Which is 2 Acres and a half. Begining at a Certain pillar of ſtones Which is the most Southerly Corner and Runing Eaſt 34 Degrees North on Meadow Lott No. 6. 38 rod there Making an Angle and Runing North 36 Degrees Weſt on Common Land 16 rod there making an Angle and Runing ſouth 42 degrees West on Common Land 38 rod to apillar of Stones on the upland there making an Angle and and Runing ſouth 36 Degrees Eaſt on Common Land 7 rod and a half to Where it Began furvayed By Nathan Heywood and approved of By the Committee viz Joſiah Willard Edward Hartwell Jonathan Willard Nathan Heywood

Recorded Sept the 3d 1731

℔ Edward Hartwell Clerk

Lunenburg May the 17th 1729 Laid out by the Committee appointed twenty three acres and Eighty four rod of third Divifion Land to John Heywood arifing from houfe Lott Number fix and adjoyning to his 2d Divifion and it bounds north on the abovefaid heywoods own fecond Divifion weft on the Land of nathan Heywood. fouth on Lancafter old town and Eaft on the Land of Benjamin Cory beging at a Chefnut tree marked for the fouth weft Corner of his 2d Divfion and runing fouth five degrees Eaft forty fix rod to a pillar of ftones there making a Corner and Runing Eaft twenty Degrees fouth fixty feven rod to a pillar of Stones there making an Angle and runing north five Degrees Weft feventy five rod to a ftake there making an Angle and Runing Weft five Degrees fouth fixty rod to Where it began furvayed by Nathan Heywood and approved of by the Committee viz Edward Hartwell Jofiah Willard and Nathan Heywood.

Recorded May ye 29th 1729

℔ Edward Hartwell Clerk.

[6] JAMES COLBERN of

Granted unto James Colbern by the Committee appointed by the Greate and General Court to aLott and Grant out the Lands Within the Town of Lunenburg to Grantees   Within faid town for a houfe Lott bearing Number 7 toGether Withall the Rights and Divifions of Land and meadow that beLongs thereto or fhall arife therefrom

Lunenburg December the 24th 1729.

Houfe Lott No 7. furvayed for James Colbourn Houfe Lott No 7 the Contents of Which is 46 acres and 25 rod begining at ftake fet up for the moft foutherly Corner and runing Eaft 29 Degrees north 18 rod on pools' Lott there making an Angle and runing north 29 Degrees Weft 119 rod on the High way there making an Angle and runing Weft 30 degrees fouth 64 rod partly on the old meeting Houfe land there making an angle and runing fouth 4 degrees West 27 rod on Hills Lott there making an angle and runing Eaſt 21 degrees ſouth 59 rod Croſs the meadow there making an angle and runing ſouth 10 degrees West 63 rod to where it began ⅌ nathan Heywood ſurvayer approved of by Edward Hartwell Jonathan Willard nathan Heywood

Recorded ſeptember yᵉ 16, 1737

⅌ Edward Hartwell Clerk

Lunenburg June the 26. 1729

Laid out by the Committee appointed three acres and 135 rod of Land to James Colbourn to make up what is wanting in his Houſe Lott N⁰ 7. begining at a Certain piller of ſtones near to Hills Houſe and runing north 4 degrees Eaſt 19 rod on ſaid hills Lott there making an angle and runing Eaſt 30 degrees north 37 rod there making an angle and runing ſouth 20 Degree eaſt 16 rod to ſaid Colbourns Line to where it began 44 rod

ſurvayed by Nathan Heywood and approved of by the Committee viz Edward Hartwell Jonathan Willard

Recorded September the 16ᵗʰ 1737.

⅌ Edward Hartwell Clerk

[6²]   Lunenburg January the 22ᵈ 1730/1.

2ᵈ Diviſion No 59.   ſurvayed for James Colbern ſecond Diviſion number 59 on the ſoutherly part of flat Hill the Contents of Which is 57 acres and a half Begining at a Certain ſtake ſet up for the moſt Weſterly Corner and runing North 17 Degrees Eaſt on Land Left for a highway 62 rod to a ſtak there making an Angle and Runing Eaſt 31 Degrees ſouth on Lott Number 58 152 rod to a ſtake in Groton Line there making an Angle and Runing ſouth 17 degrees Weſt on ſaid Line 62 rod to a ſtake there making an Angle and runing Weſt 31 degrees north on Lott Number 60 152 rod to Where it began. Survayed by Nathan Heywood and approved of by the Committee viz Joſiah Willard Edward Hartwell Jonathan Willard and Nathan Heywood

Recorded December the 27ᵗʰ 1732

⅌ Edward Harwell Clerk

Proprietors' Records.

[7] THE HEIRS OF MAJ^{ER} FLAGG of

Granted to the Heirs of Major Eleizer Flagg by the Committee appointed by the Greate and Generall Court to alott and Grant out the Lands Within the town of Lunenburg to Granttee fourty five acres of Land Within faid town for a Houfe Lott No Eight to Gether with all the Rights and Divifions of Land beLonging thereunto or arifeing therefrom

January the 5th 1729

Survayed for Jonathan Pool Esq Claimer Houfe Lott No 8 the Contents of Which is 45 Acres begining at a ftake fet up for the most foutherly Corner and Runing Eaft 28 Deg 30 minits north 160 rod on Burbeens Lott there making an angle and Runing north 28 Deg 30 min Weft 45 rod on the High Way there making an Angle and runing West 28 Deg 30 mints fouth 160 rod partly on Colberns Lott and partly on the minifterael Lott there making an Angle and runing South 28 Deg 30 min Eaft 45 rod to Where it began

Survayed by Nathan Heywood and approved of by the Committee viz Edward Hartwell Jofiah Willard Nathan Heywood Jonathan Willard and Benoni Boynton

Recorded April the 16th Anno Domini 1731

℗ Edward Hartwell Clerk

Meadow Lott No 2

furvayed for Jonathan poole Esqr Claimer meadow Lott No 2. in horfsmeet meadows the Contents of Which is fix acres butted and bounded as Difcribed by plan begining at a pillar of ftones and runing fouth 10 degree West 22 rod to a pillar of ftones there making an angle and runing Weft 38 degrees North 65 rod to a ftake there making an Angle and runing East 30 degree fouth 63 rod to Where it began

furvayed by nathan Heywood and approved of by the Committee above faid

Recorded June the 14th 1731

℗ Edward Hartwell Clerk

part of the 4th division that belong to House Lott No 8 above said is Recorded at page 56 in the second part of this book

[7²] JONATHAN POOL ESQ^R
Lunenburg April the 27th 1730.

2d Division
No 4

Laid out by the Committee appointed 180 Acres of Land for a second Division N° 4 and a third Division beLonging to house Lott No 8. to Jonathan Pooll Esqr Claimer in the Westerly part of said township Begining at a Certain Maple tree Marked for the Northeast Corner and runing south 15 Deg East on Land of John and Timothy Poole 165 rod there Making an Angle and runing West 15 Deg south on Land of John Bewer 152 rod and on Common Land 28 rod to a stake there making an Angle and runing North 15 Deg West on Common Land 160 rod to a bunch of Maple trees there making an Angle and runing East 15 Degree North on Common Land 180 rod to where it began survayed by Nathan Heywood and approved by the Committee viz Josiah Willard Jonathan Willard Nathan Heywood and Edward Hartwell

Recorded April the 15th in the year of our Lord one thousand seven Hundred and thirty one

℔ Edward Hartwell Clerk

½ 4th
Division

December the 15th 1769 Laid out by the Committee appointed Ebenezer Harrington Claimer fifty acres of Land in Fitchburg being one half of a forth division which did belong to the right of Eleazer flagg Poole a rising from house Lott No Eight there being two rod allowance in the Length and also in the width of it for roads going through the same.

it begins at a pine tree marked for the nor west Corner of it in the East Line of Phinehas Hartwells Land and runs south three degrees East Eighty rod bounding on said Hartwells Land all the way Excepting Eight rod which it Extends fur ther south to a heap of stones then it runs East three Degree^s north bounding on Common Land one hundred and two rod to a heap of ſtones then it runs north three Degrees Weſt bounding on Common Land Eighty two rod to a heap of ſtones on a Large Rock by the Brook then it runs Weſt three degrees ſouth Bounding on Common Land one hundred and two rod to the pine tree first mentioned   by Nathan Haywood ſurvayer

 allowed of by the Committee and ordered to be Recorded

          Edward Hartwell
          Nathan Heywood
          Ephraim Pearce

  Recorded December the 25th 1769

          ℔ Edward Hartwell
          Propriator Clerk

[8]   JAMES BURBEEN of
Houſe Lot Granted to James Burbeen by the Committee appointed by the greate and General Court to alot and Grant out the Lands Within the town of Lunenburgh to Grantees fourty five acres of Land within ſaid town for a houſe Lot bareing Number nine to Gether with all the Rights and Diviſions of Land belonging thereunto and the said Houſe Lot Bounds one Hundred and ſixty Rod ſoutherly on Lot number ten and northerly on the highway and partly on Lot number Eight Easterly on ye high way and Weſterly on the Land Left for a way It begins at a pillar of Stones and runs Eaſt twenty Eight deg North one hundred ſixty rod to a pillar of ſtones there making an Angle and Runing north twenty Eight Degrees Weſt fourty five rod to a pillar of ſtones there making an Angle and runing West twenty Eighty degr. ſouth one Hundred and ſixty rod to a pillar of ſtones there making an Angle and runing ſouth twenty Eight degr. Eaſt fourty five rod to where it began and Laid out by the committee above ſaid

2d Diviſion A ſecond Diviſion Lot bareing Number one
No : 1 ſcituate at the Noreaſt Corner of ſaid town and the Contents is ſeventy acres and it Bounds northerly on north town Line Eaſterly on Groton Line ſoutherly on

second Devision Westerly on second Division Number two beginning at a pillar of stones and and Runing south seventeen degr. West one Hundred and Sixty Eight rod to to a pillar of stones there making an Angle and Runing West thirty two degr North one hundred and one Rod to a pillar of stones there making an Angle and Runing north thirty seven degr. East one Hundred and sixty one rod to a pillar of stones there making an Angle and Runing East thirty two degr. south fourty three Rod to where it began. survayed by Nathan Heywood and recorded March the thirteenth day in the year of our Lord one thousand seven Hundred and twenty nine thirty by order of the Committee viz. Josiah Willard Edward Hartwell Jonathan Willard and nathan Heywood the said second Division is Coupled to the House Lot above said by ye General Courts Committee

        Edward Hartwell Clerk.

    Lunenburg August the 18th 1729.

3^d Division Laid out by the Committee appointed one Hundred acres of third Division Land to the Right of Mr James Burbeen Near the Moonusnouck hill begining at a hemlock tree and Runing West fourty degr south one Hundred Rod there Making an Angle and runing North fourty deg^r West one Hundred and sixty Rod there making an Angle and runing East fourty degr North one Hundred rod there making an Angle and Runing south fourty degr East one Hundred and sixty rod to where It began survayed By Nathan Heywood and approved of by the Committee viz Josiah Willard Edward Hartwell and Nathan Heywood

 Recorded March the 20th day In the year of our Lord one thousand seven hundred and twenty nine thirty

       ℞ Edward Hartwell Clerk

Meadow Lott No 7. Laid out by the General Courts Committee to Mr James Burbeen meadow Lot No seven Lying in Lunenburgh 6 acres and In that meadow Called Clay pit meadow and is Coupled to house Lott No: 9: and is Bounded northerly on Mr Allens Lott Westerly on the Land of Ephraim Wetherbe foutherly on f^d Wetherbes meadow Lott No 6 and Eafterly on the land of Jofeph Page. and It begins at a ftake fet up for the northweft Corner and runs fouth twenty, nine deg. thirty min Eaft fourteen rod to a ftake there making an Angle and Runing Eaft twenty nine Degree North 80 Rod to a ftake there making an Angle and Runing North twenty nine degr. Weft ten rod to a ftake there making an Angle and Runing Weft twenty seven degr fouth Eighty rod to where It began

Survayed by Nathan Heywood and approved on by the Committee viz Edward Hartwell Jofiah Willard and Jonathan Willard

Recorded March the twenty feventh day in the year of our Lord one thoufand feven hundred and thirty.

         Edward Hartwell Clerk

[9]
47
L^t
No
10

Houfe Lott
No 10

JOSHUA HUTCHINS of
To William Clark Esqr for three common rights after the fecond division, arrising from House Lotts Number three number Nineteen and Number Seventy five.

Granted unto Joshua Hutchins by the Committee appointed by the Greate and General Court to a Lot and Grant out the Lands Within the town of Lunenburgh to grantees fourty four acres and ninety two rod for a houfe Lot bareing number ten to gether with all the rights of Divifions of Land belonging there unto Within the townfhip of Lunenburgh

BeGining at a pillar of ftones and a ftake fet up for fouth Corner and Runing North twenty nine Degr Weft fourty five Rod to a pillar of ftones there making an Angle and Runing East twenty Eight degr thirty minints North one Hundred and fifty nine rod to a pillar of Stones there making an Angle and Runing fouth twenty Eight Degr thirty minit Eaft fourty five rod to a ftake there making an Angle and Runing Weft twenty Eight Degr thirty min fouth one Hundred and fifty Eight rod on Wetherbes Lot to where It Began and the faid Lott Bounds Wefterly on highway northerly on Burbeens Lot Eafterly on highway foutherly on the Land of Ephraim Wetherbe furvayed by Nathan Heywood and approved of by the Committee viz Edward Hartwell Nathan Heywood Jofhua Hutchins and Jofiah Willard

Recorded March the the twenty fifth day In the year of our Lord one thoufand feven Hundred and thirty

⅌ Edward Hartwell Clerk

2d
Nº 29

Lunenburgh February ye 23^d 1729/30 furvayed for Jofhua Hutchins a 2^d Divifion number twenty nine Lying Eafterly from pearl hill meadows adjoyning to the North Town Line Begining at a pillar of Stones in the north town Line Erected for the Eafterly Corner and runing fouth thirty two deg West one Hundred and forty five rod to a pillar of Stones Bounding on a fecond divifion there making an Angle and runing Weft thirty two deg North fixty feven rod to a pillar of ftones there making an Angle and runing North thirty two deg Eaft one Hundred and and fourty five rod to the north town Line Bounding on unDevided Land making an angle and runing Eaft thirty two deg fouth fixty feven rod on the North town Line to Where Survayed by Nathan Heywood and approved of by the Committee viz Jofiah Willard Edward Hartwell and Jofhua Hutchens

Recorded october the twenty third Day in the year of our Lord one thoufand feven Hundred and thirty

⅌ Edward Hartwell Clerk.

3d divifion

Lunenburgh April the 23^d 1729 Laid out to William Lawrance by the Committee appointed by the proprietors fourteen acres and one Hundred and forty Eight rod of third Divifion Land to the right number Eleven on the Northerly fide of Mulpus. begining at a pillar of Stones and runing North twenty five deg Eaft forty rod to a pillar of ftones there making an Angle and runing Weft thirty 8 rod to a pillar of ftones there making and an Angle and runing Weft thirty feven deg North fifty fix rod to a pillar of ftones there making an Angle and runing weft forty deg fouth ten rod there making an Angle and runing fouth Eight teen deg weft twelve rod there making an Angle and runing Eaft thirty three deg fouth ninety four rod to Where it began furvayed by Nathan Heywood and approved of by the Committee viz Edwd Hartwell Benoni Boynton and hilkiah boynton this plan comprehending fome meadow of John hills

  recorded october the 21st Anno domini 1730
     by me Edward Hartwell Clerke

[9²]   Lunenburg January the 11th: 1730/31

Meadow Lott No. 4 Mulpus

  Survayed for Jofhua Hutchins meadow Lott Number 4 In uper mulpus meadows the contents of Which is 5 acres begining at a Certain red oak tree marked for the fouth Corner and runing North 2 degrees Eaft on Meadow Lott Number three 50 rod to a ftake there making an Angle and runing Weft 16 degrees north 20 rod to a ftake there making an Angle and Runing fouth 1 degree Eaft on Meadow Lott No 5 48 rod to a pillar of ftones there Making an Angle and runing Eaft 27 degres fouth 18 rod to Where it Began furvayed by Nathan Heywood and approved of by the Committee viz Edward Hartwell Jofiah Willard Jonathan Willard and Nathan Heywood.

  Recorded December the 29th annoque Domini 1731
     ℗ Edward Hartwell Cler

[10]   WILLIAM LAWRANCE of
   Lunenburgh December the 24th 1729

5 Acres Mulpus falls

  Laid out by the Committee appointed five acres of Land at Mulpus falls to Ephraim Wetherbe Claimer to make up what is Wanting his houfe Lots number eleven and number twelve

  Begining at a pillar of ftones and a Cartain chery tree near the falls and Runing fouth fourty three degr Weft Six rod on Capt Gould there making an Angle and Runing West five degr fouth twelve rod to a pine tree on Capt Gould there making an Angle and Runing Eaft twenty fix deg^r fouth twenty two rod there making an Angle and

Runing North thirteen deg^r Weſt fifteen rod and a half to the fore mentioned Cherry tree thence runing North twelve deg^r Weſt thirty one rod on Capt Gould there making an Angle and Runing Eaſt twenty five deg^r ſouth fourty ſix rod on Auſtan to a black oak tree there making an Angle and Runing ſouth thirty rod on fiſk to a pine tree there making an Angle and Runing north thirty ſeven deg^r Weſt to a white oak tree thirty nine rod there making an Angle and Runing ſouth fourty three degr Weſt to where It Began

Survayed by Nathan Heywood and approved by the Committee viz Edward Hartwell Jonathan Willard and Joſiah Willard

Recorded March the twenty fourth day in the year of our Lord one thouſand ſeven Hundred and thirty

₽ Edward Hartwell CLerk.

Houſe Lott No 11 12   Granted to William Lawrance By the Committee appointed by the Greate and General Court to a Lot and grant out the Lands within the townſhip of Lunenburgh to Grantees fourty four acres and a quarter of Land Within ſaid town for a houſe Lott bareing Number Eleven to gether With all the rights and Diviſion of Land Belonging thereunto

Lunenburgh December the 11th 1729 Survayed for Ephraim Wetherbe Claimer two Houſe Lotts and a meadow Lott the number of the houſe Lotts are Eleven and twelve the Contents of both is Eighty four Acres and three quarters.

Lott Number twelve begins at a Small Elm tree at the End of the meadow Lott and runs Weſt twenty nine Degr ſouth on aſtains Lot one hundred and ſixty four rod to a ſtake there making an Angle and Runing north twenty nine Deg^r Weſt Eighty five rod and a half to a ſtake Croſs both the Lotts there making an Angle and runing Eaſt twenty Eight Degr thirty min North one hundred and ſixty five rod on Hutchins Lott there making an Angle and runing ſouth thirty ſeven Degr Eaſt fourty ſix rod on the Highway to a Cheſnut tree there making an Angle and Runing ſouth twenty Eight Degr thirty min

Eaſt fourty rod and a half to Where It Began. the
meadow Lott begins at a ſtake in the End of
Meadow the Houſe Lott Eight rod and two rod on
auſtins Lott there making an Angle and Runing Eaſt
twenty nine Degr North on Auſtins and pages meadow
Eighty rod there making an Angle and runing North
twenty nine Degr Weſt on Joſeph Page ten rod there
making an Angle and Runing twenty nine Deg^r ſouth
Eighty Rod to Where it Began the Contents of the
Meadow Lott is five acres ſurvayed by Nathan Heywood
and approved of by the Committee viz Joſiah Willard
Edward Hartwell Nathan Haywood Jonathan Willard
and Joſhua Hutchens Recorded march the twenty fifth
Day In the year of our Lord one thouſand ſeven Hundred
and thirty

℗ Edward Hartwell Clerk.

[11]   PHINEAS PARKER of
Houſe Granted to Phineas Parker By the Com-
Lott No 12. mittee appointed by the greate and General
Court to a Lott and Grantt out the Lands Contained
Within the townſhip of Lunenburg to Grantees fourty
acres and a half of Land Within ſaid town for a Houſe
Lott Baring Number twelve to gether With all the Rights
and Diviſions of Land Belonging thereunto

Lunenburgh January the 10th 1729/30

2^d Diviſion Survayed for Robart Ffyfe Claimer a ſecond
No 41. Diviſion number 41 Laid out by the General
Courts Committee to Phineas Parker and Coupled to
houſe Lot number twelve Begining at a pillar of ſtones
Erected for the North weſt Corner and runing Eaſt thirty
two Deg^r ſouth fourty five rod on Burbeens Lott there
making an angle and Runing ſouth ſeventeen degr Weſt
one Hundred and fifty three rod on Groton Line there
making an angle and runing Weſt thirty two deg north
one Hundred and ten rod there making an Angle and
Runing north fourty one degr thirty min Eaſt one Hundred and fifty one rod to Where it began the Contents of
this Lott is ſeventy one acres and one hundred and fifteen

rod furvayed by Nathan Heywood and approved of By the Committee Edward Hartwell Jofiah Willard Jonathan Willard and Nathan Heywood

Meadow No 4 Lower Mulpus

furvayed for Robart ffyfe Claimer meadow Lot Number four belonging to houfe Lott Number twelve Lying in Lower Mulpus meadows Begining at a ftake fet up for the fouth weft Corner and runing Eaft twelve Degr thirty Min fouth fifty rod and a half there making an Angle and Runing Eaft thirty degr north twenty five rod there making an Angle and Runing Weft twelve degr thirty min north Eighty four rod there makeing an Angle and runing fouth twenty feven degr Eaft twenty two rod to where it Began

furvayed by Nathan Heywood and approved of by the Committee viz Jofiah Willard Jonathan Willard Nathan Heywood

Recorded march the twenty fift day in the year of our Lord one thoufand feven Hundred and thirty by me
Edward Hartwell Clerk.

Lunenburgh August the 12th 1729

3d Divifion

Laid out Phineas Parker by the Committee appointed one Hundred and twenty Acres of third Divifion Land belonging to Houfe Lot number twelve and is on the fowwefterly part of the apple tree Hill begining at a pillar of ftones Erected in Mr Pages Line and Runing North Eight Degr Eaft one Hundred and thirty three rod on faid Line to faid Pages nor weft Corner there making an Angle and Runing Weft Eigh degr North one Hundred and fifty rod to a pillar of ftones there making an Angle and Runing fouth Eight Degr Weft ninety four rod Crofsing the River twice at an Elme tree there making an Angle and Runing fouth thirty feven degr Eaft fifty four rod to a With hazele tree there making an Angle and runing Eaft Eight degr fouth one Hundred and thirteen rod to Where it Began

furvayed by Nathan Haywood and approved of by the Committee viz Edward Hartwell Nathan Heywood and Hilkiah Boynton —

Proprietors' Records. 19

Recorded march the twenty fifth day In the year of our Lord one thouſand ſeven Hundred and thirty
₱ Edward Hartwell Clerk

[11²]   Lunenburg november yᵉ 29 1731.

4ᵗʰ Diviſion   Laid out by the Committee appointed ten acres of fourth Diviſion Land to Robart Fyffe Claimer ſouth from his third Diviſion and adjoyning thereto ſixty rod and all the other Lines are bounding on the River and the ten acres is allmost all Entervail

Land ſurvayed by nathan Heywood and approved of by the Committee to witt Joſiah Willard Jonathan Willard and Edward Hartwell
Recorded march the 22ᵈ : 1731/2
₱ Edward Hartwell Clerk.

Lunenburg November the 30ᵗʰ 1731.

4ᵗʰ Diviſion Land.   Laid out by the Committee appointed ſeventy acres of fourth Diviſion to Robert Fyffe Claimer the right ariſing from houſe Lott No 12 and also the ten acres a bove ſaid is Laid out upon the ſaid right No 12 the ſeventy acres begins at a Certain Elm tree marked for the ſouth weſt Corner of his own third Diviſion and runs north 8 deg weſt on sᵈ third Diviſion ſeventy ſeven rod to a pillar of ſtones there making an Angle and runing Weſt 27 Deg north 56 ʳᵒᵈ to a black oak tree there making an Angle and runing Weſt 10 Degrees north on Land of Mr thurſtin 80 rod to a pillar of ſtones there making an Angle and runing ſouth Eight Degrees Weſt on Common Land 86 rod to a maple tree there making an Angle and runing East 12 Degrees ſouth 133 rod to Where it began

ſurvayed by Nathan Haywood and approved of by the Committee viz Joſiah Willard Edward Hartwell and Jonathan Willard
Recorded March the 22ᵈ anno Domini 1731/2
₱ Edward Hartwell Clerk

this Land Lyeth on the northerly ſide of the Role ſtone hill — —

[12]   DANIEL AUSTAIN

Houſe Lott   Granted to Daniel Auſtain by the Com-
No 13   mittee appointed by the Great and General
Court to a Lott and and grant out the Lands within the townſhip of Lunenburgh to Granttees forty three acres and a quarter within ſaid town for a Houſe Lott No thirteen to Gether with all the Rights and Diviſions of Land beLonging thereunto

               Lunenburgh february the 28th 1729/30.

Meadow   Survayed for Daniel Auſtain His Houſe
No 4   Lott Number thirtteen the Contents of Which is forty three Acres and a quarter alſo Laid by the committee a piece of Land adjoyning to make up what is Wanting in his houſe Lott. alſo furvayed his meadow Lott the Contents of which is fix acres and a quarter they joyning to gether begining at heape of ſtones which is y^e ſouth eaſterly Corner and runing North twenty nine Degrees Weſt forty three rod to a ſtake there making an angle and Runing Eaſt twenty Eight degrees North on Wetherbes Lott one hundred and fixty three rod to a heep of ſtones there making an Angle and Runing ſouth twenty nine degrees Eaſt on Wetherbe meadow two rod there making an Angle runing Eaſt twenty nine degrees north on the ſaid wetherbes meadow fixty Eight rod there making an Angle and runing ſouth Eleven degrees Eaſt on Joseph Pages meadow twenty one rod to a ſtake there making an angle and Runing Weſt twenty fix degrees ſouth on John fifks meadow forty five rod to a white oke tree there making an Angle and runing ſouth thirty degrees Weſt nineteen rod to the End of the Houſ Lott there making an Angle and runing ſouth twenty nine degrees East Eleven rod to a ſtake there making an Angle and Runing Weſt twenty nine degrees ſouth one Hundred and fixty three rod to where it began

     Survayed by Nathan Heywood and approved of by the Committee viz Edward Hartwell Nathan Heywood Joſiah Willard and Jonathan Willard

     Recorded August the ſeventh Day in the year of our Lord one thouſand ſeven Hundred and thirty

               by me Edward Hartwell Clerk

Lunenburgh April the 23ᵈ 1729.

third Divifion' Land — Laid out for Daniel Auftin by the Committee appointed to the right thirteen one hundred and nineteen acres and forty rod of third Divifion Land Lying on the Northerly fid of Mulpus begining at a pillar of ftones and Runing Eaft twenty five degrees fouth one Hundred and Eighty rod to a pillar of Stones; there making an Angle and Runing north twenty five degrees Eaft one Hundred and fix rod to a pillar of ftones there making an angle and Runing weft twenty five Degrees North one Hundred and Eighty rod to a pillar of ftones. there making an Angle and Runing fouth twenty five Degrees West one Hundred and fix rod to where it began.

furvayed by Nathan Heywood and approved of by the Committee viz

Edward Hartwell Benoni Boynton and Hilkiah boynton

Recorded August the feventh Day in the year of our Lord one thoufand feven Hundred and thirty

₱ Edward Hartwell Clerk

[12²] Lunenburg march the 23ᵈ 1730 — — —

2ᵈ Divifion No 50. — furvayed for Daniel Auftin 2ᵈ Divifion No 50 the Contents of which is 56 acres and three quarters Cituate and Lying on flat hill Begining at pillar of ftones Erected for the fouth Corner and runing north 17 degrees Eaft on Land of Archeebild mac-fedrich 150 rod to a ftake and heep of ftone there making an Angle and runing West 32 degrees north 61 rod to a pillar of ftones there making an Angle and runing fouth 18 degrees West on Lott No. 51: 149: rod to a ftake there making an angle and runing Eaft 31 degree fouth 64 rod to Where it Began

furvayed by Nathan Heywood and approved of by the Committee viz Jofiah Willard Edward Hartwell Jonathan Willard Nathan Heywood.

Recorded august the 16ᵗʰ annoque Domini 1731

₱ Edward Hartwell Clerk.

[13]   SAMUEL PAGE.

Granted to famuell Page by the Committee appointed by the Greate and General Court to aLott and Grant out the Lands within the Town of Lunenburg to Grantees one hundred and Eleven acres and one quarter for two Houfe Lotts within faid Townfhip for two Houfe Lotts namly fifty one and fifty two togather with all the Divifions of upland and meadow that belong thereto or fhall arife therefrom within the townfhip of faid Lunenburg.

Houfe Lott Lunenburg october the 26th 1747 furvayed
No: 51.   for the Heirs of Mr Samll Page above faid
   52.   Late of sd Lunenburg Deceafed the two Houfe Lotts which The faid famuell Page Died Poffeft of being Number fifty one and fifty two the Contents of Bouth being one hundred and Eleven acres and a quarter there being forty five pearch taken out by the town for a town way as pict out by this plan faid Lotts Begins at a Certain white oak tree marked for the fouth weft Corner of faid Land and runs north twenty three Degrees Weft on Capt Jonathan Willard and on the Town road and Robert Clarks Land one hundred and thirty feven rod to a Little walnut tree then it Runs Eaft twenty nine Degrees north on faid Clarks Land one hundred and fifty rod to a pillar of ftones then it Runs fouth one Degree Eaft on Land belonging to the Heirs of Jonas Gibfon Deceafed two hundred and Eight rod to a pillar of ftones on the Back fide of Aaron Browns fhop then it Runs then it Runs Weft Eight Degrees north on the Town Road feventy four Rod to where it begun

℔ Nathan Heywood furvayor and allowed on and ordered to be put upon Record by the Committee viz Nathan Heywood Edward Hartwell and
       December ye 4th 1747 then Recorded
              ℔ Edward Hartwell proprietors clark

[13²]   Lunenburg, April the 14th 1729.
3d Divifion   Laid out to famuell Page by the Commit-
No. 51   tee Eighty acres and fifty rod of third Divifion Land at the apple tree hill the Right arifing from

Houfe Lott No fifty one begining at a pillar of ftones and runing Eaft nine Degrees north Eighty one rod to a pillar of ftones there making and an angle and runing fouth nine Degrees west Eighty two rods to a pillar of ftones there making an Angle and runing Weft ten degrees fouth Eight rod there making an Angle and runing fouth ten degrees Eaft twenty one rod there making angle and runing fouth nine Degrees Weft fifty one rod there making an Angle and runing Weft nine Degrees North Eighty one rod there making an Angle and runing north nine Degrees Eaft one hundred and fixty rod to where it began

       Nathan Heywood furvayer

 approved of by the Committee viz Jofiah Willard Benoni Boynton Ifaac Farnsworth

 Recorded the 19th Day of may Annoque Domini 1729
      pr Edward Hartwell Clerk.

    Lunenburg october the 26th 1747.

2d Divifion   furvayed fecond Divifion Number fixty two
No 62   arifing from Houfe Lott Number 51 and is the most northerly Lott which is in the pofsefsion of Mofes Mitchel and nathaniel Page and Contains fixty two acres and one hundred and thirty Eight rod it begins at a pillar of ftones which is the most foutherly Corner of faid Lott and runs north fixteen Degrees Eaft on Land Left for a highway fixty four rod to a pillar of ftones then runs Weft twenty nine degrees north on Land of William Alexander one hundred and fixty two rod to a pillar of ftones then runs fouth fixteen Degrees Weft on Land of Robert Clark fixty four rod to a pillar of ftones then it Runs East twenty nine Degrees fouth on fecond Divifion No 61 – one hundred and fixty two rod to where it began

 furvayed by Nathan Heywood and allowed by the Committee Nathan Heywood Edward Hartwell December the 4th 1747. then Recorded

      ℔ Edward Hartwell
       proprietors Clerk

 the other Land of Mr famuell page are Recorded in the fecond part of this Book at page 41

[14]   THOMAS HILL.

House Lott   Granted to Thomas Hill By the Committee
No 15   appointed By the Greate and General Court to
alott and Grant out the Lands Within the townſhip of
Lunenburg to Granttees 47 acres & 138 rod for Houſe
Lott Number fifteen the meadow Lott in ſaid Houſe Lott
together withall the Rights and Diviſions of upland and
meadow within the Townſhip of Lunenburg that belongs
to or ſhall ariſe from ſaid Lott

April the 5th 1743. ſurvayed for John Hill of Boston
Esq. Claimer Houſe Lott No 15 the meadow Lott within
ſaid Lott and is bounded as followeth to witt Weſterly on Land of Samuell Davies ſoutherly on ye miniſterial
House Lott Eaſterly partly on the ſaid miniſterial Houſe
Lott and partly on ye Land of James Colbern Robert
Speer and Abel platts and northerly on Northfield road
ſo Called Begining at a ſtake ſet up for the ſoutheaſt
Corner and runs Weſt forty Six rod to a ſtake and heap
of ſtones then runing north one hundred and fifty Eight
rod to a ſtake and heap of ſtones then runing Eaſt fifty
one rod to a ſtake and heap of ſtones then runing ſouth
two degrees West one hundred and fifty nine rod to where
it began

ſurvayed by Jonathan Hubbard Jur allowed and approved of By the Committee and ordered to be recorded
viz

Edward Hartwell
Hilkiah Boynton
Nathan Heywood
Jonathan Willard

Recorded November ye 11th 1743

℗ Edward Hartwell Clerk

Lunenburg September the 2d 1729.

3d Diviſion   Laid out to Zacheas Hill one hundred and
twenty Eight acres and ninety rod nine acres
being to make up what is wanting in his Houſe Lott
begining at a Crotched oak tree and Runing ſouth 5
degrees Weſt 121 rod to an oak tree there making an

angle and Runing Eaſt five Degrees ſouth one hundred and ſeventy rod there making an Angle runing North five Degrees Eaſt one hundred and twenty one rod on John Hills Lott there making an Angle and Runing Weſt five Degrees North one hundred and ſeventy rod to where began partly on Capt Willards Land and partly on undevided Land ſurvayed by Nathan Heywood and approved of by the Committee viz Edward Hartwell Isaac Farnsworth and Jonathan Willard

Recorded october the 22ᵈ 1742

℔ Edward Hartwell proprietors Clerk

[14²]   Lunenburg June the 17ᵗʰ 1730
2ᵈ Diviſion   Survayed for Thomas Hill 2ᵈ Diviſion Nº
No 32   32. the Contents of Which is 54 Acres begining at a ſtake and heep of ſtones Which is the ſoutherly Corner and Runing West 31 deg 30 minits north 57 rod there there making an Angle and runing North 30 Deg. Eaſt on Lott No 31. 152 rod there making an Angle and Runing Eaſt 31 deg 30 min ſouth on the North range of Lotts 57 rod there making an Angle and Runing ſouth 30 Deg West on Lott No 33. to Where it Began.

ſurvayed by Nathan Heywood and approved of By the Committee to Witt Joſiah Willard Edward Hartwell Jonathan Willard and Nathan Heywood.

Recorded May the 26. 1732

℔ Edward Hartwell Cler.

Lunenburg April yᵉ 28ᵗʰ 1731

4ᵗʰ Diviſion   Laid out by the Committee appointed 86 acres of Land to Zacheus Hill Claimer in the Weſterly part ſaid townſhip for a fourth Diviſion ariſing from houſe Lott No 15 adjoyning to ſᵈ Zacheus Hills third Diviſion beging at a Certain pillar of ſtones in the Line of ſaid 3ᵈ Diviſion and runing Eaſt 5 deg ſouth on ſᵈ third Diviſion 76 rod to a maple tree there making an Angle and and Runing north 5 deg East on Land of William Clark Esqʳ 238 rod to a pillar of ſtones there making an Angle and runing West 35 deg ſouth on ſᵈ Clarks Land 59 rod to a ftake and heap of ftones there making an Angle and runing fouth 12 deg Weft on land of thomas Heale Esqr and David Wait 108 rod to where it Began. Survayed by Nathan Heywood and approved of by the Committee viz Jofiah Willard Edward Hartwell and Jonathan Willard Recorded May the 26th 1732

℔ Edward Hartwell Cler

May the 26th 1744. we whofe Names are under written making fearch and taking a Critical furvay of the fourth Divifion above pland viz Zacheus Hills and finding wanting in meafur Eight acres and an half and have therefore Laid out faid Eight acres an a half on the fouth fide of of faid Hills 3^d Divifion an hundred and feventy rod in Long and Eight rods wide to make up faid Deficient Lott

℔ Nathan Heywood furvayor

approved of by the Committee viz Edward Hartwell Nathan Heywood an
May the 28th 1744 Recorded ℔

Edward Hartwell proprietors Clerk

[15]   THOMAS KIMBAL

Granted to Thomas Kimbal by the Committee appointed by the Greate and General Court to a Lott and Grant out the Lands Within the town of Lunenburg to Grantee   acres for a houfe Lott bearing No 16 to gether with all the rights and Divifions of Lands belonging thereto or arifeing therefrom.

Lunenburg March ye 24th 1729/30

2^d Divifion   furvayed for Thomas Kimbal a fecond Di-
No 24   vifion No 24 the Contents of Which is fifty two acres and a quarter

Begining at a ftak and a heap of ftones Erected for the South Corner and runing north twenty Eight Deg Eaft on Lott number twenty three one hundred and fifty rod to a ftak there making there making An Angle and Runing Weft thirty one deg thirty minits north on the

North town Line fifty six rods to a ftake there making an Angle and runing fouth twenty nine degrees Weft one hundred and fifty rod on Lott No 25 there making an Angle and runing Eaft thirty one degree thirty minits fouth fifty feven rod and a half to Where it began

Surveyed by Nathan Heywood and approved of by the Committee viz Jofiah Willard Edward Hartwell Jonathan Willard and nathan Heywood

Recorded march the 26. annoque Domini 1731

₱ Edward Hartwell Clerk

[16] JONATHAN WOODMAN.

Granted unto Jonathan Woodman by the Committee appointed by the Greate and General Court to a Lott and Grant out the Lands Within faid town to Granttees for a houfe Lott to gether Withall the rights and Divifions of Land be Longing there to or arifing there to from

Lunenburg March the 25th 1729 $\frac{30}{}$

2^d Divifion   Survayed for Capt Jonathan Woodman a
No 40   fecond Divifion Lott No 40 : Lying near perhams meadow the Contents of which is 51 acres and a half Begining at a Certain White oak tree ⁓ marked for the fouth weft Corner and Runing West to a White oak tree 54 rod Bounding Chifly on Capt Jofeph Goulds first Divifion there making an Angle and runing Weft 31 deg 30 minits North 8 : rod to a ftake there making an Angle and runing north 27 Degrees Eaft : 157 : on Brewers Lott to a ftake there making an Angle and runing Eaft : 31 : deg : 30 : minits fouth on fecond Divifion Land : 60 : rod to a read oak tree there making an Angle and runing South 29 Degrees West on Goulds Lott : 128 rod to Where It began

Survayed by Nathan Heywood and approved of by the Committee viz Jofiah Willard Edward Hartwell Jonathan Willard and Nathan Heywood.

Recorded october the 11th annoque Domini 1731 :

₱ Edward Hartwell Cler

[**16²**] Lunenburg May the 21ˢᵗ 1737

2ᵈ Divifion Survayed for Collº Jofiah Willard Claimer
No 82. 2ᵈ Divifion No 82 (arifing from Houfe Lott No 5.) now in pofsefsion of Capᵗ Jonathan Woodman Containing 55 acres Begining at a Certain Red oak tree marked for the Eafterly Corner of faid Woodmans other Divifion and runs fouth 32 deg West on faid Divifion 128: rod to a White oak tree then runs Eaft 105 rod bounding partly on Capᵗ Jofeph Gould partly on Jonathan Dows Esqʳ and partly on John White to a hemLock tree then runing north 28 deg 30 min Eaft on Jonathan Wheeler 75 rod to a White oak tree thence runing Weft 31 deg 30 min north on the north range. 86. rod to Where it began

℔ Nathan Heywood Survayer

approved of Edward Hartwell Jofiah Willard and Jonathan Willard Committee

Recorded may the 23ᵈ 1737

℔ Edward Hartwell Clerk

June 21ᶠᵗ 1773.

Laid out by the Committee appointed twenty four acres and an half of Land in Fitchburg to George Kimball Claimer to make up what is wanting in the fecond Divifion Lott number forty it being an Equivelent therefor It Begins at a beach tree marked and ftands on the northry fide of the Road that Leads up to Benjamin Frofts Dwelling Houfe and in the Eafterly Line of faid Frofts Land and runs Eaft three Degrees north bounding on Common Land feventy rod to a heap of ftones thence north three Degrees Weft Bounding on Common Land fifty-six rod to a heap of ftones thence Weft three degrees fouth on Common Land feventy rod to a heap of ftones By the Brook which is faid Frofts north eaft Corner then it runs fouth three degrees Eaft Bounding on faid Frofts Land fifty fix rod to where it began

furvayed by Nathan Heywood and approved of and ordered to be Recorded by us Nathan Heywood Ephraim Pearce and Eleazer Houghton Committee

Recorded June the 25ᵗʰ 1773

By me Edward Hartwell Proprietors Cleark

[17] SAMUEL WARREN.

[18] JOSIAH BAILEY.

Houſe Lott
No 19

Granted unto Joſiah Bailey Houſe Lott nomber nineteen within the town of Lunenburg by the Committee appointed by the Great and General Court to alott and Grant out the Lands Within ſaid town it Being forty two acres and one hundred and thirty nine rod to gather With all the rights and Diviſions that belong thereto or ſhall ariſe there from and the ſaid Houſe Lott Begins at a heap of ſtones Which is the Norweſt Corner and runing ſouth 1 degree Weſt on John Hills Lott 154 rod there making an Angle and runing Eaſt on Woborn farm 44 rod and ½ to a Cheſnut tree there making an Angle and and runing North one Degree Eaſt on Lott Number 18. 154 rod there making an Angle and runing Weſt 44 rod and a half to Where it Began

Survayed by Nathan Haywood and approved of By the Committee viz Joſiah Willard Edward Hartwell Jonathan Willard and Nathan Heywood

Recorded march y^e: 1: 1733/4

℔ Edward Hartwell Clerk

[18²] Lunenburg January the 11th 1730/31

Meadow
Lott No 3.
mulpus.

Survayed for Joſiah Bayley meadow Lott Number 3 in uper mulpus the Contents of Which is 6 acres and (114) rod Begining at red oake tree marked at the ſouth Corner and runing Eaſt 27 Degrees North on the upland thirty three rod to a pine tree there making an Angle and Runing North 9 West on Meadow Lot No. 2 37 rod to a pillar of Stones there making an Angle and Runing West 10 degrees ſouth by the upLand 15 rod to a pine tree there making an angle and runing Weſt 16 degrees North 7 rod and a half to a ſtake there making an Angle and Runing ſouth 2 Degrees Weſt on Meadow Lott No: 4: 50 rod to Where It Began

Survayed by Nathan Heywood and approved of By the Committee viz Joſiah Willard Jonathan Willard Edward Hartwell and Nathan Heywood.

Recorded December the 29th: 1731:

℔ Edward Hartwell Cler

Lunenburg March the 24th 1729/30

2d Divifion No 23. Survayed for Jofiah Bailey a fecond Divifion No. 23. the Contents of Which is 52. Acres and a quarter

Begining at a ftake and a pillar of ftones Erected for the fouth Corner and Runing North 28 Degrees Eaft on Lott No 22 150 rod to a ftake there making an Angle and runing West 31 deg 30 minits north on the north town Line 56 rod there making an Angle and Runing fouth 28 degrees West on Lot Number twenty four 150 rod to a ftake there making an Angle and runing Eaft 31 degree 30 minits fouth 57 rod to Where It Began.

Survayed By Nathan Heywood and approved of By the Committee viz Jofiah Willard Jonathan Willard Nathan Heywood and Edward Hartwell

Recorded December the 29th annoque Domini 1731

₱ Edward Hartwell Cler

[19] JOHN HILL

Houfe Lott 20. Granted to John Hill By the Committee appointed By the Greate and General Court to aLott and Grant out the Land Within the Townfhip of Lunenburgh to Granttees fourty one acres and : 139 rod of Land Within faid Townfhip for a houfe Lott baring Number twenty to gether With all the Rights and Divifions of Land belonging thereunto

Lunenburg June the 12th 1730 furvayed for John Hill Houfe Lott Number twenty the Contents of Which is fourty one Acres and 139 rod. Begining at a heap of ftones Which is the North eaft Corner and Runing fouth one Degree Weft on Josiah Baleyes Lott one Hundred and fifty four rod there making an Angle and Runing Weft fourty three rod and a half on Woborn farm there Making an Angle and Runing North one Degree Eaft on Calfs Lott one hundred and fifty four rod there making an Angle and runing Eaft on Northfield road fourty three rod and a half to where it began furvayed by Nathan Heywood and approved of by the Committee viz Josiah Willard Jonathan Willard Edward Hartwell and Nathan Heywood

Recorded December the feventeenth Day in the year of our Lord one thoufand feven hundred and thirty

Edwd Hartwell Clerk

Lunenburgh June the 17th 1730

2^d Divifion
33.

furvayed for John hill fecond Divifion Number thirty three the Contents of Which is fifty three acres and a half. Begining at a ftake and and heep of ftones Which is the Southerly Corner and Runing Weft thirty one Degrees thirty minits North fifty fix rod and a half there making an angle and Runing north thirty degrees Eaft on Lott Number thirty two one Hundred and fifty two rod there Making an Angle and Runing Eaft thirty one Degrees thirty minits fouth on the North range fifty fix rod and a half there making an Angle and runing fouth thirty degrees Weft on Lott Number thirty four one hundred fifty two Rod to Where It Began furvayed by Nathan Heywood and approved of by the Committee Jofiah Willard Jonathan Willard Edward Hartwell and nathan heywood

Recorded Defember the feventeenth Day in the year of our Lord one thoufand feven hundred and thirty

Edwd Hartwell Clerk

Lunenburg September 2^d 1729, to John hill

3^d Divifion

Laid out by the Committee appointed one Hundred and twenty acres of third Divifion Land arifing from houfe Lott Number twenty

Begining at a Hemlock tree and Runing Weft five Degrees north one Hundred and fifty nine rod on third Divifion Land Laid out to Capt Jofiah Willard there Making an Angle and Runing fouth five Degrees Weft one Hundred and twenty one rod there making an Angle and Runing Eaft five Degrees fouth one hundred and fifty nine rod to a White pine tree there making an angle and runing north five degrees Eaft one hundred and twenty one rod to Where It began

Survayed by Nathan Heywood and approved of by the Committee viz Edward Hartwell Jonathan Willard and Isaac Farnsworth

Recorded December the feventeenth Day in the year of our Lord one thoufand feven Hundred & thirty

⅌ Edwd Hartwell Clerk

[Inserted between pages 19 and 19².]

This may Certify whome it may Concerne that we Jofhua Billings Junr and Ruben Billings Did inadvertently Cut Down A Hemlock tree which was marked for the Northeaft Corner of John Hills 4th Divifion lot arifing from Houfe lot No 20 and is Recorded in the 19th page of the proprietors book, and is alfo the foutheaft Corner of a lot of land Laid out to Col^o Jofiah Willard and Recorded in page 16 of the proprietors 2^d book

   (signed)   Joshua Billings Junr
   (signed)   Reuben Billings.

We the under figned, owners of the lands Ajacent to the above mentioned Hemlock Confidering the above mentioned Hemlock to be of Great importance to be kept in Remembrance (it being the only original bound, for a Great Distance from this place) Did afsemble immediately and Erect a large heap of Stones around the Stump, and we Defire the proprietors Clerk to Seal thefe lines into the proprietors Book facing page 19th So that whoever in future should look for the bounds of Ether of the above mentioned lots may se that the bound is Renewed as above mentioned

     (signed)   Thos Evans ⎫ owners
Afhby Sep^tr ye 26th 1795. Israel gibson ⎪ of the
     (signed)   Asa Kendall ⎬ Ajacent
     (signed)   Jacob Puffer ⎭ Lands

[19²] Lunenburg January the 11 1730/31

Meadow Lott No 2 a quarter

Survayed for John Hill meadow Lott No 2 in mulpus uper meadows next to the faid Way. the Contents of Which is 4 acres and Begining at a pine tree marked for the fouth

weſt Corner and runing north nine Degrees West on meadow Lott No 3 : 37 rod to a heap of ſtones there making an Angle and runing Eaſt one Degree North on upland 13 rod to a pine ſtumpe there making an Angle and Runing ſouth 42 Degrees Eaſt on upland 19 rod there making an angle and Runing ſouth ten Degrees Weſt on upland 8 rods there making an angle and ſouth East 6 rod and a half to a pine tree there making an angle and runing ſouth 35 Degrees West Croſing the Brook 12 rod to a pine tree there making an Angle and Runing West one Degree ſouth 16 rod to Where it Began ſurvayed By
         Nathan Heywood

and approved of by the Committee viz Joſiah Willard Edward Hartwell Jonathan Willard and Nathan Heywood

 Recorded September the 3ᵈ anno Domini 1731
      ₱ Edward Hartwell
         Clerke

     December the 3ᵈ 1731.

4ᵗʰ Diviſion Laid out by the Committee appointed thirty acres and one hundred rod of Land to John Hill for part of his fourth Diviſion ſcituat Lying and being by the norweſterly ſide of the perl hill being Chiefly Swamp Beginning at a Certain Black oake tree marked for the Eaſt Corner which is the Corner of Collᵒ Browns Land and runing west thirty one Degrees thirty minits north on Hugh Scotts Land ſeventy rod to a beach tree there making angle and runing ſouth thirty one degrees thirty minits weſt on Common Land ſeventy rod to a pillar of ſtones by a Cheſnut tree there making an Angle and runing Eaſt thirty one degrees thirty minits ſouth on Common Land ſeventy rod to the aforeſaid Collᵒ Browns Land there making an Angle and runing north 31 degrees Eaſt on ſaid Browns Land ſeventy rod to where it began
      ₱ nathan Heywood ſurvayor

and approved of by the Committee viz Edward Hartwell Ephraim Pearce and Jonathan Willard
 Recorded December yᵉ 16ᵗʰ 1738
     ₱ Edward Hartwell Clerk

february 4
1737/8
4th Divifion

Laid out to John Hill forty acres and an half of Land in the northwesterly part of faid townfhip for part of a forth divifion arifing from Houfe Lott No twenty Begining at a hemlock tree marked for the Eaft Corner of faid Land and runs Weft thirty two degrees north on Land Laid out to Collo Jofiah Willard 222 rod to a maple tree then runs fouth twelve digrees Weft on Land belonging to the Heirs of Collo Brown thirty three rod then runs Eaft thirty two Degrees fouth on the fecretarys Land two hundred and twelve rod then north thirty two degrees Eaft thirty rod to where it began

₱ Nathan Heywood furvayor

And approved of By the Committee viz Edward Hartwell Jonathan Willard and Jofiah Willard.

Recorded December the 16th 1738

₱ Edward Hartwell Clerk

[20]   JOHN CALF

House Lott
No 21

Granted unto John Calf by the Committee appointed by the Greate and General Court to a Lott and Grant out the Lands Contained Within the Townfhip of Lunenburg to Granttee thirty Eight Acres and a quarter Within faid town for Houfe Lott bearing Number 21 to Gether With all the Rights and Divifions of Land and meadow that beLongs thereto or fhall arife therefrom

Recorded march ye 7th 1732/3

₱ Edward Hartwell Clerk

Lunenburg April the 24th 1733.

Survayed for Mr Jonas Clark Claimer Houfe Lott No 21 the Contents of Which is thirty Eight acres and a quarter

Begining at a Certain Chefnut tree marked for the Northeaft Corner of faid Lott and runing West on Northfield Road 43 rod to a pillar of ftones there making an angle and runing fouth on mr Heals Lott 154 rod to to a pillar of ftones thence runing East on Woborn farm 38 rod to a pillar of ftones thence runing north one Degree Eaft on John Hill Lott 154 rod to Where it Began   furvayed By Nathan Heywood and approved of By the Committee viz Jofiah Willard Edward Hartwell Jonathan Willard and Nathan Heywood

Recorded March ye 7th 1733/4

₱ Edward Hartwell Clerk

Lunenburg october ye 25th 1736.

Meadow Lott No 3.   furvayed meadow Lott No 3. in Lower Mulpus belonging to the right of John Calf the Contents of which is five acres Begining at a white pine tree marked for the Eafterly Corner and runing fouth 20 degrees Weft 35 rod to a ftake by the Brook then runing Weft 4 deg^r north by the Brook 23 rod to a ftake then runing North 4 degrs West by meadow Lott No 2: 16 rod to a black burch tree then runs East 37: Deg^{rs} north on a pine ridge and fwamp 36: rod to fmall maple tree then runs fouth 43 deg^{rs} Eaft on fwamp ten rod to where it began

By Nathan Heywood fur.

approved of By the Committee viz Edward Hartwell Jonathan Willard

Recorded November ye 8th 1736

₱ Edward Hartwell propr: Clerk

[20^2]   Lunenburg. March the 24th 1732/3

2^d Divifion No 27   Survayed for John Calf a 2^d Divifion number twenty feven the Contents of Which is fifty two acres and a half.

Begining at a ftake and heap of ftones Erected for the fouth Corner and runing north 30 Degrees Eaft on Lott Number 26 150 rod to a ftake there making an Angle and Runing Weft 31 degrees 30 minits north on the north town Line 56 rods there making an Angle and Runing fouth 30 degrees West on Lott No 28 150 rod to a ftake there making an Angle and runing East 31 degrees 30 minits fouth 56 to Where it began.

furvayed by nathan Heywood and approved of by the Committee viz Jofiah Willard Edward Hartwell Jonathan Willard and Nathan Heywood

Recorded December ye 29th 1733

₱ Edward Hartwell Clerk

Lunenburg April ye 24th 1733.

3^d Divifion   Laid out to mr Jonas Clark Claimer by the Committee appointed 120 Acres of third Divifion Land arifing from Houfe Lott No 21 Cituate and Lying on the Southerly fide of the River Begining at a ftake which is John Heywoods foutheaft Corner of his third Divifion and Runing Eaft 42 Degrees South by the River 90 rod there making an Angle and runing West 33 degrees fouth 14 rod to Goodridges Corner there making an Angle and runing fouth 42 Degrees Eaft on Goodridges Lott 10 rods there making an Angle and runing West 11 degrees fouth on houghtons Lott 83 rod there making an Angle and runing West 19 Degrees fouth on Common Land 146 rod there making an Angle and runing North 15 Degrees West on Common Land 96 rod there making an Angle and runing Eaft 15 Degrees north Chiefly on John Heywoods Lott 189 rod to Where it Began furvayed by Nathan Heywood and approved of by ye Committee viz. Jofiah Willard Edward Hartwell & Jonathan Willard

Recorded march ye 7th 1733/4

℔ Edward Hartwell Clerk

The other Lands belonging to this Right are Recorded in the fecond part of this Book at page 35.

[21]   THOMAS HALE.

Granted to Thomas Hale by the Committee appointed by the Greate and General Court to a lott and Grant out the Lands Within the Town of Lunenburg to Granttee forty five acres of Land Within faid town for a houfe Lott No : 22 to gether With all the Rights and Divifions of Land belonging thereto or arifeing therefrom — —

Lunenburg April the 24 : 1733.

Houfe Lott No 22   Survayed for Thomas Hale Houfe Lott No. 22 the Contents of Which is 45 Acres Begining at a Certain pillar of ftones Erected for the North eaft Corner and runing West 44 rod to a pillar of ftones and runing from thence fouth 2 Degrees West on m^r prefcotts Lott 154 rod to a pillar of ftones thence runing Eaft on Woborn farm 50 rod to a pillar of ftones thence runing north on the Lott now beLonging to m^r Jonas Clark 154 rod to Where it Began

furvayed by Nathan Heywood and approved of By the Committee viz Jofiah Willard Edward Hartwell and Nathan Heywood

Recorded March ye 7th 1733/4

℗ Edward Hartwell Clerk

Lunenburg June the 17th 1731.

2^d Divifion No 38. furvayed for Thomas Hale 2^d Divifion N° 38. the Contents of Which is 52 Acres and a quarter. begining at hemlock tree Which is the foutherly Corner and runing Weft 31 deg 30 minits North 57 rod there making an Angle and runing North 30 Deg Eaft on Lott No 37. 152 rod there making an Angle and runing Eaft 31 degree 30 min fouth on the North range of Lotts 52 rod there making an Angle and runing fouth 28 Degrees West on Lott No: 39: 152: rod to Where it began.

furvayed by Nathan Heywood and approved of by the Committee to witt Jofiah Willard Edward Hartwell Jonathan Willard and Nathan Heywood

Recorded May the 28th 1731

℗ Edwd Hartwell Clerk

[21^2]   Lunenburg April ye 26. 1731

3^d Divifion & 4th Divifion Laid out by the Committee appointed 195 acres of Land In the Westerly part of f^d townfhip for a third and fourth Divifion to Thomas Hale Esqr arifeing from houfe Lott No 22 Begining at a Certain Beach tree Marked for the north west Corner and Runing South 12 Degrees West on Land of Samuell Brown Esqr 165 rod to a ftake and heep of ftones there making an Angle and runing Eaft 12 Degrees fouth on Land of David Wait 190 : rod to a pillar of ftones there making an Angle and Runing North 12 Degrees Eaft on Common Land 165 rod to a ftake and heep of ftons there making and Angle and Runing West : 12 : Degrees north on Land of Jofiah Willard 190 rod to Where it began furvayed by Nathan Heywood and approved of by the Committee viz Jofiah Willard Edward Hartwell and Jonathan Willard

Recorded September the 11th anno Domini 1731
₱ Edward Hartwell Clerk

Lunenburg May the 8th 1731

Meadow Lott furvayed for thomas Hale Esqr Meadow
Mulpus Lott No : 1 in Mulpus meadows the Contents of which is 6 acres and a half. Begining at a Certain pillar of Stones Erected for the North Corner and runing fouth 38 Degrees West on Mr Thirsting meadow 32 : rod to the upland there making an Angle and runing fouth by the upLand : 40 : rod there making an Angle and runing Eaft on meadow Land of Walter Beeth 25 rod to a ftake there making an Angle and runing Weft 30 Degrees north : 9 : rod by the up Land there making an Angle and runing north 19 Degrees West on the up Land : 6 : rod there making an Angle and runing north 4 degrees Eaft on the upland : 18 : rod there making an Angle and runing north 37 Degrees East 18 rod on the upland there making an Angle and Runing North 18 Degree West on the upland 25 rod to Where it began

furvayed by Nathan Heywood and approved of by the Committee viz Josiah Willard Edward Hartwell Jonathan Willard and Nathan Heywood.

Recorded October the 11th annoque Domini 1731
₱ Edward Hartwell CLer

[22] THE REV^D MR ANDREW GARDNER of Lunenburgh
47   To William Clark Esqr For a Seccond division of Sixty Acres Number eighty arrising from House lott N° one and bounded as by Plan given in with the Deed

To Ditto   For two third divisions of Two hundred and forty acres, arrising from House lotts Nomber one and number Eighty four lying East of Neesepegesuck ponds

To Ditto   For two Common rights after the third division arrising from House lotts Number One & number Eighty four

Lunenburg January the 9th 1729/30

Houſe Lott No 84

Survayed for the Revrend m^r andrew Gardner Claimer Houſe Lott Number 84. the Contents of Which is 51 acres and a half Begining at a ſtake ſet up for the north eaſt Corner and runing Weſt 2 Degrees ſouth 120 rod on Groute Lott there making an Angle and runing ſouth 15 degrees Eaſt 68 rod on Woborn farm Line there making an Angle and runing Eaſt 4 Degrees North 134 rod on Jonathan Willards Lott there making an Angle and Runing North 23 degrees Weſt 31 rod on pages Lott there making an Angle and runing north 29 Degrees Weſt 27 rod to Where it Began

Survayed by Nathan Haywood and approved by the Committee viz Joſiah Willard Edward Hartwell Jonathan Willard and Nathan Heywood

Recorded February the 22^d anno Domini 1733/4

₱ Edward Hartwell proprietor Clerk

Lunenburg January the 18th 1730/31

meadow Lott No 1.

Survayed for m^r Andrew Gardner Claimer meadow Lott No 1 in Cattaconamoug meadows on Both ſides Massapoog brook the Contents of Which is 5 acres and a quarter Begining at a Certain popler tree marked for the moſt northerly Corner and runing West 24 degrees ſouth on Land of Eleazer Houghton 34 rod to a ſtake there making an angle and runing ſouth 19 Degrees Eaſt on Land of ſ^d Houghton 20 rod to a ſtake there making an Angle and runing Eaſt 9 degree north on Land of ſaid Houghton 34 rod to a ſtake there making an Angle and runing north 19 degrees Weſt on medow Lott number two twenty Eight rod to Where it began

ſurvayed by Nathan Heywood and approved of by the Committee viz Joſiah Willard Edward Hartwell Jonathan Willard and Nathan Heywood

Recorded February ye 22^d 1733/4

₱ Edward Hartwell Clerk.

[22²] Lunenburg June the 17th 1730:

Second Divifion No 31 — furvayed for the Reverend Mr Andrew Gardner Claimer 2d Divifion Number 31 : the Contents of Which is 54 acres

Begining at a ftake and heap of ftones Which is the foutherly Corner and Runing West 31 deg 30 min North 57 rod there making an Angle and Runing North 30 deg East 152 rod there making an Angle and runing East 31 deg 30 fouth on the North range 57 rod there Making an Angle and Runing fouth 30 deg West on Lott No. 32 : 152 : rod to Where it Began furvayed Nathan Heywood and approved of By the Committee viz Jofiah Willard Edward Hartwell Jonathan Willard and Nathan Heywood
Recorded December the 29th Anno Domini 1731

℗ Edward Hartwell Cler

Lunenburg april ye 10th 1730.

Houfe lot No 14 — furvayed for the Revd Mr Andrew Gardner Claimer Houfe Lott Number 14 the Contents of which is 45 acres Begining at a ftake fet up for the foutherly Corner and runing Eaft 30 degrees North on mr pages Lott 168 rod to a White oak tree there making angle and runing North 29 Degrees West on the Clay pitt Land 45, rod there making an Angle and runing west 31 degrees fouth on Daniel Auftins Lott 168 there making an Angle and runing fouth 29 degrees East 40 rod to Where it Began

furvayed by Nathan Haywood and approved of by the Committee viz Jofiah Willard Edward Hartwell Jonathan Willard and Nathan Heywood
Recorded February ye 22d 1733/4

℗ Edward Hartwell proprietors Clerk

[23] ROBERT PAUL

Houfe Lott No 24. — Granted unto Robart Paul by the Committee appointed by the Greate and General Court to a Lott and Grant out the Lands Within the town of Lunenburg to granttees thirty nine Acres and a half of Land Within faid town for a houfe Lott Number twenty four to gether With all the Rights and Divifions of Land that belongs thereto or fhall arife therefrom

Lunenburg November ye 24th 1731.

Survayed for Hugh Scot Claimer houſe Lott Number 24 the Contents of Which is thirty nine Acres and a half. Begining at a Certain Chesnut tree marked for the northeasterly Corner and Runing West 43 : rod to a pillar of Stones bounding on Land left for a highway called northfield road there making an Angle and runing ſouth 2 degrees 30 degrees West on Robart Cummings Lott N° 25: 147: rod to a pillar of ſtones there making an Angle and runing East on Woborn farm 44 rod to a pillar of ſtones there making an Angle and runing north 3 Degrees Eaſt on m^r preſcotts Lott 147 rod to Where it Began

ſurvayed by Nathan Heywood and approved of by the Committee viz Edward Hartwell Nathan Heywood Jonathan Willard and Josiah Willard

Recorded December the 6th Anno Domini 1731

₱ Edward Hartwell Cler

Lunenburg November the 23^d 1731

2^d Diviſion   ſurvayed for hugh Scot Claimer ſecond
No 30   diviſion number 30. the Contents of Which is 51 acres and a half belonging to houſe Lott 24 Begining at a Certain Stake and heape of Stones Erected for the ſouth eaſt Corner and runing West 31 Degrees 30 minits north 56 rod to a ſtake and pillar of ſtones there making an Angle and runing North 31 degrees Eaſt 150 rod to a pillar of Stones there making an Angle and runing Eaſt 31 Degrees 30 minits South on the north range of Lotts 55 rod to a pillar of Stones there making an Angle and Runing South 31 degree West on Lott No 31: 150 : rod to Where It Began Survayed by nathan Heywood and approved of By the Committee Edward Hartwell Nathan Heywood Jonathan Willard Josiah Willard

Recorded December the 6: 1731

₱ Edward Hartwell CLer

Lunenburg November the 23^d 1731.

Meadow Lott   Survayed for huge Scot Claimer the Meadow Lott belonging to Houſe Lott Number 24 In pearl hill meadow at the Lower End of ſaid meadow the Contents of Which is fix acres and three quarters Containing fom upland. Begining at a Certain pine tree marked for the Most Wefterly Corner and runing North 35 Deg Eaft 78 rod to a pine tree there making an Angle and runing fouth 30 Degrees Eaft 20 rod to a White oak tree there making an Angle and runing fouth 40 Degrees Weft 67 rod there making an Angle and running West 24 Degrees north on Meadow Land 12 rod to Where it Began

⅌ Nathan Heywood Survayer

approved of by the Committee Edward Hartwell Nathan heywood Jonathan Willard Jofiah Willard.

Recorded December the 15th anno Domini 1731

⅌ Edward Hartwell Clerk

[23²] Lunenburg November ye 23d 1731.

Houfe Lott No. 24.

Laid out by the Committee appointed 235 Acres of Land northerly from pearl Hill to Hugh Scott Claimer arifeing from Houfe Lott No. 24 for a third Divifion and a fourth Divifion and to make up What is Wanting in the Houfe Lott and fecond Divifion in Cluding a fmale corner of meadow belonging to another Lott.

Begining at a Certain ftake in faid meadow and runing North 31 deg. 30 minits Eaft on Mr Allens Land 145 rod to the town Line there making an angle and Runing West 31 degrees 30 minits north on faid town Line 260 rod the other two Lines being parralel and Bounding Wefterly on Common Land and fowweft By Collonel Brown and Josiah Willard Esqr.

Survayed by nathan Heywood and approved of By the Committee viz Josiah Willard Edward Hartwell Jonathan Willard Nathan Heywood

Recorded May the 25th Anno Domini 1732

⅌ Edward Hartwell Cler

[24] CAPT. JOSIAH WILLARD of Lunenburgh

47

To William Clark Esqr for two Seccond divisions of One hundred and twenty Acres arrising from House Lotts number and pland with his lott bought of the Revd Mr Gardner & part of his own third division

47   To Ditto – – for four third divisions of Four hundred & Eighty Acres arrising from House lotts Number Forty Six number Fifty three, Number Eighty five & Number Eighty Six —

[24²]   Lunenburgh April the 11th 1730.

Second Divifion No. 6.   Survayed for Capt Josiah Willard the Land Where he now DweLs the Contents of which is one hundred and fivety acres and a half.

Second Divifion No. 5.   Begining at a ftake fet up for the foutheafterly Corner and runing Weft, twenty Degrees forty minits fouth on Land of Eleazer Houghton fivety nine rod there making an Angle. and runing North twenty fix degr West on Land of f^d Houghton fifty Eight rod there making an Angle and runing weft feven degrees North on Land of Said Houghton fixty rod there making an Angle and runing North fixteen degrees Weft Eighty three rod on Woborn Line there makeing an Angle and runing Eaft twenty feven degrees North two Hundred and fix rod on Land of Jonathan Willard, there Making an Angle and runing South Eight Degrees Weft one hundred and twenty Nine rod on Land of the afore f^d Josiah willard there making an angle and runing fouth three degrees Weft Eighty three rod to Where it began.

Survayed by Nathan Heywood and approved on by the Committee viz Josiah Willard Jonth Willard Edward Hartwell Nathan Heywood and there is a Lowance in the above f^d Land for a highway four rod wide

Recorded September the tenth Day in the year of our Lord one thoufand feven hundred and thirty — — —

       ℔ Edward Hartwell Clerk

4th Division   Laid out to Lt. Edward Hartwell and to Capt Josiah Willard by the Committee apointed by the proprietors of Lunenburgh three Hundred acres of fourth Divifion Land Scituate neer to the middle of Lunenburgh Townfhip at aple tree hill the rights arifeing from Houfe Lott Number Seventy three and part of the right Eighty Seven and from Houfe Lott Number fixty and part of the fifty feven—Begining at a pillar of ftones Erected for a Corner and runing Eaft twenty Seven deg. fouth fifty two rod to a pillar of ftones and then runs Eaft nine degree fouth one Hundred and fixty two rod on Ffyefs Lott to a pillar of Stones there runing North twenty feven deg Eaft one hundred and Eighty one rod on faid hartwells Lott to a pillar of Stones and then runs weft fifteen deg north one hundred and one rod to a mark and then runs weft fourty four deg North fifty two rod to a pillar of ftones and then runs Weft thirty five degrees fouth ninety four rod to a pillar of ftones and then runs north fifteen deg West one one Hundred and fifty five rod to a pillar of Stones and Bounds on Daniel Thuftain to where it began furvayed by Nathan Heywood and approved of by the Committee viz Edward Hartwell Jofiah willard and Jonathan willard

Recorded october the 20th day in the year of our Lord one thoufand feven Hundred and thirty
                    ℔ Edward Hartwell Clerk

The other Lands of Colo Jofiah Willard are at page 8 in the fecond part of this book and fo on.

[25]   JOSIAH WILLARD ESQ^R of Boston

Houfe Lott   Granted unto Josiah Willard Esqr by the
No 26.   Committee appointed By the Greate and General Court to a Lott and Grant out the Lands Within the town of Lunenburg to Grantee 57 acres and a quarter of Land Within faid town for a houfe Lott Number 26 to Gether withall the rights and Divifions of Land that beLongs thereto or fhall arife therefrom ; &c.

Lunenburgh June 16th 1730.

Survayed for Josiah Willard Esqr Houfe Lott No 26 on the fouth fide of North field Road the Contents of Which is 57 Acres and a quarter Begining at a pillar of Stones Which is North eaft Corner and Runing Weft on f^d Road 58 rod there making an Angle and Runing fouth on Land of John Wood 158 rod there Making an Angle and runing Eaft 58 rod there Making an Angle and runing North 158' rod to Where it Began. Survayed by Nathan Heywood and approved of by the Committee viz Josiah Willard Edward Hartwell Jonathan Willard and Nathan Heywood

Recorded May the 28th annoque Domini 1731 p^r
Edward Hartwell Clerk.

Lunenburg November ye 7th 1730.

Houfe Lott No. 36. Survayed for Josiah Willard Esqr of Boston Claimer Houfe Lott Number thirty fix the Contents of which is fourty four acres and a half Begining at a Certain pillar of tones Erected for the fouth eaft Corner and runing runing North 4 degrees West on Lott No 35 160 rod there making an Angle and Runing West 46 rod there making an Angle and Runing fouth 4 degrees Eaft on lot number 37 160 rod to a pillar of Stones there making an Angle and Runing Eaft on Land Left for a high Way 45 rod to Where it began.

Survayed by Nathan Heywood and approved of by the Committee viz Josiah Willard Jonathan Willard Edward Hartwell and Nathan Heywood.

Recorded December ye 29th 1732
₱ Edward Hartwell Clerk.

September the 5th 1743.

2^d Divifion No 77. Survayed for the Honourable Josiah Willard Esqr a fecond Divifion Loott in Lunenburg being N^o feventy feven Confisting of fifty one acres and an half Begining at a pillar ftones which is the north Corner of faid Lott and runs fouth on Robert Commings Lott two hundred and ten rod to a pillar of ftones then Eaft on m^r Birds Land forty two rod to a pillar of ftones then it runs north on Abraham Whitneys Land one hundred and Eighty four rod to a pillar of stones then it runs weft thirty one Degrees and an half North on Land of Jonas Clark Esqr forty nine rod to where it began

₱ Nathan Heywood Survayor

Allowed by the Committee viz Edward Hartwell, Nathan Heywood and Jonathan Willard

Recorded october the 15th 1743.
⅌ Edward Hartwell
Proprietors Clerke

[25²] Lunenburg, March the 24th 1730/31
3d & 4th Divifions.
Laid out by the Committee appointed two Hundred and ninety acres of Land to Jofiah Willard Esqr and madam Hannah Willard his Wife for each of them a third Divifion and and for him the faid Jofiah Willard a forth Divifion arifeing from Lott No. 26 and madam Willards from No 35, Begining at a black oak tree marked for the fowweft Corner of houfe Lott No. 38 and runing Weft on Land Lefe for a high Way 41 rod to a White oake tree there making an Angle and runing fouth on Land of John Wood 99 rod to a pillar of ftones there making an Angle and runing West 12 Degrees fouth on Dorchefter fairm 97 rod to a pillar of ftone there making an Angle and runing North on Land Laid out to Capt Josiah Willard 67 rod to a maple tree there making an Angle and runing Eaft 33 rod to a pillar of ftones there making an Angle and runing north on Land Laid out to Mr Gardner 230 rod to a hemLock Tree there making an Angle and runing Weft on Land of faid Gardner 37 rod to a pillar of ftones there making an Angle and runing Eaft 40 degrees North on Gibsons Land 102 rod to a pillar of ftones there making an Angle and runing north 14 degrees West 67 rod to a pillar of ftones there an Angle and runing Eaft on a Line of 2d Divifion 135 rod to a pillar of ftones there making an Angle and runing fouth on 2d Divifion Land 151 rod to a pillar of ftones there making an Angle and runing West on first Divifion Land 55 rod to a Chefnut tree there making an Angle and runing fouth on first Divifion Lott No 38. 160 rod to Where it began

Survayed by Nathan Heywood and approved of by the Committee wit Edward Hartwell Jofiah Willard Jonathan Willard and Nathan Heywood.

Recorded June the 12th Anno Domini 1731
Edward Hartwell Clerk.

[26] JONATHAN DOWSE. ESQ^R of Charlestown

Houſe Lott No 27. Granted to Jonathan Dowse Esqr by the Committee appointed By the Greate and General Court to a Lott and Grant out the Lands Within the townſhip of Lunenburgh to Granttees fourty five acres of Land Within ſaid town for a houſe Lott Number twenty ſeven together With all the Rights and Diviſions of Land belonging there unto

Lunenburg. August the 13th 1730.

Survayed for Jonathan Dowse. Esqr Houſe Lott Number twenty ſeven the Contents of Which was fourty five acres Begining at a Cartain pillar of Stones Which was Erected for the Southeaſt Corner and Runing Weſt fourty five rod to a tree there Making an Angle and runing North one Degree West one hundred and ſixty rod to a pillar of ſtones there making an angle and runing Eaſt fourty five rod to a pillar of ſtones there making an Angle and runing ſouth one degree East one hundred and ſixty rod to Where it began

Survayed by Nathan Heywood and approved of by the Committee viz Josiah Willard Edward Hartwell Jonathan Willard and Nathan Heywood.

Recorded December the third Day in the year of our Lord one thouſand ſeven hundred and thirty

℗ Edward Hartwell Clerk

Lunenburgh November ye 6th 1730.

Meadow Lott No 14 mulpus. Survayed for Jonathan Dowse Esqr a Meadow Lott Number fourteen in uper Mulpus Meadow the Contents of Which is two acres and ſixty five rod begining at a ſtak Which is the Most Southerly Corner and runing Eaſt nine degrees thirty mints North thirty rod to a ſtak there making an Angle and runing north two degree Eaſt twelve rod to a ſtake there Making an Angle and Runing West ten degrees ſouth thirty five rod there making an Angle and runing ſouth nineteen Degrees Eaſt twelve rod to where it began.

Survayed by nathan Heywood and alowed by the Committee Edward Hartwell Jonathan Willard nathan

Heywood and
Recorded December the third Day in the year of our Lord one thoufand feven Hundred and thirty.
℔ Edward Hartwell Clerk.

[26²] Lunenburgh, November the 6th 1730.

2d Divifion No 18 and 4th Divifion Survayed for Jonathan Dows Esqr fecond Divifion Number Eighteen the Contents of Which is fixty acres and fixty four rod in Cluding part of meadow Called perrums meadow alfo Laid out by the Committee appointed one Hundred acres of Land adjoyning to faid fecond Divifion for a fourth Divifion to faid Dows and Eight acres more in part to make up what is Wanting in his meadow Lott and In the fecond Divifiion by reafon of the fecound Divifion in Cludeing fom meadow belonging to other men begining at a red oak tree marked for the Wefterly Corner and runing north thirty one Degrees Eaft one hundred and fifty one rod to a pillar of ftones there making an Angle and runing Eaft thirty one Degrees thirty minits South on the north town Line one Hundred and Eighty two rod to a pillar of ftones there making an Angle and runing fouth thirty : 5 : degrees Weft one Hundred and fifty one rod to a pillar of Stones there making an Angle and runing West thirty one Degree thirty minits north one hundred and feventy fix rod to Where it began. furvayed by Nathan Heywood and approved of by the Committee viz Edward Hartwell, Jonathan Willard. Nathan Heywood and

Recorded December the third Day in the year of our Lord one thoufand feven Hundred and thirty
℔. Edward Hartwell Clerk.

Lunenburgh November the 8th 1729.

3d Divifion Laid out by the Committee appointed one hundred and nineteen acres and a half of third Divifion Land to Jonathan Dows Esqr within the townfhip of Lunenburgh the right a Rifeing from houfe Lott number twenty feven Begining at a burch tree and runing fouth thirty three Degree Weft one Hundred and

Eighty three rod to a pillar of ſtones there making an Angle and Runing Weſt fifty rod to a pillar of ſtones there making an angle and runing north five degrees Eaſt one hundred and ſixty three rod to a hemlock tree there making an Angle and runing Eaſt five degree ſouth fifty two rod to a pillar of ſtones there making an Angle and runing north five degree Eaſt Eighty rod to a pillar of ſtones there making an Angle and runing ſouth fourty five degree Eaſt one Hundred and twenty rod to where it began.

Survayed by Nanthan Heywood and approved of by the Committee viz Joſiah Willard Edward Hartwell and Isaac Farnsworth

Recorded December the the third day in the year of our Lord one thouſand ſeven hundred and thirty

₱ Edward Hartwell Clerk

[27]   CAPT JOSEPH GOULD.

Houſe Lott No 28.
   Survayed for Capt Joseph Gould Claimer Houſe Lot Number twenty eight the Contents being fourty five acres and ninety rod.

  begining at a beach tree marked for the ſouth Eaſt Corner and Runing North one hundred and ſixty two rod to a pillar of ſtones there making an Angle and Runing Weſt fourty five rod to a pillar of ſtones there making an Angle and Runing South one Hundred and ſixty two rod to a pillar of ſtones there making an Angle and runing Eaſt fourty five rod to Where It Began.

Survayed By Nathan Heywood and approved of by the Committee viz Joſiah Willard Edward Hartwell Nathan Heywood and Jonathan Willard.

Recorded March the thirteenth day In the year of our Lord one thouſand ſeven Hundred and twenty-nine thirty by me

        Edward Hartwell Clerk

meadow Lott No 1.
  Laid out to Capt Joseph Gould Claimer ſeven acres of meadow and fifty ſix rod with upland and Reckoned to him for his meadow Lot and Lyeth above Mulpus falls and is Number one

and is Coupled to the houfe Lot above faid. Begining at a ftake in Jofeph Pages Line and Runing East thirty Eight Deg^r fouth twenty rod to a ftake there making an Angle and Runing Eaft three Deg^r thirty mints North seventeen rod to a pillar of ftones there making an Angle and Runing north fourty three Deg^r Eaft fix rod to a Cherry tree there making an Angle and Runing north twelve Degrees Weft thirty feven rod to a pillar of ftones there Making an Angle and runing Weft ten deg^r fouth twenty five rod to a pillr of ftones there making an Angle and Runing fouth nine deg Weft twenty-five rod to where It Began.

furvayed By Nathan Heywood and approved of by the Committee viz Jofiah Willard Edward Hartwell, Jonathan Willard and Nathan Heywood.

Recorded march the thirteenth Day in the year of our Lord one thoufand feven Hundred and twenty nine thirty by me

        Edward Hartwell
           Clerk

Lunenburgh. March ye 24th 1729/30

Second No
Divifion 26
No 26

Survayed for Joseph Gould Claimer a fecond Divifion No 26 the Contents of Which is fifty one acres and three quarters begining at a maple tree marked for the fouth Corner and Runing North twenty nine Degrees Eaft on fecond Divifion No twenty five one hundred and fifty rod to a ftake in the North town Line there making an Angle and Runing Weft thirty one Dege and thirty min North on the North town Line fifty fix rod to a ftake there making an Angle and Runing fouth thirty Deg^r Weft on fecond Divifion No twenty feven one Hundred and fifty Rod to a ftake there making an Angle and Runing Eaft thirty one Deg^r and thirty min fouth fifty Eight Rod to Where It Began

Survayed By Nathan Heywood and approved of by the Committee viz Jofiah Willard Edward Hartwell Nathan Heywood Jonathan Williard

Recorded April the twenty third Day annoque Domini one thoufand feven Hundred and thirty

        pr Edward Hartwell Clerk.

[27²] Granted unto Nathan Towns by the Committee appointed by the Greate and General to a Lott and Grant out the Lands Within the town of Lunenburgh to Granttees fourty five acres of Land Within Within said town for a House Lott number twenty to Gether With all the rights and Divisions of Land belonging thereunto
Recorded May the 18th 1730. by me
Edward Hartwell proprietors Clerke

Lunenburg April ye 26. 1729

3d Division   Laid out for Capt Joseph Gould Claimer by the Committee appointed and Impowered by the Proprietors of the town of Lunenburgh ninety one acres and thirty two rod for a third Division of Land the Right arising from house Lott Number twenty Eight and is Bounded all Round by Common Land and It begins at a stake marked for the norwest Corner and Runing south one Hundred and twenty Eight rod to a stake Marked for the sowwest Corner there making an Angle and Runing East one Hundred and fourteen rod to a White oke tree there making an Angle and Runing North one Hundred and twenty Eight Rod to a stake marked for northwest Corner from thence Runing West one Hundred and fourteen rod to where it began.

Survayed by Nathan Heywood and approved of by the Committee viz. Edward Hartwell Josiah Willard and Jonathan Willard.

Recorded May the Eighteenth day in the year of our Lord one thousand seven hundred and Thirty by me
Edward Hartwell Clerk -

Lunenburgh May the 16th 1730.

4th division   Laid out by the Committee appointed ninety four acres of Land for a forth Division to Capt Joseph Gould Claimer Ariseing from House Lott No twenty Eight and to make up what is Wanting in his second Division adjoyning to his third Division Begining at a White oak tree marked for the south east Corner of said third Division and Runing North 40 rod on said third

Divifion there making an Angle and Runing Eaft feventeen Degrees fouth on Common Land fixty Rod there making an Angle and Runing fouth feventeen degrees Weft on Stow Line Eighty nine rod there making an Angle runing Weft on Common Land one Hundred and fixty five rod there making An angle and Runing North one Hundred and ninety rod there making an angle and Runing East twenty rod to faid third Divifion norweft Corner there making an Angle and Runing South on faid third Divifion one Hundred and twenty Eight rod there making an Angle and Runing Eaft on faid third Divifion one Hundred and fourteen rod to where It began.

furvayed by Nathan Heywood and approved of by the Committee viz Jofiah Willard, Edward Hartwell and Jonathan Willard

Recorded May the twenty feventh day in the year of our Lord one thoufand feven Hundred and thirty

₱ Edward Hartwell Clerk.

[28]   JOHN GOODRIDGE

Granted to John Goodridge by the Committee appointed by the Greate and General Court to alott and Grant out the Lands within the Townfhip of Lunenburg to Grantees Houfe Lott No : 29 :

[28²]

2ᵈ Divifion   Granted to Abraham Whitney by the Com-
No 76   mittee appointed by the Greate and General Court to a Lott and Grant out the Lands within the Town of Lunenburg to Grantees fecond Divifion Number feventy fix within the Townfhip of Lunenburg and alfo meadow Lott number nine Weft of uper mulpus and all the after Rights and Divifions that beLong to Houfe Lott No twenty nine.

Lunenburg may the 10ᵗʰ 1745.

furvayed for Abraham Whitney fecond Divifion Lott No 76 in faid Townfhip Begining at a pillar of ftones which is the moft north eafterly Corner of faid Lott and runs West thirty one degrees north on Arrington Gibſons ſecond Diviſion fifty ſix rod and a half to a heap of ſtones, then runs ſouth one degree Weſt one hundred and Eighty two rod on ſecond Diviſion belonging to the Honourable Joſiah Willard Esqr then it runs Eaſt fifty ſix rod and an half on Land of Mr Benj^a Bird Chiefly to a Cheſnut tree then runs north two degrees Weſt on Land of William Jones one hundred and fifty four rod to where it began and it Contains fifty five acres.

ſurvayed by Nathan Heywood and allowed of by the Committee viz Edward Hartwell Jonathan Willard & Nathan Heywood.

Recorded may the 21st 1745

℔ Edward Hartwell proprietors Clerk

[29] JOHN BREWER.

Granted to John Brewer by the Committee appointed by the Greate and general Court to a Lott and grant out the Lands within the Townſhip of Lunenburgh to Granttees forty three acres of Land within ſaid town for a houſe Lott bareing number thirty to gether with all the rights and diviſions of Land belonging thereunto.

Lunenburgh June the 9th 1730.

Houſe Lott No. 30.   ſurvayed for John Brewer Houſe Lott Number thirty the Contents of which is forty three acres. Begining at a ſtake and heap of ſtones which is the ſouth weſt Corner and runing North two deg Weſt on Lott Number thirty one one Hundred and fifty five rod there making an Angle and runing Eaſt forty five rod there making an Angle and runing ſouth one Hundred and fifty five rod on Lott No twenty nine there making an Angle and runing Weſt forty four rod to where it began

Survayed by Nathan Heywood and approved of by the Committee viz Josiah Willard, Edward Hartwell Nathan Heywood and Joſhua Hutchens

recorded october the 21^t anno Domini 1730.

℔ Edward Hartwell Clerk

Lunenburgh. June the 9th 1730.

2d Divifion
No 39

Survayed for John Brewer fecond Divifion Number thirty nine the Contents of Which is forty Nine Acres. Begining at a ftake and a heep of ftones Which is the foutherly Corner and runing Weft thirty one deg thirty minits North fifty two rod there Making an Angle and runing North twenty Eight deg Eaft on Lott number thirty Eight one Hundred and fifty one rod there making an Angle and runing Eaft thirty one deg thirty minits fouth on the north range of Lotts fifty one rod there making an Angle and runing fouth twenty feven deg Weft on Woodman Lott one Hundred and fifty one rod to Where it began

furvayed by Nathan Heywood and approved of By the Committee viz Josiah Willard Edward Hartwell Nathan Heywood and Joshua Hutchens

Recorded october 21th Anno Domini 1730.

℗ Edward Hartwell Clerk

Lunenburgh. August the 14th: 1729

3d Divifion
Land

Laid out to John Brewer Claimer by the Committee appointed three hundred and fixty acres of third Divifion Land the right a rifeing from the Houfe Lotts No: thirty number Eight three and fixty one and is aboute a mile Wefterly from the appletree hill begining at black oak tree marked for for the fouthefterly Corner and runing Weft 15 deg fouth 5 rod to a pillar of ftones there making an Angle and runing Weft thirty fore deg North fifteen rod to a red oak tree there Making an Angle and runing fouth thirty four deg Weft Eighteen rod making an Angle and runing Weft fifteen deg fouth feventy two rod to a Hornwood tree there making an Angle and runing fouth fifteen deg Eaft fixty five rod to a ftake there making an Angle and runing Weft fifteen deg fouth two Hundred and thirty two rod to a pillar of ftones there making an Angle and runing North 4 deg Eaft two hundred and thirty rod to a maple tree there making an Angle and runing Eaft fifteen deg North two Hundred and fixty rod to a pillar of ftones there making an Angle and runing fouth fifteen d. Eaſt one hundred and fifty two rod to where it began bounded all round on Common Land

ſurvayed By Nathan Heywood and approved of by the Committee viz Joſiah Willard Edward Hartwell and Nathan Heywood.

Recorded october the 22^d in the year of our Lord one thouſand ſeven hundred and thirty

⅌ Edward Hartwell Clerk.

[29²]

4th Diviſion Land

Laid out to John Brewer Claimer by the Committee appointed two Hundred and ſeventy four acres and a half of Land on the Northerly ſide of Mr Preſcotts third diviſion two hundred and fourty acres of Which Land is three fourth diviſions ariſeing from houſe Lotts number thirty number Eighty three & number ſixty one and thirty four acres and a half of which Land is to make up what is wanting in ſaid Brewers first and ſecond diviſion

begining at M^r preſcotts north eaſterly Corner and runing Weſt fifteen degree north on ſ^d preſcotts Land two hundred and fourty rod there making an Angle and runing north fifteen degrees Eaſt on Common Land one hundred and Eighty three rod there making an Angle and runing Eaſt fifteen degrs ſouth on Common Land two hundred and fourty rod there making an Angle and runing ſouth fifteen degrees Weſt one hundred and Eighty three rod to where it began

ſurvayed by Nathan Heywood June the 10th 1730 and approved of by the Committee viz Joſiah Willard Edward Hartwell and Jonathan Willard.

recorded December the third day in the year of our Lord one thouſand ſeven hundred and thirty

⅌ Edward Hartwell Clerk.

[30]

Houſe Lott No 31

NATHANIEL HARRIS.

Grantted to Nathaniel Harris by the Committee appointed by the Greate and General Court to a Lott and grant out the Lands Within the

Townſhip of Lunenburgh to granttees fourty three acres of Land Within ſaid town for a Houſe Lott baring number thirty one to gether with all the rights and Diviſions of Land belonging thereunto

Lunenburgh June the 10th 1730.

Survayed for Nathaniel Harris Houſe Lott Number thirty one the Contents of Which is fourty three acres. Begining at a tree and a heape of ſtones which is the ſouth weſt Corner and runing North two degree Weſt on Lott num^{br} thirty two one hundred and fifty five rod there making an angle and runing Eaſt fourty four rod and a half there making an Angle and runing ſouth two degrees Eaſt on Lott number thirty. one Hundred and fifty five rod there making an Angle and runing Weſt fourty four rod and a half on Northfield Road to Where it Began

Survayed by Nathan Heywood and approved of by the Committee viz Josiah Willard, Edward Hartwell Jonathan Willard and Nathan Heywood.

Recorded November the twenty ſix day in the year of our Lord one thouſand ſeven Hundred and thirty

₱ Edward Hartwell Clerk.

Lunenburg June the ſeventeenth 1730.

2^d Diviſion Lott No 37

Survayed for Nathaniel Harris ſecond Diviſion number thirty ſeven the Contents of Which is fifty four acres Begining at a ſtake and a heape of ſtones which is the ſoutherly Corner and runing weſt thirty one Degrees thirty mints North fifty ſeven rod there making an angle and runing north thirty degr East on Lott number thirty ſix one hundred and fifty two rod there making an angle and runing Eaſt thirty one degr thirty minits ſouth on the North range of Lotts fifty ſeven rod there making an angle and runing ſouth thirty deg^r Weſt on Lott number thirty Eight one hundred and fifty two rod to where it began.

Survayed by Nathan Heywood and approved of By the Committee viz Joſiah Willard Edward Hartwell Nathan Heywood and Joshua Hutchens.

Recorded November the twenty fix Day in the year of our Lord one thoufand feven Hundred and thirty
₱ Edward Hartwell Clerk

Lunenburg April yᵉ 8ᵗʰ 1729

2 : 3ᵈ Divifions   Laid out to Mʳ Nathaniel Harris by the Committee appointed one hundred and fixty acres of third Divifion Land belonging to two Rights number thirty one and feventy one. Begining at a Pillar of ftones in Lancafter Line and runing upon faid Line Weft twenty Eight Degree fouth one hundred and fixty rod to apillar of ftones there making an Angle and Runing North twenty Eight deg Weft one Hundred and fixty rod to a pillar of ftones there making an Angle and Runing Eaft twenty Eight Degrees North one Hundred and fixty rod to apillar of ftones there making an Angle and Runing fouth tweenty Eight Degrees Eaft one hundred and fixty rod to where it began

Survayed by Nathan Heywood and approved of by the Committee viz Josiah Willard Edward Hartwell Benoni Boynton Nathan Heywood and Jofhua Hutchens

Recorded December the 15ᵗʰ anno Domi 1730
₱ Edward Hartwell Clerk

[30²] Granted to Nathaniel Harris by the Committee appointed by the greate and General Court to a Lott and Grant out the Land within the The Townfhip of Lunenburgh to Granttees fourty feven Acres and a quarter of Land on flat hill for a fecond Divifion bearing Number fixty feven to gether With all the Divifions and grants of Land and medows within the Townfhip of Lunenburg aforefaid that fhall arife from houfe Lott Number feventy one

Lunenburg November the 2ᵈ 1730.

2ᵈ Divifion   Survayed for Mʳ Nathaniel Harris fecond
No 67.   divifion number fixty feven the Contents of which is fourty feven acres and a quarter of Land Lying on flat hill Begining at a ftak and heape of ftones

Erected for the moſt ſoutherly Corner and Runing North ſeventeen degrees Eaſt on Land Left for a highway ſixty 7 Rod there making an Angle and Runing Weſt thirty one Degrees thirty Min North on Lott number ſixty Eight one hundred and twenty Eight Rod there making an Angle and Runing ſouth ſeventeen deg Weſt ſixty rod there making an Angle and and Runing Eaſt thirty one degs thirty minits ſouth on Lott number ſixty ſix in 2ᵈ Diviſion one Hundred and twenty Eight Rod to Were It Began

Survayed by Nathan Heywood and approved of by the Committee viz Edwᵈ Hartwell Jonathan Willard Joſiah Willard and Nathan Heywood

Recorded December the fifteenth Day in the year of our Lord one thouſand ſeven Hundred and thirty

℘ Edwᵈ Hartwell Clerk

Lunenburg November the 2ᵈ 1730.

2ᵈ Diviſion No 66. ſurvayed for Mʳ Nathaniel Harris Second Diviſion Number ſixty ſix upon flatt Hill the Contents of Which is fourty ſeven acres of Land and a half. Begining at a ſtak and Heap of ſtones Erected for the moſt ſoutherly Corner and runing north ſeventeen degrees Eaſt on Land Left for a high way ſixty one rod there making an Angle and Runing Weſt thirty one Degs thirty minits North on Lott Number ſixty ſeven which is the Lott above ſaid one hundred and twenty Eight Rod there making an Angle and runing ſouth ſeventeen degrees Weſt ſixty one rod there making an Angle and runing Eaſt thirty one deg thirty minits ſouth on Lott number ſixty five one Hundred and twenty Eight Rod to Where it began

Survayed by Nathan Heywood and approved of by the Committee viz Edwᵈ Hartwell Jonathan Willard Joſiah Willard and Nathan Heywood

Recorded December the fifteenth Day in the year of our Lord one thouſand ſeven Hundred and thirty

℘ Edward Hartwell Clerk

[31] ARCH.ᴬ MACPHEADRIS & JOHN SCOTT.

Granted unto Arch.ᵃ Macpheadris & John Scott by the Committee appointed by the Greate and General Court to a Lott and Grant out the Lands Within the townſhip of Lunenburg to Granttees fifty one acres of Land and a quarter Within ſaid town for a Houſe Lott bearing Number 32 there being a Lowance in it for a two rod road together with all the Rights and Diviſions of upland and meadow that belongs thereto or that ſhall ariſe therefrom.

Entered January 13ᵗʰ 1729:

₱ Edwᵈ Hartwell proprietors Clerk

Lunenburg october the 31ᵗʰ 1747

Houſe Lott No 32. ſurvayed for John Scott Houſe Lott Number thirty two which Contains fifty one acre and a quarter there being allowance in it for a two rod road it begins at a pillar of ſtones which is the ſouth eaſt Corner of ſaid Lott and it Runs north two Degrees West on Land of Eſqʳ Harris one hundred and ſixty four rod to a pillar of ſtones then it runs Weſt one Degree ſouth on Land of William Jones fifty one rod to a pillar of ſtones then it runs ſouth three Degrees thirty minits Eaſt on Land of Arrington Gibſon one hundred and ſixty three rod to a pillar of ſtones then it runs Eaſt forty nine rod to where it began

ſurvayed by Nathan Heywood and approved of by the Committee viz Nathan Heywood Edward Hartwell

Recorded December the 17ᵗʰ 1747

₱ Edward Hartwell proprietors Clerk

Lunenburg June the 5ᵗʰ 1729.

3 Diviſion Laid out by the Committee appointed fifty acres of third Diviſion Land to John ſcott ariſing from Houſe Lott No: 32: And Lyeth Near the Menoofnock Hill begining at a pillar of ſtones and Runs north 28 Degrees Weſt fifty rod to a pillar of ſtones there making an angle and runing Eaſt twenty Eight Degrees north 160 rod to a pillar of ſtones there making an Angle and and Runing ſouth 28: Degrees Eaſt 50: rod to a

pillar of ſtones there making an angle and runing Weſt 28 Deg^r ſouth 160 : rod upon Nathaniel Harriſes Line to where it began

ſurvayed by me Nathan Heywood and approved of by the Committee viz Edward Hartwell Jonathan Willard and Nathan Heywood

Recorded November the 5th 1747

℘ Edward Hartwell
proprietors Clerk.

[31²] Lunenburg January the 13th 1729/30

2^d Diviſion
No 49.

ſurvayed for Archabald Mackfeddrich a ſecond Diviſion Lott No : 49 : the Contents of Which is 63 acres and 70 rod begining at a ſtake ſet up for the Weſt Corner and runing north 27 deg Eaſt 157 rod there making an Angle and runing Eaſt 32 degrees ſouth 65 rod on ffyfes Lott there making an Angle and Runing ſouth 27 deg West 157 rod to a ſtake there making an Angle and Runing Weſt 32 north 65 rod to Where It began

ſurvayed by Nathan Heywood

Lunenburg January the 13th 1729:/30

3^d Diviſion

Laid out by the Committee appointed 55 acres of third Diviſion Land to archabald Mackfadrich ariſeing from houſe Lott No 32 and is adjoyning to Groton Line begining at a ſtake ſet up for the Weſt Corner and Runing North 27 Degrees Eaſt 157 rod on his own ſecond Diviſion there making an Angle and runing Eaſt 32 deg. ſouth 45 rod on ffyfes Lott there making an Angle and runing Weſt 32 deg north 68 rod to Where it Began

ſurvayed by Nathan Heywood and approved of by the Committee to Wit Edward Hartwell Joſiah Willard Nathan Heywood and Jonathan Willard

Recorded December the 29th Annoque Domini 1731.

℘ Edward Hartwell Cler.

Laid out for John Scott of Lunenburg fifty acres of Land to the Right of the ſaid John ſcott and Archabel

Macfedris the Right arifing from from Houfe Lott Number thirty two and is in full of what was wanting in in the forth Divifion that belonged to faid Right. begining at a Chefnut tree and runs north forty five Degrees Eaft partly on Common Land and partly on Land of William Rufsell one hundred and twenty two Rod to a ftak and heap of ftones then Runs Weft forty five Degrees north on Common Land fixty rod to a beach tree then Runs fouth forty five Degrees Weft on Common Land one hundred and twenty two rod to a ftake and heap of ftones then runs Eaft forty five Degrees fouth on Common Land forty five rod to where it began

Survayed by Benjamin Bellows Junr furvayor Laid out by the Committee appointed for that purpose viz
$\begin{cases} \text{Edward Hartwell} \\ \text{Jonathan Willard} \\ \text{Ephraim pearce} \end{cases}$

Entered november 22^d 1742
₱ Edward Hartwell proprietors Clerk

[32]   TIMOTHY GIBSON

Houfe Lott No. 33   Granted unto Timothy Gibson by the Greate and General Courts Committee who was appointed to a Lott and Grant out the Lands Within the town of Lunenburg to Granttees forty four acres and a half of Land Within f^d town for a houfe Lott bearing Number 33 together With all the rights and Divifions of Land belonging thereto or arifeing therefrom and also Granted unto the faid Timothy Gibson by the Committee appointed by the Greate and General Court to

Houfe Lott No 72   aLott and Grant out the Lands Within the town of Lunenburg to Granttees forty fix acres and a quarter Within faid town for a houfe Lott bareing No 72. to Gether With all the rights and Divifions of Land that belongs thereto or fhall arife therefrom

Lunenburg November the 7th 1730.

Survayed for Timothy Gibson Houfe Lott Number 72 the Contents of Which is forty fix acres and a quarter Begining at a ftake which is the Most Northerly Corner and Runing Weſt 31 deg ſouth on Benjamin Goodridges Lott 45 rod there making an Angle and runing ſouth 25 Degrees Eaſt on Farnſworths Lott 168 rod to a ſtake there making an Angle and runing East 27 deg north on Ephraim pearces Land 42 rod there making an Angle and runing north 24 degrees Weſt on ſaid pearces Land 172 rod to Where it Began

Survayed by Nathan Heywood and approved of by the Committee viz Joſiah Willard Jonathan Willard, Edward Hartwell and Nathan Heywood Recorded December the 30th Anno Domini 1731

₱ Edward Hartwell Cler.

Lunenburg November the 7th 1730.

ſurvayed for Timothy Gibson Houſe Lott Number 38 the Contents of Which is forty four acres and a half Begining at a ſtake which is the ſouth eaſt Corner and runing north 3 deg West on John Scots Land 160 rod to a ſtake there making an Angle and runing Weſt on Joneses Land 45 rod to a ſtake there making an Angle and runing ſouth 3 deg Eaſt on Lott No 34 : 160 rod there making an Angle and runing Eaſt on the highway 45 rod to Where it Began

ſurvayed by Nathan Heywood and approved of by the Committee to wit Edward Hartwell Nathan Heywood Jonathan Willard and Joſiah Willard

Recorded December the 30th annoque Domini 1731

₱ Edward Hartwell Cler

Lunenburg June the ye 17th 1730.

2d Diviſion No 34.

ſurvayed for Timothy Gibson 2d Diviſion Number 34 the Contents of Which is 53 acres and a halfe Begining at a ſtake and heep of ſtones Which is the ſoutherly Corner and runing Weſt 31 degr 30 minits north 56 rod there making an Angle and runing north 30 deg Eaſt 152 rod on Lott No 33 there making an Angle and runing Eaſt 31 deg 30 minits ſouth on the north range of Lotts 57 rod there making an Angle and runing ſouth 30 degrees West on Lott No 35. 152 rod to Where It began

Survayed by Nathan Heywood and approved of by the Committee viz Josiah Willard Jonathan Willard Edward Hartwell and Nathan Heywood

Recorded December ye 31th anno domini 1731

₱ Edward Hartwell Clerk

[32²] Lunenburg March the 18th 1730/1

2^d Divifion   Survayed for Timothy Gibson 2^d Divifion
No 69   number 69 the Contents of Which is 60 acres In the fouth eaft part of the townfhip Begining a red oak tree which is the fouth eaft Corner of faid Lott and runing north 6 deg West partly on the Land of Benjamin Cory and partly on the Land of David pearce 161 rod to a ftake there making an Angle and runing West 5 deg fouth on Land of f^d pearce 59 rod to a ftake there making an Angle and runing fouth 18 deg East on Land of Capt Willard 160 rod to a ftake there making an Angle and runing East 5 degrees north partly on Common Land and partly on Land of John heywood 61 rod to Where It began

furvayed by nathan Heywood and approved of By the Committee viz Josiah Willard Edward Hartwell Nathan Heywood and Jonathan Willard.

Recorded the 31st day of December annoque Domini 1731.

₱ Edward Hartwell Clerk

Lunenburg April the 17th 1729.

3^d Divifion   Laid out to Timothy Gibson by the Committee appointed two peices of third Divifion Land the Rights arifeing from houfe Lott Number thirty three and feventy two. Lying near the Eaft fide of the pearl hill begining at a pillar of ftones and runing Eaft one hundred and forty one rod to a pillar of ftones there making an Angle and runing north Eighteen Degrees Eaft two hundred rod to a pillar of ftones there making an Angle and runing West nineteen Degrees north thirty fix rod to a pillar of ftones there making an Angle and runing fouth thirty nine Degrees West two hundred and fixty five rod to Where it began the other Lott Begins at an oak tree ſtanding in the Line of the first Lott and runing South forty Degree Eaſt one hundred and twenty Eight rod to a pillar of ſtones there making an Angle and runing Eaſt forty Degrees north one hundred and ſix rod to a pillar of ſtones there making an Angle and runing north forty Degree Weſt one hundred and ninety five rod to a pillar of ſtones there making an Angle and runing ſouth Eighteen Degrees West upon the first Lott one hundred and twenty five rod to Where it began   Nathan Heywood ſurvayer

approved of by the Committee viz Joſiah Willard Edward Hartwell and Jonathan Willard

Recorded may the 29th 1729

℗ Edward Hartwell Clerk

the other Lands of the ſaid Mr Timothy Gibson are Recorded in ſecond part of this book at page 37.

Leiut. Josiah Jones of Weston.

Granted unto Lieut Josiah Jones by the Committee appointed by the Greate and General Court to a lott and Grant out the Lands Within the townſhip of Lunenburg to Grantees 44 acres and an half of Land Within ſaid town for a houſe Lott No. 34 to gether with all the Rights and Diviſions of Land and meadow that belong thereto or ſhall ariſe therefrom

Lunenburg November the 7th 1730

Houſe Lott No 34

ſurvayd for Joſiah Jones Houſe Lott the Contents of which is 44 acres and an half begining at a Certain ſtake ſet up for the ſouth Eaſt Corner and runing North 3 degrees West on Houſe Lott No 33 160 rod to a ſtake there making an Angle and runing West 45 rod to a ſtake there making an Angle and runing ſouth 3 Degrees Eaſt on Lott No 35. 160 rod to a pillar of ſtones there making an Angle and Runing Eaſt on Land Left for a high way 45 rod to Where it began

ſurvayed by Nathan Heywood and approved of by the Committee viz Joſiah Willard Jonathan Willard Edward Hartwell and Nathan Heywood

Recorded December ye 15th 1732.

℗ Edward Hartwell Clerk

[34] in trust for Mad*m* Willard of Boston.

Houſe Lott
No 35.

Granted to Jacob Wendell Esqʳ and mʳ Joſeph Brandon feoffee in trust for Mrs Hannah Willard of Boston for the uſe of her and her heirs and assigns by the Committee appointed by the Greate and General Court to a Lott and Grant out the Lands Within Town of Lunenburgh to Granttees forty four Acres and a half for a Houſe Lott Number 35 to Gether With all the Rights and Diviſions of Land beLonging thereunto or ariſeing therefrom

Lunenburg November 7ᵗʰ 1730.

ſurvayed for Jacob Wendell Esqʳ and Mʳ Joſeph Brandon fefees Houſe Lott No: 35 the Contents of Which is 44 Acres and a half Begining at a Certain pillar of ſtones Ereced for the ſouth Eaſt Corner and Runing North 3 degree Weſt on Lott No 34. 160 rod to a pillar of ſtones there making an Angle and runing Weſt 46 rod to a pillar of ſtones there making an Angle and runing ſouth 4 degrees Eaſt on Lott No: 36: 160 rod to a pillar of ſtones there making an Angle and Runing Eaſt 44 rod to Where it began

Surveyed by Nathan Heywood and approved of by the Committee viz Joſiah Willard Edward Hartwell Jonathan Willard and Nathan Heywood.

Recorded april the 20ᵗʰ annoque Domini 1731

℔ Edward Hartwell Clerk

Lunenburg November the 2ᵈ 1730

ſecond
Diviſion
No 68

ſurvayed for Maddam Willard 2ᵈ Diviſion No 68. on flatt hill the Contents of Which is 46 Acres and three quarters

Begining at a ſtake and Heep of ſtones Which is the Moſt ſoutherly Corner and runing North 17 degrees Eaſt on Land Left for a highway 60 rod there making an Angle and runing Weſt 31 deg 30 minits North 128. there making an Angle and runing ſouth 17 degr Weſt 60 rod there making an Angle and Runing Eaſt 31 deg 30 mins ſouth on Lott No: 67: 128 rod to Where it began furvayed by Nathan Heywood and approved of by the Committee viz Edward Hartwell Nathan Heywood Jonathan Willard and Jofiah Willard.

Recorded May the 28th 1731

℔ Edward Hartwell Clerk

[34²]   Lunenburg May the 29th 1731

Meadow Lott No 5.   Survayed for Maddam Hannah Willard meadow Lott No 5. in mulpus meadows the Contents of Which is four acres. Begining at a Certain ftake fet up for the fouth weft Corner and runing Eaft 10 degrees fouth on meadow Land one hundred and two rod to a ftake there making an Angle and runing West thirty feven degrees north near the Brook twenty rod to a ftake there making an Angle and runing West 6 Degrees north on Mr Clark Meadow Lott Eighty five rod to a ftake on the upland there making an Angle and runing fouth on the upland four rod to Where it began

furvayed by Nathan Heywood and approved of by the Committee viz Jofiah Willard Edward Hartwell Nathan Heywood and Jonathan Willard

Recorded March the 4th Anno Domini 1731

℔ Edward Hartwell Clerk.

[35]   DAVID GOULD.

Granted unto David Gould by the Committee apointed by the Great and General Court to alott and Grant out the Lands Contained in the townfhip of Lunenburg to Grantees 44 acres and a half for a houfe Lott baring Number 36.

[36]   BENJAMIN CORY of Lunenburg.

Granted to Benjamin Cory By the Committee appointed by the Greate and General Court to aLott and Grant out the Lands Within the town of Lunenburg to Granttees forty four acres and a quarter number 37 toGether With all the rights and Divifions of Land arifeing therefrom or belonging thereto

Lunenburg November ye 7th 1730.

Houfe Lott
No 37

Survayed for Benjamin Cory Houfe Lott Number 37 the Contents of Which is 44 acres and a quarter begining at a Certain heap of Stones Erected for the fouth Eaft Corner and runing north 4 degrees Weft on Lott No 36. 158 rod there making an Angle and Runing Weft 45 rod to apillar of ftones there making an Angle and Runing fouth 4 deg Eaft on Lott No 38 158 there Making an Angle & runing Eaft on Land Left for a high Way 45 rod to Where it Began

furvayed by Nathan Heywood and approved of by the Committee viz Jofiah Willard Edward Hartwell Jonaathan Willard and Nathan Heywood

Recorded May the 26th 1732

℔ Edward Hartwell Cler

Lunenburg March the 18 1730/1

2^d
Divifion
No 71

furvayed for Benjamin Cory fecond Divifion Number No 71 the Contents of which is 70 acres Begining at a ftake which is the fowweft Corner and runing north 5 degree Weft on Land of Capt Willard 160 rod to a ftake there making an Angle and runing weft 5 Degrees fouth on Land of Li^t Hartwell 70 rod to a dead white pine tree there making an Angle and Runing fouth 5 Degrees Eaft on Land of John Heywood 160 rod to a ftake there making an Angle and runing Eaft 5 Degrees north on land of faid Cory 70 rod to where it began

furvayed by Nathan Haywood and approved of by the Committee viz Jofiah Willard Edward Hartwell Nathan Heywood and Jonathan Willard

Recorded February ye 6th 1722/3

℔ Edward Hartwell Clerk

[36²]   Lunenburg May the 17th 1729

3d Divifion

Laid out to Benjamin Cory by the Committe appointed thirty Eight acre and one Hundred and forty one rod of third Divifion Land the Right arifeing from houfe Lott No 37 and adjoyning to his 2^d divifion and it bounds north on the Land of the above faid Cory. Weft on the land of John Heywood fouth on Lancafter old townfhip and Eaft on the Land of Josiah Willard

Begining at a ftake which is the fouthweft Corner of his 2^d Divifion and runing fouth five Degrees Eaft feventy five rod to apillar of ftones there making an Angle and Runing Eaft twenty degrees fouth feventy feven rod to a pillar of ftones there making an Angle and runing north five Degrees Weft one hundred and Eight rod there making an Angle and Runing Weft five degrees fouth feventy rod to Where it began

furvayed by Nathan Heywood and approved of by the Committee viz Jofiah Willard Edward Hartwell and Hilkiah Boynton

Recorded may the 31th 1729

℔ Edward Hartwell Clerk

Lunenburg March the 18th 1730/1

Laid out to Benjamin Cory by the Committee appointed Eleven Acres and a quarter of Land in the foutheafterly part of faid townfhip for an Equevilent to the town way which gos through his fecond Divifion

Begining at a red oak tree which is the fouth eaft Corner of Gibsons Lott and Runing Eaft 5 Degrees North on land of John Heywood 25 rod and a half to a ftake and heep of ftones there making an Angle and runing north on Captain Goulds Land 63 rod to a ftake there making an Angle and runing Weft on Land of David pearce 32 rod to a ftake there making an angle and Runing fouth 6 degrees Eaft on Land of the aforefaid Gibson 65 rod to Where it began

Survayed by   and approved of by the Committee viz Jofiah Willard and Jonathan Willard

Recorded February ye 6th 1732/3

℔ Edward Hartwell Cler

[37]   NATHAN HEYWOOD

Granted to Nathan Heywood by the Committee appointed by the Greate and General Court to aLott and Grant out the Lands Within the town of Lunenburg to

Granttee fifty one acres and a quarter of Land Within faid town for a houfe Lott bareing number thirty Eight to gether with all the rights and Divifions of Land and meadow beLonging thereto or arifeing therefrom

Lunenburg February the 24th 1729/30.

Houfe Lot No 38.   Survayed for Nathan Heywood Houfe Lott No 38. the Contents of Which is fifty one acres and a quarter Begining at a pillar of ftones Erected for the Northeafterly Corner and runing West fourty nine rod to apillar of ftones there making an Angle and runing fouth one hundred and fifty two rod to an oak tree there making an Angle and runing Eaft fifty nine rod to a pillar of ftones there making an Angle and and runing North five deg Weft one hundred and fifty three rod to Where it began bounded fouth on Northfield Road Eaft on on Lott No 37 north and Weft on third Divifion Land furvayed by Nathan Heywood and approved of by the Committee viz Jofiah Willard Edward Hartwell Jonathan Willard and Nathan Heywood

    recorded February the 25th annoque Domini 1730/31

Edward Hartwell Clerk

2^d Divifion No 73   The Land of Nathan Heywood where he now Lives is fivety nine acres and a half of fecond Divifion Land and feventeen ares and a half of third Divifion Land all arifeing from houfe Lott No. 38.

Begining at a Certain Chefnut tree marked for the fouth Eafterly Corner of the fecond Divifion and runing fouth five degrees Eaft on Land of John Heywood fourty fix rod to a pillar of ftones in Lancafter Line there making An Angle and runing on faid Line to the Corner of faid townfhip there making An Angle and runing on the Line of f^d Lancafter new grant one hundred and feventy Eight rod to a pillar of ftones there making An Angle and Runing Eaft five Deg North on Liue^t Hartwells Land feventy nine rod to a pillar of ftones there making an Angle and runing fouth four deg Eaft on Land of the aforefaid John Heywood one Hundred and fixty rod to Where it Began

surveyed by Nathan Heywood and approved of by the Committee viz Edward Hartwell Josiah Willard Jonathan willard and Nathan Heywood
Recorded March the 17th annoque Domini 1730/31
₱ Edward Hartwell Clerk

[37²] Lunenburg February ye 18th 1730/31

Meadow Lott   surveyed for Nathan Heywood His Meadow Lott belonging to House Lott No thirty Eight Lying Within William Wallases House Lott the Contents of Which is six Acres begining at a Certain pine tree marked for the south east Corner and Runing East thirty four deg thirty min North sixteen Rod and a half to a pine stump there Making an Angle and Runing North thirty degrees East Eight rod to a pine stump there Making An Angle and runing North twenty three Deg West fourteen rod to a black oak stumpe there making an Angle and Runing North East Eighteen rod to an Elm stump there making an Angle and Runing south forty deg East nine rod to a pine stump there making an Angle and Runing south six deg West thirteen rod to a stak there making an Angle and runing East thirty two Dege south fourty rod to a heep of stones in borman's Line there making an Angle and runing West one deg south sixty three rod to where it began bounding all round on said Wallases Land

surveyed by Nathan Heywood and approved of by the Committee viz Josiah Willard Jonathan willard Nahan Heywood and Edward Hartwell
Recorded march the 17th anno Domini 1730/31
Edward Hartwell Clerk

Lunenburg February the 4th 1729/30

meadow.   Laid out for Nathan Heywood by the Committee appointed one Acre and 17 rod of Meadow Land on the East side of Mr Bormans farm in part of the Equevelent for the Town way going in his home Lott

Begining at Catacoonamoug brook in the afore said farm Line and runing North sixteen deg East on sd Line twenty two rod to the brook again. there making an Angle and runing Eaſt fourty deg ſouth upon the brook ſixteen rod there making an Angle and runing weſt forty degrees ſouth upon the Brook fourteen rod there making an Angle and runing Weſt twelve deg ſouth on the brook Eight rod to where it began.

ſurvayed by nathan heywood and approved of by the Committee viz Joſiah Willard Jonathan Willard Edward Hartwell.

Recorded march the 17th 1730/31

Edward Hartwell CLerk

The other Lands of the aboveſᵈ Heywood are in the ſecond part of this book at page — 21.

[38]   Ministerial Lott.

Lunenburg April yᵉ 24th 1733

Survayed the miniſterial Houſe Lott the Contents of which is ſixty five acres and three quarters begining at a Certain pillar of Stones Erected for the Northeaſt Cornner of Woburn Farm and Runing South 15 Degrees East on ſaid farm 147 rod to a pillar of ſtones thence Runing Eaſt 28 Degrees north on Isaac Farnsworths Lott 62 rod thence Runing North 28 degrees Weſt on pools Lott 38 rod to a ſtake thence runing Eaſt 28 Degrees north on ſaid pools Land 75 rod to a ſtake thence Runing Weſt 42 Degrees north on Isaac Farnsworth meadow Lott 69 rod to a ſtake in the meadow thence runing West 46 rod to a ſtake thence Runing Weſt 4 Degrees ſouth 44 rod to where it Began

ſurvayed By Nathan Haywood and approved of By the Committee viz. Joſiah Willard Edward Hartwell and

Recorded april the 9th 1736

℔ Edward Hartwell Cler

Laid out by the Committee appointed fifty four acres and a half of Land in the ſoutheaſterly Cornner of the Townſhip of Lunenburg for part of the miniſterial Land Begining at a pillar of ſtones Erected for the Corner of ſaid Townſhip and runs North 17 degrees East on ſtow Line. 102. rod to apillar of ſtones then runs weſt on Capt Goulds Land 116 rod to a pillar of ſtones then runs ſouth on Land of Nathan Heywood 40 rod to a pillar of ſtones then runs weſt on ſaid Heywoods Land 12 rod to a pond then runing by ſaid pond 38 rod to Lanceſter Line then runing Eaſt 17 Degrees ſouth on Lancaſter Line 85 rod to where it Began.

ſurvayed By Nathan Heywood and approved of By the Committee viz Joſiah Willard Jonathan Willard and Edward Hartwell

Recorded April the 9th 1736.

₱ Edward Hartwell Cler

[38²]   Lunenburg October ye 2^d 1732

2^d Diviſion   Survayed ye Miniſteariel 2^d Diviſion number 45 the Contents of which is 55 acres and a half Begining at a Certain pillar of ſtones Erected for y^e ſouth Corner and runing North 30 degrees Eaſt on 2^d Diviſion N° 44. 150. rod to a pillar of ſtones thence runing West 31 degrees 30 min. North on ye North range of 2^d Diviſions 64 rod thence runing ſouth 26 Degrees West on 2^d Diviſion N° 46. 151. rod to a pillar of ſtones thence runing Eaſt 31 degrees 30 minuts ſouth 54 rod and a half to Where it began   ₱ Nathan Heywood ſurvayer and approved of by the Committee viz Joſiah Willard Edward Hartwell Jonathan Willard and Nathan Heywood

Recor^d march ye 10th 1734

₱ Edward Hartwell Clerk

Laid out by the Committee appointed for that purpoſe 68 acres of Land in the Eaſt part of the townſhip of Lunenburg for part of the miniſterial Land Granted by the Great and General Court Begining at a pillar of ſtones in ſtow Line Juſt By Groton ſouth weſt Corner and runing by Groton Corner and runing north 17 Degrees Eaſt on Groton Line 308 rod to Catacoonamoog brook then runs up the Brook 26 rod then runing by and bounding on Catacoonamooge meadow 88 rod till it Coms to

Ephriam pearces, Land then runs Eaft 25 degrees fouth on faid pearces Land 6 rod to a ftake and heape of ftones then runs fouth 4 degrees Weft on faid pearces Land 77 rod to a ftake then runs Weft 25 degrees north on faid perces Land 20 rod to a pine tree then runs fouth 42 degrees Weft on on Land of Nathaniel page 91 rod to a ftake then runs fouth 34 rod on Capt Goulds Land to a pillar of ftones then runs Eaft 17 degrees fouth on faid Goulds Land 90 rod to where it Began

furvayed By Nathan Heywood and approved of by the Committee viz. Josiah Willard Edward Hartwell and Jonathan Willard

Recorded april the 9th 1736

℘ Edward Hartwell Cler

[39]   JEREMIAH ALLEN ESQ^R of Boston

Granted unto Jeremiah Allen Esqr by the Committee apointed by the Greate and General Court to aLott and grant out the Lands Within the Town of Lunenburgh to grantees forty nine ares and a half for a houfe Lott and Meadow Lott all in one Intire piece Lying in faid town and the Houfe Lott is bareing Number forty the f^d houfe Lott to gether with all the rights and Divifions of Land and meadow belonging thereunto or arifing therefrom within faid Townfhip are granted unto ye f^d Jeremiah allen by the Committee above faid

Lunenburg march ye 23^d 1730

Houfe Lot
No. 40

Survayed for Jeremiah allen Esqr houfe Lott No – 40 With the meadow Lott Lying in and by the fame the Contents of the Whole being forty nine acres and a half Begining at Certain popler tree marked for the Eafterly Corner and runing North 26 Degrees Weft on Land of Joseph page 50. rod to a white oak tree there making an Angle and runing Weft 26 Degree fouth on Land of John Heywood 160 rod to a pillar of ftones there making an Angle and runing fouth 29 Degrees Eaft on Land of Ephraim Wetherbe and Daniel auftin 49 rod to a heep of ſtones there making an Angle and runing Eaſt 21 Degrees North on Burbeens meadow Lott 84 rod to a ſtake there making an Angle and runing North 9 Degrees Eaſt on Land of ſaid Joseph page 5 rod to a ſtake there making an Angle and runing Eaſt 25 Degrees North on Land of ſaid page 70 rod to Where it began.

ſurvayed by Nathan Heywood and approved of by the Committee viz Edward Hartwell Nathan Heywood Josiah Willard and

Recorded may the first day anno Domini. 1731
℔ Edward Hartwell Clerk

Lunenburg January the 22ᵈ 1730/1

2ᵈ Diviſion Survayed for Jeremiah allen Esqʳ 2ᵈ Diviſion
No 57 No 57 on the ſoutherly ſide of flatt hill the Contents of which is 57 acres and a half. Begining at a ſtake which is the most weſterly Corner and runing North 17 deg Eaſt on Land Left for a high way 61 rod and a half to a ſtak there making an Angle and runing Eaſt 31 degrees ſouth on Lott Number 56. 152. rod to a ſtake in groton Line there making an Angle and runing ſouth 17 Degrees Weſt on ſaid Line 62 rod to a ſtake there making an Angle and runing Weſt 31 Degrees North on Lott No: 58. 152 rod to Where it began

ſurvayed by Nathan Heywood and approved of by the by the Committee viz

the bounds of this Lott ⎧ Edward Hartwell
Includs 6 acres of meadow ⎪ Josiah Willard
of Nathaniel Harwoods ⎨ Jonathan Willard &
this Lott being but 57 ⎩ Nathan Heywood
Acres and a half

Recorded May the first Day anno Domini. 1731
℔ Edward Hartwell
proprietors Clerk

[39²] Lunenburg February the 23ᵈ 1729/30

meadow Lotts Laid out by the Committee appointed 135 Acres of third Diviſion Land to the Right of Jeremiah Allen Esqr three meadow Lotts and alowance

Proprietors' Records. 75

for Wayes Exceped in faid Lott Cituate by and In Cluding the pearl hill meadow.

Begining at a pillar of ftones in the Line of the north town being Erected for the Eafterly Corner of faid Lott and Runing fouth 32 deg. Weft by 2ᵈ Divifion Land of Jofhua Hutchens 145 rod to a pillar of ftones there making an Angle and Runing West 32 deg north 149 rod to a ftake on Common Land there making an Angle and and Runing north 32 deg Eaft 145 rod to the north town Line bounding on Common Land there making an Angle and runing Eaft 32 deg fouth on faid Line 149 rod to Where It Began.

furvayed by Nathan Haywood and approved of by the Committee viz

        Josiah Willard
        Edward Hartwell
        Nathan Heywood
Recorded December the 30ᵗʰ annoque Domini 1731
    ℔ Edward Hartwell Cler

    Lunenburg october the 12ᵗʰ 1747.

Laid out by the Committee appointed Eleven acres and one 100 rod in faid Townfhip near the pearl hill meadows to make up whats an Equivilent for what is wanting in the Honourable James Allin fecond Divifion on flatt hill Number 57 which hath Nathaniel Harwoods meadow Contained in it it begins at a piller of ftones fixteen rod from the foutheaft Corner of faid Allins 135 acres and runs Weft 32 deg north on faid Land twelve rod to a heap of ftones then it runs fouth 31 degs Weft 160 rod on Mʳ William Browns Land to a heep of ftones then it runs Eaft 9 degrees north on Common Land 15 rod to a heap of ftones thence runs north 31 degrees Eaft on fecond Divifion Land 150 rod to where it began furvayed by Nathan Heywood approved of by the Committee viz Nathan Heywood Edward Hartwell

Recorded December the 15ᵗʰ 1748
    ℔ Edward Hartwell Clerk

[40]   JOSEPH PAGE of

Houſe Lott No 41 and Meadow Lott

Granted to Joſeph Page by the Committee appointed by the Greate and General Court to a Lott and Grant out the Lands within the town of Lunenburgh to grantees fifty two acres and forty four Rod for a Houſe Lott Bareing Number forty one together With all the rights and Diviſions of Land beLonging thereunto — —

Survayed for Joseph Page January the 14th 1729 $\frac{}{30}$ Houſe Lott No forty one the Contents of Which is fifty two Acres and forty four rod and a meadow Lott and a piece of third Diviſion Land ariſeing from the above ſaid Houſe Lott which are ten acres and ſeventy five rod the Contents of the Whole being ſixty two Acres and one Hundred and nineteen rod all in one intire piece highwayes going through the ſame. Begining at a ſtake ſet up for the ſouth Corner of the Houſe Lott and Runing Thirty ſeven degrees thirty minits Eaſt one Hundred and ſixty rod on fiſk Lott making an Angle and runing Weſt thirty ſix degrees thirty minits North twenty Eight rod and a half partly on Capt Goulds meadow Lott and partly on Common Land, making an Angle and runing Weſt thirteen degrees ſouth one hundred and ſeven rod and a half to a pillar of ſtones bounding Chiefly on Land Laid out to ſaid page making an Angle and Runing ſouth twenty ſix degrees ſeventy ſix rod on ſtiles and Allen making an Angle and Runing Weſt twenty five degrees ſouth on Allen ſeventy two rod there making an Angle and Runing ſouth fourteen Degrees Weſt ſix rod there making an Angle and runing ſouth twenty nine Degrees Eaſt twenty one rod and a half on burbeen and wetherbe. making an Angle and runing Weſt twenty nine Degrees ſouth twelve rod on Wetherbe. making an Angle and runing ſouth Eleven degree Eaſt twenty one rod on Auſtan making an Angle and Runing Eaſt twenty degrees North thirty one rod on fiffs meadow making an Angle and Runing north ſix Degrees Eaſt twenty ſix rod making an Angle and Runing Eaſt fifteen Degrees ſouth thirty one rod to Where it began furvayed by Nathan Heywood and approved of by the Committee viz Josiah Willard Edward Hartwell Jonathan Willard and Nathan Heywood

Recorded August the feventh Day in the year of our Lord one thoufand feven hundred and thirty

℔ Edward Hartwell Clerk.

Lunenburgh april ye 22^d 1729.

Laid out to Joseph Page by the Committee twelve acres and one hundred and thirty nine rod of third Divifion Land with a Lowance for a highway belonging to houfe Lott Number forty one adjoyning to his houfe Lott beginning at apillar of ftones and Runing East thirty five degrees North fifty nine rod there making an Angle and runing Weft thirty three degrees north forty nine rod there making an Angle and Runing West twenty Eight Degrees fouth thirty four rod there making an Angle and Runing fouth twenty Eight Degrees Eaft forty Eight rod to where it began

furvayed by me Nathan Heywood and approved of by the Committee viz Jofiah Willard, Edward Hartwell and Isaac Farnsworth

Recorded August the feventh Day in the year of our Lord one thoufand feven Hundred and thirty.

℔ Edward Hartwell CLerk

[41] JOHN FISK of

Granted to John Fisk by the Committee appointed by the Greate and General Court to a Lott and Grant out the Land Within the town of Lunenburgh to Granttees forty Eight acres and twenty five rod for a houfe Lott and meadow Lott Lying in the Houfe Lott together with all the rights and Divifions of Land beLonging thereunto —

Lunenburgh January the 26th 1729/30

Hofe Lott furvayed for John Fisk four pieces of Land
No 42 the first was his houfe Lott Number forty two the Contents of which is fourty Eight acres and twenty-five rod Begining at a ftake fet up for the norweft Corner

and runing Eaſt 36 degrees thirty minits ſouth fifty rod on the highway there making an Angle and runing north thirty : 7 : Eaſt one hundred and fourty nine rod ſixty nine rod on Whetneys Lott and Eighty rod on Common Land making an Angle and runing north twenty degrees Weſt fifteen rod on Common Land making an Angle and runing Weſt fourty degrees North thirty five rod to a ſtake in the meadow there making an Angle and runing ſouth thirty ſeven degree thirty minits weſt one hundred and ſixty rod on Joseph Pages Lott to where it Began the ſecond peice was one acre and a half adjoyning to the aboveſaid houſe Lott. begining at a Cheſnut tree marked for Whitneyes Corner and runing ſouth forty two Degrees Eaſt ſeven rod and a half on Common Land to a Cheſnut tree there making an Angle and runing North thirty nine Degrees thirty minits Eaſt twenty two rod to a popler tree on Common Land there making an Angle and runing North Ten degrees Eaſt nineteen rod on Common Land to a pine tree which is a rangeing mark for his houſe Lott there making an Angle and runing ſouth thirty ſeven Degrees Weſt on his own houſe Lott thirty Eight rod to Where it Began the third piece was three acres and ſeventy two rod on the other ſide of the highway one acre and one hundred thirty five rod to make up what is wanting in the houſe Lott the Remainder is third Diviſion Land begining at a White oke tree and Runing Weſt twenty four Degrees North twenty three rod to a ſtake there making an Angle and Runing ſouth four Degree Weſt twenty Eight rod to a ſtake there making an Angle and runing ſouth twenty four Degrees Weſt thirty ſix rod to a White oke tree there making an Angle and Runing North thirty ſeven deg Eaſt ſixty three rod to where It began

2d Diviſion

3d Diviſion

Survayed by Nathan Heywood and approved of by us the ſubſcribers and ordered to be recorded viz Josiah Willard Edward Hartwell Hilkiah Boynton Jonathan Willard and Nathan Heywood

Recorded August the Eight Day in the year of our Lord one thouſand ſeven Hundred and thirty

p^r Edward Hartwell Clerk

[41²] Lunenburgh January the 26th 1729/30

Meadow Lott No 3. ſurvayed for John Fisk Claimer meadow Lott No three which belonged to the right formerly was William Blunts and begins a greate White oke tree at the easterly End of the Meadow and runing North twelve Degrees Weſt three rod to a ſtake there making an Angle and Runing Weſt twenty Degrees ſouth partly on pages and on Auſtins meadow ſeventy five rod to a White oke tree there making an Angle and Runing ſouth fourty one Degrees Eaſt on the Clay pitt Land thirteen rod to a ſtake there making an Angle and runing Eaſt nineteen Degree thirty minits North ſixty rod to a ſtake there making an Angle and runing North twenty five Degrees Eaſt fourteen rod to Where it began

Survayed by Nathan hewood and approved of by the Committee viz Joſiah willard Edward Hartwell Hilkiah Boynton Jonathan Willard and Nathan Haywood

Recorded August the Eight Day in the year of our Lord one thouſand ſeven Hundred and thirty

Pr Edward Hartwell Clerk

Lunenburgh June the 16th 1729.

3d Diviſion Laid out by the Committee appointed twenty Eight ares and ninety ſix rod of third Diviſion Land to John fiſk ariſeing from houſe Lott No fourty two on the Northerly ſide of mulpus begining at a black oke tree and runing ſouth thirty rod to a pine tree there making an Angle and runing ſouth thirty Degrees Eaſt thirty rod to a pine tree there making an Angle and runing Eaſt twenty Degrees thirty mints ſouth ten rod to a tree there making an Angle and runing ſouth fourty two Degrees Eaſt ſixty rod to a little pine tree there making an Angle and runing North ninteen degrees Eaſt ſeventy ſix rod to a pillar of ſtones there making an Angle and runing Weſt twnty five degrees North Eighty ſix rod to where it began

ſurvayed by nathan Heywood and approved of by the Committee viz Joſiah willard Edward Hartwell Nathan Heywood and Jonathan Willard

Recorded August the Eight Day in the year of our Lord one thoufand feven hundred and thirty

₱ Edward Hartwell Clerk

The other Lands of the above faid John Fifk are Recorded in the fecond part of this book at page 23.

[42] JONATHAN WHITNEY. of

Granted to Jonathan Whitney By the Committee appointed by the Grate and General Court to a Lott and Grant out the Lands within the town of Lunenburg to Granttees fifty acres of Land Within faid town for a Houfe Lott Number forty five to gether with all the Rights and Divifions of Land that fhall arife therefrom or be Longs thereto

Lunenburg Sep^t ye 5th 1733.

Houfe Lott No 45. Survayed for Jonathan Whitney Houfe Lott Number 45 the Contents of Which is 50 acres Begining at a pillar of ftones Erected for the North Corner and Runing fouth 24 Degrees Eaft. 56. rod to a pillar of ftones bounding on the Highway thence runing fouth 36 Degrees Weft on Jacob Goulds Lott. 164. to a pillar of ftones thence runing North 24 degrees Weft on Jonas Gibfons Land 57 rod to a pillar of ftones thence runing north 37 Degrees Eaft : 164 : rod to Where it Began furvayed by Nathan Heywood approved of By the the Committee viz Jofiah Willard Jonathan Willard Edwd Hartwell and Nathan Heywood

Enterd with the Records in the proprietors Book may the 4th annoque Domini 1734

₱ Edwd Hartwell proprietors Clerk:

Lunenburg. Sep^{tm} ye 5th 1733.

Meadow Lott No 2. furvayed for Jonathan Whitney meadow Lott No 2 the Contents of Which is 4 acres and ¾ Begining at a ftake and heape of ftones Erected for the weft Corner and runing Eaft 20 degrees north on John Fifks meadow Lott 63 rod to a ftake thence runing fouth 32 degrees Weft on Land Land Left for away 24 rod to a pillar of ftones then runing Weft 24 degrees fouth on m^r prefcootts Land 34 rod then runing North 46 Degrees Weft on m^r prefcotts Land 18. rod to Where it Began

furvayed by Nathan Heywood and approved of By the Committee viz Jofiah Willard Jonathan Willard & Edwd Hartwell and Nathan Heywood

entered with the Records in the proprietors Book May the 4.th annoque Domini 1734.

₱ Edward Hartwell
pro Clerk

[42²] Lunenburg December ye 7.th 1731

Houfe Lott No. 43

furvayed for Jonathan Whitney Houfe Lott No: 43. the Contents of Which is 22 Acres ¾

Begining at a Certain heap of ftones which is the moft Wefterly Corner of faid Lott and runing North 36 degrees Eaft on John Fifks Lott 70 rod to a Chefnut tree there making an Angle and runing fouth 28 Degrees Eaft partly on faid fifks Land and partly on Common Land 56 rod to a pillar of ftones there making an Angle and runing fouth 37 degrees Weft on Thirftins Lott 71. to a black oak tree there making an Angle and runing north 30 Degrees weft 26 rod to a Chefnut tree there making an Angle and runing North 24 degrees Weft 24 rod to a white oak tree there making an Angle and runing north 20. degrees Weft. 6. rod to Where it Began

₱ Nathan Heywood furvayer

approved of by the Committee viz Jofiah Willard Jonathan Willard Edward Hartwell and Nathan Heywood

Record may ye 4.th 1734.

₱ Edwd Hartwell pro.^r Clerk

[43] BENJAMIN PRESCOT of Salem

Houfe Lott No 44

Granted to the Reverend Mr Benjamin Prefcott By the Committee appointed By the Greate and General Court to aLott and grant out the Lands within the town of Lunenburgh to Granttees forty nine acres and a quarter of Land Within faid town for a houfe Lott No forty four to gether With all the Rights and Divifions of Land Belonging there unto

Lunenburgh April the 10th 1730.

ſurvayed for the Rnd Mr Benja Preſcott Houſe Lott Number forty four the Contents of Which is forty nine acres and a quarter begining at a White oak tree for the Weſterly Corner. and Runing ſouth thirty degrees Eaſt fifty five rod to a ſtake and a heep of ſtones there making An angle and Runing North thirty ſeven degrees Eaſt one Hundred and ſixty rod. there making an Angle and Runing Weſt thirty ſix degrees North fifty rod. there making An Angle and Runing Weſt ſixteen degree north ſix rod there making an Angle and Runing ſouth thirty ſix degree Weſt one hundred and thirty five rod to where It began

ſurvayed by Nathan Heywood and approve of by the Committee viz Joſiah Willard Edward Hartwell Nathan Heywood and Jonathan Willard.

Recorded June the fifth day in the year of our Lord one thouſand ſeven hundred and thirty by me

Edward Hartwell CLerk

Lunenburgh April the 10th 1730.

Second Diviſion No : 44 : ſurvayed for the reverend Mr Benja Preſcott a ſecond Diviſion Lott No: 44 which is Coupled to the houſe Lott a bove ſaid by the General Courts Committee the Contents of Which is fifty one acres and one hundred and Eight rod. Begining at a Certain ſtake ſet up for the moſt ſoutherly Corner and runing North thirty degrees Eaſt one hundred and forty ſix rod bounding on a Lott of Eleazar Boynton there making an Angle and Runing Weſt thirty one Degree thirty minits North on John fiſks Lott fifty five rod to a pillar of ſtones there making an Angle and Runing ſouth thirty one Degrees Weſt on ſecond Diviſion one Hundred and forty ſix rod to a ſtake there making an Angle and Runing Eaſt thirty one Degrees thirty minits ſouth fifty ſeven rod to Where it Began

ſurvayed by Nathan Heywood and approved of by the Committee viz Edward Hartwell Nathan' Heywood Joſiah willard and Jonathan willard.

Recorded october the tenth day in the year of our Lord one thoufand feven Hundred and thirty by me
                              Edwd Hartwell Clerk

                    Lunenburgh June the 11th 1730.

Meadow   furvayed for the Revd Mr Benj^a Prefcoott
No 1 in   meadow Lott No. one in Clay pit meadow
Clay pit   and alfo Laid out by the Committee appoint-
meadow   ed *[Eight] acres and *[3 quarters] of Land
adjoyning thereto to make up what is Wanting in his fecond Divifion the Contents of the whole is Eight acres and fifty one rod Begining at a Cartain White oak tree marked for ye fouth Corner and runing North thirty degrees Weft on m^r Gardner and on aftains Lott fifty fix rod there making an Angle and runing North twenty fix degrees thirty mints Eaft on faid Aftain twenty two rod to a White oak tree there making An Angle and runing
                   fouth forty one degrees thirty minits Eaft on
Mr Fifks and on Whitneys meadow thirty one
prefcootts
other Lands   rod there making an Angle and runing Eaft
are Recorded   twenty degrees North on Whitneys meadow
in ye fecond   41 rod there making an Angle and runing
part of this   fouth thirty fix degrees Weft on f^d mr pref-
book at   cotts Houfe Lott feventy one rod to where It
page 5   Began

furvayed By Nathan Heywood and approved of by the Committee viz Jofiah willard Edward Hartwell Nathan Heywood and Jonathan Willard. — — — — —

Recorded October the tenth Day in the year of our Lord one thoufand feven Hundred and thirty
                         By me Edward Hartwell Clerk

[43^2]   Lunenburgh May ye 28th 1730 -

4th Laid out by the Committe appointed
Divifion   Eighty Acres of Land to the Rev^d m^r Benjamin Prefcott for a forth Divifion arifeing from the right or houfe Lott No forty four Cituate and and Lying foutheafterly from his third Divifion. begining at a Chefnut tree

---
*In the original the words in brackets are stricken out.

Which is the fouth Eaft Corner of faid third Divifion and runing runing fouth feventeen deg Eaft on Land alreaddy Layed out Eighty one rod there making an Angle and runing Weft forty Degrees fouth Chiefly on Common Land a houndred rod there Making an Angle and runing North forty degrees Weft on Common Land forty rod there making an Angle and runing North nine Degrees Weft on Common Land one hundred and forty rod there making an Angle and and runing Eaft fifteen degrees fouth on the afore faid third Divifion one hundred and three rod to Where it Began

furvayed By Nathan Heywood and approved of By the Committee viz Jofiah Willard Edward Hartwell and Jonathan Willard.

Recorded October the 10th 1730 —
by me Edward Hartwell Clerk

Lunenburgh April ye 14th 1729.

3d Divifion   Laid out to Benjamin Prefcott Clark Claimer by the Committe appointed one hundred and feventeen acres and a hundred and twenty rod of Land for a third Divifion the right arifeing from houfe Lott number ten. Cituate at the aple tree hill Begining at a pillar of ftones and runing North twenty five deg Eaft one hundred and feventy two rod to a pillar of ftones there making an angle and runing Eaft twenty five degrees fouth one hundred and twenty rod to a pillar of ftones there making an Angle and runing fouth twenty five degrees weft one hundred and forty two rod to a pillar of ftones there making an Angle and runing West nine degres North one hundred and twenty two rod to where it Began

furvayed by Nathan Heywood and approved of by the Committ viz Jofiah Willard Edward Hartwell and Nathan Heywood

Recorded october the tenth Day in the year of our Lord one thoufand feven hundred and thirty —— ——
₱ Edward Hartwell CLerk

Proprietors' Records.

Lunenburgh February the twenty feventh. 1729/30—

3ᵈ Divifion   Laid out by the Committee appointed one Hundred and twenty ares of third Divifion Land to the Reverend Mʳ Benjamin Prefcott. arifeing from the right number forty four fcituate and Lyeth towards the fouthweft Corner of faid Townfhip. Begining at a Cartain Cheftnut tree marked for the foutheaftly Corner and runing north fifteen degrees Eaft on Common Land one hundred and fixty rod to a heepe of ftones there making an angle and runing weft fifteen degree north one hundred and twenty rod on Common Land there making an angle and runing fouth fifteen degrees weft on Common Land one hundred and fixty rod making an angle and runing Eaft fifteen degree fouth on Common Land one hundred and twenty rod to where it began.

furvayed by Nathan Heywood and approved of by the Committee Jofiah Willard Edward hartwell and Nathan Heywood

Recorded october the Eight Day in the year of our Lord one thoufand feven hundred and thirty ———

₱ Edward Hartwell Clerk

[44]   JONATHAN WHITNEY Junior of

[45]   MOSES GOULD of

Granted unto Moses Gould by the Committee appointed by the Great and General Court to a Lott and Grant out the Lands Contained Within the townfhip of Lunenburg to Granttees 49 acres for a Houfe Lott Number 46 to Gether With all the Rights and Divifions of upland and meadow that beLongs thereto or that fhall arife there from.

Recorded December yᵉ 27. 1732.

₱ Edward Hartwell Cler—

Lunenburg September the 5ᵗʰ 1733.

Houfe Lott   Surveyᵈ for Jacob Gould Claimer Houfe
No. 46   Lott No. 46. the Contents of which is 49 acres. Begining at the moft northerly Cornner and runing fouth 36. degrees weft on Jonathan whitneys Land 164 rod to a pillar of ftones then runing fouth 24 deg

Eaft on Gilfons Land 55 rod and a half to a ftake then runs north 35 degrees Eaft on George Wheelers Land 164 rod to a heep of ftones then runing North 24 degrees Weft on the high way 54 rod to Where it Began

℔ Nathan Haywood Survayer

and approved of by the Committee viz Jofiah Willard Edward Hartwell Nathan Heywood and Jonathan Willard Recorded January the 28th 1734

℔ Edward Hartwell Clerk

[45²] Lunenburg March ye 23^d: 1730 31

2^d Divifion furvayed for mofes Gould 2^d Divifion No. 52 on flatt hill the Contents of Which is 53 Acres Begining at a pillar of ftones Erected for the fouth West Corner and Runing Eaft 31 degree fouth 59 rod to a ftake there making an Angle and runing North 17 Degrees 30 minits Eaft on Lott No. 51 : 148 rod to a ftake there making an Angle and runing Weft 31 degrees North 60 rod to a ftake there making an Angle and runing fouth 18 Degrees Weft 148 rod to Where it Began

furvayed by Nathan Heywood and approved of By the Committee viz Jofiah Willard Edward Hartwell Jonathan Willard and Nathan Heywood

Recorded march ye 7th 1733./4

℔ Edward Hartwell Clerk

[46] WILLIAM WHEELOR of

Granted to William Wheeler by the Committee appointed by the Great and General Court to a Lott and Grant out the Lands within the Town of Lunenburg to Granttees fifty one acres and an half of Land within faid Townfhip for a houfe Lott No. 47 together with all the wrights and Divifions of Lands that beLongs thereto or fhall arife therefrom.

Lunenburg March the 5th 1744.

Houfe Lott Then furvayed for William and Francis No 47 ·Allexander Claimers Houfe Lott Numer forty feven originally William Wheelers Lying in Lunenburg afore faid Containing fifty one Acres and an half it begins at a pillar of ſtones Erected for the moſt northerly Corner of ſaid Lott and runs ſouth thirty ſix degrees Weſt on Jacob Goulds Land and on Land belonging to the Heirs of Jonas Gilſon Deceaſed one hundred and ſixty Eight rod then it runs ſouth twenty four degrees Eaſt on ſaid Gilſons Land and on Land belonging to John ſwan fifty ſeven rod and an half then it runs north thirty ſix degrees Eaſt on Land of Mr Robert Clark one hundred and ſixty Eight rod to appillar of ſtones then it runs north twenty four degrees Weſt on a highway fifty ſeven rod and an half to where it firſt began

℔ Nathan Heywood ſurr

approved of by the Committee viz Nathan Heywood Jonathan Willard and Edward Hartwell

Recorded may the 21ſt 1745

℔ Edward Hartwell proprietors Clerk

Lunenburg march the 6th. 1744.

2d Diviſion No. 63

Then ſurvayed for William and francis Alexander Claimer ſecond Diviſion Number ſixty three in Lunenburg afore ſaid Cituate and Lying on the ſoutherly ſide of flatt Hill Containing ſixty one acres it begins at appillar of ſtones Erected for the moſt ſoutherly Corner of ſaid Lott and runs Weſt thirty one degree thirty minuts north on Land of Nathaniel Page and Moſes Mitchel one hundred and ſixty one rod to a ſtake and heap of ſtones then it runs North ſixteen Degrees Eaſt on Land of Mr Robert Clark ſixty four rod to a heap of ſtones then it runs Eaſt thirty one degrees thirty minuts ſouth on Land of William and Joſeph Moffet one hundred and ſixty one rod then it runs ſouth ſixteen degrees Weſt on a highway Laid out between the Lotts ſixty four rod to where it began.

℔ Nathan Heywood ſur

approved of by the Committee viz

Nathan Heywood
Jonathan Willard &
Edward Hartwell

Recorded may the 21ſt 1745.

℔ Edward Hartwell proprietors Clark

[47] **WILLIAM CLARK ESQ^R of Boston.**

Houſe Lott
No. 48

Granted to William Clark Esqr by the Committee appointed by the greate and General Court to a Lott and Grant out the Lands Within the Townſhip of Lunenburgh to Granttees forty nine acres of Land within ſaid Town for a houſe Lott bearing number forty Eight to gether With all the Rights and Diviſions of Land belonging thereunto — — —

Lunenburgh May the 4th 1730.

ſurvayed for William Clark Esqr Houſe Lott Number forty Eight the Contents of Which is forty nine Acres. Begining at a heep of ſtones near the South ſide of the Houſe by the High Way. and runing Eaſt ten Degrees thirty minits ſouth twenty rod to a ſtake there making an Angle and runing North thirty ſeven degrees Eaſt on Beaths Lott one Hundred and fifty one rod to a maple tree. there making an Angle and runing north thirty three Degrees thirty minits Weſt fifty five rod to a ſtak near Wheelers fraim there making an Angle and runing ſouth thirty ſix Degrees thirty min Weſt one hundred and ſixty rod to a ſtak there making an Angle and runing ſouth twenty four degrees Eaſt thirty ſeven rod to where it Began

The other lands of m^r Clark are in y^e ſecond part of this book at page one : 2 :

ſurvayed by Nathan Heywood and approved of by the Committee viz Josiah Willard Edward Hartwell Jonathan willard and Nathan Heywood

Recorded the twenty third Day of November In the year of our Lord one thouſen ſeven Hundred and thirty

℔ Edward Hartwell Clerk

[47²] By His Common Right, as an original Proprietor. by lott being Number forty Eight. . . . 48.
22 By The Revd Mr Andrew Gardner. for a Seccond diviſion of Sixty Acres. number Eighty, arriſing from House Lott Number One and bounded as by plan given in with the deed . . . .

24 By Capt Josiah Willard for two Seccond divisions of One hundred and twenty Acres arrising from House Lotts Number   and pland with the Lott bought of the Reverend Mr Gardner and part of his third division . . . .
22 By the Reverend Mr Andrew Gardner. for two third divisions of Two hundred and forty Acres arrising from House Lotts Number One and number Eighty four, lying East of Neesepegesuck Ponds. . . .
24 By Capt Josiah Willard for four third divisions of. Four hundred and Eighty Acres arrising from House Lotts Number Forty Six Number Fifty four Number Eighty five and Number Eighty Six . . . . . .
9 By Joshua Hutchins for three Common Rights after the Seccond division arrising from House Lotts Number Three Number Nineteen. and Number Seventy five.
22 By the Reverend Mr Andrew Gardner for two Common rights after the third division arrising from House lotts Number One and Number Eighty four. .

[48]   WALTER BEATH of Lunenburgh.

first   Granted unto Walter Beath by the Com-
fecond   mittee appointed by the Greate and and Gen-
third   eral Court to a Lott and Grant out the
Divifion
              Lands Within the townfhip of Lunenburg to
Granttees forty five acres of Land Within faid town for a houfe Lott Number forty nine to gether With all the Rights and Divifion of Land and meadow arifing therefrom or belonging thereto The Land of Walter Beath in Lunenburg the Contents of Which is two hundred and twenty two acres there being a first fecond and third Divifion. Begining at a Certain white pine tree near the Lower end of Mulpus meadows and runing Weft 30 Deg fouth by the meadows 72 rod to a ftake there making an Angle and runing fouth one Deg Eaft near faid meadows 71 rod to a ftake there making an Angle and runing Weft on Heals meadow Lott 25 rod to a ftake there making there making an Angle and runing north on Said Heals meadow 26 rod to a pillar of ftones there making an Angle and runing Weft 36 Deg fouth on thirf-

Proprietors' Records.

tins Land 50 rod to a pillar of ſtones there making an
Angle and runing ſouth thirty three Deg Eaſt
on m^r Clark Land thirty three rod to a maple tree there making an Angle and runing
ſouth 37 Deg Weſt on ſaid Clarks Land 151
rod. to a ſtake there making an Angle and
runing Eaſt 10 Deg ſouth partly on the road which goeth
to Groton 108. rod to a ſtake there making an Angle and
runing ſouth 17 Degs West on ſaid Clarks Land 50 rod
to a ſtake there making an Angle and runing Eaſt 31 Degrees 30 minits ſouth on ſaid ſecond Diviſion Land 143
rod to a ſtake there making an Angle and runing north
ſeventeen deg^r Eaſt on ſaid ſecond Diviſion Land ſixty four
rod to a ſtake there making an Angle and Runing Weſt
31 Degs 30 minit north on Harwoods Land 143 rod to a
ſtake there making an Angle and runing North 17 Degs
Eaſt on 2^d Diviſion Land 136 rod to a ſtake there making an Angle and Runing Weſt 17 Degs north on ſaid
Harwoods Land 40 rod to a ſtake there making an Angle
and Runing North 17 Degres Eaſt on ſ^d harwoods Land
40 rod to a ſtake there making an Angle and Runing Eaſt
17 Degs ſouth on ſ^d Harwood Land 40 rod to a ſtake
there making an Angle and runing north 17 Degrees Eaſt
on 2^d Diviſion Land 199 rod to a ſtake and pillar of
ſtones there making an Angle and Runing Weſt 31 Degres
north on 2^d Diviſion Land 44 rod to a ſtake there making
an Angle and Runing ſouth 10 Degrees Weſt on Common
Land 78 rod to Where it began approved of by the
Committee viz Edward Hartwell Jonathan Willard Nathan Heywood and Benoni Boynton

miſtake 33: should have been 83 on Clark

Recorded December the 15th 1732.

℔ Edward Hartwell Clerk

[48²] Lunenburg May the 9th 1729 — — —

Meadow Lott   Laid out to Walter Beeth by the Commit-
No   tee appointed 5ᵃ = 52 ^{rod} of Meadow Land
and ſom up Land tow acres to make up What is Wanting In his Houſe Lott and three quaters and the remaider
is third Diviſion Begining at a ſtake in the meadow and
runing North 1 deg 30 mints Eaſt 70 rod to a pillar of

ſtones there making an Angle and runing Weſt 34 deg ſouth 18 rod to a White oake tree there making an Angle and runing ſouth 59 rod to apillar of ſtones there making angle and runing Eaſt 3 deg ſouth 13 rod to Where it began ſurvayed by Nathan Heywood and approved of by the Committee viz Joſiah Willard Jonathan Willard and Edward Hartwell

  Recorded June the first anno Domini 1731.
℔ Edward Hartwell Clerk.

[49]   DANIEL THURSTAIN of
Houſe Lott   Granted unto Daniel Thurſton by the Com-
No. 50   mittee appointed by the Greate and General Court to a Lott and Grant out the Lands Within the town of Lunenburg to Granttees thirty four acres and fifty Rod Within ſaid town for a houſe Lott and meadow Lott all in one Intire piece to Gether With all the after Draughts and Diviſions ariſeing there from or belonging thereto. and the ſᵈ Houſe Lott is Number (50) and Begins at a ſtak and heap of ſtones and runs ſouth twenty four Deg Eaſt 101 rod to a ſtake there making an Angle and runing ſouth 36 deg 30 mint Weſt 36 rod there making an Angle and runing ſouth 18 Degrees 30 min Eaſt 14 rod there making an Angle and runing West 36 Deg ſouth 20 rod there making an Angle and Runing north 24 deg West 104 rod there making an Angle and runing north 36 Deg 30 min Eaſt 60 rod to a ſtake and heap of Stones to Where it Began ſurvayed By Nathan Heywood July the 22ᵈ. 1729 and approved of By the Committee viz Edward Hartwell, Joſiah Willard Jonathan Willard Nathan Heywood and Joſhua Hutchens

  Recorded march yᵉ 3ᵈ 1729/30
℔ me Edward Hartwell Cler

Lunenburg october yᵉ 2ᵈ 1732.

2ᵈ Diviſion   Survayed Daniel Thirſtin 2ᵈ Diviſion No.
No 46   46. the Contents of which is 64 acres. Begining at a certain Heap of Stones Erected for the ſouth Corner and Runing North 26 Degrees Eaſt on on yᵉ miniſteriel 2ᵈ Diviſion 151. rod to a pillar of ſtones thence run-

ing Weſt 31. degrees. 30. minits north on the northerly range of Lotts 67 rod thence runing ſouth 27 Degrees Weſt on 2ᵈ Diviſion No. 47. 151 rod. to a pillar of Stones thence runing Eaſt 31 degrees 30 minits ſouth 68 rod to Where it Began. pr Nathan Heywood ſurvayer.

allowed and approved of by the Committee viz Joſiah Willard Edward Hartwell Jonathan Willard and Nathan Heywood

Recored December the 5ᵗʰ 1732

pʳ Edward Hartwell Clerk

[49²]   Decᵐ 29. 1729.

3ᵈ Diviſion   Laid out By the Committee appointed 135 acres and 60 rod of third Diviſion Land to Daniel Thurſton belonging to Houſe Lott No. 50) 15 acres and 110. rod of Which Land is to make up what is wanting in his houſe Lott and 119 acres & 110 rod of third Diviſion Land belonging to ſaid Houſe Lott.

Begining at a pillar of ſtones Erected for the ſouth Weſt Corner and Runing north 10. Deg Eaſt nineteen rod there making an Angle and runing north 34 deg 30 minits Eaſt 20 rod there making an Angle and Runing weſt 34 Degrees 30 minits north 70 rod there making an Angle and runing north 10 Degrees Eaſt 230. rod to a black oak tree there making an Angle and runing Eaſt 10 Degrees ſouth 80 rod there making an Angle and runing ſouth 10 Degree Weſt 272. rod to a black oake tree there making an Angle and runing Weſt 10 Degrees north 80. rod to Where it Began

ſurvayed by nathan Heywood and approved of By the Committee viz Edward Hartwell Nathan Heywood and Jonathan Willard

Recorded march yᵉ 3ᵈ 172/30

℔ Edward Hartwell Cler

Lunenburg November yᵉ 30ᵗʰ 1731.

4ᵗʰ Diviſion   Laid out by the Committee appointed 86 acres of Land to Daniel Thurſton for a 4ᵗʰ diviſion ariſeing from Houſe Lott No. (50) adjoyning to his own 3ᵈ Diviſion Begining at a White pine tree marked for the most foutherly Corner and runing West 34 degrees 30 min north on Land of Jonathan Willard 72 rod to a black oak tree there making an Angle and runing north 10 deg Eaft on Common Land 200 rod to a pillar of Stones there making an Angle and runing Eaft 10 degrees fouth on Common Land 64 rod. to a read oak tree there making an Angle and runing fouth ten degrees West on the aforefaid third Divifion 230. rod to Where it Began

₱ Nathan Heywood fur

approved of By the Committee viz Jonathan Willard Edward Hartwell and James Jewell

Recorded June ye 23^d anno Dommini 1732

₱ Edward Hartwell Cler

[50]   JONAS GILSON of

Granted to Jonas Gilson by the Committee appointed by the Greate and General Court to a Lott and Grant out the Lands within the Townfhip of Lunenburg to Granttees forty five acres of Land within faid Townfhip for a houfe Lott Number fifty three together with all the Divifions of upland and meadow that belongs there to or fhall arife therefrom within faid Town.

Lunenburg November the 30th 1747.

Houfe Lott No. 53   furvayed Houfe Lott Number fifty three be longing to the Heirs of Jonas Gilson Late of Lunenburg Deceafed it Contains forty five acres it begins at a Certain white oak tree marked for the moft north eafterly Corner and runs Weft twenty nine Degrees fouth on Land of Robert Clark twenty four rod to a heap of ftones which is pages north Eaft Corner then it runs fouth one Degree Eaft on pages Line two hundred and Eight rod to a heap of ftones by the north fide of Aaron Browns fhop then it runs Eaft Eight Degree fouth on the town road forty rod and an half to a ftump then it runs north four Degrees Weft on fecond Divifion Land of faid Gilsons two hundred and fixteen rod then runs North thirty Degrees Weft twelve rod to where it began

₱ Nathan Heywood furvayer

and allowed of by the Committee viz Nathan Heywood Edward Hartwell and Jonathan Willard
Recorded December the 24th 1747
₱ Edward Hartwell
₱ proprietors Clerk

Lunenburg November the 30th 1747.

Meadow Lott No 3

ſurvayed for the Heirs of Jonas Gilson Late of Lunenburg Deceaſed meadow Lott number three belonging to Houſe Lott No: 53: ſcituate and lying in the meadow Called turkey Hill meadow the Contents of which is ſix acres and 54 rod it begins at a Certain Dead tree marked for the ſouth Corner and runs Eaſt twenty ſeven Degrees thirty minuts north on meadow Laid out to ſamuell page Late of Lunenburg Deceaſed forty three rod then it runs north twenty four Degrees Weſt on Land of William Allexander twenty ſix rod to a ſtake then runs Weſt twenty ſeven Degrees thirty minuts ſouth on Meadow origional Capt Jonathan Willards but now belonging to the Heirs of the ſaid Jonas Gilson thirty ſix rod to a white oak tree then it runs ſouth ten Degrees Eaſt on ſaid Gilsons ſecond Diviſion Land twenty ſeven rod to where it began
₱ Nathan Heywood ſurvayer
allowed of by the Committee viz Edward Hartwell Nathan Heywood and Jonathan Willard.
Recorded December the 25th 1747
₱ Edward Hartwell proprietors Clerk

[50²] Lunenburg November the 30th 1747.

2^d Diviſion No 97

ſurvayed part of a ſecond Diviſion Number 97 belonging to the Heirs of Jonas Gilson Late of Lunenburg Deceaſed and is adjoyning to His firſt Diviſion and Contains twenty ſeven acres

it begins at a Certain white pine buſh by the bever Damm of Turkey Hill meadow and runs north nine Degrees Weſt twelve rod then it runs Weſt nine Degrees ſouth twelve rod then it runs north Eighteen Degrees thirty minuts Weſt Eleven rod then it runs Weſt twenty ſeven Degr north twelve rod then it runs Weſt thirty one

Degrees fouth ten rod and a half then it runs fouth thirteen Degrees Weft fix rod then it runs Weft twenty fix Degrees fouth twelve rod then it runs north twenty Degrees thirty minuts Weft Eight rod then it runs north twenty three Degrees Eaft twelve rod to a ftump then it runs north twelve Degrees thirty minuts Eaft nine rod to a dead tree all the afore mentioned Lines bounding on the meadow Lotts belonging to the Heirs of famuell page Late of Lunenburg Deceafed then it runs north ten Degrees Weft on meadow Lott belonging to the faid Gilfons Heirs twenty feven rod to a white oak tree then it runs North fix degrees Weft on Meadow Lott now belonging to the faid Gilfons Heirs but originally Capt Jonathan Willards thirty fix rod to a black oak tree then it runs Eaft twenty feven Degrees thirty minuts north on faid meadow three rod and an half then runs north Eight Degrees Weft on Common Land fixty nine rod then it runs north twenty four Degrees Weft Eleven rod to a heap of ftones then it runs north thirty Degrees Weft forty three rod then it runs fouth four Degrees Eaft on faid Gilfons Houfe Lott two hundred and fixteen rod to a ftump by the road then it runs Eaft one Degree north by the Town Road feventy rod to where it began

₱ Nathan Heywood furvayer

allowed of in order for Recording by the Committee viz Nathan Heywood Edward Hartwell and Jonathan Willard. Recorded December the 25th 1747.

₱ Edward Hartwell proprietors Clerk

[51]   JACOB STILES of

Houfe Lott   Granted to Jacob Stiles by the Committee
No 56   appointed by the Greate and General Court to alott and Grant out the Land Within the town of Lunenburgh to Granttees fourty five acres and fixty Rod of Land Within faid town for a houfe Lott baring Number fifty fix to gether Withall the rights and Divifions of Land belonging there too or arifeing there from — —

Survayed for Jacob Stiles Houfe Lott Number fifty fix the Contents of Which is fourty five acres and fixty rod.

Begining at a pillar of ſtones Which is the Moſt northerly Corner of houſe Lott number fifty ſeven which ſaid Stiles purchaſed of Capt Joſiah Willard and weſt thirty ſix deg South one Hundred and fourty ſeven rod upon the Northerly Line of the afore Said Lott to the pillar of ſtones which is the Corner of both Lotts there making an Angle and runing north thirty Degrees Weſt fifty four rod to a hemlock tree there making an Angle and and Runing Eaſt thirty two degrees north one hundred and fifty four rod there making an Angle and runing ſouth twenty one deg Eaſt fourty four rod and a half to Where it began —

Survayed by Nathan heywood and approved of by the Committee viz Edward Hartwell Joſiah Willard Benoni Boynton Hilkiah Boynton

Recorded December the twenty third Day in the year of our Lord one thouſand ſeven hundred and thirty — —

₱ Edward Hartwell Clerk

Meadow No Lott 7 uper mulpus
ſurvayd meadow Lott Number ſeven ſcituate in uper Mulpus the Contents of which is four acres and and hundred and thirty rod and it is diſcribed with meadow Lott nomber Eight as they ware both ſurvayed to gether for m^r Nathaniel woods who bought the ſaid meadow Lott Number ſeven of the above ſaid ſtiles and both meadow Lotts are diſcribed at page 52 which is m^r Woods page and the Said meadow Lott Number ſeven was Coupled to Jacob ſtiles houſe Lott Number 56. by the general Courts Committe

Edward Hartwell Clerk

Lunenburgh may y^e. 15. 1729

3^d Diviſion No 56
Laid out by the Committee appointed fourteen acres and thirty Eight rod of third Diviſion Land to Jacob Stiles Ariſeing from Houſe Lott Number fifty ſix. begining at a pine tree and runing South ſeven Deg Weſt thirty: ſeven .rod there making an Angle and Runing Weſt twenty Eight Deg South one hundred and Eight rod upon Lancaſter new Grant Line there making an Angle and and runing North thirty Degres Weſt nine rod there Making an Angle and Runing Eaſt

thirty feven Degree north one hundred and thirty two rod to Where it began

furvayed by Nathan Heywood and alowed by the Committee viz Edward Hartwell Isaac Farnsworth and Jonathan Willard

Recorded December the twenty fourth Day in the year of our Lord one thoufand feven hundred and thirty — —

℘ Edward Hartwell Clerk

[51²]   Lunenburgh Auguft ye 18th 1730

2^d Divifion   Survayed for Jacob Siles fecond divifion
No 10   number ten the Contents of Which is fifty three Acres and a quarter begining at a ftump and a ftake it being the moft foutherly Corner and runing north thirty one degrees Eaft on No 9 one Hundred and fourty nine rod to a ftake there making an Angle and Runing Weft thirty one deg thirty minits north on the North town Line fifty Eight Rod there making an Angle and runing fouth thirty five deg Weft on No Eleven one hundred and fourty nine rod there making an Angle and Runing Eaft thirty one degrees 30 minits South on Meadows and upland fifty fix rod to Where it began. furvayed by Nathan Heywood and approved by the Committee viz Edward Hartwell Josiah Willard Jonathan Willard and Nathan Heywood. Recorded December the twenty fix day in the year of our Lord one thoufand feven Hundred and thirty

℘ Edward Hartwell Clerk

Lunenburgh May the 15th 1729

Houfe   furvayed for Jacob Stiles Claimer Houfe
Lott   Lott Number — 57 — the Contents of Which
No 57   is thirty feven acres and Eighteen rod begining at a pine tree and Runing Weft thirty feven degrees fouth one hundred and thirty two rod to a black burch tree there making an Angle and runing North thirty deg Weft fourty four rod to a pillar of ftones there making an Angle and Runing Eaft thirty fix degr North one hundred and fourty feven rod there making an Angle and

runing south twenty one degrees East thirty rod to a pillar of stones there making an Angle and runing south seven deg West nineteen rod to Where it began. survayed by Nathan Heywood and approved of by the Committee Josiah Willard Edward Hartwell Jonathan Willard and nathan Heywood
Edward Hartwell Clerk

Lunenburg March the 19th 1730/1

3^d Division   Layed out by the Committee appointed one hundred and thirteen acres of Land on the West side of Dorchester farm in said township to Jacob Stiles for his third Division belonging to house Lott No 56 and for an Equevilent to What is wanting In his house Lott and In his 2^d Division and In his Meadow Lott Begining at Certain Elme tree in said Dorcherster Line and runing West 42 degr south on Common Land 123 rod to a pitch pine tree there making an Angle and runing East 37 deg south on Common Land 16 rod to a stake and heape of Stones there making an Angle and Runing south 7 deg West on Common Land 52 rod to a White pine tree there making an Angle and runing south 34 deg East on Common Land 130 rod to a pillar to a pillar of stones there Making an Angle and Runing East 30 degrees North on Common Land 55 rod to Dorchester there making an Angle and runing north 10 degrees West on said Dorchester 225 rod to Where it began

survayed by Nathan Heywood and approved of by the Committee viz Edward Hartwell Jonathan Willard and Nathan Heywood

Recorded January the 24th anno Domini 1731/2
℔ Edward Hartwell Clerk

[52]   NATHANIEL WOODS of

Granted to Nathaniel Woods by the Committee appointed by the Greate and General Court to aLott and grant out the Lands Within the Town of Lunenburgh to granttee forty five acres of Land within said town for a houfe Lott Bareing Number fifty Eight to gether with all the rights and Divifions of Land belonging there unto

Hofe Lott No 58.   Houfe Number fifty Eight Bounds Norwefterly on the Land of Edward Hartwell 100 & feventy two rod and it Bounds northeafterly 55 rod on the Land of Jacob Stiles fouth eafterly on the Line between Lancafter new grant and Lunenburgh fouthwefterly on Common Land.

Lunenburgh auguft the 18th 1730

2d Divifion No 11   Survayed for Nathaniel woods fecond Divifion No Eleven the Contents of Which is fifty four acres and a quarter — — —

Begining at a pillar of ftones which is the Wefterly Corner and runing North thirty four deg Eaft on Woods Lott one Hundred and forty nine rod to a pillar of ftones there Making an Angle and runing Eaft thirty one deg thirty Min. fouth on the North Town Line fifty Eight rod and ½ to a pillar of ftones there making an Angle and runing fouth thirty five deg Weft on ftiles Lott one Hundred and fourty Nine rod to a pillar of ftones there Making an Angle and runing Weft thirty one deg thirty minits North fifty feven rod to where It began. alfo aded by the Committee a piece at the fouth wefterly end of faid Lott in part to make up What is Wanting in fd Lott. Confifting of one acre and a quarter and twelve rod — Begining at a ftake on the fouth fide of the brook Which is the corner of fome Land Laid out to Benoni Boynton thence runing North forty two deg Eaft ten rod to the Corner of fd 2d divifion there Making an Angle and runing Eaft thirty one deg thirty mins fouth on faid Divifion and fo bounding on faid Divifion on one fide and on the other fide on the Brook furvayed by nathan Heywood and approved of by the Committee

                                  Jofiah Willard
                                  Edward Hartwell
                                  Jonathan Willard
                                  & Nathan Heywood

Lunenburgh January the 6th 1729/30. — —

Meadow
No 8
meadow 7

ſurvayed for Nathaniel Woods Claimer two Meadow Lotts the one being Number Eight Laid to his houſe Lott the other being Number ſeven which ſd Woods bought of Jacob Stiles both ſcituate in uper mulpus the Contents of one being ſix acres and a ¼ the other being four acres and one hundred and thirty rod begining at pillar of ſtones Which is the Northerly Corner and runing Eaſt thirty one deg thirty Min. ſouth Croſs the Ends of both meadow Lotts thirty nine rod there making an Angle and runing ſouth twenty Eight deg. Weſt fifty four rod there making an Angle and runing Weſt twenty four rod there making an Angle and runing North thirteen deg Eaſt ſeventy one rod to Where It began

ſurvayed by Nathan Heywood and approved of by the Committee viz Joſiah Willard Edward Hartwell Jonathan Willard and Nathan Heywood

Recorded october the twenty Ninth in the year of our Lord one thouſand ſeven Hundred and thirty

℔ Edward Hartwell Clerk

[53]   Peter Harwood of.

Houſe Lott
No 59

Granted unto Peter Harwood By the Committee appointed By the Greate and General Court to a Lott and Grant out the Lands Within the town of Lunenburgh to Granttees fourty five Acres of Land Within Said Town for a houſe Lott Numbur fifty nine to to gether With all the Rights and Diviſion of Land belonging there unto. Laid out to Nathaniel Harwood Claimer By the Committee appointed thirty five acres of Land ſcituat Eaſterly from the apple tree hill it being a part of the Houſe Lott No. 59 and it is bounded northweſterly on Common Land Eighty rod ſouthweſterly it Bounds on Common Land ſeventy two rod ſouth eaſterly it Bounds on Common Land ſixty two Rod Northeaſterly It Bounds on John Whitneys houſe Lott Recorded by order of the Committee viz Joſiah Willard Edward Hartwell Hilkiah Boynton and Jonathan Willard and Survayed By Sam[ll] Jones. Recorded December the twenty second Day in the year of our Lord one thousand seven hundred and thirty

₱ Edward Hartwell Clerk

Lunenburgh May the Eighth Day 1729 — — —

House Lott Laid out to Nathaniel Harwood Claimer ten acres of first Division Land to make up the whole of the above sd house Lott No 59. Begining at a pillar of stones and Runing North Eighteen Deg East fourty Rod to a pillar of stones there making an Angle and runing West Eighteen Degrees North fourty rod to a pillar of stones there making an angle and Runing south Eighteen Degrees West fourty rod to a pillar of stones there making an Angle and Runing East Eighteen deg south fourty rod to Where it began — Survayed by Nathan Heywood and approved of by the Committee viz Edward Hartwell Josiah willard Jonathan willard and Nathan Heywood

Recorded December the twenty second Day in the year of our Lord one thousand seven Hundred and thirty

₱ Edward Hartwell Clerk

Lunenburgh November 2[d] 1730

2[d] Division No 65 Survayed for Nathaniel Harwood Claimer second Division Number sixty five on the flatt hill the Contents of Which is fourty seven acres and a half begining at a stake and Heap of Stones Which is the Most southerly Corner and runing North seventeen Deg East on Land Left for a highway sixty rod there making an Angle and runing west thirty one degrees thirty minits north on Lott No sixty six one hundred and twenty Eight rod there making an angle and and runing south seventeen Degrees West on Beaths Land sixty one rod there making an Angle and runing East thirty one degres thirty minits south one hundred and twenty Eight rod to Where it began Survayed by nathan heywood and approved of by the Committee viz Josiah willard Jonathan willard Edward Hartwell and Nathan Heywood

Recorded December the twenty fecond Day in the year of our Lord thoufand feven hundred and thirty . . .
By me Edward Hartwell Clerk.

[53²] Lunenburgh December the 28th 1729 - - - - —

3d Divifion   Laid out by the Committee appointed fixty fix acres and fixty rod of third Divifion Land to Nathaniel Harwood Claimer arifeing from houfe Lott No 59—lying between pearl hill and apple tree hill. begining at a pillar of ftones at the Corner of Land Laid out fd Harwood and runing weft twenty five degres north one hundred and Eighteen rod on Whitneys Land there making an Angle and and runing fouth twenty five deg Weft one hundred rod there making an Angle and runing Eaft fifteen degr fouth one hundred and nineteen rod there making an Angle and runing north twenty five degres Eaft Eighty rod on faid harwoods Line to Where it began Survayd by nathan heywood and approved of by the Committee viz Edward Hartwell Josiah Willard Jonathan Willard and Nathan Heywood

Recorded December the 22d annoque Domini. 1730.
℔ Edward Hartwell Clerk

Lunenburg December the 18th 1730.

meadow Lott No. 1 beaver pond meadows   Survayed for Nathaniel Hawood Claimer meadow Lott No. 1. in Beaver pond meadows the Contents of which is fix acres. begining at a Certain take and heape of ftones on the Westerly fide of faid meadow Lott and Runing fouth 30 Degree on a pine ridge 8 rod there making an Angle and runing Eaft 24 Degrees fouth on fd pine ridge 17 rod to Groton Line there making an Angle and runing fouth 17 deg Weft on sd Line 32 rod to a ftake there making an Angle and runing Weft 31 dege 30 minits north on 2d Divifion Land 12 rod there making an Angle and runing north by the upland 4 rod there making an Angle and runing weft 40 dege north on the upland ten rod there making an Angle and runing north 25 Degrees

Eaſt on the upland 16 rod there making an Angle and runing weſt 20 Degrees North 4 rod by the upland there making an Angle and runing Weſt 34 degre ſouth 14 rod by the upland there making an Angle and runing Weſt 40 degrees north by the upland. 6. rod there making an Angle and runing north 48 Degrees Eaſt by the upland 4 rod there making an Angle and runing north 22 rod there making an Angle and runing Eaſt 40 Degree north by the upland 5 rod to an oake ſtumpe there making an angle and runing ſouth 45 Degrees Eaſt on meadow 18 rod to Where it Began

Survayed By Nathan Heywood and approved of by the Committee viz Joſiah Willard Edward Hartwell Jonathan Willard and Nathan Heywood

Recorded October the 8th annoque Domini. 1731.

₱ Edward Hartwell Cler

Lunenburg December the 18th 1731.

3d Diviſion Laid out by the Committee appointed 80 acres of Land to nathaniel harwood Claimer — for part of a third Diviſion ariſeing from houſe Lot No. 59: and to make up what is found wanting in his 2d Diviſion Begining at a Certain White oake tree marked toWard the northweſt Corner of said Land and runing north 17 Degrees Eaſt 23 rod to a ſtake which is prescott Corner and making an Angle and runing Eaſt 32 Degrees ſouth on ſaid prescotts Line 115 rod there making an Angle and Runing South 32 Degree Weſt on Common Land .119. rod to Ensign Willards Land there making an Angle and runing West 30 Degrees north partly on ſaid Willards Land 29 rod there making an Angle and runing West 43 Degrees 30 minits north on Common Land 92 rod there making an Angle and runing north 40 Degrees Eaſt on Common Land 80 rod to Where it Began. Survayed by Nathan Heywood and approved of by the Committee viz Edward Hartwell Jonathan Willard Joſiah Willard and Nathan Heywood

Recorded october the 8th annoque Domini. 1731.

₱ Edward Hartwell Cler

[54] BENONI BOYNTON of

[54²] Lunenburgh October the 14th 1730 — —

4th Divifion Laid out By the Committee appointed two Hundred acres of Land to Elifha Smith Claimer the right arifeing from houfe Lott number Eighty one Hundred and twenty acres of Which Land is third Divifion. and Eighty acres of which Land is fourth Divifion fcituate and Lyeth in the Wefterly Part of faid townfhip. Begining at a Cartain ftake and Heepe of ftones Erected for the Southeaft Corner and runing North fifteen degr Weft on Common Land one hundred and fixty rod to a pillar of ftones there making an Angle and runing Weft fifteen Degr fouth on Common Land two Hundred rod to a pillar of ftones there making an Angle and runing fouth fifteen degrees Eaft on Common Land one Hundred and fixty rod to pools Land there making an Angle and runing Eaft fifteen degr north two hundred rod one hundred and Eighty rod on the Land Laid to three of the pools and twenty rod on Common Land to where it began furvayed by Nathan heywood and approved of by the Committee viz Jofiah Willard Edward Hartwell and Jonathan Willard

Recorded November the twenty feventh Day in the year of our Lord one thoufand feven hundred and thirty
₱ Edward Hartwell Clerk

Lunenburg January ye 11th 1730/1

meadow Lott No. 5 in uper mulpus
Survayed for Benoni Boynton meadow Lott No 5 in upper mulpus the Contents of which is five acre.

Begining at a red oak tree marked on the wefterly fide of faid meadow Lott and runing Eaft 31 Degrees fouth 31 rod and a half to a pillar of ftones there making an Angle and runing north one Degree Weft on meadow Lott Number four. 48 rod to a ftake there making an Angle and runing Weft 38 Degrees north nine Rod and a half to a ftake there making an Angle and

Runing South 25 degrees Weſt 43. rod to Where it began Survayed by nathan Heywood and approved of by the Committee viz Josiah Willard Jonathan Willard Nathan Heywood & Edward Hartwell
 Recorded December the 9th 1732.
℔ Edward Hartwell Clerk

[55]   WILLIAM WALLIS

 Granted unto William Wallis By the Committee appointed by the Greate and General Court to a Lott and Grant out the Lands Within the town of Lunenburgh to Grantees Houſe Lott No 62 together With all the rights and Diviſions of Land beLonging there unto or ariſeing there from. and the ſaid Houſe Lott N⁰ 62 falling within Lancaſter new Grant. the Committee appointed by the proprietors of the town of Lunenburg for that purpors Laid out to the ſaid William Wallis ſixty acres of Land Within ſaid Lunenburg for an Equevilent for his houſe Lott afore ſᵈ

Houſe Lott   January the 13th 1730$\frac{31}{}$ ſurvayed for Wil-
No. 62   liam Wallis Houſe Lott No. 62. Includeing Nathan Heywoods meadow Lott. the Contents of the Whole is 67. Acres and a half — — — Begining at a Certain White oak tree marked for the Northeaſt Corner and Runing ſouth 2 deg 30 minits Eaſt fifty nine rod to a ſtak there making an Angle and runing West thirteen degree thirty minits ſouth partly on Bormans farm Eighty nine rod to a ſtak there making an Angle and runing West 2 deg 30 minit ſouth on ſaid farm ſeventy Eight rod to a ſtake there making an Angle and runing North 2 degs 30 mits Weſt ſixty five rod to a ſtak there making an Angle and runing Eaſt 6 deg North one hundred and ſixty ſix rod to Where it began. ſurvayed by Nathan Heywood and approved of by the Committee viz Joſiah Willard Edward Hartwell Jonathan Willard and Nathan Heywood. Jonathan Hartwell
 Recorded March yᵉ 26. annoque Domini. 1731.
℔ Edward Hartwell Clerk

Lunenburg march yᵉ 24. 1729$\overline{30}$

2ᵈ Divifion No 25

furvayd for William Wallas fecond Divifion No. 25 the Contents of Which is 53 Acres. Begining at a maple tree marked for the Weft Corner and runing Eaft 31 degr 30 mints fouth 57 rod and a half to a heep of ftones there making an Angle and runing North 28 deg 30 min Eaft on Lott No. 24. 150. rod to a ftake there making an Angle and and runing West 31. deg. 30. mini North on the North town Line 56 rod to a ftake there making an Angle and runing fouth 30. deg Weft. 150 rod to Where it Began

furvayed by Nathan Heywood and approved of by the Committee viz Edward Hartwell Hartwell Jofiah Willard Jonathan Willard and Nathan Heywood — —

Recorded March yᵉ 26 Annoque Domini. 1731

⅌ Edward Hartwell Clerk — —

*the other Lands of the faid William Wallas are Recorded at page 33 in the in the 2ᵈ part of this Book.

[55²] Lunenburg December the 16ᵗʰ 1729.

3ᵈ Divifion

Laid out to William Wallas by the Committee appointed 55 acres and 94 rod of third Divifion Land the right arifeing from houfe Lott No 62. begining att a ftake fet up for the fouth weft Corner of faid wallases first divifion and runing weft 2 deg fouth 82 rod Chiefly on bormans farm there making an Angle and runing north 25 deg weft 94 rod on Houghtons 2ᵈ Divifion there making an Angle and runing Eaft 18 degres north 30 rod Cheifly on Land Laid out to Houghton to make up what was wanting in his firft Divifion Lott there making an Angle and runing Eaft 72 rod on Common Land there making an Angle and runing fouth 3 deg Eaft 32 rod on Land Laid out to Capᵗ Jofiah willard to a pine tree there making an Angle and runing Eaft 8 deg north 20 rod there making an Angle and runing fouth 62 rod to Where it begun on faid Wallases first divifion

furvayed by Nathan Heywood and approved of by the Committee — viz Edward Hartwell Jofiah Willard Jonathan Willard and Nathan Heywood

---

*In the original this was written in the margin.

Recorded March the 26 annoque Domini. 1731.
℔ Edwd Hartwell Clerk

Lunenburg December the 16th 1729.

3^d Divifion   Laid out by the Committee appoinited 31 acres and 72 rod of third Divifion Land to William wallas arifeing from houfe Lott No. 62. Begining at a pillar of ftones Erected for the Norweft Corner and runing fouth one degree Eaft 55 rod to a white oak tree on Land Laid out to Haftings there making an Angle and runing Eaft 7 Degr north 28 rod to a white oak tree on fd wallases first divifion there making an Angle and runing fouth 2 deg Eaft 59 rod on faid wallases firft Divifion there making an Angle and runing weft 13 deg fouth 8 rod to a white pine tree marked for Bormans Corner there making an Angle and runing fouth 16 deg weft 7 rod on Bormans farm there making an Angle and runing Eaft 10 degr fouth 12 rod on Common Land there making an Angle and runing north 18 deg Eaft 40 rod to a black oake tree on Common Land there making an angle and runing Eaft 34 deg north 63 rod on Common Land there making an Angle and runing Weft 26. deg north 109 rod on third divifion Land Laid out to fam^ll page to where it began furvayed by Nathan Heywood and approved of by the Committee viz Edward Hartwell Jonathan willard and Nathan heywood

Recorded march the 26. annoque Domini 1731.
Edwd Hartwell Clerk

Lunenburg January the .13th $17\frac{31}{30}$.

3^d Divifion   Laid out by the Committee appointed 13 acres of third Divifion Land to make up What is wanting in William Wallafes third Divifion. arifeing from Houfe Lott No 62. adjoyning to faid Wallafes meadow Lott begining at a Certain pine tree marked on the Eafterly part of faid Land and runing north 11 deg on Common Land 76 rod to a burch bush which is dodges Corner there making an Angle and runing fouth 16 deg Weft on Bormans farm 71 rod there making an Angle and runing fouth 40 deg Eaft by the brook 20 rod there making an Angle and runing fouth 35 deg Weft on faid Wallafes own meadow 38 rod there making an Angle and runing 43 deg Eaft on faid meadow Lott 18 rod there making an angle and runing North 29 deg Eaft Cheifly on fd meadow Lott 60 rod to where it began Survayed by Nathan Heywood and approved of by the Committee viz Jofiah Willard Jonathan Willard and Edward Hartwell and Nathan Heywood

Recorded March the 26th annoque Domini 1731

⅌ Edwd Hartwell Clerk

[56]   JOHN HAISTINGS of
march the 28th 1766.

furvayed for Andrew mitchel Claimer the Land where he now Dwells in the Eafterly part of Lunenburg the Contents of which is fifty two acres it Begins at a Litle white oak tree which is the northeaft Corner of it and runs Weft Eight Degrees fouth ninty two rod bounding parly on Land of John Richards and parly on Land belonging to the Heirs of Robert Clark Deceafed to a heap of ftones then it runs fouth two Degrees Eaft ninty one rod Bounding on the the Land belonging to the faid mitchel to a heap of ftones then it runs Eaft ten Degrees north ninty two rod bounding on Land belonging to m^r James Gordon to a ftake and heap of ftones in the road thence north two Degrees Weft ninety four rod to the firft mentioned white oak tree bounding Chiefly on or all the way on Common or undivided Land furvayed by Nathan Heywood furvayer approved of by the Committee viz Edward Hartwell Joshua Hutchings and Nathan Heywood and ordered to be Recorded.

Recorded April the 3^d 1766.

⅌ Edward Hartwell
Proprietors Clerk

[57]   SCHOOL LOTT.

Laid out for the ufe of the fchoole in Lunenburg one hundred and fixty nine acres of Land on the Eafterly fide of pearl hill it begins at a heap of ftones being foutherly or foutheasterly Corner of faid Land and runs North feventy one rod on Land formerly belonging to Robert Commings to a heap of ftones then it runs Weft thirty one degrees north one hundred and thirty three rod bounding on the Land of feveral fecond Divifions thence Weft fourteen degrees fouth one hundred and Eleven Rod bounding on Land formerly belonging to Col? Brown thence runs fouth nineteen Degrees Weft twenty three rod on Land belonging to the Heirs of Capt John Gibson Deceafed thence Weft nineteen Degrees north five rod on faid Gibson thence fouth fixteen degrees Weft Eight rod then it runs forty degrees Eaft on Land of Reuben Gibson one hundred and ninty five rod then it runs north fourteen degrees Weft fixty feven rod on Land formerly belonging to Secretary Willard thence Eaft one hundred and forty rod on faid Willards Land to where it began furvayed by Nathan Heywood and approved of and ordered to be Recorded by Edward Hartwell Nathan Heywood and Benj$\underline{a}$ Goodridge

Recorded February the 22^d 1764

℔ Edward Hartwell proprietors Clark

[58]   DAVID PEARCE of

Granted unto David peace by the Committee appointed by the greate and General Court to a Lott and grant out the Lands within the town of Lunenburgh to Granttees forty nine acres and a half of Land Within faid town for a houfe Lott bareing Number 65 together with all the rights and Divifions of Land belonging thereunto.

Houfe Lott No. 65   Survay^d for David pearce houfe Lott Number 65 the Contents of which is forty nine acres and a half. Begining at a ftake fet up for the fouth Eaft Corner and runing Weft 26 Degree fouth on Jofhua Goodridges Lott 48 rod to a ftake there making an Angle and runing North 26 Degrees Weft on Benjamin goodridges 2^d Divifion and on James Jewells Land. 168 rod to a ftake there making an Angle and runing Eaft 24 Degrees North party on the woborn farm and partly on the goare of Land by woborn farm 47 rod to a pillar of ftones there making an Angle and runing fouth

26 Degrees Eaſt on Farnſworth Lott 166 rod to Where it began

ſurvayed by Nathan Heywood and approved of by the Committee to viz Edward Hartwell Joſiah Willard Jonathan Willard and Nathan Heywood

Recorded may the first Day annoque Domini. 1731

℔ Edward Hartwell Clerk

Lunenburg December ye 30th. 1730.

Houſe Lott No 88

ſurvayed for David Pearce Claimer Houſe Lott No —— 88 and the ſecond Diviſion belonging to ſaid Houſe Lott they both Lying together in one Intire piece the Contence of the Whole being 121 Acres and a half. Begining at a pillar of ſtones Which is the Norweſt Corner and Runing Eaſt 5 Degrees North partly on Ephraim Pearce and Partly on Land of Eleazer Houghton 110 rod to a ſmall pine tree there Making an Angle and runing South 22 deg Eaſt on Bormans farm 37 rod to a White oak tree there Making an Angle and Runing ſouth 7 Degrees Eaſt on third Diviſion Land belonging to the ſame right 106 rod to a ſtake there making an Angle and runing Weſt 6 Degres 30 min ſouth on Land of Gibſon and Richardson 126 rod to a ſtake there making an Angle runing North 5 degrees 30 minits Weſt on Land of Lt Hartwell 163 rod to Where it began

ſurvayed by Nathan Heywood and approved of by the Committee viz Joſiah Willard Edward Hartwell Jonathan Willard and Nathan Heywood. Recorded may the 28th. 1731.

℔ Edward Hartwell Clerk.

Lunenburg December the 30th. 1730.

4^d Diviſion

Laid out by the Committee appointed 34 acres of 4th Diviſion Land to David pearce Claimer in the ſouth eaſt part of ſaid township ariſeing from houſe Lott No. 88: begining at a Certain ſtake Which is the ſouth Eaſt Corner and runing Weſt partly on Capt Goulds Land and partly on Common Land 82 rod to a ſtake there making an angle and runing north 7 degree Weſt on Gibſons Land 62 rod there making an

Angle and runing Eaſt on third Diviſion Land Laid out to the ſame right 100 rod there making an Angle and runing ſouth 20 Degres Weſt on Land of Nathaniel page 62 to Where it began. ſurvayed by Nathan Heywood and approved of by the Committee viz. Edward Hartwell Jonathan Willard and Joſiah Willard
  Recorded May the 28th 1731.
                    ℔ Edward Hartwell Clerk
*The other Lands of David pearce are Recorded in the ſecond part of this Book at page 31

[58²] Lunenburg December the 30th 1730: . . .

4th Diviſion   Laid out to David Pearce Claimer by the Committee appointed 13 acres and a half of fourth Diviſion Land in the ſoutheaſterly part of ſaid townſhip ariſeing from houſe Lott Number. 88: . . .
  Begining at a pillar of ſtones in Bormans Line it being the moſt Weſterly Corner and runing Eaſt 12 degrees North on ſaid Bormans Line 55 rod to a pillar of ſtones there making an Angle and runing north 16 Degrees Eaſt on ſd Bormans Land 12 rod there making an Angle and runing Eaſt 20 deg ſouth on CattaCoonamog brook 20: rod there making an Angle and ſouth 20 Degres Eaſt on meadow Land Laid to Lᵗ Hartwell 28 rod there making an Angle and runing Weſt 25 Degres on Land belonging to Nathaniel page 50 rod there making an Angle and runing Weſt 43. degree North on third Diviſion Land Laid to the ſame right No 88 : 50 : rod to Where it began. ſurvayed by Nathan Heywood and approved of by the Committee viz Edward Hartwell Joſiah Willard and Jonathan Willard.
  Recorded May the 28th anno Domini. 1731.
                    ℔ Edward Hartwell Clerk

Lunenburg December the 15th 1729.

2ᵈ Diviſion   ſurvayed for David Parce a ſecond Diviſion
No 86   number 86 the Contents being 54 acres and a quarter. Begining at a pillar of Stones Erected for the north Eaſt Corner and runing ſouth 30

---
*In the original this was written in the margin.

deg Eaſt 96 rod on Ephraim Pearces ſecond Diviſion there making an Angle and Runing Weſt 5 deg ſouth 132 rod Chiefly on Lt Hartwells Land making an Angle and runing north 25 deg 30 min West 49. rod on Joſhua Goodridges Land there Making an Angle and Runing Eaſt 25 deg 30 min North 118 rod to Where it Began partly on Harris and partly Gibſon ſurvayed by Nathan Heywood and approved of by the Committee viz Edward Hartwell Jonathan Willard Joſhua Hutchens Nathan Heywood and Joſiah Willard

Recorded January the 17th Day annoque Domini 1731/2
℔ Edward Hartwell Clerk

Lunenburg Sep^{temr} ye 25th 1731.

4th Diviſion   Laid out by the Committee appointed forty five ares of fourth Diviſion Land in y^e ſoutheaſterly part of ſaid townſhip to Ephraim Pearce ariſeing from houſe Lott No. 88. Begining at a Certain ſtake and heep of ſtones in Lancaſter Line which is Erected for the ſouthweſterly Corner of ſaid Land and runing Eaſt 23 degrees ſouth on ſaid Line 88 rod to the Littele pond there making an Angle and runing north 21 degrees Eaſt by ſaid pond 13 rod to a ſtake there making an Angle and runing north on Land of Nathan Heywood 38 rod to a ſtake there making an Angle and runing Weſt on Land of Capt Gould 14 rod to a ſtake there making an Angle and runing north on ſaid Goulds Land 58 rod to a pillar of ſtones there making an Angle and runing Weſt partly on Land of Ebenezer Richardſon and partly on Common Land 72 rod there making an Angle and runing ſouth 5 degrees Eaſt partly on ſaid Richardſons 2^d Diviſion and partly on Common Land 77 rod to where it began ſurvayed
℔ Nathan Heywood

approved of by the Committee viz Edward Hartwell Ephraim Pearce and Jonathan Willard.

Recorded December ye 22^d: 1732.
℔ Edward Hartwell Clerk

[59] The Heirs of SAMUEL FARNSWORTH deceased

Granted to the Heirs of Samuell Farnsworth deceafed by the Committee appointed by the Greate and General Court to a Lott and Grant out the Lands Within the townfhip of Lunenburg to Grantees   acres Within faid townfhip for a Houfe Lott Number (66) to Gether with all the rights and Divifions of Land arifeing there from and belonging thereunto

February the 17th 1730/1

Houfe Lott No. 66.
Then furvayed the Houfe Lott No. 66. Laid out to Samuell Farnsworth by the General Courts Committee it being the Lott which faid Farnsworth Bult a Houfe and field upon it bounds foutheafterly on   north easterly on   Norwefterly on Land Laid out to Jofiah Willard and fouthwefterly moftly on Benjamin Goodridges Lott a Little peice bounds on Land Left for a Highway.

It begins at a Chefnut a mark for faid Goodridges Lott and Runs and Runs fouth eafterly ten rod to a red oak then North eafterly forty two Rod to a heap of ftones then Nor wefterly one Hundred and fifty fix rod to a heap of Stones: then wefterly forty feven Rod to a Heap of ftones and then It runs fouth eafterly to Where it first began 157 rod. furvay^d ℔ Jonas Houghton and approved of by the Committee viz Jofiah Willard Nathan Heywood Jonathan willard and Edward Hartwell

Recorded December the 14th 1732.

℔ Edward Hartwell

Cler ——

[59²]   October the 2^d & 3^d 1730.

3^d & 4th Divifion
Laid out to the Right of Samuell Farnsworth two Hundred and fifteen acres in Lunenburg viz one hundred and fifteen acres for the 3^d Divifion and one hundred acres for the fourth Divifion of upland. (there is allowed for in faid Land five acres for a high way and thirty acres Laid out to Nathaniel Harwood. It Bounds foutherly part on Dorchefter farm part on Common Eafterly partly on fd farm

It Begins at heep of ftoons in the north Line of faid farm near to the northeaft Corner of It and Runs north twenty fix rod to a heep of ftoons then Wefterly two hundred and twenty five rod to a heep of ftones then norwefterly one hundred and fixty rod to a heep of ftoons then fouthwefterly ninety five rod to a heep of ftoons then foutheafterly one hundred and forty fix rod to a heep of ftoons then foutherly wefterly one hundred and ninety three rod to a heep of ftoons then Eafterly fifty one rod to a heep of ftoons then foutherly Eighty rod to a heep of ftoons and thirty rod to a heep of ftoons then Eaft ten Degrees north fourty Eight rod to faid Dorchefter farm and then it runs northerly by faid farm two hundred and Eighty five rod and Eafterly two Hundred fixty and two rod to Where it began

furvay^d ⅌ Jonas Houghton and approved of by the Committee viz Jofiah Willard Jonathan Willard Nathan Heywood and Edward Hartwel

Recorded December ye 14th 1732

⅌ Edward Hartwell Clark

[60] BENJAMIN GOODRIDGE of Lunenburg

Houfe Lott No. 67

Granted unto Benjamin Goodridge By the Committee appointed by the Greate and General Court to aLott and Grant out the Lands Within town of Lunenburg to Granttee forty one Acres and feventy one rod of Land for a Houfe Lott bareing number fixty feven to gethere Withall the Rights and Divifions of Land belonging there unto or a Rifeing therefrom Within the townfhip of Lunenburg

Lunenburg December the 15th 1729

furvayed for Benjamin Goodridge Houfe Lott Number 67 the Contents of Which is forty one acres and feventy one rod Begining at a pillar of ftones Erected for the North Corner and runing fouth 25 Degrees 30 min Eaft. 149. rod on Ephraim Pearces Houfe Lott there making an Angle and runing Weft 25 Degrees 30 min. fouth 44 rod on Gibfons Lott there making an Angle and runing North 25 deg. 45. min Weft 149 rod on farnsworth Lott there making an Angle and runing Eaſt 25 deg 30 min North 45. rod on Willards Land to Where it Began ſurvayed by Nathan Heywood and approved of by the Committee viz Edward Hartwell Nathan Heywood Joſiah Willard and Jonathan Willard

Recorded January the 17th Day annoque Domini. 1731/2

₱ Edward Hartwell Cler

Lunenburg November the 19th 1734

Laid out by the Committee appointed one hundred acres of fourth Diviſion Land to the Heirs of Philip Goodridge Deceſt Scituate and Lying Weſterly from Role ſtone hill. Begining at a ſtake and heep of ſtones Erected for the ſouth Weſt Corner of ſaid Land

Lunenburg February 25: 1736/7

2d Diviſion
No 91

ſurvayed for Benjamin Goodridge ſecond Diviſion No. 91 ſcituate and Lying neer maſhapooge pond Containing Eighty five acres in the whole there being four meadow Lotts included in it. and allowance for ways to them begining at a Certain pine tree marked for moſt ſoutherly Corner of the ſame and runs Eaſt Eighteen degrees north on upland and swamp and pond belonging to the ſaid goodridge one hundred and ſixteen rod the Corner ſhould be aboute ten rods in the pond then runs north twenty ſix degrees Weſt on Land now belonging to Joſhua Goodridge and John Divoll 97 rod to a ſtak then runs Weſt three degrees ſouth on Land of ſaid Divoll and his own Land ſeventy Eight rod to a white pine ſtump where the ſaid Goodridge got a greate Deal of Good timber then runs Weſt three Degrees North on ſaid Goodridge fifty Eight rod then ſouth thirty one Degree Eaſt on Lancaſter Line one hundred and thirty rod to where it began ſurvayed by Nathan Heywood approved of By the Committee viz Edward Hartwell Jonathan Willard

Recorded ſeptember the 31ft 1750.

₱ Edward Hartwell
proprietors Clerk

[60²] Lunenburgh April the. 27ᵗʰ 1730 . . . .

the 300 ares   Laid out to Benjamin Goodridge by the Committee appointed by the proprietors of Lunenburgh three Hundred acres of Land Granted to the said Goodridge for the payment of the proprietors Debts also thirty two acres for an aquivelent for half a meadow Lott be Longing to the sᵈ Goodridge. scituate and Lyeth aboute a mile Westerly from the aple tree Hill Begining at a Certain Rock by yᵉ river and runing north thirty seven degrees East on Common Land to the Corner of Jonathan Willards Lott there making an angle and runing West thirty four Degrees thirty minites North on said Willards Lott one Hundred and fifty two Rod there making An Angle and Runing North thirty four Degree thirty minits East on sd Willards Land one Hundred and Eighty two rod there Making An angle and runing West fifteen Degrees south on John Brewers Lott seventy nine rod there making an Angle and runing south fifteen degʳ East on sd Brewers Lott sixty Eight rod there making an Angle and runing West fifteen degr south on sd Brewers Land two Hundred forty four rod there making an Angle and Runing south thirty five degrees west on Common Land two hundred and one Rod there making an Angle and runing East fifteen degrees North on Common Land one Hundred and thirty rod there Making an Angle and runing by the river to where It Began survayed by Nathan Heywood and approved of by the Committee viz Josiah Willard Edward Hartwell and Isaac farnsworth

Recorded July the 3ᵈ day in the year of our Lord one thousand seven Hundred and thirty by me — — — —
Edward Hartwell CLerk — — —

Lunenburgh august the 15ᵗʰ 1729.

third Divi<u>n</u>   Laid out for Benjamin Goodridge by the Committee appointed Eighty Eight acres and ninety nine rod of third division Land ariseing from house Lott No sixty seven southerly from apple tree hill on the other side of the river begining at a heap of stones and Runing East fifteen degrees North one Hundred and seventy two rod to a pillar of stones there making an Angle and Runing North one Degree Weft fixty three rod there making an Angle and Runing Weft fifteen degrees North fixty three rod to a poplar tree thre making an Angle and Runing Weft twenty feven degrees fouth 140 rod to a pillar of ftones there making an Angle and runing fouth twenty degrees Eaft fixty two rod to where it began —— furvayed by nathan Heywood and approved of by the Committee viz Edward Hartwell Jonathan Willard and Nathan Heywood

Recorded the Eight Day of July in the year of our Lord one thoufand feven Hundred and thirty by me
Edward Hartwell Clerke — — —

Lunenburg Auguft ye 11th 1729:

3^d Divifion   Laid out for Benjamin Goodridge 12 acres and 15 rod of third Divifion Land be Longing to houfe Lott No 67 and is on the Wefterly fide of Maffapoge pond begining at a ftake fet up for the Corner of his fecond Divifion and runing north 44 dege Weft 12 rod to Lancafter Line there making an Angle and Runing fouth 30 Degrees Eaft on faid Line 114 rod to a black oak tree there making an Angle and runing north 8 dege Weft 77 rod by faid pond there there making an Angle and Runing North 29 degrees Weft 18 rod there making an Angle and runing Weft 6 degrees fouth 30 rod on the afore faid fecond Divifion Line to Where it Began furvayed By Nathan Heywood and approved of by the Committee viz Jonathan Willard Edward Hartwell and Nathan Heywood. — — —

Recorded December 29th annoque Domini. 1731
₱ Edward Hartwell Cler

[61]   Ephraim Peirce Junr of

[62]   Samuel Bennet of.

Houfe Lott No. 69   Granted unto Samuell Bennit by the Committee appointed by the Greate and General Court to a Lott and Grant out the Lands Within the Townfhip of Lunenburg to Granttees thirty Eight Acres and three Quarters of Land Within faid town for a houfe Lott No 69 to gether With all the Rights and Divifions of Land belonging there unto or arifeing there from. A platt of the feverail divifions of Land of Eleizer Houghton Claimer Where he now Lives the Contents of the whole is one hundred and fivety 7 acres and the Contents of Each particuler is Set Down in Each perticuler platt and the out fide Lines fet fourth by points of Compas. Begining at a Certain pillar of Stones by the gravill pitt near Capt Jofiah Willards Sawmill and runing Eaft 7 deg fouth on Land of fd Capt Josiah Willard 59 rod to a pillar of ftones there making an Angle and Runing fouth 25 deg 30 Eaft on Land of f^d Willard 58 rod to a ftak Which is the Corner of the meadow Lott there making an Angle and Runing Eaft 20 degrees north on meadow of faid Willard 60. rod. to a ftake there making an Angle and Runing fouth 17 Deg Eaft 28 rod to a pine tree there making an Angle and runing Eaft 25 deg north three rod and a half to a heep of ftones there making an Angle and runing fouth 17 degrees Eaft 35 rod to a pine tree there making an angle and runing fouth 38 deg Weft on Woodmans meadow Lott 18 rod to a popler tree there making an angle and runing Weft 24. deg. fouth on Auftins meadow Lott 34 rod to a ftake there making an Angle and runing fouth 18 deg Eaft on faid Auftins meadow Lott 20 rod to a ftake there making an Angle and runing Eaft 9 deg North on feverail meadow Lotts a 106 rod to a heep of ftones on the other fide of Cataconamoug Brook there making an Angle and runing fouth 2 Deg Eaft 35 rod to a ftake there making an Angle and runing Weft on Wallafes Land 97 rod to a heap of ftones there making an angle and runing Weft 20 Degrees fouth on faid Wallases Land four rod to a pine tree there making an Angle and runing Weft 18 Degs fouth on faid Wallases Land 26 rod to a ftake there making an angle and runing fouth 25 Degrees Eaft on faid Wallases Land 94 rod to a ftake there making an Angle and runing Eaft 6 deg North on f^d Wallases Land 8 rod and a half to a white oak tree Which is Bormans Corner there making an Angle and runing fouth 19 degrees Eaft on f^d Bormans

Proprietors' Records. 119

Line 138 rod to a pillar of ſtones there making an Angle and runing Weſt 5 Degrees ſouth on Ephraim Pearces Land 30 rod to a ſtake
there

[**62²**] there making an Angle and runing North 25 degrees Weſt on pearces Land 280 rod to a ſtake there making an Angle and runing Eaſt 25 Degrees 30 minits north on Land of ſaid pearce 14 rod to a ſtake there making an angle and runing north 25 degrees 30 mints Weſt on Land of ſᵈ pearce 143. rod to Where it began a high Way going through ſᵈ firſt Diviſion

Survayᵈ by Nathan Heywood and approved of by the Committee viz Joſiah Willard Jonathan Willard Edward Hartwell and Nathan Heywood
Recorded May the 7ᵗʰ annoque Domini. 1731
℔ Edward Hartwell Clerk

Lunenburg april yᵉ 10ᵗʰ 1729

3ᵈ Diviſion   Laid out to Eleazer Houghton Claimer by the Committee appointed 89 acres and 51: rod for a third Diviſion ariſeing from houſe Lott No. 69 Begining at a pillar of ſtones and runing Weſt ten Degrees ſouth 80. rod to a pillar of ſtones there making an angle and runing north 10 Degrees Weſt 160 rod to a heape of ſtones there making an angle and runing Eaſt 10 Degrees north 83 rod to a pillar of ſtones there making an Angle and runing ſouth 39 Degrees Eaſt to a pillar of ſtones. 51. rod there making an Angle and runing ſouth 113 rod to Where it Began Laid down by me me Nathan Heywood ſurvayer and approved of By the Committee Edward Hartwell Hilkiah Boynton and nathan Heywood
Recorded march yᵉ 7ᵗʰ 1733./4
℔ me Edward Hartwell Clerk

Lunenburg November the 19ᵗʰ 1734

4ᵗʰ Diviſion   Laid out by the Committee appointed ſeventy acres of fourth diviſion Land to Eleazer Houghton Claimer ariſeing from houſe Lott No. 69. ſcituate Lying Weſterly from Role ſtone hill. Begining at a

Certain hemLock tree marked by ye River fide which is Nathaniel Harris Esqr and John Whitneys Corner and runing Eaft 15 degrees fouth on faid Harris and Whitney 134 rod to a pine tree then runing fouth 15 degrees Weft on faid Harris and Whitneys 98 rod to a ftake then runing Eaft 15 degrees fouth on John Brewer 59 rod to a ftake then runing north 8 degrees Eaft on Land now Laid out to the Heirs of philip Goodridge Deeceft 178 rod then Runing Weft 10 degrees fouth on Common Land 184 rod to Where it began

℞ Nathan Heywood fury^r and approved of by the Committee viz Jofiah Willard Edward Hartwell and Jonathan Willard

Recorded January the 31^{ft} 1734/5

℞ Edward Hartwell Clerk

[63]   PHILIP GOODRIDGE

Houfe Lott No. 70

Granted unto Philip Goodridge by the Committee appointed by the Greate and General Court to a Lott and Grant out the Lands Within the town of Lunenburg to Granttees .50. acres and .148. rod of Land Within faid town for a Houfe Lott No. 70. and meadow Lott to Gether Withall the rights and Divifions of Land belonging there unto or arifeing there from

Lunenburg March the 26th 1730. . . . .

Houfe Lott and meadow Lott is all in one Intire peice which is: a. 50 and R. 148

furvayed for Jofhua Goodridge Claimer Houfe Lott Number 70 the Contents of Which is .50. acres and one Hundred and forty Eight rod. Begining at a ftake in the Meadow Which is the fouthwefterly Corner and Runing Eaft 26 degrees North on Pearces Land 48 rod to a Chesnut tree there making an Angle and Runing North 27 Degrees West on Farnsworth Lott .168. rod to a ftake there making an Angle and Runing West 26. fouth on the Lott that Benjamin Goodridge now Pofsefses 48 rod to a ftake there Making an Angle and Runing fouth 27 Degrees Eaft 168. rod to Where it Began. furvayed by Nathan Heywood and approved of By the Committee viz Edward Hartwell Jonathan Willard Nathan Heywood and Joſiah Willard — —

Recorded the 11th Day of October annoque Domini. 1731

℞ Edward Hartwell Cler

Lunenburg March the 26. 1730

2d Diviſion No 85

Survayed for Joſhua Goodridge Claimer a ſecond Diviſion No. 85 the Contents of Which is fourty acres. Begining at the ſoutherly part of Maſhapoge pond being the Weſterly Corner of ſaid ſecond Diviſon and Runing ſouth .5. Degrees Eaſt on Lt Hartwells Land 27 rod to a cheſnut tree there making an Angle and runing Eaſt .5. Degree north on ſaid Hartwells Land 94 rod to a ſtake there making an Angle and runing north 27 degrees West partly on pearces Land and partly on ſaid goodridges first Diviſion 159 rod to the pond there making an Angle and runing by the pond to Where it Began Survayed By Nathan Heywood and approved of by the Committee viz Edward Hartwell Jonathan Willard Nathan Heywood and Joſiah Willard

Recorded October ye 11th annoque Domini. 1731.

℞ Edward Hartwell Cler

Laid out to Joshua Goodridge an Equevilent for the town way Laid through his firſt and ſecond Diviſion Land Laid out in the ſoutheaſterly part of ſaid Townſhip the pice Containing thirty acres of pine Land Laid out by the Committee appointed viz Edward Hartwell and Jonathan Willard and Nathan Heywood ſurvayer. and it Begins at a Certain pine tree on the ſoutherly ſide of Cataconamoug meadows below the ridge hill and runs Weſt on Common Land 25 rod yn runs ſouth 3. degrees Eaſt on Land of Nathaniel page 95 rod yn Weſt 26 rod on ſaid pages Land then ſouth on Capt Goulds Land 60 rod then north 42 Degrees Eaſt on Common Land 91 rod then north .8. degrees Eaſt on Land of Ephraim Pearce 20. rod then North .15. degres Weſt on ſaid pearces Land .68. rod to where it Began

Recorded march 25th 1735.

℞ Edward Hartwell proprietors Cler

[63²] Lunenburg april yᵉ 10ᵗʰ 1729

3ᵈ Divifion   Laid out for Heirs of Philip Goodridge Deceft. by the Committee appointed one hundred and Twenty acres and a hundred and twenty feven rod of third Divifion Land five acres belonging to the Houfe Lott. Begining at a pillar of ftones Erected for Jewells North weft Corner and runing fouth 28 Degrees Eaft thirty four rod to a pillar of ftones there making an Angle and runing Weft twenty five degrees fouth one hundred rod to a pillar of ftones There making an Angle and runing north one hundred and thirteen rod to a pillar of ftones there making an Angle and Runing North thirty nine Degrees Weft Sixty rod to a pillar of ftones there making an Angle and Runing Eaft twenty Eight Degrees North to a pillar of ftones fixty two rod there making an Angle and Runing fouth forty nine degrees Eaft one hundred and forty three rod to a pillar of ftones there making an Angle and Runing Weft twenty Eight Degrees South fixty five rod to where it began Laid Down by Nathan Heywood fuʳʸ and approved of By the Committee viz Edward Hartwell Jofiah Willard and Hilkiah Boynton

Recorded January the 14ᵗʰ annoque Domini. 1734/5
₱ Edward Hartwell proprietors Clerk

Lunenburg November yᵉ 19ᵗʰ 1734

4ᵗʰ Divifion   Laid out by the Committee appointed one hundred acres of fourth divifion Land to the Heirs of Philip Goodridge Deceaft. fcituat & Lying Wefterly from Role ftone hill Begining at ftake and heep of ftones Erected for the fouthweft Corner of faid Land and Runing Eaft 15 degrees fouth on Land of John Brewer 65 rod to a ftake in a fwamp then Runing Eaft 13 degrees 30 minuts North on Land of Colˡᵒ Fitch 53 rod to a ftake then Runing North 11 degrees Weft on Common Land 193 rod then Weft 10 degrees fouth on Common Land 53 rod then fouth 8 degrees Weft on Land Now Laid out to Eleazer Houghton 178. rod to Where it Began ₱ Nathan Heywood furvayer

Lieut. Edward Hartwell of Lunenburgh Dr.

Granted unto said Lt Edward Hartwell by the Committee appointed by the Great and General Court to allot and Grant out the Lands within the Town of Lunenburgh to Grantees of sixty acres of Land in said Town for a House Lot Number Eighty Seven with all the Rights and Priviledges belonging thereunto, and there being Laid out adjoyning to said house Lot, thirty sixty acre Lots being second Division the one being number Sixty three and is Coupled to the House Lot above said, the other in Number Seventy three and is Coupled to House Lot Number Seventy three, and also five Meadow Lots five acres Each within the Land above said, and the three forty acre Lots together with the two meadow Lots Lyeth in one intire piece scituate near to the southeasterly side of Lunenburgh and is Containing on Hundred and ninety acres, and it Beginnes at a Chesnut tree marked in the northwest Corner then making an Angle and Running south five degrees East one hundred and sixty five rod to a Chesnut to a Stake markt an Angle and Running East five degrees North one hundred and seventy rod to a pillar of Stones making an Angle and Running North five degrees West one hundred and sixty five rod to a pillar of Stones there making an Angle and Running West five degrees South one hundred and seventy rod to where it began, and it bounds North on the Land of Ephraim Pearce and Philip Goodridge West on the Common Land South on the Land of Nathan Heywood, John Heywood and Benjamin Bragg East on the Land of Jacob Pearce ⅌ Samuell Jones Surveyor

Received January the first day in the year of our Lord one thousand seven hundred and twenty Eight nine by order of the Committee Viz Josiah Willard Edward Hartwell, Jonathan Hubbard Samuel Hutchins Hilkiah Boyington and Adam Heywood

⅌ Edward Hartwell Clerk

Granted to Edward Hartwell by the Committee appointed by the Great and General Court to allot and Grant out the Lands within the Town of Lunenburgh to Grantees forty five acres of Land within the said town, his House Lot to gether with all Rights and Privilidges belonging thereunto, and is the Third House Lot bounded Northerly on Farmerston Farm, Southerly on Common Land Southerly on the Land of Ishaac Woods, and the said Third Lot is bearing Number Seventy three and begins at a pillar of Stones made for a Corner from thence west thirty nine rod, with one hand, and sixty rod to a pillar of Stones made for a Corner, from thence runs forty five rod to a Chesnut tree made for a Corner, from thence runs one hundred and sixty rod to a pillar of Stones made for the southeast Corner then runs forty five rod to where it began Surveyed by Samuell Jones

Received by order of the Committee appointed to make the Book of Records for the Town of Lunenburg viz Josiah Willard Edward Hartwell Samuel Boyington Jonathan Willard Samuel Hutchins Hilkiah Boyington and Adam Heywood Received the 4th day of January A.D. 1728/9

⅌ Edward Proprietors Clerk

Granted unto Edward Hartwell by the Committee as pointed by the Inhabitants of the town of Lunenburg the second one acre of meadow Land Lying and scituate within the town and is adjoyning to the westerly side of Mr. Kermans them on the second five acre way Lot Lot twenty six Hartwell's said Hartwells Land, and is measured and alowed of said land and there begins at a pine tree and Runs West Eleven degrees South twenty six rod there making an Angle and Runing South fifteen degrees West twenty three rod there making an Angle and Runing East ten degrees North thirty five rod there making an Angle and Runing West thirty three rod near northeasterly surveyed to the it began surveyed by Nathan Heywood and approved of by the Committee viz Josiah Willard Edward Hartwell and Jonathan Willard Recd on march the twenty seventh day in the year of our Lord one thousand seven hundred and thirty

⅌ Edward Hartwell Clerk

Proprietors' Records.

and approved of by the Committee viz
      Jofiah Willard
      Edward Hartwell &
      Jonathan Willard
 Recorded January ye 31^ft 1734/5
     ℔ Edward Hartwell Clerk

 Laid out By the Committee appointed fixty acres of Land to the Heirs of philip goodridge Deceaft to make up what is wanting in faid Goodridges fecond Divifion Cituat and Lying in the fouth part of Lunenburg. Begining at a ftake fet up for foutheafterly Angle of faid Goodridges third Divifion and runing weft 25 Degrees fouth on faid third Divifion 100 pole to a ftake then runing fouth 28 Degrees Eaft Chifly on Thomas Richardfons Land 102 pole to a stake then runs Eaft 28 Degres north on Common Land 100 pole to a ftake then runs 28 Degrees Weft on land of Jofiah White 94 pole to where it Began. furvayed by Nathan Heywood and approved of By the Committee viz Edward Hartwell Jonathan Willard and Jofiah Willard
 Recorded march the 16th 1735/6
     ℔ Edward Hartwell pro^r Clerk

[64] Liev^t. Edward Hartwell of Lunenburgh

Houfe Lott Granted and Laid out to Edward Hartwell by the Committee appointed by the greate and General Court to a Lot and Grant out the Lands Within the Town of Lunenburgh to Granttees fixty acres of Land In faid town for a Houfe Lot Number Eighty feven. with all the Rights and Divifions belonging thereunto. and there being Laid out adjoyning to faid houfe Lot two fixty acre Lots being fecond Divifions the one being number Ninety three and is Coupled to the Houfe Lot above faid. the other is Number Eighty Nine and is Coupled to Houfe Lot Nomber feventy three and alfo two meadow Lots five acres Each within the Land above faid. and the three fixty acres Lots to gether with the two meadow Lots Lyeth in one Intire piece fcituate near to the foutheafterly fide of Lunenburgh and is Containing one Hundred and ninety acres and It Begins at a Chefnut tree marked for the norweſt Corner there making An Angle and Runing fouth five degrees Eaſt one Hundred and fixty five rod to a Chefnut tree there making an Angle and Runing Eaſt five degrees North one Hundred and ninety rod to a pillar of ſtones there making an Angle and Runing North five degrees Weſt one Hundred And fixty five rod to a pillar of ſtones there making an Angle and Runing Weſt five degrees ſouth one Hundred and ninety rods to where It began. and it Bounds North on the Land of Ephraim Pearce and Philip Goodridge Weſt on the Common Land fouth on the Land of Nathan Heywood John Heywood and Benjamin Cory Eaſt on the Land of David Pearce ⅌ Samuell Jones frvayer

Recorded January the third day in the year of our Lord one thouſand feven Hundred and twenty Eight nine by order of the Committee viz Joſiah Willard Edward Hartwell Jonathan Willard Joshua Hutchins Hilkiah Boynton and Nathan Heywood

. . . . . Edward Hartwell Clerk —

Houſe Lot no 73

Granted to Edward Hartwell by the Committee appointed by the greate and General Court to alot and Grant out the Lands within the town of Lunenburgh to granttees forty five acres of Land within ſaid town for a houſe Lot to gether with all Rights and Diviſion be Longing there unto and the ſaid Houſe Lot Bounds Northerly on Dorcheſter farm Weſterly on Common Land foutherly on the Land of Nathaiel woods and the ſaid Houſe Lot is bareing Number feventy three and Begins at a pillar of ſtones made for a Corner from thence runs weſt thirty ſix degree fouth one hunder and fixty rod to a pillar of ſtones made for a corner from thence runs forty five rod to Chefnut tree made for a Corner from thence runs one hundred and fixty rod to a pillar of ſtones made for the foutheaſt Corner then runs forty five rod to where it began furvayed by famuell Jones

Recorded by order of the Committee appointed to make a Book of Records for the Town of Lunenburg viz

Jofiah Willard Edward Hartwell Benoni Boynton Hilkiah Boynton Jonathan Willard Jofhua Hutchings and Nathan Heywood Recorded the 4th Day of January A. D. 1728/9
₱ Edward proprietors Clerk

Lunenburgh february the 10th 1729/30

Meadow Laid out to Edward Hartwell by the Committee appointed by the Proprietors of the town of Lunenburgh for that purpors five acres of meadow and fwompey Land fcituate within the town above faid and adjoyning on or neer the Eafterly Line of Mr Bormans fairm for the average in part the way being Laid through faid Hartwells Land and is accepted and allowed by faid town and It Begins at a pine tree and Runs Weft Eleven deg fouth nineteen rod there making an Angle and Runing fouth fixteen degr Weft twenty five rod there making an Angle and Runing Eaft ten degr thirty min north fifty five rod there making an Angle and Runing Weft thirty three degr north thirty four rod to where It Began — furvayed By Nathan Heywood and approved of by the Committee viz Jofiah Willard Edward Hartwell and Jonathan Willard. Recorded march the twenty feventh day in the year of our Lord one thoufand feven hundred and thirty
₱ Edward Hartwell Clerk

[64²] Laid out to Edward Hartwell By the Committee appointed by the proprietors of Lunenburgh for that purpurs thirty feven acres and a half of third

3d Divifion Divifion Land Within faid town the Right arifeing from houfe Lott Number Eighty feven and It Bounds Eaft on the Land where faid Hartwell now Lives on, north on Mafsapog Pond Weft on Lancafter new Grant and fouth on Land Laid out to Nathan Heywood it Extends the fouth Line of faid Hartwells Land where he now Lives to fd Lancafter new Grant twenty rod and from thence it Runs Northward to faid mafsapog Pond by faid Hartwells Land and Land of Goodridges and faid new grant furvayed By Jonas Houghton and approd of by the Committee viz Jofiah Willard Jonathan Willard and Nathan Heywood

Recorded march the twenty fixth Day in the year of our Lord one thoufand feven Hundred and thirty

₱ Edward Hartwell Proprietors – Clerk . . .

Lunenburgh march the 5th 1729

3d Divifion   Laid out to Edward Hartwell fourty feven acres of third Divifion Land arifeing from houfe Lott number. 87. by the Committee appointed for that porpos and it is Bounded all round By Common Land begining at a pillar of ftones & Runing fouth thirty five degr Eaft one Hundred and fixty rod to a pillar of ftones there making an Angle and Runing Eaft thirty five degr North fourty feven rod to a pillar of ftones there Making an Angle and Runing North thirty five Degr Weft one Hundred and fixty rod to a pillar of ftones there making an Angle and Runing Weft thirty degr fouth fourty feven rod to where It began. the faid 47 acres is fcituate within ye town of Lunenburgh near to the South Weft End of the pearl hill taking in a fwompe a Crofing the north Branch of Lancafter north River furvayed By Nathan Heywood and approved on by the Committee viz Jonathan Willard Jofiah Willard and Edward Hartwell –

Recorded March the twenty fixth Day in the year of our Lord one thoufand feven Hundred and thirty

pr Edward Hartwell Clerk – – –

Lunenburgh June the 7th 1729

Laid out to Edward Hartwell by the Committee appointed ten acres of third Divifion Land It Being Cheifly meadow belonging to houfe Lott Number Eighty feven begining at a ftake and Runing fouth one Degr Eaft fifty one rod there making making an Angle and runing North thirty fix degr thirty min. Eaft fourty two rod there making an Angle and Runing north twenty fix rod there making an Angle and runing north twenty degr Weft twelve rod there making an angle & runing Weft Eight degr north thirty two rod there making an Angle

and runing fouth feventeen dgr Eaft twenty fix rod to where It Began and the faid ten acres of meadow Bounds Wefterly on meadow Lott number three foutherly on Common Land Eaft on the Cataconamoug Brook and northerly on Common Land and fd ten acres Lyeth above Cataconamoug pond furvayed by Nathan Haywood and approved on by the Committee viz Nathan Heywood Jonathan Willard and Jofhua hutchens Recorded march the twenty fixth Day in the year of our Lord one thoufand feven Hundred and thirty
⅌ Edward Hartwell Clerk

Lunenburgh June the 25th 1729

3d divifion   Laid out to Edward Hartwell by the Committee appointed twenty fix acres and Eighty four rod of third Divifion Land to the right Number Eighty feven begining at a pillar of ftones and runing North twenty fix degr Weft fifty five rod and a half to a pillar of ftones there making an Angle and Runing Weft thirty five degr fouth feventy Eight rod to a pillar of ftones there making an Angle and Runing fouth twenty fix degr Eaft fifty five rod and a halfe to a pillar of ftones there making an angle and runing Eaft thirty five degr North feventy Eight rod to where it Began — furvayed by Nathan Heywood and approved on by the Committee viz Jofiah Willard Nathan Heywood and Edwd Hartwell. Recorded March the twenty fixth Day in the year of our Lord one thoufand feven Hundred and thirty
p^r Edward Hartwell Clerk — —

The other Lands of the above faid hartwell are Recorded at page 17 in the fecond part of this Book.

the above faid half acre and 4 rod belongs to 3^d Divifion arifing from houfe Lott No. 73 and part of that right

[65]   ELNATHAN JONES of

Granted unto Elnathan Jones by the Committee appointed by the Greate and General Court to a Lott and Grant out the Lands Within the town of Lunenburg to Granttees a houfe Lott Within faid town Number 74. to gether With all the Rights and Divifions of Land and meadow that belongs thereto or fhall arife there from within the townfhip of Lunenburg a fore faid

Recorded feptember the 2ᵈ 1732.

₱ Edward Hartwell Clerk

Houfe Lott No. 74

Survayed for Jonathan Wheeler Claimer Houfe Lott Number 74 Contains fifty three acres and ¼ begins at a poplar tree marked for the moft foutherly Corner of faid Lott and runs Weft 31 degrees 30 minits north on land of John White fixty rod to a heap of ftones then runs north 37 degrees Eaft one hundred and fifty rod to a heap of ftones then Runs Eaft 31 degrees 30 minuts fouth on the town line fifty five rod to a heap of ftones then runs fouth 35 degrees Weft on fanderfons Lott one hundred and fifty rod to Where it began by nathan Heywood furvayer

approved of by the Committee viz Edward Hartwell Jofiah Willard Jonathan Willard & Nathan Haywood

Recorded December the 20ᵗʰ 1739.

₱ Edward Hartwell Clerk

2ᵈ Divifion No 14

Survayed for Jonathan Wheeler Claimer fecond Divifion Number fourteen the Contents fifty Eight acres and ¼ begining at a White oak tree marked for the northerly Corner of faid Lott from thence runs fouth thirty degrees Weft on Capᵗ Woodmans Lott feventy fix rod to a hemlock tree then runs Eaft nine rod and an half on Land of John White then runs fouth on faid White one hundred and twenty rod then runs Eaft thirty Degrees North feventy two rod then runs North on faid White one hundred and thirty rod to a heap of ftones then runs Weft thirty one Degrees and an half north on faid fecond Divifion Land forty rod to where it began by Nathan Heywood

approved of by the Committee viz Edward Hartwell Jofiah Willard Jonathan Willard and Nathan Heywood

Recorded December the 20ᵗʰ 1739.

₱ Edward Hartwell Clark

[65²] furvayed for Jonathan Wheeler Claimer meadow Lott Number fix in uper mulpufs Contains five acres and a quarter Begining at a maple tree marked for the moft northerly Corner of faid Lott from thence runs fouth twenty two degrees Eaft on upland twenty fix rod then runs fouth twenty nine Degrees Weft on upland forty rod to the Brook then bound upon the Brook to where it began. by Nathan Heywood and approved of by the Committee viz Edward Hartwell Jofiah Willard Jonathan Willard Nathan Heywood
Recorded December the 22ᵈ : 1739

meadow.
Lott
No. 6
uper mulpos

℗ Edward Hartwell Clerk

4th Divifion   Laid out by the Committee appointed one hundred acres of Land in Lunenburg Lying neer the fouth Weft Corner of faid Townfhip for Jonathan Wheeler Claimer it being for a fourth Divifion arifing from Houfe Lott Number feventy four Begining at a Certain white pine tree marked for the North weft Corner of faid Land and Runs Eaft twelve Degrees fouth on Common Land one hundred and thirty fix rod to a ftake then runs fouth fifteen degrees Weft on Land of the Revᵈ Mʳ Benjamin Prefcott one hundred and Eight rod to a ftake then Runs fouth twelve Degrees Weft on Common Land to a ftake then runs Weft twelve Degrees North on Land Laid out at the fame time to Jonathan Poole Esqʳ one hundred and thirty one rod then Runs North twelve Degrees Eaft on the General Courts Committees farm one Hundred and twenty rod to where it began

℗ Nathan Heywood furvayer

and approved of by the Committee viz Edward Hartwell Ephraim Pearce Jonathan Willard and Jofiah Willard.
Recorded December yᵉ 22ᵈ 1739.

℗ Edward Hartwell Clerk

the fourth Divifion above Recorded to Jonathan Wheeler proves to be Laid out in Land that was Laid out before to the Reverend Mʳ Benjamin Prefcoutt therefore the Committee have Laid out the faid fourth Divifion in another place and have ordered the Records of the above faid fourth Divifion to be null and void.

[66]   JOHN WOOD. of

Granted unto John Wood by the Committee appointed by the Great and General Court to alott and Grant out the Lands Within the townfhip of Lunenburg to Granttees forty five acres of Land Within faid townfhip for a houfe Lott bearing Number feventy five to Gether with all the rights & Divifions both of up Land and meadow that be Longs thereto or fhall arife there from within the townfhip of Lunenburg afore faid

Lunenburg March the 1ft 1728/9

Houfe Lott No. 75   Laid out to Mr John Wood by the Com_ mittee appointed by the proprietors of the town of Lunenburg for that purpofe forty five acres of Land Within faid town for a houfe Lott in the Lew of that Lott which was taken by Lancafter new additinal Grant the faid Lott bearing Number feventy five and it bounds fouth on Woborn farm Eaft on the Land of Jofiah Willard Esqr of Boston north on Northfield road Weft on Common Land and partly on Dorchefter farm and it begins at a ftake and heap of ftones made for the northweft Corner and from thence runs fouth one hundred and twenty rod to Dorchefter farm from thence runing to the Corner of faid Dorchefter farm and from thence runing to Woborn farm and then runing Eaft thirty fix rod to a pillar of ftones from thence runing north one hundred and fixty rod to a pillar of ftones from thence runing Weft to where it Began. furvayed by famuell Jones and approved of By the Committee viz Jofiah Willard Edward Hartwell and Jonathan Willard. Recorded august the 30th 1729.

℔ Edward Hartwell Clerk

[67]   EDWARD EMERSON Esqr of

Houfe Lott 78   Granted unto Edward Emerfon by the Committee appointed by the Greate and Generall Court to a Lott and Grant out the Lands Within the Townſhip of Lunenburg to Granttee fourty five acres for a houſe Lott N⁰ 78 With all the rights and Diviſions of Land belonging thereunto

february the 25ᵗʰ 1728/9.

By order of the Committee for the Laying out of an aquivelent for the Loſt Lotts. (that was Laid out in Lancaſter additional Grant of Land) Haveing Laid out fourty five acres for the Lott N⁰ 78 Which Lies north Eaſterly from apple tree hill nere against the ſouth end of one of the perl hills and it is bounded round by undevided Land It begins at a hemLock tree ſtanding by a brook: then ſouth Eighty rod to a red oke tree then Weſt ninety rod to a heep of ſtones and then north to Where it first began

ſurvayed by Jonas Houghton and approved of by the Committee viz Joſiah Willard Edward Hartwell Jonathan Willard and nathan Heywood. Recorded December the twenty ninth Day in the year of our Lord one thouſand ſeven Hundred and thirty

₱ Edwᵈ Hartwell Clerk

Lunenburg June the 12ᵗʰ 1730:

2ᵈ Diviſion 21   Survayed for Edward Emerſon ſecond Diviſion No 21 the Contents of Which is fourty ſeven acres and a half. Begining at a ſtak and heap of ſtones Which is the ſouth Corner and Runing North thirty one Deg Eaſt on Lott No: 20: 147 rod there making an Angle and Runing Weſt thirty one Deg thirty minits North on the North town Line fifty five rod there making an Angle and Runing South twenty Eight Deg Weſt on John Whitneys Lott 147 rod there making an Angle and Runing Eaſt thirty one deg thirty Minits South fourty Seven rod to Where it began

ſurvayed by Nathan Heywood and approved of by the Committee viz Joſiah Willard Edward Hartwell Jonathan Willard and Nathan Heywood.   .   .   .   .   .

Recorded December the 29ᵗʰ Day in the year of our Lord one thouſand ſeven Hundred and thirty

₱ Edward Hartwell Clerk

[67²] Lunenburgh December the 9ᵗʰ 1730 - - -

3 & 4 Divifion

Laid out by the Committee appointed two Hundred and fifteen acres of third and fourth Divifion Land to Edward Emerson. arifing from Houfe Lott Number Seventy Eight. in the Weft part of the townfhip — — ——

Begining at Certain Red oak tree marked for Collº Browns Southeaft Corner and Runing fouth four Degres Weft on John Brewers Land one Hundred and twenty two Rod to a pillar of Stones there making an Angle and Runing Weft twelve Degres North on the Land of Robert Comin two Hundred and ninety rod to the Weft Line of faid townfhip there making an Angle and Runing North twelve Deg Eaft on faid Line one hundred and twenty rod there Making an Angle and Runing Eaft twelve Deg fouth on Collº Browns Land two Hundred and feventy feven Rod to Where It Began. Survayed By Nathan Heywood and approved of by the Committee viz Edward Hartwell Jofiah Willard Jonathan Willard and Ephraim Pearce

Recorded December the twelfe day in the year of our Lord one thoufand feven hundred and thirty

℘ Edward Hartwell Clerk

may the 24ᵗʰ 1744.

then Laid out to the Heirs of Edward Emmerfon Deceaft thirty fix acres of Land in Lunenburg allowance for a two rod road to go through the fame which Land is to make up what is wanting in the fecond Divifion No: 21: belonging to the Heirs of faid Emmerfon it begins at a fmall white oak tree marked for the fouth Corner of Land belonging to the Heirs of John White Late of Lunenburg Deceafed and it runs Weft ten Degrees fouth 31: rod on faid Whites Land to a white burch thence Extending faid Line to the river thence runing down the river and bounding on the river till it Comes to a White oak tree marked then it runs Eaft ten Degrees north on Common Land 13 rod to a pine tree marked then it runs North ten Degrees Weft 72. rod on Common Land and 66: rod on Land of Ephraim pearce to where it began furvayed by Nathan Heywood and allowed by the Committee viz Jonathan Willard Nathan Heywood and Edward Hartwell

Recorded may the 28th 1744.

℘ Edward Hartwell proprietors Clark

[68] JOHN WHITNEY of
Houfe Lott number 76   Granted by the Committee appointed by the greate and General Court unto John Whitney fourty five ares of Land for a Houfe Lott to gether With all the rights and Divifions of Land beLonging thereunto Within the Townfhip of Lunenburgh

Lunenburgh April the 9th 1729 — — —

Laid out for John Whitney by the Committee apointed two Lotts fourty four acres and a hundred and one rod for a Houfe Lott number feventy fix and Eighty acres and fifty one rod for a third Divifion the first Lott being at a pillar of ftones and runing north twenty five degr Eaft fourty fix rod to a pillar of ftones there making an Angle and runing Eaft twenty five degres fouth one hundred and feventy five rod to a pillar of ftones there making an Angle and runing upon Dorchefter Line fixty rod there making an angle and runing Weft twenty five degrees north to where It began

3d Divifion   the third Divifion Lott begins at the fame place where the other Lott ends and runs Weft twenty five degres North one hundred and twenty two rods there making an angle and runing Eaft thirty five degr north fifty four rod there making an Angle and runing north thirty five degrees Weft feventy two rod there making an Angle and runing Eeaf twenty five degres North Eighty four rods there making an angle and Runing fouth twenty degre Eaft one hundred and fourty four rod to a pillar of ftones there making an Angle and Runing fouth twenty five deg Weft forty fix rod to Where it began aproved of by the Committee and furvayed by Nathan Heywood. viz Edward Hartwell Nathan Heywood and Jofiah Willard and Jonathan Willard Recorded December the 15th anno. Domini. 1730:

℘ Edward Hartwell Clerk

Lunenburg June the 12th 1730:

2d Divifion 22 — No Survayd for John Whitney fecond Divifion No 22 the Contents of Which is fifty acres of Land. — Begining at a ftak and a heap of ftones Which is the fouth Corner and runing North twenty Eight Degs Eaft on Emerfons Lott one Hundred and fourty feven rod there making an Angle and Runing Weft thirty one degr thirty minits North on the North Town Line fifty five rod there Making an angle and Runing South twenty Eight degrs Weft one Hundred and fourty feven Rod there Making an Angle and Runing Eaft thirty one Deg thirty minit fouth fifty five rod to Where it Began. furvayed by Nathan Heywood and approved of by the Committee viz Jofiah Willard Edward Hartwell Joshua Hutchens and Nathan Heywood

Recorded December the fifteenth Day in the year of our Lord one thoufand feven hundred and thirty

℔ Edward Hartwell Clerk

[68²] Lunenburgh November the 7th 1730

3. 4th Divifions — Laid out by the Committee appointed three Hundred Acres of Land to Nathaniel Harris and to John Whitney in the fouthweft part of faid Townfhip. two Hundred and fourty acres for three fourth Divifions two for faid Harris arifeing from Houfe Lotts Number thirty one and feventy one and one for faid Whitney arifeing from his own houfe Lott N⁰ 76 and fixty acres of faid Land is to make up What is found wanting in there former Divifions. Begining at a Certain hemlock tree marked for the moft Northerly Corner Standing by the River fide. and Runing Eaft fifteen degrees South on Common Land one hundred and thirty four rod to a pine tree there making an Angle and Runing fouth fifteen deg Weft on Common Land ninety Eighty rod to a pillar of ftones and a ftake there making an Angle and Runing Weft fifteen Deg north on John Brewers Land one Hundred and twelve rod there making an Angle and Runing fouth fifteen degr West on faid Brewers Land one Hundred and Eighty three rod there making an Angle and Runing Weft fifteen degrees North partly on the Land

Proprietors' Records. 135

Laid out to ye Reverend Mr Prefcott and partly on Common Land two Hundred and five rod to a hemLock tree by the River. thence runing by and bounding on the river three Hundred and thirty fix rod upon a ftraight Line to Where It Began furvayed by Nathan Heywood and approved of by the Committe Edward Hartwell Jonathan Willard James Jewell and Jofiah Willard . . . .

Recorded December the fifteen Day in the year of our Lord one one thoufand feven Hundred and thirty

℔ Edwd Hartwell Clerk

[69]   JONATHAN WILLARD of
Houfe lot   Granted to Lie^{vt} Jonathan Willard by the
No 89   Committee appointed by the Greate and Gen-
and 79   eral Court to alott and Grant out the Lands Contained Within the townfhip of Lunenburg to Granttees Houfe Lott Number Eighty nine and alfo Houfe Lott Number Seventy nine to Gether withall the Rights and Divifions of upland and meadow that belongs to both the faid Lotts or fhall arife therefrom Within the townfhip of Lunenburg a bove faid

Lunenburg Auguft the 29th 1729.

2^d Divifions   furvayed for Jonathan Willard the Land
No 7 & 8   on which his houfe Standeth and the Land there a bouts being Laid out for two 2^d Divifions the one being number feven and the other being Number Eight which was Laid out for forty five acres and alfo houfe Lott Number Eighty nine. the Contents is 183 acrs & a half Begining at a pillar of ftones and runing north 13 degrees Weft .220. rod on Woborn Line to apillar of ftones there making an Angle and Runing Eaft 4 degrees north 130 rod to a pillar of ftones there making an Angle and runing fouth 23 degrees 30 minits Eaft 100 rod to a White oak tree there making an Angle and Runing Eaft 7 degrees 30 minits fouth 67 rod to a pillar of ftones there making an Angle and runing fouth 8 degrees 40 minits West 34 rod to a pillar of ftones there making an Angle and runing Weft 26 Degrees fouth two hundred rod to Where it Began

furvayed by Nathan Haywood and approved of By the Committee viz Edward Hartwell Jonathan Willard Nathan Heywood and

Recorded January the 17th 1732/3

₱ Edward Hartwell Clerk

Lunenburg January the 7th 1729/30.

3d Divifion   Laid out by the Committee appointed 45 acres of third Divifion Land to Enfign Jonathan Willard belonging to the Rights No 79 & 89⅔ five acres belongs to another right begining at a fpruce tree near Groton Line and Runing Weft 30 Deg North 90 rod there making an Angle and runing fouth 30 Degrees West 80 rod there making an Angle and Runing Eaft 30 Deg fouth 90 rod to apine tree there making an Angle and Runing north 30 Deg Eaft Eighty rod to where it began furvayed by Nathan Heywood and approved of by the Committee. viz Jofiah Willard Edward Hartwell Nathan Heywood and Jonathan Willard.

Recorded December ye 15th 1732

₱ Edward Hartwell Clerk

the other Land of the faid Willard are Recorded at page 43 in the fecond part of the Book

[69²]   Lunenburg october the 27th 1729.

3d Divifion   Laid out by the Committee appointed two hundred acres of third Divifion Land arifeing from houfe Lotts No 79 and 89. begining at a pillar of ftones by a black oak tree and runing fouth 34 Degrees 30 minits weft 200 rod to a white oake tree there making an Angle and runing weft 34 Degrees 30 minits north 160 rod to a pillar of ftones there making an Angle and runing north 34 Degrees 30 minits Eaft 200 rod to a red oak tree and a pillar of ftones there making an Angle and runing Eaft 34 Degrees 30 minits fouth 160 rod to Where it began furvayed by nathan Heywood and approved of by the Committee viz Jofiah Willard Edward Hartwell Nathan Heywood and Jonathan willard

Recorded December ye 9th 1732

₱ Edward Hartwell Clerk

Lunenburg April the ye 27. 1731.

4th Divifion   Laid out by the Committee appointed 100 acres of Land in the Wefterly part of faid townfhip to Enfign Jonathan Willard for a fourth Divifion arifeing from houfe Lott No 79 begining at a Certain maple tree marked and mentioned in in the plan and runing Eaft 17 Degrees fouth on Common Land 118 rod to hills fouth weft Corner there making an Angle and runing north 5 Degrees Eaft on faid hills Lott 101 rod to a pillar of ftones there making an Angle and Runing weft 12 Degrees North on land of David wait 179 rod to a pillar of ftones there making an Angle and Runing fouth 12 Degrees Weft Chiefly on Land of Samuell Brown Esqr 87 rod to a pillar of ftones there making an Angle and runing Eaft 15 Degrees north on land of Elifha fmith 68 rod to a fmale horn wood tree there making an Angle and runing fouth 15 Degrees Eaft on Land of faid fmith 22 rod to Where it began furvayed by Nathan Heywood and approved of by the Committee viz Jofiah Willard Edward Hartwell and Jonathan Willard.

Recorded December the 9th 1732.

℔ Edward Hartwell Clerk

Lunenburg october ye 21^ft 1732.

Laid out by the Committee appointed 15 acres of Land in the eafterly part of faid townfhip to Lt Jonathan Willard (which) with five acre as Laid out to the faid willard fom time before. is in ftead of half a meadow Lott which he the faid Willard purchafed of John Heywood. it begins at a Certain Stake fet up in the Line of the Land Laid out to Jacob Gould and Runs fouth 30 Degrees Weft partly on faid Land and partly on Common Land 80 rod to apine tree on a ridge hill thence runs north 43 degrees partly on Common Land and partly on Wallafes meadow Lott 48 rod upon a ftraight Line to apine tree which is faid Wallafes Corner thence runing north 28 Degre Weft on Common Land 5 rod to apine tree thence Runing Eaft 42 Degres north 66 rod on Common Land to a little ftake thence runs Eaft 30 Degrees

fouth on Common Land 30 rod to Where it began ⅌
Nathan Heywood furvayer
and approved of by the Committee Jofiah Willard Edward Hartwell and Jonathan Willard.
Recorded December. 11th 1732.
⅌ Edward Hartwell Clerk

[70] EBEN^R WHEELOR & JONA^N BALL of.

No. Houf Lott 81

Granted unto Ebenezer Wheeler and Jonathan Ball by the Committee appointed by the greate and General Court to a Lott and Grant out the Lands Within the town of Lunenburg to Granttees fifty three acres within faid town for a houfe Lott Number Eighty one togather With all the Rights and Divifions of Land that fhall arife therefrom or Belongs thereto

Lunenburg December the 6th 1731.

Survayed for Jonathan ball and Ebenezer Wheeler Houfe Lott Number Eighty one and fecond Divifion Number Eighty four Boath Belonging to one Right. the Contence of the whole is one hundred and nine acres and a halfe there being (53.) acres in the houfe Lott and (56.) in the fecond Divifion . . . .

Begining at a Certain ftake and heape of ftones Erected for the moft foutherly Corner and runing Eaft .30. Degrees north on Benoni Boyntons Land. 190. rod to apine tree there making an angle and Runing north ten Degrees Weft on Lott No. 87. 21. rod and a halfe to ftake and heap of ftones there making an Angle and Runing Eaft 30 Degrees north on faid Lott number 87. 74. rod to a pillar of ftones there Making an Angle and Runing Weft 31 Degree 30 minits North on the Range Line 165. rod to a ftake and pillar of ftones there making an Angle and runing fouth 130 rod on Number 83. in 2^d Divifion to a ftake there making an Angle and Runing Weft 30 Degrees fouth on faid 2^d Divifion 72 rod to a ftake and heape of Stones there making an Angle and Runing fouth on Land Left for a highway .40. rod to a pillar of ftones there making an Angle and runing West : 9 Degrees ſouth on ſᵈ highway : 20 : rod there Making an Angle and Runing ſouth three Degrees Weſt on Common Land 26 rod to Where it Began . . . . . ℗ Nathan Heywood ſur ᵛʳ

approved of by the Committee viz Edward Hartwell Nathan Heywood Joſiah Willard and Jonathan Willard
Recorded December the 15ᵗʰ annoque Domini. 1731
℗ Edward Hartwell Cler.

Lunenburg Auguſt yᵉ 19ᵗʰ 1732

3ᵈ Diviſion Laid out by the Committee appointed 85 acres of 3ᵈ Diviſion Land ſouth eaſterly from the apple tree hill to Ebenezer Wheeler and Jonathan Ball ariſeing from Houſe Lott No. 81. Begining at a pillar of ſtones Erected for the moſt ſoutherly Corner and runing Eaſt 10 Degrees north on Common Land 30 rod to a White oak tree there there making an angle and runing north 10 Degrees Weſt 96 rod on Land of Ephraim pearce to apine tree there making an Angle and runing Eaſt 10 Deg north on Land of ſᵈ pearce 100 rod to a pillar of ſtones there making an Angle and runing north 10 deg weſt on Common Land 80 rod to a pillar of ſtones there making an Angle and runing Weſt 10 Deg ſouth 136 rod to a pillar of ſtones there making an Angle and runing ſouth 10 Deg Eaſt on Common Land 70 rod to a pillar to a pillar of ſtones theremaking an Angle and runing ſouth 38 Deg Weſt on Common Land 39 rod to a hemlock tree by the river thence runing Down the river to where it began.

ſurvayᵈ by Nathan Heywood and approved of by the Committee viz Edward Hartwell Jonathan Willard and Nathan Heywood.

Recorded auguſt the 24ᵗʰ 1732.
℗ Edward Hartwell Clerk

this third Diviſion is more fully diſcribed in the ſecond part of this book at page 30 and is one hundred acres allowed by ye Committee

[70²] Lunenburgh May the fixth day 1730

4th Divifion   Laid out by the Committee appointed one Hundred and Eighty five acres and one Hundred rod of forth divifion Land to Ebenezer Wheeler and Jonathan Ball Claimers arifeing from the Rights No fifty nine and No fixty three Including Necepegeefuck fow weft pond there being a Lowance for the fame . . . .

Begining at a Certain maple tree marked for the Northerly Corner and runing fouth thirty two Degrees Weft on Common Land two Hundred and feventy rod. there making an Angle and Runing Eaft thirty two degrees fouth on Common Land one Hundred and ten rod there making an Angle and runing north thirty two degree Eaft on Common Land two Hundred and feventy rod there making an angle and runing Weft thirty two deg north on the North town Line one Hundred and ten rod to Where It Began Survayed by Nathan Heywood and approved of by the Committee viz Jofiah Willard Edward Hartwell and Jonathan Willard. Laid out by the Committee ap-

4th Divifion   pointed ninety two acres and one Hundred and thirty rod of fourth divifion Land to Ebenezer Wheeler and Jonathan Ball to the right No Eighty one Including part or all the northeasterly nefepegeefuck pond. Begining at a pillar of ftones Erected for the Eafterly Corner and Runing weft thirty two degrees north on the north town Line feventy rod there making an Angle and runing fouth thirty two degrees Weft two hundred and feventy rod there making an angle and runing Eaft thirty two degrees fouth on Common Land fourty two rod there making an Angle and Runing North thirty Eight degree Eaft on m^r Clark's Land and on Common Land two Hundred and feventy two rod to where it Began furvayed by Nathan Heywood and approved of by the Committee viz Jofiah Willard Edward Hartwell and Jonathan Willard. . . . .

Recorded July the 3^d Day in the year of our Lord one thoufand feven Hundred and thirty by me

Edward Hartwell Clerk—

may the 23ᵈ 1732.

Laid out by the Committee appointed twenty acres of Land to Ebenezer Wheeler and Jonathan Ball as an addition to there Land by Reason of two ponds which Lyeth therein Lying on the north weſt ſide of ſaid Land 170 rod in Length and 19 rod in Bredth and is bounded northerly on the town Line Weſterly on Common Land ſoutherly on Common Land and Eaſterly on the Land of the fᵈ Wheeler and Ball ſurvayed by nathan Heywood and approved of by the Committee viz Edward Hartwell Joſiah Willard Recorded June the 5ᵗʰ 1732.

℔ Edward Hartwell Cler—

[71]   Isaac Farnsworth of

Houſe Lott No 82   Granted to Isaac Farnsworth by the Committee appointed By the Greate and General Court to a Lott and grant out the Lands Within the Townſhip of Lunenburgh to granttee ſixty one acres and a half of Land within ſaid town for a houſe Lott baring number Eighty two to gether with all the rights and Diviſions of Land belonging thereunto.

Lunenburg August the 13ᵗʰ 1730– . . . .

ſurvayed for Iſaac Farnsworth Houſe Lott number Eighty two the Contents of Which is ſixty two acres. Begining at a ſtake and Heape of ſtones Which is the ſouutheaſt corner and runing Weſt one Degree thirty minits North on Lott Number Eighty three one hundred and four rod pillar of ſtones there making an Angle and runing North fifteen degs Weſt on Woborn farm one hundred and ſix rod to a pillar of ſtones there Making an Angle and Runing Eaſt twenty Eight degrees north on the miniſterial Lott or Common Land ſixty two rod there making an Angle and runing ſouth twenty nine degrees Eaſt partly on pools and partly on Burbeens and partly on Wetherbes Lotts one hundred and fifty three rod to to Where it began A high Way being Laid out four rod Wide Within the Laſt Line mentioned from the ſoutheaſt Corner to the a fore ſaid Burbeens Lott there being a

Lowance in y̌e Lott for the ſame ſurvayed by nathan Haywood and approved of by the Committee viz Joſiah Willard Edward Hartwell Jonathan willard and Nathan Heywood

Recorded December the firſt day in the year of our Lord one thouſand ſeven Hundred and thirty

℈ Edward Hartwell Clerk

Lunenburg January y̌e 5. 1729.

Meadow Lott No. 3   ſurvayed for Isaac Farnsworth meadow Lott No. 3 in Horſe meate meadows the Contents of Which is ſix acres. Begining at a Certain ſtake and heape of ſtones Erected for the ſouth Corner and runing north ten degrees Eaſt on Colborns Land 22: rod to a ſtake there making an Angle and runing West 38 degrees North on pooles meadow Lott 65: rod to a ſtake there making an Angle and runing ſouth three degrees Weſt on hills meadow Lott 13 : rod to a ſtake there making an Angle and runing ſouth 45: degree Eaſt on the miniſterial Land and meadow 68 rod to Where it Began. ſurvayed by Nathan Heywood and approved of by the Committee viz Joſiah Willard Edward Hartwell Jonathan Willard and Nathan Heywood.

Recorded June the 14th annoque Domini. 1731

℈ Edward Hartwell Clerk

[71²]   Lunenburg March the 23d 1730 31/—

2d Diviſion No. 51   Survayed for Isaac Farnſworth 2d Diviſion No 51. on flatt hill the Contents of Which is 55 acres and a half — — Begining at a Certain pillar of ſtones Erected for the ſouth Corner and runing North 18 degrees Eaſt on Lott No. 50. 149 rod to a pillar of ſtones there making an Angle and runing Weſt 31 degrees North 61 rod and a half to a pillar of ſtones there making an Angle and Runing ſouth 17 dege 30 minits Weſt on Lott No 52: 148 rod to a pillar of ſtones there making an Angle and runing Eaſt 31 degrees ſouth 63 rod and a half to Where it began.

ſurvayed by Nathan Heywood and approved of By the Committee viz Joſiah Willard Edward Hartwell Jona-

than Willard and Nathan Heywood. Recorded June the 14th . . . . . annoque Domini. 1731
₱ Edward Hartwell Clerk

Lunenburg April the 9th 1729. — — —

3d Divifion Laid out to Isaac Farnsworth by the Committee appointed and Impowered by the proprietors of Lunenburg 80. Acres of third Divifion Land arifeing from houfe Lott No. 82 : Lying Weft from perl hill brook begining at a Chefnut tree marked for the fouth weft Corner and runing North 160 : rod to a pillar of ftones there making an Angle and runing Eaft : 80 : rod to a pillar of ftones there making an Angle and runing fouth 160 rod to a pillar of ftones there making an Angle and runing Weft. 80 : rod to Where it began

furvayed by Nathan Heywood and approved of by the Committee to viz Jofiah Willard Benoni Boynton and Jofhua Hutchens.

Recorded June the 14th annoque Domni 1731
pr Edward Hartwell Clerk

[72] JOHN GROUT of.
Lunenburg March the 15th 1732 3/

Houfe Lott No 83

Survayd for John Grout Houfe Lott Number 83 the Contents of Which is .53. acres and a quarter there being alowance in faid Lott for a high way four rod wide Begining at a pillar of ftones which is the fouth eaft Corner and runing Weft 2 Deg fouth on Lott Number 84. 122 rod to Woborn farm thence runing north 15 degrees weft on faid woborn Line 82. rod to a pillar of ftones thence runing Eaft one Degree thirty minits fouth on Lott Number 82. 104 rod to a pillar of ftones thence runing fouth 29 Degrees Eaft Chiefly on Lott Number twelve 83 rod to Where it began

Survayed by Nathan Heywood and approved of by the Committee viz Jofiah Willard Jonathan Willard Benoni Boynton Hilkiah Boynton Nathan Heywood.

Recorded april the 27th 1733.
₱ Edward Hartwell Clerk

[72²] Lunenburgh June the 16th 1729. . . .

medow Lot

Laid out to John Grout by the Committee appointed five acres and ten rod of meadow beLonging to the right No Eighty three It Lyeth southerly from Col? Tayers meadow Lott. Begining at a pillar of ftones and runing fouth one Degree fifteen minits ·Eaft thirty rod to a maple bufh there making an Angle and Runing Eaft one Degree fifteen minits north twenty feven rod to a pillar of ftones. there making an Angle and Runing North one Degree fifteen minits Weft thirty rod there making an Angle and Runing Weft one degree fifteen minits fouth twenty feven Rod to where it began. furvayed by nathan heywood and approved by the Committee viz Jofiah willard Edward Hartwell and Jonathan Willard

Recorded September the fifth Day in the year of our Lord one thoufand feven hundred and thirty

℔ Edward Hartwell Clerk

[73]

Houfe Lott 84

SAMUEL AUSTAIN of

Granted to Samuell auftin by the Committee appointed by the Greate and General Court to a Lott and Grant out the Lands Within the town of Lunenburg to grantees (51) acres of Land Within faid town for a houfe Lott to gether With all the Rights and Divifions Belonging there unto Recorded January yᵉ 10th 1732/3

℔ Edward Hartwell Clerk

Mr Gardner

Houfe Lott No. 23

Granted to mr andrew Gardner by the Committee appointed by the Grate and General Court to alott and Grant out the Lands Within the town of Lunenburg to Granttee 43 acres for a houfe Lott Number 23 within the town of Lunenburg to gether With all the Rights and Divifions of upLand and meadow that belongs thereto or shall arife there from.

Lunenburg January the 12th 1730/31

ſurvayed for the Rnd m^r Andrew Gardner Houſe Lott Number 23 on the ſouth ſide Northfield road the Contents of Which is 43 acres. Begining at a Certain Cheſnut tree marked for the Northweſt Corner and runing ſouth 3 Degrees Weſt on Lott Number 24. 155 rod to a pillar of ſtones there making an Angle and runing Eaſt on Woborn farm 45 rod to a ſtake there making an Angle and runing North 3 degrees Eaſt on Lott No: 22 : 155. rod to a ſtake there making an angle and runing Weſt on ſaid Northfield road 44 rod to Where it began

ſurvayed By Nathan Heywood and approved By the Committee viz Joſiah Willard Edward Hartwell Jonathan Willard and nathan Haywood Recorded February ye 25th 1733./4.

℗ Edward Hartwell Clark

[73²] Mr Andrew Gardner

Granted to m^r Andrew Gardner By the Committee appointed By the Greate and General Court to alott and Grant out the Lands Within the town of Lunenburg to Granttees 44 acres and a quarter number one ſcituate Lying and being within the townſhip of Lunenburg in the County of Worceſter for ahouſe Lott together With all ye Rights and Diviſions of up Land and meadows that beLongs thereto or ſhall ariſe there from

Recorded october ye 30th 1732

℗ Edward Hartwell Clerk

Lunenburg January the 12th 1730/31

House Lott N° 1   ſurvayed for the Ren^d mr andrew Gardner the miniſters Lott No. 1. the Contents of which is forty four acres and a quarter Begining at a heape of ſtones which is the ſouth Corner and Runing north 29 degrees Weſt 45 rod and a half to a ſtump there making an angle and runing Eaſt 31 degrees north partly on Land of Benoni Boynton 159 rod to aſtake there makeing an angle and runing ſouth 29 degree Eaſt 44 rod to a heap of ſtones there making an

Angle and runing Weſt 31 degrees ſouth on Hilkiah Boyntons Lott 159 rod to Where it began. ſurvayed by Nathan Heywood and approved of By the Committee viz Joſiah Willard Edward Hartwell Jonathan Willard and Nathan Heywood Recorded February yᵉ 25. 1733/4
℔ Edward Hartwell Clerke

Lunenburg January the 22ᵈ 1730/31

2ᵈ Diviſion No 58

ſurvayed for Rnd mʳ andrew Gardner Claimer 2ᵈ Diviſion No. 58. the Contents of Which is 57. acres and a half. Begining at a ſtake and heap of ſtones which is the Weſterly Corner and runing North 10 degrees 30 minits Eaſt on Land Left for a high Way 62 rod to a ſtake there making an Angle and runing Eaſt 31 Degrees ſouth on 2ᵈ Diviſion No: : 152. rod to aſtake there making an Angle and runing ſouth. 17. degrees Weſt on Groton Line 62 rod to a ſtake there making an Angle and runing Weſt 31 degrees North on Lott No. 59: 152 rod to Where it Began

ſurvayed By Nathan Heywood and approved of By the Committee viz Edward Hartwell Joſiah Willard Jonathan Willard and Nathan Heywood

Recorded February yᵉ 25ᵗʰ 1733/4
℔ Edward Hartwell Clerk

[74] WILLIAM TAILER ESQᴿ of Dorchester

Granted William Tayler Esqʳ by the Committee appointed by the Greate and General Court to a Lott and Grant out the Lands Within the town of Lunenburg to Granttee 56 acres and ¾ for a Houſe Lott No 53 to gether Withall the rights and Diviſions of Land beLonging there unto.

Lunenburg November the 2ᵈ 1730

Houſe Lott No. 53

ſurvayed for Coˡˡ William Tayler Houſe Lott No 53 upon flat Hill the Contents of Which is fifty ſix Acres and three quarter. Begining at a ſtake and heep of ſtones Which is the Weſterly Corner and Runing North 17 Degrees Eaſt on Land Left for a high Way ſixty rod there making an Angle and runing

Eaſt 31 Deg 30 min ſouth 153 rod to Groton Line there making an Angle and Runing ſouth ſeventeen Dege Weſt on ſaid Line 60 rod there making an Angle and runing Weſt 31 Deg 30 minits North 153 rod to Where it began. ſurvayed by Nathan Heywood and approved of by the Committee to viz Edward Hartwell Joſiah Willard Jonathan Willard and Nathan Heywood — —

Recorded April the 16th annoque Domni. 1731.

℔ Edward Hartwell Clerk

Lunenburg June the 16th 1729

meadow

Laid out to William Tayler Esqr five acres & ten rod of meadow belonging to the right No. 53 and is Northerly from mulpus meadows. — — Begining at a White oak tree and Runs ſouth one Degree 15 mints Eaſt 30. rod. there making an Angle and runing Eaſt one Degree 15 minits north 27. rod there making an angle and runing North one Deg 15. min West 30 rod there making an Angle and Weſt one Degree 15 minits ſouth to Where it began. Survayed by Nathan Heywood and approved of by the Committee to Witt Edward Hartwell Joſiah Willard and Jonathan Willard. . . .

Recorded April the 16th anno Domini. 1731.

℔ Edward Hartwell Clerk

[74²] Lunenburg November the 2d 1730.

2d Diviſion
No 54

Survayed for Coll Tayler a ſecond Diviſion on flat Hill No. 54 the Contents of Which is 56 acres and three quarters. Begining at a ſtak and heepe of ſtones Which is the Weſterly Corner and Runing north 17 Degs Eaſt on Land Left for a high Way 60. rod there making an Angle and runing Eaſt 31 deg 30 mints ſouth on Lott No. 53 : 153. rod there making an Angle and runing ſouth 19 Deg Weſt on Groton Line 60 rod there making an Angle and runing Weſt 31 deg 30 mints north on Coll Thaxters Lott 150 rod to Where it began

ſurvayed by Nathan Heywood and approved of by the Committee viz Joſiah Willard Jonathan Willard Edward Hartwell and

Recorded April the 16th annoque Domini. 1731.

℔ Edward Hartwell Clerk

[75] SAMUEL THAXTER Esq.ʳ of Hingham.

Houfe Lott
No. 55

Granted to Samuell Thaxter Esqʳ By the Committee appointed by the Greate and General Court to a Lott and Grant out the Lands Within the town of Lunenburg to Granttee 55 acres of Land Within faid Town for a Houfe Lott Baring No 55 to Gether Withall the Rights and Divifions of Land be Longing there unto. furvayed for Co^ll Samuell Thaxter Esqʳ Houfe Lott No. 55. the Contents is 55 acres and it Lyeth on flatt hill within the town of Lunenburg. Begining at a ftak and heep of ftones Which is the Wefterly Corner and Runing North 17 Deg Eaſt on Land Left for a high Way 61 rod there making an Angle and Runing Eaft 31 Deg 30 fouth on Coll Tylers Lott No. 54. 150. rod there making an Angle and runing fouth 19 Deg Weft on Groton Line .60. rod there making an Angle and Runing Weft 31 Deg 30 min North on Lott No .56. 150 rod to Where it began Survayed by Nathan Heywood and approved of by the Committee viz Edward Hartwell Jofiah Willard Jonathan Willard and Nathan Heywood. Recorded april the 16ᵗʰ Annoque Domni. 1731.

℞ Edward Hartwell Clerk

Lunenburgh November the 2ᵈ 1730.

2ᵈ Divifion
No 56

Survayed for famell Thaxter Esqʳ a fecond Divifion No. 56. on flatt Hill the Contents of which is 53 acres and three quarters. begining at a ftak which is the moft Wefterly Corner and runing north 17 deg Eaft on Land Left for a high way 61 rod there making an Angle and runing Eaft 31 Deg 30 min South on Lott No. 55. 150 rod to Groton Line there making an Angle and runing fouth 17 Deg Weft on faid Line 58. rod to a ftake there making an Angle and runing Weft 31 deg 30 mint North 150 rod to where it began

Survayed by Nathan Heywood and approved of by the Committee viz Jofiah Willard Edward Hartwell Jonathan Willard and Nathan Heywood

Recorded Aprill yᵉ 16ᵗʰ 1731.

℞ Edward Hartwell Clerk

[76] EPHRAIM PEIRCE of Lunenburg

Granted to Ephraim Peirce by the Committee appointed by the Greate and General Court to a Lott and Grant out the Lands Within the town of Lunenburgh to granttees fourty three acres of Land Within faid town for a houfe Lott bareing Number Sixty Eight to gether Withall the rights and Devifions of Land belong there unto —

Lunenburgh December the 15th 1729

Houfe Lott No. 68 furvayed for Ephraim Pearce Houfe Lott Number Sixty Eight above Said. the Contents is fourty three acres Beggining at a pillar of ftones by the gravel pit at Capt Willards Sawmill and Runing fouth twenty five degr thirty min Eaft one Hundred and fourty three rod on Houghtons Lott there making an Angle and Runing Weft twenty five Degr thirty Min fouth partly on houghton fecond Divifion but Chiefly on Second Divifion belonging to faid lot fourty fix rod and a half there making an Angle and Runing North twenty five degr thirty min. Weft one Hundred and fourty nine rod on Benjamin Goodridges Lott there making an Angle and Runing Eaft fixteenth degr north fourty fix rod on Capt Jofiah Willards Land to where It Began furvayed by nathan Heywood and approved of by the Committee viz Edward Hartwell Nathan Heywood Jofiah Willard and Jonathan Willard

⅌ Edward Hartwell Clerk

Laid out to the above faid Ephraim Pearce a fecond Divifion Divifion number Eighty feven and is Coupled to the houfe Lot above faid and the Contents is fixty two acres begining at a ftake fet up in the fouth End of the Houfe Lott and Runing fouth twenty five degr Eaft two Hundred and Eighty rod on houghtons fecond Divifion there making an Angle and Runing Weft five Degr fouth fourty rod there making an angle and runing north thirty Degr Weft ninety six rod on fecond Divifion No Eighty fix there making an Angle and Runing Eaft twenty five degrees and thirty min: north twelve rod on Gibsons Lott there making an Angle and runing north twenty five deg: Weſt one Hundred and ſeventy rod on gibſons Lott there making an Angle and Runing Eaſt twenty five Degrees thirty Min North thirty two rod on the afore ſd Houſe Lott to where It began ſurvayed By Nathan Heywood and approved of by the Committee viz Edward Hartwell Nathan Heywood Jonathan Willard and Joſiah Willard. Recorded March the twenty ſeventh day in the year of our Lord one thouſand ſeven Hundred & thirty

℗ Edward Hartwell Clerk

Houſ Lott No. 88   Granted to Ephraim Pearce by the By the Committee appointed by the Greate and General Court to a Lott and Grant out the Lands Within the town of Lunenburgh to Granttee ſixty acres of Land Within ſaid town for a Houſe Lott No 88. to Gether Withall the Rights and Diviſions of Land beLonging there to or ariſeing there from. . . . .
Recorded may the 28th 1731.

℗ Edward Hartwell Clerk

Lunenburg march the 23d 1729/30.

Laid out by the Committee appointed for that purpose Eleven acres and a half of Land to Ephraim Pearce Claimer to make up what is Wanting in his ſecond Diviſion Number Number Eigty ſix Lying near Cataconamoug meadows begining at pine tree marked for the norweſt Corner and runing ſouth 15 Degrees Eaſt 68 rod to a pillar of ſtones there making an angle and runing ſouth 8 degree weſt 20 rod to pine tree there making an angle and runing Eaſt 25 Degrees ſouth 20 rod to a pillar of ſtones there making an angle and runing north 4 deg Eaſt 77 rod to a heap of ſtones there making an angle and runing weſt 25 degrees north Chiefly on Wheelers meadow 40 rod to Where it began four Lines are bounded on Common Land ſurvayed by Nathan Heywood and approved of by the Committee viz Edward Hartwell Jonathan Willard and
Recorded March ye 22d 1732/3

℗ Edward Hartwell Cler . . .

Proprietors' Records.

[76²] Lunenburgh April the 5th 1729 ———

3d Divifion Laid out to Ephraim Pearce by the Cômmittee appointed Eighty acres of third Divifion Land. Arifeing from houfe Lott Number fixty Eight being foutheafterly from apple tree hill Beging at a pine tree marked for the norweft Corner and Runing fouth ten Deg Eaft one hundred and fixty rod there making an Angle and Runing Eaft ten Deg North fixty rod there making an Angle and Runing North three degrees thirty mini Eaft one Hundred and fixty four rod there Making an Angle and Runing Weft ten deg fouth one Hundred rod to Where it Began furvayed by Nathan Heywood and approved of By the Committee viz Edward Hartwell Jonathan Willard and Hilkiah Boynton and Nathan Heywood. Recorded December the thirty first. Day in year of our Lord one thoufand feven Hundred and thirty

℔ Edward Hartwell Clerk

Lunenburg march yᵉ 23ᵈ 1729/30

For road and deficient. Laid out by the Committee appointed for that purpose 36 Acres of Land to Ephraim pearce for allowance for a town way Laid out in his Lotts and for wat is wanting In the faid Lotts fcituat Lying and being near Cattaconamoug pond.

Begining at a pine tree marked for the Eafterly Corner and runing fouth 17 Degrees weft 44 rod to the brook there making an Angle and runing fouth 39 Degrees Weft by the Brook 26 rod there making an Angle and runing North 44 degrees Weft 120 rod to a pine tree there making an Angle and runing North 45 Degrees Eaft 36 rod to a pillar of ftones there making an Angle and Runing Eaft 30 Degrees fouth Chiefly on Land Laid out to Jonathan Willard 100 rod to Where it Began   furvayed by nathan Haywood and approved of By the Committee viz Edward Hartwell Jofiah Willard and Jonathan Willard Recorded January yᵉ 4th 1733/4

℔ Edward Hartwell Cler

[78]   Nathaniel Page of Lunenburgh
March the 23ᵈ 1729=30

third Divifion   Laid out by the Committee appointed Eighty fix acres and a Half of third Divifion Land to Nathaniel Page Claimer arifeing from Houfe Lott Number fifty two fcituate and Lying near Cataconamoug Meadows and Including one meadow Lott alowed to be Eight acres. the Plan Confifting of ninety four acres and a half Begining at a ftake and Heap of ftones Erected for a Corner of the Meadow Lott and Runing Weft twenty five Degrees fouth on Common Land fourty Eight Rod to a White oak tree there Making An angle Runing Eaft fourty Degrees fouth on third Divifion Land Laid out to David Pearce twenty one rod to an afh tree there Making An angle and Runing fouth feventeen Degʳ Weft Cheifly on Land of faid Pearce one Hundred and fixty rod there Making An angle and Runing Eaft party on the Land of Cap Jofeph Gould one Hundred and twenty Rod to a ftake there Making An angle and Runing North three Degrees Weft on Common Land one Hundred and fixty five rod to a heepe of ftones on the Ridge hill By the pond. there making An angle and Runing Weft twelve rod on Common Land. there Making An angle and Runing South thirty fix Degrees thirty minits Weft on meadow Land Laid out to Lᵗ Hartwell thirty Eight Rod there making An angle and Runing north one Degree Weft on faid Hartwells Meadow fifty one Rod to Where It began furvayed by Nathan Heywood and approved by the Committee viz Edward Hartwell Jofiah Willard and Jonathan Willard.   .   .   .   .   .   .

Recorded May the twenty fixth day in the year of our Lord one thoufand feven Hundred and thirty . . .
         ℔ Edward Hartwell Clerk . . .

Lunenburg November the 20ᵗʰ 1729.

3ᵈ Divifion   Laid out by the Committee appointed feven acres and a quarter of third Divifion Land to Jonathan Page Claimer belonging to the Right No : 52 : begining at a pillar of ftones at mʳ Clarks Corner and runing fouth thirty feven degrees Weft Eighty rod to a maple tree there making an Angle and and runing Eaft fix Degrees north fixty two rod to a pillar of ftones there making an Angle and runing Weft thirty three Degrees north thirty two rod to a white oak tree there making an Angle and runing north Eighteen Degrees fifteen minuts Eaft fourty two rod to where it began

furvayed by Nathan Heywood
and approved of by the Committee viz Edward Hartwell Jonathan Willard and Nathan Heywood

Recorded may the 25th 1744.

₱ Edward Hartwell Proprietors Clerk

[79]   JAMES JEWELL of Lunenburgh

Granted unto James Jewell by the Committee appointed by the Greate and General Court to a Lott and Grant out the Lands Within the town of Lunenburg to granttees feventy acres of Land Within faid town for a fecond Divifion Number Sixteen which faid Committee Coupled to House Lott number two and the above faid fecond Divifion Number fixteen is Granted unto the above Named James Jewell to gether with the meadow Lott and all the rights and Divifions of Land arifing from the a fore faid houfe Lott Number two. and alfo the a fore faid Committee Granted unto the above Named James Jewell fecond Divifion Number thirty one which fecond Divifion was Coupled to houfe Lott No thirty fix .   .   .   .

Lunenburgh May the Eight 1730.

No furvayed for James Jewell his fecond Divi-
2^d Divifion 16 fion Number fixteen the Contents of Which is feventy acres and a half begining at Woborn Corner and Runing Weft fourty Deg north on Woborn Line twenty five rod there making an Angle and Runing Weft thirty degs thirty minits fouth on hastings Lott thirty feven rod there making an Angle and runing fouth thirty one deg Eaft on Lancafter Line feventy rod there making an Angle and Runing Eaft two deg thirty minits fouth on Land of Benjamin goodridge fifty Eight rod there making

an Angle and runing Eaſt ſeven degres north on Land of ſaid goodridge Eighty two rod there making an Angle and runing north twenty ſix deg^r thirty minits Weſt on Land of ſaid goodridge one hundred and Eleven rod there making an Angle and runing Weſt thirty degres ſouth on Woborn Line Eighty nine rod to Where it began ſurvayed by nathan Heywood and approved of by the Committee Edward Hartwell Joſiah Willard nathan Heywood and Jonathan Willard

Recorded December the twenty ſecond Day in the year one thouſand ſeven hundred and thirty

₱ Edward Hartwell Clerk

Lunenburg May the 8th 1730 . . . . .

4th Diviſion Laid out by the Committee appointed one Hundred Acres of Land to James Jewell part of Which Land is to mak up his third Diviſion one Hundred and twenty acres and the Remainder is for his fourth Diviſion ariſeing from house Lott No two and is ajoyning to his third Diviſion begining at a black oak tree marked for the Easterly Corner of his third Diviſion and runing Weſt twenty Eight degres ſouth on his third Diviſion Lott one hundred and fourty ſeven rod there making an Angle and runing north twenty Eight Degrees weſt partly on Harriſes and partly on Scotts and partly Common Land one hundred and fifty five rod there making an Angle and runing Eaſt twenty Eight deg north on Common Land one hundred and nine rod there making an Angle and runing ſouth ten deg Eaſt on Eleazer houghtons Land one hundred and ten rod there making an Angle and runing Eaſt ten degrs north on ſaid houghtons Land Eighty rod there making an angle and runing ſouth Eighteen deg Eaſt on Common Land twenty four rod to where it began ſurvayed by nathan Heywood and approved of by the Committee viz Edward Hartwell Jonathan willard nathan heywood and James Jewell

Recorded December the 22^d annoque Domini 1730.

₱ Edward Hartwell Clerk

Proprietors' Records. 155

[79²] Lunenburg April yᵉ 4. 1729

3ᵈ Divifion Laid out to James Jewel by the Committee appointed for that purpors two picefes of third Divifion Land the Contents of one being one hundred acres and ninety two rod the other being Eighty acres both Lying upon Lancafter Line yᵉ first Begins at a pillar of ftones and runs West 28 Degrees fouth 149 rod to a pillar of ftones there making an Angle and runing north 28 Degrees Weft 108 rod to a pillar of ftones there making an angle and runing Eaft 28 Degrees north 149 rod to a pillar of ftones there making and an Angle and runing fouth 28 Degrees Eaft 108 rod to a pillar of ftones where it began the other Runing the fame points and being Eighty Rods upon Lancafter Line and 160 rod upon the other Lines furvayed by nathan Heywood and approved of by the Committee viz Jofiah Willard Edward Hartwell and Jonathan Willard.

Recorded December yᵉ 9ᵗʰ 1732.

℔ Edward Hartwell Cler.

[80] HARVARD COLLEDGE.

Lunenburgh December yᵉ 26 : 1729

Laid out by the Committee appointed two Hundred and fifty Acres and fourty four rod of Land in the Northeafterly part of faid townfhip to Harvard Colledge. begining at a pillar of ftones Erected for the moft foutherly Corner and runing North thirty two degrees Eaft one hundred and forty two rod on fecond devifion belonging to John fifk there Making an Angle and Runing Weft thirty two Degrees North two Hundred and Eighty two rod on the North town Line there making an Angle and runing fouth thirty two Degrees Weft one Hundred and forty two rod on Common Land there Making an Angle and runing Eaft thirty two degrees fouth two Hundred and Eighty two rod to Where it began. furvayed by Nathan Heywood and approved of by the Committee. viz Jofiah Willard Edward Hartwell Jonathan Willard and Nathan Heywood

Recorded Auguft the feventh day in the year of our Lord one thoufand feven Hundred and thirty . . . .

By me Edward Hartwell Proprietors CLerk

[81]   Samuell Brown Esqr of Salem

Lunenburgh December the 7th 1730 — — —

3d Divifion   Laid out by the Committee appointed fix Hundred and twenty acres of third Divifion Land the Right arifeing from Houfe Lotts Number Eleven twenty nine fifty Eight fourty one and fourty five — — Laid out to the Hlb: Samuell Brown Esqr Claimer at the Northweft Corner of faid Townfhip Begining at apillar of ftones which is the northweft Corner of faid town fhip and runing Eaft thirty two degree fouth on the Line of faid townfhip three Hundred and fourty rod to a ftak and heepe of ftones there Making an Angle and runing fouth twelve degrees Weft on Common Land two Hundred and two rod to a heape of ftones there making an Angle and runing Weft twenty nine degree north on Capt Jofiah Willards Land one hundred and fourty Eight rod to a heape of ftones there making an Angle and runing fouth twenty nine Deg Weft on the Land of faid Willard one hundred and Eighty nine rod to a maple tree there Making an Angle and Runing Weft twelve degrs North on the Land of William Clark Esqr one Hundred and twenty rod to apillar of ftones there making an Angle and runing North twelve degr Eaft on the Weft Line of faid townfhip four Hundred and fifty five rod to where it began   furvayed by nathan Heywood and approved of by the Committee Edwd Hartwell Jofiah willard Ephraim pearce & Jonathan willard

Recorded December the 14th in the year of our Lord one thoufand feven Hundred and thirty

                     ℗ Edward Hartwell Clerk

Lunenburgh December the 7th 1730 . . . .

4th Divifion   Laid out by the Committee appointed fix Hundred and fourty Acres of Land to the HLb. Samuell Brown Esqr Claimer in the Weft part of faid townfhip the Rights a Rifeing from Houfe Lotts Number Eighteen thirty four feven fifty three thirty fix Eleven twenty nine and fifty Eight and ye above faid Land is Laid out for fourth Divifion Land Begining at a ſtake and heape of ſtones Erected for for the northeaſt Corner and Runing Weſt twelve deg north on Land of William Clark Esqr three hundred and twenty rod to the Weſt Line of ſaid town ſhip there making an Angle and Runing ſouth twelve deg Weſt on ſaid Line three hundred and twenty rod to a heap of ſtones there making an Angle and runing Eaſt twelve deg ſouth on Common Land three Hundred and twenty rod to a pillar of ſtones there making an Angle and Runing north twelve deg Eaſt on Common Land three Hundred and twenty rod to where It began

ſurvayed by nathan Heywood and approved of by the Committee Edwd Hartwell Joſiah willard Jonathan willard Eph^a pearce

Recorded December the 14th anno Domini 1730

₱ Edward Hartwell Clerk

[81²]   Lunenburgh February the 24th 1729.   .   .   .

3^d Diviſion   Laid out by the Committee appointed five Hundred and fifty acres of third Diviſion Land at and on the north End of the pearl hill to Samuell Brown Esqr Claimer the rights ariſeing from Houſe Lotts number Eighteen thirty four seven fifty three and ſeventy acres of the right Number thirty ſix — — Begining at a Cartain White pine tree marked for the Weſterly Corner and Runing Eaſt thirty two degrees ſouth two Hundred and thirteen rod to a pillar of ſtones bounding on Common Land there making an Angle and runing north fourty Degree Eaſt twenty rod on Gibsons Lott to a pillar of ſtones which is Gibsons Corner there making an Angle and runing Eaſt fourteen Degr North on Common Land one Hundred and ſixty two rod to a pillar of ſtones there Making an Angle and Runing north thirty two degrees Eaſt on Common Land one Hundred and Sixty rod to a pillar of ſtones there Making an Angle and Runing Weſt thirty two degree north partly on Land Laid out to Jeremiah Allen Eſq^r and partly on Common Land three Hundred and thirty rod to a black oak tree there making an Angle and runing ſouth thirty two degrees Weſt two hundred and ninety four rod to Where it began. ſurvayed by Nathan Heywood and approved of by the Committee to witt Joſiah Willard Edward Hartwell Jonathan willard and Nathan Heywood Recorded December the twelve day in the year of our Lord one thouſand ſeven hundred and thirty

⅌ Edward Hartwell Clerk

Lunenburgh December the 8th 1730.

4 division   Laid out by the Committee appointed four Hundred and fifty acres of fourth Diviſion Land to Samuell Brown Esqr Claimer ⸺ ⸺ ⸺

Which Land Ariſes from Houſe Lotts Number thirty Eight thirty three ſeventy two : 68 : 41 : and 45 and there is 20 acres of 4th diviſion Land in Coll^o Browns third Diviſion plan at the town corner that belongs to these rights in the Weſterly part of ſaid town ſhip begining at a Certain ſtake and heap of ſtones ſet up for Eliſha Smiths ſouth Weſt Corner and Runing Weſt fifteen deg ſouth on Juſtis pools Lott one Hundrd and twelve rod to a bunch of Maple trees there making an Angle and Runing South fifteen Degree Eaſt on ſ^d pools Lott one hundred and ſixty rod to a pillar of ſtones there Making and an Angle and and Runing Eaſt fifteen Degrees North on ſaid pools Lott twenty Eight rod there making an Angle and Runing ſouth four Degrees Weſt on John Brewers Land one Hundred and fourteen rod to a red oak tree there making an Angle and Runing Weſt twelve Deg North on Emerſons Land two Hundred and ſeventy ſeven rod to the Weſt Line of ſaid townſhip there Making an Angle and runing North twelve Deg Eaſt on ſaid Line three hundred and twenty rod there making an Angle and Runing Eaſt Eighteen deg ſouth Juſtice preſcotts Land 270 rod to where it began ſurvayed by Nathan Heywood and approved of by the Committee viz Edward Hartwell Josiah willard Jonathan willard and Ephraim pearce

Recorded December the 14th 1730: by me

Edward Hartwell Clerk

[82]   Benjamin Prescott Esqr
                  Lunenburgh December the 8th 1730.

4th Divifion   Laid out by the Committee appointed three Hundred and twenty acres of fourth Divifion Land to Benjamin Prefcott Esqr Claimer in the Weft part of f^d Townfhip the rights arifeing from Houfe Lotts Number fourty three. fifty one. fifty two and Eighty two Begining at a Cartain Stak and heape of ftones which is Coll^o Browns foutheaft Corner and Runing fouth twelve Degrees Weft on Common Land feventeen rod to a ftak and heap of ftones there making an Angle and runing Weft fifteen Degrees fouth on Elifha Smiths Land one Hundred and fourty rod to a heape of Stones there making an An Angle and Runing South fifteen Eaft on faid Smiths Land one Hundred Sixty rod to a pillar of Stones there Making an Angle and Runing Weft Eighteen degrees North on Land of Coll^o Brown two Hundred and fixty feven rod to the Weft Line of Said Townfhip there Making an Angle and runing north twelve degrees Eaft on Said Line one Hundred and ninety three rod there making an Angle and runing Eaft twelve degrees fouth on Coll^o Browns Land three Hundred and twenty rod to where it began furvayed by nathan Heywood and approved of by the Committee viz Josiah Willard Edward Hartwell and Jonathan Willard

      Recorded December the 14th 1730.

                       ℔ Edward Hartwell Clerk

[83]   Robert Comin of Concard
                  Lunenburgh December ye 9th 1730.

3d
4th Divifion   Laid out by the Committee appointed one Hundred and ninety feven acres of third and forth Divifion Land to Robart Comin Claimer in the Weft part of faid townfhip the right arifeing from Houfe Lott number twenty five. Begining at a Certain pillar of ftones Which is the Eaft Corner and Ruuing fouth thirty four Deg thirty Minits Weft on Land belonging to Coll^o Thomas Fitch one hundred and thirty rod to a Maple tree there Making an Angle and Runing Weft twelve Degs

North two Hundred and fourty Rod to the Weſt Line of ſaid townſhip there making an Angle and Runing North twelve Degr Eaſt on ſaid Line one Hundred and nineteen rod there making an Angle and Runing Eaſt twelve Degrees ſouth on Emerſons Land two Hundred and ninety Rod to Where it Began

Survayed by Nathan Heywood and approved of by the Committee viz Joſiah willard Edward Hartwell Jonathan Willard and Ephraim Pearce

Recorded December the 12th in the year of our Lord one thouſand ſeven hundred and thirty

℔ Edwd Hartwell Clerk

ſeptember the 5th 1743.

2^d Diviſion No. 78

ſurvayed for Robert Commings Claimer a ſecond Diviſion Lott of Land Lying in Lunenburg Conſiſting of fifty Eight acres and one half ſaid Lott being No 78. and begins at a pillar of ſtones which is Joſeph Woods ſoutheaſt Corner and is the moſt Northerly Corner of ſaid Lott and runs ſouth 236. rod partly on the Honble Joſiah Willards Land to apillar of ſtones then Runs Eaſt on m^r Birds Land. 42 : rod to a pillar of ſtones then it runs North on the ſaid Joſiah Willards Land being a ſecond Diviſion Lott No : 77 : 210 : rod to a pillar of ſtones then it runs Weſt 31 : deg & ½ north on Land of Jonas Clark Eſq^r 49 : rod to where it began

℔ Nathan Heywood ſurvayer

allowed by the Committee viz Nathan Haywood Edward Hartwell and Jonathan Willard.

Recorded May 25th 1744.

℔ Edward Hartwell proprietors Clerk

Lunenburg october ye 25th 1736

medow Lott No. 2 lower mulpus

ſurvayed for Robert Comming Claimer meadow Lott No : 2 in Lower mulpus being 5 : acres of meadow and Containing a pine ridge of upland begining at a Certain ſtake by the brook and runs North 4 : degrees Weſt on No : 3 : 16 rod to a black burch tree then runs Eaſt 37 : deg. north on ſaid No : 3. 36 rod to a Little maple tree then runs north 43. dege : Weſt on ſwamp and upland 30 rod to apine tree then runs Weſt 6 : Degrees ſouth on meadow Lott No: 1: 19 rod to the brook then Runs down the brook to where it began

        Nathan Heywood ſurvayer

approved of by yᵉ Committee viz Jonathan Willard Nathan Haywood Edward Hartwell

Recorded may yᵉ 25ᵗʰ 1744 :

      ℔ Edward Hartwell proprietors Clerk

[84]   JOHN AND TIMOTHY POOLS
    Lunenburg March the 24ᵗʰ 1729/30

2ᵈ Diviſion   ſurvayed for John and Timothy Pools
No 28   Claimers a 2ᵈ Diviſion No : 28 the Contents of Which is 52 Acres and it Begins at a ſtake and Heep of Stones Erected for the South Corner and runing North 30 degr Eaſt on 2ᵈ Diviſion No 27. 150 rod to a ſtak in the North Town Line there making an Angle and runing Weſt 31 Deg 30 min North on ſd Line 55 rod there making an Angle and Runing ſouth 31 deg Weſt on Lott No. 29. 150. rod to a ſtake there making an angle and runing Eaſt 31 Deg 30 min ſouth 56 rods to Where it began. Survayed by Nathan Heywood and approved of by the Committee viz Edward Hartwell Joſiah Willard Jonathan Willard and Nathan Heywood. Recorded April the 16ᵗʰ Day Annoque Domini. 1731.

        ℔ Edward Hartwell Clerk

    Lunenburg April yᵉ 28ᵗʰ 1730.

3ᵈ Diviſion   Laid out by the Committee appointed 120 acres of Land for a third Diviſion to John and Timothy Pools Claimers. ariſeing from houſe Lott No 4. in the Weſterly part of ſaid townſhip begining at a ſtake and a heep of ſtones ſet up for John brewers noreaſt Corner and runing North 15 Deg Weſt on Common Land 160 rod to a ſtake and heep of ſtones there making an angle and runing Weſt 15 deg ſouth on Common Land 120 rod to a maple tree there making an Angle and runing ſouth 15 deg Eaſt on Juſtice pools Land 160 rod to John Brewers Line there making an Angle and runing

Eaft 15 Deg North on Said Line 120 rod to Where it began furvayed by Nathan Heywood and approved of by the Committee viz Jofiah Willard Edward Hartwell Jonathan Willard and Nathan Heywood. Recorded April the 16th Day Annoque Domini. 1731 . . . ——
⁋ Edward Hartwell Clerk

[84²] Laid out to Capt Timothy Pool Claimer to the Rights of James Burbeen one hundred acres of Land in Lunenburg for a fourth Divifion fcituate
4th Divifion and Lying in the fouth wefterly part of faid Townfhip and partly on the Hill Called manoofnock hill Begining at a ftake fet up for the moft foutherly Corner of faid Land and runs North forty four degr. Eaft on Land Laid out to alexander Forfter Claimer feventy two rod to a ftake then Runs North feventeen degrees Weft on faid forfters forty rod to a hemlock tree then runs Eaft Seventeen degrees north on faid forster Eighty rod to a black oak tree then runs north ten degrees Weft on Common Land feventy rod to a hemlock tree then runs Weft forty degrees fouth on the afore faid James Burbeens third Divifion one hundred rod then runs north forty degrees Weft on faid Burbeens third Divifion Seventy rod to a White oak tree then runs fouth twenty two Degrees Weft on Land Laid out to the faid Timothy and John Pools Claimers one hundred and forty fix rod to a ftake then runs Eaft twelve degrees fouth on the Town Line Eighty three rod to Where it began
⁋ Nathan Heywood Survayer
and approved of by the Committee viz Edward Hartwell Ephraim Pearce and Jonathan Willard.
Recorded the 27th Day of November A. D. 1738
⁋ Edward Hartwell Clerk

4th Divifion Laid out by the Committee appointed to John and Timothy Pool Claimers ninty five acres of Land in Lunenburg to wards the fouth weft Corner of faid Townfhip for a fourth Divifion arifing from houfe Lott No. 4. Including ten acres Laid out to Edward Hartwell Esqr. Begining at a ftake and heape of ftones fet up for the foutherly Corner of faid Land and runs north twenty two degrees Eaft on Land Laid out to the afore faid Timothy pool one hundred and forty fix rod to a white oak tree then then Runs north forty degrees Weft on Land Laid out to James Burbeen fixty nine rod to a black oak tree then runs fouth twenty fix degrees Weft on Common Land one hundred and ninty Eight rod to a ftake then runs Eaft twelve degrees fouth on the town line one hundred and five rod to where it began

by Nathan Heywood furvayer
and approved of by the Committee viz Edward Hartwell Jonathan Willard and Jofiah Willard.
Recorded December ye 16th 1738

₱ Edward Hartwell Clerk

[85]   DAVID WAITE:
Lunenburgh april ye 27 1731

Divifion 4th Laid out to David Waite Claimer by the Committee appointed Eighty acres of fourth Divifion Land in the Wefterly part of faid town fhip the Right a Rifeing from houfe Lott No 89: Begining at a Certain Black oake tree Which is Marked for Hills Norwefterly Corner and runing Eaft 5 Degrees fouth on faid hills Land 13 rod to a pillar of ftones there making an Angle and runing North 12 Degrees Eaft 43 rod to apillar of ftones there making an Angle and runing Weft 12 Degrees North on Land of thomas Heall Esqr 190 rod to a pillar of ftones there Making an Angle and runing fouth 12 Degrees Weft on Land of Samuell Brown Esqr 70 rod to a pillar of ftones there making an Angle and Runing Eaft 12 degree fouth on Land of Enfign Jonathan Willard 179 rod to a pillar of ftones there making an Angle and runing North 5 Degrees Eaft on Land of the afore faid hill 26 rod to Where it began

Survayed by Nathan Heywood and approved of by the Committee viz Jofiah Willard Jonathan Willard and Edward Hartwell

Recorded May the 27th Annoque Domini. . . 1731

₱ Edward Hartwell Clerk

[86]   JONATHAN POOR of Newbery – – – ——

Granted unto Jonathan Poore by the Committee appointed By the Greate and General Court to a lott and Grant out the Lands Within the town of Lunenburg to Grantees 52 acres and 80 rod for a Houſe Lott No 54 together With all the Deviſions of Land and rights ariſeing from ſaid Houſe Lot as bove ſaid

 Recorded May yͤ 16: 1731:
        Edward Hartwell Clerk

    Lunenburg April the 11th 1730. — ——

Houſe No Survayed for Capt Joſiah Willard Claimer
Lott 54 houſe Lott Number 54: the Contents of Which is 52 ares and a half Begining at a Certain pine tree marked for the ſouth weſterly Corner and runing Eaſt 8 degree ſouth on Land of the aforeſaid Willard 49 rod. there making making An Angle and runing north 9 Degrees Eaſt 160 rod there making an Angle and runing Weſt 10 degree North on the high Way 51 rod there Making an Angle and runing ſouth 8 degree Weſt Chiefly on Land of ſaid Willard 160 rod to Where it began

    Survayd by Nathan Haywood

and approved of by the Committee viz Joſiah Willard Edward Hartwell Jonathan Willard and Nathan Heywood

 Recorded May the 28th annoque Domini. 1731.
       ℔ Edward Hartwell Clerk

[86²] GENERAL COURTS COMMITTEE
    Lunenburg June the 11th 1731

Courts   Laid out by the Committee appointed one
Committees thouſand Acres of Land in the ſouthweſt Cor-
Land   ner of ſaid townſhip to the Greate and General Courts Committee viz the Hlb William Tayler Esqr the Hlb Samuell Thaxter Esqr Colͦ Francis Fullam Esqr and mr Benjamin Whitemore and Capt John ſheple Granted to them by the proprietors for there former Good ſervice in ſaid townſhip . . . .

Begining at a pillar of ſtones Erected for the Corner of ſaid townſhip and runing Eaſt 12 degrees ſouth on the ſouth Line of ſaid townſhip 400 rod to a Cheſnut tree

there making an Angle and runing north 12 degrees Eaſt on Common Land 400 rod to a White pine tree there making an Angle and runing Weſt 12 degrees north on Common Land 400 rod to a maple tree there making an Angle and runing ſouth 12 degrees Weſt on the town Line 400 rod to Where it began ſurvayed by Nathan Heywood and approved of by the Committee viz Edward Hartwell Joſiah Willard Isaac Farnsworth Ephraim Wetherbe and James Jewell
Recorded June the 14th annoque Domini. 1731. . .
₱ Edward Hartwell Clerk

Lunenburg June the 9th 1741.

Then the above Named Col francis Fullam Eſqr the only ſurviver of the above named Gent went and Renewed the bounds of the above ſaid thouſand acres and at ſame time took with him Capt William ſtrobridge Jonathan Hubburd Jur ſurvayer and I the ſubſcriber and ran the lines and Renewed the bounds and Cut down ſevral trees and the above ſaid Colo Francis Fullam Eſqr then Took poſſeſsion of the ſaid thouſand acres in the preſence of the afore ſaid William Strobridge Jonathan Hubburd and Before me
Edward Hartwell Proprietors Clerk

[87]　　　Jonathan Wheeler of
Lunenburgh october ye 4th 1729. . . . .

3d Diviſion　　Laid out By the Committee appointed to Jonathan Wheeler of Lancaſter Claimer 104 acres a ½ of third Diviſion Land ariſeing from the Right No. : 74 : Begining at a Walnut tree and Runing Weſt 155 rod to a pillar of ſtones there making an Angle and runing north 33 degrees Eaſt 183 rod to a beach tree there making an Angle and runing ſouth 45 degrees Eaſt. 141 rod to a pillar of ſtones there making an angle and Runing South 40. degrees Weſt 70 rod to Where it Began.

Survayed By Nathan heywood and approved of by the Committee viz Edward Hartwell Josiah Willard and Jonathan Willard. Recorded Sept the 11th anno Domini 1731
₱ Edward Hartwell Cler.

Proprietors' Records.

Lunenburg June the 16th 1749

4th Divifion   Laid out by the Committee appointed one hundred and thirty acres of Land in faid Town to Jonathan moor Claimer in the Wefterly part of faid Town one Hundred acres of which is for a fourth Divifion arifing from houfe Lott Number 74 and thirty acres to make up what is wanting in faid Houfe Lott and in the fecond Divifion belonging thereto: it Begins at a Certain black oak tree marked for Daniel Thurftins fouthweft Corner and runs north ten Degrees Eaft on faid thurftins two hundred rod to a heap of ftones on a Ledge of Rocks then it runs Weft twenty feven Degrees north one hundred and fixty Eight rod on Common Land to a maple tree marked then it runs fouth fifteen Degrees Eaft two hundred and fifty one rod partly on uptons Land and partly on John Brewers Land to a heap of ftones then it Runs Weft 15 degrees fouth on faid Brewer five rod to a heap of ftones then it runs Eaft thirty four degrees and an half fouth on Land Laid out to Capt Jonathan Willard but now in the poffefsion of the Honourable Andrew oliver fixty three rod to where it began   furvayed by Nathan Heywood and approved of by the Committee viz Edward Hartwell Jonathan Willard Ephraim pearce and Nathan Heywood

Recorded June the 24th 1749

℔ Edward Hartwell proprietors Clerk

[88]   EBENEZER RICHARDSON   .   .   .

Lunenburg March the 18th 1730$\frac{1}{\ }$

12. acres
Equeetent
for Hyways

Laid out by the Committee appointed twelve acres of Land in the fow eaft part of faid Lunenburg townfhip to Ebenezer Richardfon Claimer for an Equevilent to the town wayes going through his Lott. Beginning at a Certain pitch pine tree marked Which is the north Corner and runing weft 25 Degrees fouth on Land of John heywood 46 rod to a White oake tree there making an Angle and runing fouth on Common Land 38 rod to a Chesnut bush. there making an Angle and Runing Eaft on Common Land 40

rod to a pillar of ſtones there making an Angle and runing north on Capt Goulds Land 57 rod to Where it began.
Survayed By Nathan Heywood and approved of By the Committee viz Joſiah Willard Edward Hartwell and Jonathan Willard . . .
Recorded October the 8th Annoque Domini. 1731.
℔ Edward Hartwell Cler

[88²] JONATHAN PRESCOTT Esqr of Concord Diſceſt
Lunenburg January the 7th 1729

2^d Di   Survayed for the Heirs of Major Prescot
no 60   a ſecond No — 60 belonging to Houſe Lott No: 14 being in the Eaſt part of ſaid townſhip and adjoyning to Groton Line begining at a pine tree and runing north — 17 Degree Eaſt 60 rod on Groton Line to a pillar of ſtones there making an angle and runing weſt 32 deg north 152 on a ſecond Diviſion Line to a pillar of ſtones there making an Angle and runing ſouth —— 17 degree Weſt 60 rod to a ſtake there making an Angle and Runing Eaſt 32 deg ſouth 152 to Where it began approved of By Edward Hartwell Joſiah Willard Jonathan Willard and Nathan heywood
Recorded January the firſt Day anno Domini. 1731½
℔ Edward Hartwell Cler

Lunenburg February the 27th 1729/30

3^d Diviſion   Laid out by the Committee appointed 120 acres of Land for a 3^d Diviſion to the heirs of Jonathan preſcot Esqr deceſt to the right No 14. Begining at a pillar of ſtones Erected for the Weſterly Corner and Runing South 15 degree West on Common Land 160 rod there making an Angle and runing Eaſt 15 deg ſouth on Common Land 120 rod there making an Angle and runing north 15 deg Eaſt 160 rod there making an Angle and runing Weſt 15 deg north on Common Land 120 rod to Where it Began ſurvayed by Nathan Heywood and approved of By the Committee viz Edward Hartwell Joſiah Willard Nathan Heywood and Jonathan Willard
Recorded January the firſt Day anno Domini. 1731/2
pr Edward Hartwell Cler

Lunenburg November 4th 1730

4th Divi   Laid out by the Committee appointed 100 acres of Land for a fourth Divifion to the right of Jonathan prefcott Esqr Deceft In the South wefterly part of faid townfhip Begining at a ftake and a pillar of Stones which is the Eaft Corner and runing Weft 15 Degrees north on Common Land 161 rod there making an Angle and runing North 15 degee Eaft on Common Land 151 rod to the reverend M^r prescotts Land there making an Angle and runing Eaft 15 Degree fouth on fd prescotts Land 71 rod there making an Angle and runing fouth 9 degree on faid m^r prefcott Land 140 rod there making an Angle and runing fouth 40 Dege Eaft on faid prefcotts Land 40 rod to Where it began.

furvayed by Nathan Heywood and approved of by the Committee viz Edward Hartwell Jonathan Willard Nathan Haywood and Jofiah Willard   .   .   .   .

Recorded January the first Day anno Domini 1731/2

₱ Edward Hartwell Cler

[89]   June the 25.th 1729.

3^d Divifion   Laid out by the Committee appointed 26 acres and and Eighty four rod of third divifion Land to Edward Hartwell belonging to the right No 87. begining at a pillar of ftones and runs north 26 Degrees Weft 55 rod and an half to a pillar of ftones there making an angle and runing Weft 35 degrees fouth 78 rod to a pillar of ftones there making an angle and runing fouth 26 degrees Eaft 55 rod and an half to a pillar of ftones there making an angle and runing Eaft 35 degrees north 78 rod to where it began.

furvayed by Nathan Heywood and approved of by the Committee Edward Hartwell Jonathan Willard and Nathan Heywood   Recorded April the 26th 1779

Edward Hartwell proprietors Clerk

June the 25: 1729

3^d Divifion   Laid out to Edward Hartwell, nine acres and 132 rod of third Land arifing from No. 87. it Begins at a pillar of ftones and runs Weft 37.

degrees fouth 66. rod to a pillar of ftones there making an angle and runing fouth 26. degrees Eaft 19 rod and a half to a pillar of ftones there making an angle and and runing Eaft 28 degrees north 65. rod to a pillar of ftones there making an angle and runing north 26. degrees West thirty rod to where it began. furvayed by Nathan Haywood and approved of by the Committee

Jofiah Willard
Edward Hartwell
Isaac Farnsworth

Recorded April 26: 1779.

Edward Hartwell proprietors Clerk

Lunenburg June the 5th 1729

Laid out by the Committee appointed ten acres of third divifion Land to Edward Hartwell belonging to the Right No 87 begins at a ftake and runs fouth one degree Eaft 51. rod there making an angle and runing North 36. degree 30 min Eaft 42 rod there making an Angle and runing north 20 degrees Weft 12 rod there making an Angle and runing Weft 8 degrees north 32. rod there making angle and runing fouth 17 degrees Eaft 26. rod to where it Began. furvayed by Nathan Haywood and approved of by the Committee

Nathan Heywood
Jonathan Willard
Joshua Huchings
Edward Hartwell

Recorded April 26: 1779

Edward Hartwell Proprietors Clerk

all the a bove Lands here Recorded was Recorded in this Book above forty years fince therefore this above Record is of no ufe or fervice

(feal)   [90] To Mr John Hastings on of the Proprietors of the town of Lunenburgh Greeting. These are In his Majesties Name to Require you fourthwith to Warn the Proprietors of faid Lunenburg to Meet at the Houfe of Jonathan Willard in faid town on the fifteenth Day of October next at nine of the Clock in the forenoon then and there to Confider of and act on the Severel perticulers hereafter Mentioned Which you to Gether With ten others of your faid proprietors haveing Requefted for. to Witt William Wallis Benjamin Cory John Scott Walter Beeth John Heywood Capt Josiah Willard Samuell Page Hilkiah Boynton Jofhua Hutchens and Nathan Heywood. first to Choufe a Moderater for the Goverment of faid meeting alfo to Choufe a proprietors Clerk. thirdly to Lay out thofe Lotts anew that have fallen Within the additional Grant to Lancafter or an a quivelent to fuch as have the Whole or any Part of there Lotts fallen therein. alfo to Lay out the fecond Divifions of Such Proprietors as are Not as yet Laid out. and LikeWife the meadow Lotts of all fuch as are Wanting Either in Whole or in part of Either of faid Divifions and alfo to make up any part of any of the first Divifions that fhall be found Wanting and in perticuler to Jonathan Willard apart of his fecond Divifion to the Draught feventy Nine. to John Fisk What is Wanting in his first Lott N^o fourty two and alfo to Capt Jofiah Willard anaquivelent for What is found Wanting to a Lott that Now Belongs to Jonathan Whitney. and alfo to Choose a Committee to Lay out the fame that is the Lotts and Lands above faid or any part thereof as fhall be Granted and agreed upon by the Said Proprietors. and alfo to Cominto fom method for the Calling and fummonsing of faid proprietors Meettings for the futer and further to Grant to fuch perfons a quantity of Common Land at a place Called Mulpus falls as fhall be Conveniant for the building a fawmill as fhall Ingage in faid Sarvice and Laftly to Do What is Necefsary to git anaquivilent to the town for What is Wanting for the Land Which is taken off by Lancafter addinitinall Grant that fo our townfhip May be Compleeted. fail not given under My hand and feale this twenty fifth day of September in the fecond year of his Majeftis Reign Annoque Domini. 1728 Joseph Wilder Justice of the Peace . . . .

Recorded the twentyth Day of January in the year of our Lord one thoufand feven Hundred and twenty Eight. nine

℔ Edward Hartwell Proprietors Clerk

[90²] At a Meetting Legally Warned the proprietors of the Town of Lunenburg Being Meett at the house of Jonathan Willard in faid town on the 15th of october annoque Domini. 1728 :

1 the Proprietors proceeded to Bring in there Vote for the Choice of a moderator for the Goverment of faid Meetting Which Being Examined it appeared that Capt Josiah Willard Was Choosen by a Major part of the Votes

2 The Proprietors Proceeded to the Election of a Clerk by Writen Votes Which being Examined it appeared that Edward Hartwell was Choosen by a major part of the votes } and was Sworn to the faithfull discharg of his office.

3 Voted to Lay out those Lotts a new that have fallen Within the additinel Grant to Lancafter or anaquivilent to fuch as have the Whole or any part of there Lotts fallen therein. alfo to Lay out the fecond Divifions of fuch Proprietors as are not as yet Laid out. and Likwise the meadow Lotts of all fuch as are Wanting Either in Whole or in part of Either of faid divifions and alfo to makup any part of any of the first divifions that fhall be found Wanting. and perticuler to Jonathan Willard a part of his Scond Divifion to the Draught feventy nine to John Fifk What is Wanting in his first Lott Number fourty two. and alfo to Capt Jofiah Willard anaquivilent for What is wanting in a Lott that now belongs to Jonathan Whitney and alfo to Choofe a Committee to Lay out the Lands and and Lotts above faid

4 Voted that Edward Hartwell Jonathan Willard Hilkiah Boynton Benoni Boynton and Capt Jofiah Willard be a Committee to Lay out all the Lotts and Lands above faid.

5 Voted that when and fo often as any five or more of the Proprietors of the town of Lunenburgh Shall Judge a Proprietors Meetting Necefsary and Shall make application to the Proprietors Clerk in Wrightng under there hands for a Meetting feting fourth the occation thereof Which Proprietors Clerk is hereby Impowered to grant a warrant under his hand and feale for the Calling of fuch

meetting accordingly Caufeing the fame to be posted up in Writing in fom publick place or places Within faid town Expresing the time and place foreteen Days before the Day appointed for f^d meeting

6 Voted that Sam^ll Johnfon Jeremiah Norcrofs Jacob Gould and William Jones have a Certain track of Common Land of a boute ten or twelve acres Lying adjoyning to mulpus falls for Conveniance to Build a faw mill or mills. and that the above Named perfons fhall have hold and Improve the above faid Land fo Long as they fhall Keep faid mill or Mills in Repare. Provided that the above Named Persons fhall Build and finifh faid mill or Mills Within twelve mounths after this time. Jofiah Willard Moderator — — — —

Recorded the twenty firft Day of January in the year of our Lord one thoufand feven hundred and twenty Eight. nine

℗ Edward Hartwell Proprietors Clerk

[91] at the requeft of a fufficiant number of the proprietors of the town of Lunenburg in wrighting from under there hands

{feal} These are in his Majesties Name to Warn the Proprietors of the Town of Lunenburgh to Convene at the house of Enfign Jonathan Willard in faid Lunenburg on thirds day the thirty firft Day of this Instant october at Nine of the Clock in the forenoon then and there to Elect and Depute a Comitee to Makup a Book of Records for the Proprietors of the Town of Lunenburgh and alfo to Make Satisfaction to the above Named Jonathan Willard for fom of his Land which is now Laid out for a burying place Dated at Lunenburgh october the fixteenth annoque Domini 1728.

Edwd Hartwell Proprietors Clerk

At a Meetting Legally Warned the Proprietors of the Town of Lunenburgh Being Meett at the Houfe of Enfign Jonathan Willard in faid Town on the thirty first Day of october Annoque Domini. 1728

Proprietors' Records. 173

    1 Made Choife of Capt Josiah Willard for a Moderator for the Goverment of faid Meetting . . . .

    2 Voted that Capt Josiah Willard be the firft Committee man to Make up a Book of Records for town of Lunenburgh

    3 Voted that Edward Hartwell be the fecond Committee man to Make up a Book of Records for ye Town of Lunenburgh

    4 Voted Benoni Boynton be the third Committee man to make up a Book of Records for the Town of Lunenburgh

    5 Voted Hilkiah Boynton be the fourth Committee man to make up a Book of Records for the Town of Lunenburgh

    6 Voted that Jonathan Willard be the fifth Committee man to mak up a Book of Records for ye Town of Lunenburgh

    7 Voted that Jofhua Hutchens. be the fixth Committee man to Make up a Book of Records for the Town of Lunenburgh

    8 Voted that Nathan Heywood be the feventh Committee man to make up a Book of Records for the town of Lunenburgh

                        Josiah Willard Moderator

    Recorded the twenty firft Day of January in the year of our Lord one thoufand feven hundred and twenty Eight : nine

                        ℔ Edward Hartwell Clerk

(feal) [92] To the Proprietors of the town of Lunenburg Greeting. These are In His Majesties Name to Warn you to Convene at the Houfe of Enf. Jonathan Willard in faid town on the twentieth Day of this Inftant February at nine of the Clock in the fore noon then and there to act on the feveral perticulers Hereafter mentioned . . . . .

    1 to agree upon the Granting Such fum or fums of money as fhall be Judged needfull for the Defraying all necefsary Charges arifeing Within faid propriety. and allfo

when fuch fum or fums of money fhall be paid in by faid proprietors

2 to Choufe a Collector or Collectors Who fhall be Impowered to gether fuch fum or fums of money as fhall be agreed on and Difburft the fame as he or they fhall be ordered by faid proprietors

3 to agree to Lay out a third Divifion of Land and alfo how many acres fhall be in a third Divifion and alfo how and and In What manner we fhall proceed in Laying out the faid third Divifion. and When We fhall Begin to Lay out faid third Divifion of Land . .

4 to Choufe a Committee to Lay out faid third Divifion of Land and that the proprietors Choofe fo many as they fhall think proper and Needfull to be of the Committee. and alfo What Number of the Committee fhall be thought proper to go With the furvayer to Lay out the faid third Divifion of Land Each Day

5 to agree and Vote to Enfign Jonathan Willard an a Equivilent in Land or money for the Land that is fet apart for a burying place.

Dated at Lunenburg February the 4th anno Domni 1728/9

Edward Hartwell Proprietors clerke

Recorded april the 25th Anno Domini 1729 . . .

Edward Hartwell proprietors Clerk

[93] At a Meetting Legally Warned the Proprietors of the Town of Lunenburg being meet at the houfe of Enfign Jonathan Willard in faid town on thirds Day the twentieth Day february in the year 1728/9 . . .

1 made Choice of Capt Jofiah Willard for a Moderator for the Goverment of faid meeting. . . . .

2 voted that there be Eighty acres of Land at the Leaft Laid out by the Committee that fhall be from time to time appointed and Impowered by the proprietors for that purpofe Each proprietor of fuch part of the undevided Land Within the townfhip of Lunenburg as be Longs to or arife upon Each Intire Houfe Lott and fo In proportion to him that hath a greate or a Leff Intereft in fuch undevided Land and that Each proprietor fhall

have His proportion of Land arifeing on Houfe Lott as a fore faid Laid out In one Intire piece in any part of the undevided Land that he fhall Defier and Choofe where the Land Will allow of it. and Where there is not Land fufficiant to accomodate and fatisfy fuch Proprietor in one place it may be made up in fom other place Where he fhall defier it provided fuch proprietors all Wayes make the firs Choice or pitch of fuch Land as he fhall Defier as a fore faid. and give the fame in In Wrighting to the Committee to be Impowered to Lay out the fame be fore any other perfon. not Withftanding any proprietor Defierous to take up his Proportion of Land adjoyning to his Land allredy Layed out may be perfered and Grtifyed If the Committee Judge it Reafonable. and Where any Land Defiered to Be Layed out fhall not Be In the Judgment of the Committee fo good as the Beft Loot regard being had to the fcituation as Well as to the Quality of the Land in fuch Cafe fuch proprietor fhall have fo mouch more Laid out then the proportion a fore faid as fhall make the fame Equel in vallue to the beft in the Judgement of the Committee not Exceeding fixfcore for Eighty acres . . . .

alfo voted that no preferance be given to the first Choice to be given in as a fore faid before the third day of march next at fix of the Clock in the after noon and that Where two or more of the Proprietors before the faid third Day of march next at fix of the Clock in the afternoon fhall give in there refpective pitches or Choice of one and the fame pice of Land Preferance fhall be given to fuch proprietor that fhall obtain that priviLege by Lott to be made and Drawn by the appointment of the Committee for that purpose

[93²] alfo voted that the Land aboute the Claypit be refearved to the proprietors ufe and not Laid out to any perticuler perfon

alfo Voted that Capt Jofiah Willard Livet Edward Hartwell Benoni Boynton Hilkiah boynton Jonathan Willard Jofhua Hutchens nathan Heywood James Colbern and Ifaac Farnsworth be a Committee fully Impowered With fuch able Survayer as they fhall think fit to Imploy to Lay out every proprietor his proportion of Land in manner as a bove voted and and having Laid out the fame as a fore Said and return aplan of each Lott to the proprietors Clerke figned by any three of the Committee and furvayer and that the Clerke be hereby Impowered and Diricted to Record the fame in the proprietors book.

Jofiah Willard Moderator

Recorded april the 14th anno Domini. 1729
℔ Edward Hartwell Cler

At the Requeft of a fufficiant number of the proprietors of the townfhip of Lunenburg in Writing from under there hands

[feal] These are in his Majesties Name to Warn you to Convene at the publick meeting houfe in faid town on the firft munday of february next at ten of the Clock in the forenoon to the end that being duly meet and formed they may then and there Confider of and act on the feveral perticulers hereafter mentioned. &c

1 to have the accompts of all futch to whome the proprietors is indebted for any manner of Sarvice by any perfon or perfons for the faid propriety don and performed. and accept of and allow the fame fo far as they fhall think Juft and Reafonable and order the payment thereof accordingly and agree upon the Granting and Raiseing of money and affefling the proprietors for that purpose or to a gree upon and ordering the Granting or felling of fuch parts and proportions of the said Common and undevided Land to fuch perfons as Shall appear to buy the fame as fhall be fufficiant to defray the proprietors Charges and make payment of the money that fhall be found due from the proprietors as a fore f^{d} and order the putting the fame upon record or pafsing other tittles thereof in fuch a way and manner as they fhall Judge moft Convenant and alfo Choofe and Impower proper perfons for any of the purpoffes a fore. f^{d} as they may think proper.

alfo to agree upon and ordering the Laying out of fuch apart of the Common and undevided Land in faid town as fhall be fufficiant to fatiffy the feveral owners of the Lotts of Land where the town Ways have ben all redey Laid out by the felectmen of Lunenburg and fhall be accepted and approved of By the town for the Damage they may fuftain by fuch wayes being Laid through there Lands as a fore ʳᵈ and Choofe and Impower proper perfons to Lay out the fame and Entittle fuch perfons to fuch proportions of Land accordingly Dated at Lunenburg January the 16 anno Domini. 1729/30

⅌ Edward Hartwell proprietors Cler

Recorded march yᵉ 28ᵗʰ anno. Domini. 1730.

⅌ Edward Hartwell Cler

[94] At a meeting Legally Warned the Proprietors of the Common and undevided Lands Within the townfhip of Lunenburg being meet at the publick meeting houfe in faid town on munday the fecond Day of february anno Domini 1729/30 they proceeded to bring in there votes for the Choice of a moderator for the Goverment of faid meeting Which being Examined it appeared that Liueᵗ Edward Hartwell was Chofen by a major part of the votes

1 Voted that Hilkiah Boynton be allowed the fum of	4 13 5	
2 Voted that Jofhua Hutchens be allowed the fum of	3 4 0	
3 Voted that Capᵗ Jofiah Willard be allowed the fum of	31 6 1	
4 Voted that Ephraim Wetherbe be allowed the fum of	1 12 0	
5 Voted that Livᵗ Edward Hartwell be allowed yᵉ fum of	8 10 0	
6 Voted that Nathan Heywood be allowed the fum of	2 15 0	
7 Voted that Samuell Page be allowed the fum of	0 10 0	
8 Voted that Benoni Boynton be allowed the fum of	1 5 0	
9 Voted that Isaac Farnsworth be allowed the fum of	0 14 0	

10 Voted that James Jewell be allowed the fum of	0 18 0	
11 Voted that Jonathan Willard be allowed the fum of	3 00 0	
for the Land that is Laid out for a burying place it being the faid willards Land		
12 Voted that Jofeph Wilder Esqr be allowed the fum of	1 00 0	
13 Voted that John Heywood be allowed the fum of	0 6 0	
14 Voted that Noah Dodge be allowed the fum of	0 4 0	
15 Voted that Ephraim Pearce be allowed ye fum of	0 5 0	
16 Voted that Jonas Houghton Jonathan Houghton and Ebenezer Wilder be allowed the fum of	20 0 0	
	80 2 6	

alfo Voted and Granted fuch a quantity of the Common and undevided Land Within the townfhip of Lunenburg as fhall be fufficiant to fatiffy for the Defraying of all the proprietors Charge as a bove voted

alfo Voted and Granted to Benjamin Goodridge three hundred acres of Land to be Laid out after the tenth Day of april next Infuing the Date hereof in the undevided Land Within the townfhip of Lunenburg in one piece Where the faid Goodridge fhall Choufe it. be Laid out by a Committee Choofen to Lay out the fame who fhall figne a plan thereof in order to have the above faid Land recorded in the proprietors book and the proprietors Clerke is hereby ordered and Diricted to record the fame

alfo Voted and Choofe Capt Jofiah Willard Liu^t Edward Hartwell and Ifaac Farnfworth a Committee fully Impowered to Lay out the Land above voted and Granted to the above faid Goodridge . . .

[95] alfo Voted and Granted to Lay out an Equivelent in the Common and undevided Land Within the

town fhip of Lunenburg to fatiffy the feveral owners of the Lotts of Land Where the town ways have been allredy Laid out by the felectmen of Lunenburg a fore faid and accepted and allowed by the faid town. for the Damage they fhall fufftain by fuch ways being Laid through there Land as afore f^d and that Capt Jofiah Willard Live^t Edward Hartwell and En Jonathan Willard be a Committee fully Impowered to Lay out the above faid Land and figne the feveral plans thereof and Return them to the proprietors Clerk who is hereby ordered and Directed to record the fame in the proprietors Book &c
Edward Hartwell moderator

Recorded march the 27th anno Domini 1730.
℗ Edward Hartwell Cler

[96] At the Requeft of a fufficiant number of the Proprietors of the townfhip of Lunenburg in Writing from under there hand &c To the proprietors &c.

[feal] Thefe are In his Majesties Name to Warn you to meete at the Houfe of Capt Jofiah Willard in Lunenburg afore f^d on the fecond tufeday of may next at ELeven of the Clock in the fore noon to the end being meet and duly formed they may then and there if the fee Caufe to order the Meafuring off and Recording in the proprietors book of Records that Quantity or proportion of Land which by the proprietors afore faid hath ben Given or pretented to be voted or given to the Committee appointed by the General Court to bring forward the fettlement and Grant out Lots in the faid town for there Good fervice in that affair or otherwife to Choofe and Impower men for that purpose and Give them fuch Dirictions and Inftructions for there proceeding therein as fhall then be thought Reafonable.

alfo to here the account of Mr Samuell Jones of What the proprietors are Indebted to him and order payment thereof in fuch a way and manner as they fhall think proper

alfo to agree upon and order the Devideing and Laying out of the Common and undevided Land in faid town

that fhall Remain after the former Divifions are Compleated and Choofe and Impower perfons for that porpufe and vote them fuch powers and Dirictions as they fhall think proper.
       Edward Hartwell proprietors Cler

Dated at Lunenburg
April the 23^d 1731.
Recorded april the 7th anno Domini 1732
      pr Edward Hartwell Cler

[97] At a meeting Legally Warned the proprietors of the Common and undevided Lands Within the town of Lunenburg being meet at the houfe of Capt Jofiah Willard Within the town afore faid on the Eleventh of may anno Domini. 1731. &c

1 voted and Choofe Capt Jofiah Willard moderator for the Goverment of faid meeting &c

2 Voted and Granted to the Honer.^{ble} William Tayler Coll. famuell Thaxter Coll Franis Fullam Esqr and Capt John fhiple Eight hundred acres of Land in the fow weft Corner of faid townfhip all in one Intire peace as a Gratuity for there former Good fervice purfuant to a former vote made at Groton march. 16th 1725/6

3 voted and ordered that the proprietors above faid Meafur off the Eight hundred acres of Land in the fouth weft Corner of faid township as above faid and that the faid Eight hundred acres be recorded in the proprietors book of Records

4 voted and Choofe Capt Jofiah Willard Liue^t Edward Hartwell Enfign Jonathan Willard Ephraim pearce James Jewell Ephraim Wetherbee & Ifaac farnsworth a Committee fully Impowered to Lay out the Eight hundred acres as above faid and fign the plan and Deliver the fame to the proprietors Clerke to be recorded

5 voted and Choofe Nathan Heywood furvayer to Lay out the above faid Eight hundred acres of Land

6 voted that the faid meeting be adjourned to the 26 Day of this Inftant may at Eight of the Clock in the forenoon and to meet at the houfe afore faid then and

there to Confider on the following articles and act on the fame if they fee Caufe &c.

may the 26. 1731. the proprietors a fore f^d being meet upon adjournment at the houfe of Capt Jofiah Willard as afore. f^d

then voted Granted and ordered the Eight hundred acres above mentioned be made up one thoufand acres and that m^r Benj^a Whitemore be Intitled to two hundred acres of the faid thoufand and haveing an equel proportion with the other four Gen^t m above mentioned and that ye thoufand acres be Laid out all in one intire peace as above faid and that the tow hundred acres a fore. f^d be granted to the faid m^r Whitemore as a gratuity for his former good fervice perfuant to a former vote made at Groton march the. 16. 1725/6

alfo voted that m^r famuell Jones be paid By this propriety the fum of £22 = 09—0.

alfo voted that one hundred acres of Land adjoyning to the northerly fide of y^e 1000 acres Granted to y^e General Courts Committee be fold to the higheft bider to pay to m^r famuell Jones £22 = 9–0 and the over plus if any there be for the ufe of y^e propriety. — — — —

       Josiah Willard Moderator

Recorded April the 7th anno Domini. 1732
       ℔ Edward Hartwell Cler

[98] At the Requeft of a fuffician number of the Proprietors of the Townfhip of Lunenburg In Wrighting from under there hands &c . . . .

(feal) These are In his Majesties Name to Warn the Proprietors of of Lunenburg In the County of Worcester to Conven at the Houfe of Jofiah Willard Esqr In Lunenburg a fore faid on the fecond thirdsday of November next at Eight of the Clock In the fore noon to the end that being meet and Duly formed they may Elect and Impower fom fit perfon or perfons to purches of Mr Zahariah fitch of Boston two farms Lying and Being in Lunenburg a fore faid one of which belonged to Nathaniel Walker and the other was Granted to Francis adames or of fuch other perfon or perſons as have power to Dispose of the ſame and to take deeds of Releſe or other proper Convayances of ſaid farms to the proprietors a fore ſaid or to ſuch perticuler perſon or perſons as are In the poſſeſſion of ſaid farms or either of them by virtue of any Grants of said proprietors or Record in the proprietors Book &c and to give in Exchange therefor all or any part of the Land Lately Granted by the General Court to the ſaid proprietors for the End a fore ſaid or any other Land belonging to ſaid proprietors what ſo ever and give Execute and paſs ſufficiant Convayances thereof and to Give the perſon or perſons ſo Chooſen ſuch Inſtructions and Direction and power for his proceeding therein as to them ſhall be thought proper

alſo to agree upon and Order the Deviding and Laying out all or any part of the Common Land in Lunenburg a fore ſaid to and amoungſt the proprietors a fore ſaid according to their Respective Intereaſts therein and to Chouſe and Impower proper perſons as a Committee to Divide and Lay out the ſame In ſuch Way and manner as then ſhall be agreed on

 Dated at Lunenburg   ℔ Edward Hartwell
 October the 27ᵗʰ 1731   Proprietors Clerk
 Recorded January the 17ᵗʰ 1731/2
       ℔ Edward Hartwell Clerk

[**99**] At a Meeting Legally Warned the proprietors of Lunenburg in the County of Worceſter being aſsembled at the houſe of Joſiah Willard Esqr in Lunenburg a fore ſaid on the Eleventh Day of november anno Domini 1731

firſt Voted and Chooſe Joſiah Willard Esqr Moderator for the Goverment of ſᵈ meeting &cᵉ alſo Voted and Chooſe L Edward Hartwell and Joſiah Willard Esqr or either of them a Committee fully Impowered to purches of mʳ Zachariah fitch of Boston two farms Lying and being in Lunenburg a fore ſaid the one of which belonged to nathaniel Walker and the other was Granted to frances adames or of ſuch other perſon or perſons as have power to dispose of ſᵈ farms and take deeds of Releſe or other proper Convayances of ſaid farms to the proprietors a fore ſᵈ or to ſuch perticuler perſon or perſons as are In the poſſeſſion of Said farms or either of them by virtue of any Grants of ſaid proprietors or Records in the proprietors Book &ᶜ — — —

alſo Voted and Given In Exchenge three hundred acres of the Common and undevided Land in Lunenburg a fore ſaid unto ſuch perſon or perſons as have power to diſpoſe of the ſaid adames farm as a fore ſaid and the Committee a bove ſaid are hereby Impowered and Diricted and Authorized to make, ſign and Execute in due form of Law a deed of Convayance of the ſaid three hundred acres of Land as a bove ſaid unto ſuch perſon or perſons as have power to Diſpoſe of adames farm as a fore ſaid and take a deed of the ſaid adames farm as a bove ſaid unto the proprietors uſe as before mentioned or to ſuch perticuler perſon or perſons as are in the poſſeſſion of ſaid farm or either of them as a bove ſaid &c . . .

alſo voted that the ſaid meeting be adjourned to the first Munday of December next to meet at the Houſe of Joſiah Willard Esqr in Lunenburgh a fore ſaid at Eight of the Clock in the fore noon.

Lunenburg December the: 6. 1731

the proprietors a fore ſaid being meet upon adjournment at the houſe of Joſiah Willard Willard in Lunenburg Esqr. and further adjourned to to the first munday of January next to meet at the houſe of Joſiah Willard a bove ſaid at Eight of the Clock in the forenoon.

January the third. 1731/2.

the proprietors of a bove ſaid being aſsembled at the houſe of Joſiah Willard a bove ſaid on the 3ᵈ of January 1731/2 and further adjourned to fixth day of January Current to meet at the houſe of Joſiah Willard Esqr at one of the Clock in the afternoon

January the 6ᵗʰ 1731/2

the proprietors being aſsembled at the houſe of Joſiah Willard Esqr in Lunenburg on the 6ᵗʰ day of January anno Domini. 1731/2 Whereas Lᵗ Edward Hartwell &

Jofiah Willard Esqr the Committee Choofen by the proprietors of Lunenburg a fore faid at the opening this meeting November 11th 1731. to purches of mr Zachariah Fitch of Boston two farms Lying and being in Lunenburg a fore faid one of Which belonged to Nathaniel Walker and the other was Granted to francis adames or of fuch other perfon or perfons as have power to dispose of the faid farms and to take deeds of Relefe or other proper Convayances of faid farms to the proprietors a fore faid &c. have purchefed the farm Called Walkers farm a fore faid of Mr Zachariah Fitch for one hundred and two pounds money and have Taken a
Deed

[**100**] Deed thereof to themfelves their Heirs and afsigns for ever as will appear by faid Deed by force of Which they are becom feized of faid tract of Land and Declare they are Willing to accept of that four hundred Acres of Land Lately Granted by the Greate and General Court in on or about the month of October Laft to the proprietors of Lunenburg to enable them to perfect an agreement With the heirs of James Kibby or others Concerning faid farms In Exchange for Walkers farm as a bove faid therefore

Voted that the faid four hundred acres of Land and Every part thereof be and hereby is Granted unto the faid Edward Hartwell and Jofiah Willard their heirs and afsigns for ever in Exchange for the faid farm Called Walkers farm and that Deacon Ephraim Pearce and Mr Benja. Goodridge be a Committee Authorifed and fully Impowered in the name and behalf of the proprietors a fore faid to Execute and pafs a good deed or proper and fuficiant Convayance in Due form of Law of all the the four Hundred Acres of Land Granted to the proprietors of Lunenburg as a fore faid, unto the faid Jofiah Willard Esqr and Edward Hartwell their heirs and afsigns forever
Jofiah Willard Moderator

Recorded January the 18th anno Domini. 1731/2
pr Edward Hartwell Clerk

[101.] At the Requeft of a fufficiant number of the proprietors of the Common and undevided Land Within the townfhip of Lunenburg in Wrighting under there hands

{ feal } Thefe are In his Majesties Name to Warn you to Convene and meet at the Houfe of Capt Jofiah Willard in Lunenburg a fore faid on the fecond Wednefday of april next at ten of the Clock in the forenoon then and there If they fee Caufe to vote and a gree upon the Deviding and Laying out of all or any part of the Common and undevided Land in faid town to and amongst the proprietors thereof accordingly to there feveral Intereft therein in fuch a way and manner as they fhall think Convenant. and to Choufe and Impower proper perfons as a Committee to Lay out the Land accordingly or transact any affair Relaiting thereunto and Give them and the proprietors Clerk fuch Directions and Inftructions Reaiting to the premises as may be thought proper

Dated at Lunenburg march the 19th anno Domini. 1729/30

₱ Edward Hartwell Cler

Recorded april the 18th anno Domini 1730.

₱ Edward Hartwell Cler

[102] At a Meeting Legally Warned the Proprietors of the Common and undevided Land Within the townfhip of Lunenburg being meet at the Houfe of Capt Jofiah Willard in Lunenburg a fore faid on Wednefday the 8 day of april anno Domini. 1730. & they proceeded to bring in there votes for the Choice of a moderator and Jofiah Willard was Choofen &c

Voted that there be Eighty acres of Land Laid out at the Leaft by the Committee that fhall from time to time be appointed and Impowered by the proprietors for that purpose Each proprietor of fuch part of the undevided Land Within the townfhip of Lunenburg as belongs to or arifes upon each Intire houfe Lott and fo Inproportion to him that hath a greater or a Lefs Intereft in such undevided Land and that each proprietor fhall have his proportion of Land arifeing from houfe Lott as afore.f:d Laid out in one Intire piece in any of the undevided Land that he fhall Choufe where the Land Will allow of It and Where there is not Land fufficiant to accomodate and fatiffy fuch proprietor in one place it may be made up in fom other place Where he fhall defier and Choufe it. provided all wayes fuch proprietor make the firft Choice or pitch of fuch Land that he fhall Defier as a fore .f:d and Give the fame in in writing to the Committee to be Impowered to Lay out the fame or to the proprietors Clerke who fhall enter the pitches as they are Given in. notwithftanding if any proprietor be defierous to take up his proportion of Land adjoyning to his Land all redy Laid out may be perfered and Grattifyed If the Committee Judge it Reafonable and Where the Land Defiered to be Laid out be in the Judgement of the Committee not fo good as the beft Lotts regard being had to the fcituation as Weell as to the Quality of the Land in fuch Cafe the Committee fhall have power and are Directed to Lay out to fuch proprietor fo mouch more Land then the proportion a fore faid as fhall make the fame equel in vallue to the Beft in the Judgment of the Committee not Exceeding twenty acres. nevertheLefs no preferance fhall be given to the firft Choice to be give in as a fore faid before the firft day of may next Infuing at ten a Clock in the forenoon and that Where two or more of the proprietors Before the firft Day of May as a fore faid fhall Give in there Refpective pitches or Choice of one and the fame piece of Land preferance fhall be given perticuler proprietor that fhall obtain that priviledge by Lott [103] to be made and drawn by the appointment of the Committee for that purpors.

alfo Voted the Several proprietors in the Common Land to be devided as a fore faid who fhall enterfear in there pitches attend the Committee at the houfe of Cap:t Jofiah Willard in Lunenburg on the fifth Day of may next at one of the Clock in the after noon and forthwith Determine to Whome preferance fhall be given by the Drawing of Lotts for that purpofe as before voted and If any perfons neglect to appeare or draw his Lott as above faid the Committee are to give preferance to fuch as fhall then appear any thing before voted to the Contrary not Withftanding

alfo Voted that Capt Jofiah Willard Liue^t Edward Hartwell En Jonathan Willard Ephraim pearce and James Jewell or any three of them be a Committee With fuch able furvayer as they fhall think fitt to Imploy to Lay out every proprietor his proportion of Land in manner as above Voted and haveing Laid out the fame as a fore faid return a plan of Each Lott to the proprietors Clerk figned by any three of the Committee and the furvayer and that the Clerke be hereby Impowered and Directed to Record the fame in the proprietors Book

Jofiah Willard moderator

Recorded april the 18th 1730.

℔ Edward Hartwell Cler

[**104**] Worcefter fs

To the Proprietors of the Common and undevided Land Within the Townfhip of Lunenburg in the County of Worcefter Greeting.

at the Requeft of a fufficiant Number of the proprietors of the proprietors of the Common and undevided in the townfhip of Lunenburg afore faid.

Thefe are therefore to Notify and Warn you to Convene and meet at the Houfe of Capt Jonathan Hubburd in Lunenburg afore faid on the third mon=day of Auguft next at three of the Clock in the after noon to the end that being duly meet and formed they may then and there act on the feveral perticulers hereafter mentioned viz

first To Repeal a former vote of the faid proprietors viz Voted that one hundred acres of Land adjoyning to the northerly fide of the thoufand acres of Land granted to the General Court Committee to be fold to the highest bider to pay m^r fam^{ll} Jones the fum of £22=09=&c.

alfo to order the Granting or felling of fuch part and proportion of the Common and undevided Land afore faid unto fuch perfon or perfons as fhall appear to By the fame as fhall be fufficiant to pay m.^r Sam.^{ll} Jones the fum of £22 09 00 and to Defray the proprietors Charges and make payment of the money that fhall be found due from the proprietors afore Said and order the puting the fame upon Record or pafsing other titles in fuch way and manner as they may think proper and Conveniant and alfo Choofe and Impower proper perfons for any of the faid purporfses afore faid as they think proper

alfo to agree upon and order the Meafuring of all the Common and undevided Land in faid townfhip and Lay out the fame to Each proprietor their full proportion as is all redy Granted and take an accompt of the Remaining part of the faid Common and undevided Land afore faid and Devide the fame to Each proprietor as they fhall Judge moft proper and Conveniant. Dated at Lunenburg July the 30th 1734

Edward Hartwell proprietors Clerk

Recorded January the the 11th 1734
℔ Edward Hartwell proprietors Clerk

[105] at a Meeting Legally Warned The proprietors of the Common and undevided Land Within the Townfhip of Lunenburg being afsembled at the houfe of Capt Jonathan Hubburd in Lunenburg afore faid on the 19th Day auguft anno Domini. 1734

firft Voted and Choufe Coll^o Jofiah Willard Esqr Moderator for the Goverment of Said Meeting

2^{ly} Reconfidered a former Vote of the proprietors made may the 26th 1731 viz that one hundred acres of Land adjoyning to the Northerly fide of ye thoufand acres Granted to the General Courts Committee be fold to the higheft Bider to pay m^r fam^{ll} Jones the fum of . . £22 09 00 and the over plus if any there be for the ufe of the proprity afore faid

alfo voted that the before Recited vote and all and every the Claufes therein Contained fhall from henceforth be Repealed and Revoked and are hereby Repealed and utterly made void for ever alſo Voted and Granted to Coll⁰ Joſiah Willard his Heirs and aſsigns for ever fifty acres of Land to be Layed out in the Common and undevided Land Within the Townſhip of Lunenburg afore. sᵈ Where he ſhall Chooſe it for and in Conſideration of his paying to mr ſamˡˡ Jones afore. sᵈ the ſum of   £11 = 4 = 6 which is due and owing from the propriety to ſaid Jones

alſo Voted and Granted to Edward Hartwell Esqr his Heirs and aſsigns for ever twenty five acres of Land to be Layed out in Common and undevided Land within the Townſhip of Lunenburg afore ſaid where he ſhall Chooſe it for and in Conſideration of his paying to mr ſamˡˡ Jones afore ſaid the ſum of .   .   .   .   £5 = 12 3. which is due and owing from the ſaid proprietyors to the ſaid ſamˡˡ Jones

alſo Voted and Granted to Livᵗ Jonathan Willard His Heirs and aſsigns forever twenty five acres of Land to be Laid out in the Common and undevided Land Within the townſhip of Lunenburg afore ſaid Where he ſhall Chooſe it for and in Conſideration of his paying to mʳ ſamˡˡ Jone a fore ſaid the ſum of .   .   .   .   £5—12—3 which is due and owing from the proprietors afore ſᵈ to the ſaid ſamˡˡ Jones .   .   .   .

alſo Voted that Joſiah Willard Edward Hartwell Esqr.s Livᵗ Jonathan Willard Enſign Ephraim Wetherbe and Dea Ephraim pearce be a Committee fully Impowered with an able ſurvayer as they ſhall Chooſe to Lay out all the Lands above Granted and Return plans of yᵉ ſame by them ſigned and Delivered to the proprietors Clerk Who is hereby Directed to Record the ſame

alſo voted that all yᵉ Common and undevided Land within the Townſhip of Lunenburg be meaſured and Layed out to Each proprietor his full proportion as is all redy Granted and take an accompt of the Remaining part of the ſaid Common and undevided Land aforeSaid and Devide the Same to Each proprietor as they ſhall Judge moſt proper and conveniant the Charges of the ſurvey to be paid by the propriety either in money or Land. alſo voted that Joſiah Willard Edward Hartwell Esqr.s. and Livᵗ Jonathan Willard be a Committee fully Impowered with fuch able furvayer as they fhall Choofe to Lay out and meafure the Land a bove faid and Return the feveral plans thereof to the proprietors Clerk who is hereby Diricted to Record the fame

       Jofiah Willard moderator

 Recorded the 11ᵗʰ Day of January annoque Domini. 1734

     Edward Hartwell Proprietors Clerk

[106] Lunenburg october the 17ᵗʰ 1734

Received of Col! Jofiah Willard the fum of twenty three pounds being in full of what was Due to me from the Committee and the proprietors of the Town afore faid for fervice Done for them In furveying of Land and other wife

      Received ⅌ Samuell Jones

figned In prefence
of Jonathan Hubburg
 David ftearns

Recorded march the 13ᵗʰ 1740.

   ⅌ Edward Hartwell proprietors Clerk

of which twenty three pounds paid to the above faid famuell Jones five pounds fifteen fhillings of which money was paid by Edward Hartwell which entitled him to the the twenty five acres as on the other fide of this Lefe and also five pounds fifteen fhillings paid by Jonathan Willard to Entitle him to the twenty five acres as on the other side the five pounds fifteen fhillings paid by the faid Hartwell and the faid Jonathan Willard to the above named Col? Jofiah Willard which he paid to the above faid famuell Jones together with a Eleven pounds ten fhillings of his own money which makes up the twenty three pounds paid as by the Recept above faid which mʳ Jones would have or he would not Difcharg the proprietors

 Entered and Recorded

   ⅌ Edward Hartwell proprietors Clark

Worcester ſs may the 29. 1772. at the Requeſt of a sufficient number of the proprietors of the Common and undevided Land that belongs to the Proprietors of the Town of Lunenburg to me directed Greeting

theſe are therefore In His majeſties Name to notify and warn you the ſaid Proprietors to Conven and meet at the Houſe of Li:t Phinehas Hutchings in Lunenburg afore ſaid on the fifteenth day of June next at three of the Clock in the after noon then and there being duly meet and formed.

firſt to Chooſe a Committee to Lay out all the Common and undevided Land that belongs to the proprietors afore ſaid agreeable to a Vote of the ſaid Proprietors at a Legal meeting January the eleventh day 1734. as may more fully appear upon Record.

2ly to Chooſe a proprietors Clerk if they ſee Cauſe
    Edward Hartwell Proprietors Clerk

Recorded June the 16th 1772.
    by Edward Hartwell proprietors Clerk

[**107**] at a meeting Legally Warned the proprietors of the Common and undevided Land that belongs to the Proprietors of the town of Lunenburg being aſſembled at the Houſe of Liv:t Phinehas Hutchings in Lunenburg afore ſaid on the fifteenth day June A: D. 1772

firſt voted and Chooſe Phillip Goodridge moderator for the goverment of ſaid meeting.

2ly voted that all the Common and undevided Land that belongs to the proprietors afore ſaid be meaſured and Laid out to each proprietor his full proportion as is all redy granted and alſo take an account of the remainder part of the Common and undevided Land afore ſaid and devide the ſame to each proprietor in ſuch way and manner as the Committee that ſhall be appointed to meaſur and devide the ſaid Common ſhall Judge moſt proper and Convenant. and alſo that the Charge of the ſurvaying and Laying out the ſaid Common ſhall be paid by the ſaid proprietors either in money or Land and alſo that any three of the Committee that ſhall hereafter be

Choosen to do the service afore said with such able surνayer as they shall Choose be fully Impowered to measur and Lay out the Land afore said and return the several plans thereof to the proprietors Clerk who is directed to record the same

3ly voted Edward Hartwell Benjamin Goodridge Esqrs Phillip Goodridge Eleazer Houghton Paul wetherbee Charls white John White John Hill Nathan Heywood Ephraim Pearce David Goodridge and Ephraim Wetherbee be a Committee fully Impowered with such able survayer as they shall Choose to do the a bove said service

4ly voted and Choose Joseph Hartwell Proprietors Clerk

Phillip Goodridge moderator

Recorded June the 16: 1772.

pr. Edward Hartwell proprietors Clerk

at a Legal meeting of the proprietors of the Town of Lunenburg assembled at the House of Col!. Abijah stearnes in Lunenburg march the ninth day anno domini. 1779. to act on the following articles

first voted and Chose Liut. Phillip Goodridge moderator to Govern said meeting

2ly voted to dismiss the old Committee formerly Chosen to Lay out the Common and undevided Land within the Bounds of the Township origanally Granted to the proprietors of Lunenburg.

3ly voted to Chuse seven men to be a Committee to a Certain and Lay out all the Common and undevided Lands within the Bounds of the Township origanally Granted to the origanal proprietors of said Lunenburg.

4ly Voted and Mesrs. Phillip Goodridge Aaron Willard Charls White Benjamin Redington Benjamin Goodridge Ephraim Wetherbee and Eleazer Houghton Jur to be a Committee for to perform the service afore said

5ly voted that the Committee afore said be paid for their said service either in money or Land as the proprietors shall Chuse

6ly voted that any three of the Committee afore said with such able survayer as they shall Chuse shall be fully

Impowered to Lay out the Lands and do the Bufinefs afore faid
                    Phillip Goodridge moderator
Recorded march the 15th day anno Domini. 1779
                    Edward Hartwell proprietors Clerk

[108] Worcefter fs.
at the Requeft of a fufficant Number of the proprietors of the Common and undevided Land that belongs to the proprietors of the Town of Lunenburg to me directed in writing under their hands Requefting that I would warn a proprietors meeting as foon as may be that all the Common Land belonging to the faid proprietors may be meafured and Laid out and proceeded with agreeable to votes of the faid proprietors at a Legal meeting January the Eleventh 1734. and alfo at a meeting of the faid proprietors June the 15th 1772. and whereas fome of the perfons Choofen to do the above faid fervice at the faid meeting are now Dead and others unable to do the afore faid fervice and that the fervice may be done and performed in all perticulars as fet forth and voted at both the above faid meetings the Requeft is that an addition be made to the former Committees or that the former or that the former Committees be dismist and a new Committee Choofen to do the fervice afore faid as foon as may be.

{ feal } Thefe are therefore in the Name of the Government and People of the Mafsachusets Bay to notify and warn you the above faid proprietors to meet at the Houfe of Col.º Abijah ftearnes in faid Lunenburg on the fecond tuesday of march next at two of the Clock in the after noon then and there being duly meet and formed to act on the perticuler articals hereafter mentioned

firft to Choufe a moderator for the Government of faid meeting

2ly to make an addition to the former Committee or difmifs the former Committee and Chufe a new Committee to do the above faid fervice as has been all Ready voted at the above faid meetings

3ly and the Committee to be paid for their service as voted at the afore said meeting either in money or Land.

4ly that any three of the said Committee with such able survayer as they shall Chouse be fully impowered to do the said service

Given under my hand and seal at Lunenburg this 11th day of february 1779
                    Edward Hartwell proprietors Clerk

Recorded March the 15th anno Domini. 1779
                    Edward Hartwell proprietors Clerk

at the Requeft of a sufficiant number of the proprietors of the Common Land that belongs to the proprietors of the Town of Lunenburg to me directed in writing under their hands Requefting that I would warn a proprietors meetting as soon as may be to see if the proprietors will act on the articulers hereafter mentioned.

{ seal } These are therefore in the name of the ftate of the maſſachuſets Bay to notify and warn you the said proprietors to meet at the Houſe of Col? Abijah ftearnes in said Lunenburg on monday the tenth day may next at four of the Clock in the afternoon then and there being duly meet and formed to act on the articales hereafter mentioned

1 to Chuſe a Treasurer

ly2 Chuſe a Committee to make inquirey into the trespasses don on the said proprietors Common Land and to give the said Committee such Inftructions as shall be thought proper

Given under my hand and seal at Lunenburg this 24 day of April 1779
                    Edward Hartwell proprietors Clark

Recorded July the 6th 1780
                    Edward Hartwell proprietors Clark

[**109**] at a meeting Legally Warned the proprietors of the Common Land that belongs to the proprietors of the town of Lunenburg being aſsembled at the Houſe of

Col? Abijah ſtearnes in ſaid Lunenburg on the 10th day of may. 1779 being duly meet and formed

1 voted and Chouſe Livet Phillip Goodridge moderator for the Government of ſaid meeting it was moved to Chouſe a treaſurer and paſed in the negative

2ly voted to Chuſe a Committee of three to proſecute all treſpaſses done on the proprietors Common Land a fore ſaid Namely Benjamin Redington Col? Aaron Willard and Benjamin Goodridge alſo voted that the ſaid Committee have full power to ſettle with ſuch treſpaſſers as are willing to pay ſo much as in the Judgment of the ſaid Committee is a full Conſideration for their treſpaſs and all that Refuſe ſo to ſettle with the ſaid Committee the ſaid Committee is hereby fully Impowered to proſecute all ſuch treſpaſſers according to the Rules of Law

Recorded July the 6th 1780

Edward Hartwell proprietors Clerk

Worceſter ſs

[ſeal]

At the Requeſt of a Sufficient Number of the Proprietors of the Town of Lunenburg to me Directed under their hands in writing Deſireing I would give my Warrent for Calling a proprietors meeting to act on the articles hereafter mentioned Theſe are therefore in the Name of the goverment and People of the State of the Maſsachuſetts Bay to Notifie & warn you the said proprietors to meet at the Dwelling Houſe of Mr Philip goodridge in said Lunenburg inholder on the Twelveth Day of April next at Two of the Clock in the afternoon then and there being met and duly formed to act on the Several articles hereafter mentioned

1ft to chuſe a moderator to govern said meeting

2Ly To see if the proprietors will sell so much of their Land as will pay the Debts Due from ſaid Proprietors

3ly To Chuſe a Treaſurer and Receive accompts that are Due to Perſons that have Done Service for Said Proprietors

4ly To See if the Proprietors will chuſe a Committe to Settle accomps with thoſe that have done Service or Shall Do Service for Said Proprietors and give orders on the Treaſurer for the payment of the Same.

5ly   To chufe a committe to Lay out So much of the Common Land as to make up what is wanting in the Minifterial Lott and School Lott

6ly   To See if the Proprietors will chufe a Committe to Sell the Remainder of the said Common and undevided Lands or make Devifions of the Same as Soon as the Quantity of Said Lands are known or Relative thereto as they Shall think fit

Given under my hand and Seal this Twenty Seventh Day of march Annoque Domini. 1780

At a Meeting Legally warned the Proprietors of the Common and undevided Land that belongs to the Proprietors of the Town of Lunenburg being met at the houfe of Leut Philip goodridge in Lunenburg on the Twelveth Day of April 1780

1ft   Voted & Chofe Leut Phillip goodridge Moderator to gover said meeting

Voted that the 2d 3d & 4th articles in the above warrent pafs in the Negative

5ly   Voted to Lay out Seventy one acres of Land to make up what is wanting in the School Land in the Southerly part of Fitchburg at a place Called Toffet Swamp and to make up the Minifterial Land if there is any wanting out of the Common Land adjoining to fd Lot

6th article pafed in Negative

Philip goodridge moderator

THE SECOND PART.

[Folio. 1.] WILLIAM CLARK Esqr of Boston——

2ᵈ divifion No 9   Granted to William CLark Esqr fecond Divifion number nine Which is Coupled to Houfe Lott number fourty Eight by the Committee appointed by the greate and General Court Survayed for Mʳ William Clark Esqʳ fecond Divifion number nine the Contents of Which is fourty Seven acres and one Hundred and twelve rod. Begining at a ftake and runing Weft thirty two degrees north fifty three rod to a ftak there making an Angle and runing North thirty Seven degree Eaft one Hundred and fourty two rod to a ftak and Heap of ftones there Making an Angle and runing Eaft thirty two Degrees fouth fifty Eighty rod to a pillar of Stones there making an Angle and runing fouth thirty nine degr Weft one Hundred and fourty two rod to Where it began Survayed by nathan Heywood november the 10ᵗʰ 1729 and approved of by the Committee viz Jofiah Willard Edward Hartwell Jonathan Willard and Nathan Heywood Recorded December the 1ˢᵗ Day in the year of our Lord one thoufand Seven Hundred and thirty
₱ Edward Hartwell Clerk

Lunenburgh November the 8ᵗʰ 1729

3ᵈ Divifion   Laid out to mʳ William Clark Esqʳ Claimer by the Committee appointed four Hundred acres of third Divifion Land arifeing from Houfe Lotts number nineteen number three and number feventy five and part arifeing from his own right. House Lott number fourty Eight. Begining at a black burch tree marked for the north Corner and runing South two Hundred and fourty rod to a pillar of ſtones there making an Angle and runing ſouth five degr Eaſt one Hundred and ſeventy five rod to a black oak tree there making an Angle and runing Weſt five Degrees North three Hundred and twenty rod to a pillar of ſtones there making an Angle and runing North thirty Eight degrees and thirty min- Eaſt four Hundred and ninety rod to where it began Survayed by Nathan Heywood and approved of by the Committee viz Edward Hartwell Joſiah willard and Nathan Heywood. Recorded November the 19th Day in the year of our Lord one thouſand ſeven and thirty.

℔ Edward Hartwell Clerk

Lunenburg January the 15th 1731.

Meadow Lott No 2: ſurvayed for William Clarke Esqr Claimer meadow Lott No 2: in Cattaconnamoug meadows the Contents is fore acres and 49 rod. begining at a Certain pine tree marked for the moſt north Eaſterly Corner and runing ſouth 38 deg Weſt on Land of Eleazer houghton 18 rod to a popler tree there making an Angle and runing ſouth 19 deg Eaſt on meadow Lott No. 1: 28 rod to a ſtake there making an angle and runing Eaſt 9 degrees North on Land of ſaid Houghton 25 rod to a ſtake there making an Angle and runing North 39 degrees Weſt on meadow Lotts 44 rod to Where it began ſurvayed by Nathan Heywood and approved of by the Committe viz Joſiah Willard Edward Hartwell Jona Willard and Nathan heywood this meadow Lott belongs to houſe Lott No 17 Recorded May the 17th anno Domin 1731.

Edw Hartwell Clark

[2] Lunenburgh April ye 18th 1729 — — — —

3d Diviſion Laid out by the Committee appointed fifty one ares and a half of third diviſion Land to Mr William Clark Esqr ariſeing from Houſe Lott fourty Eight — — begining at a ſtake and heap of ſtones and runing Weſt eleven degrees North one Hundred and thirty rod on a ſecond Diviſion beLonging to the afore ſaid Clark to a pillar of ſtones there making an Angle and runing fouth ninety feven rod to apillar of ftones there making an Angle and runing Eaft fix degrees north feventy Eight rod to a fmall maple tree there making an Angle and runing north thirty feven degr Eaft Eighty rod to where It began Survayed by nathan Heywood and approved of by the Committee viz Jofiah Willard Edward Hartwell and Nathan Heywood —— Recorded December the firft Day. in the year of our Lord one thoufand Seven hundred and thirty

℔ Edward Hartwell Clerk

Lunenburgh December the 7th 1730 — — —

3d & 4th Divifion

Laid out by the Committee appointed fix Hundred and fourty acres of third and fourth divifion Land to the Hlb. William Clark Esq.r the Rights a rifeing from Houfe Lotts Number five fixteen and Seventeen Begining at a Cartain White afh tree marked for the Northeaft Corner and runing Weft twelve deg north on Land Laid out to Capt Josiah Williard and Collo Brown three Hundred and twenty rod to the Weft Line of faid town fhip there making an Angle and runing fouth twelve deg Weft on faid line three hundred and twenty rod to a pillar of ftones there making an Angle and runing Eaft twelve deg fouth on Land of Collo Brown three Hundred and twenty rod to a ftak and heap of ftones there making an Angle and runing North twelve deg Eaft on Land of Capt Josiah Willard three Hundred and twenty rod to Where it began furvayed by Nathan Heywood and approved of by the Committee viz Jofiah Willard Edward Hartwell Jonathan Willard and Ephraim Pearce. Recorded December the twenty ninth Day in the year of our Lord one thoufand feven hundred and thirty

℔ Edward Hartwell Clerk

Lunenburg July the 22d 1729.

Laid out by the Committee to the right of William Clark Esqr one acre and one hundred and two rod of third Divifion Land adjoyning to his houfe Lott bounded as it is Difcribed by plan furvayed by Nathan heywood and approved of by the Committee Jofiah Willard Nathan Heywood and Edward Hartwell

Recorded May the 7th annoque Domini. 1731

℘ Edward Hartwell Clerk

[3]   WILLIAM CLARK Esqr
fecond No   Surveyed for William Clark Esqr Claimer
Divifion 79   three fecond Divifions No. 79:: No 80: No: 81

Lunenburgh November the 20th 1729 — — —

furvay^d a fecond divifion No: 79: arifeing from the houfe Lott No: 54. the Contents of Which is 55 acres and a half. begining at a pillar of ftones Erected for the foweaft Corner and runing Eaft 11 degrees fouth 130 rod to a pillar of ftones there making an angle and runing North 17 degrees eaft 65 rod to a pillar of ftones there making an Angle and runing Weft 11 degrees North 141 rod to apillar of ftones there making an Angle and runing South 7 Degrees Weft 65 rod to Where It Began furvay^d By Nathan Heywood and approved of by the Committee viz Jofiah Willard Edward Hartwell Jonathan Willard and Nathan heywood. Recorded May the 7th annoque Domini. 1731

℘ Edward Hartwell Clerk

Lunenburg November the 20th 1729 — — — —
fecond Divifion   furvayed the fecond Divifion No 80 the
No — — 80   Contents of Which is 60 acres belonging to the Minifters Lott No 1 Begining at a pillar of ftones Erected for the fouth Eaft Corner and runing North 17 degrees Eaft 125 rod to a ftake there making an Angle and runing West 11 degrees North 82 rod to a pillar of ftones there making an Angle and runing fouth 12 degrees Weft 123 rod to apillar of ftones there making an Angle and runing Eaft 11 degrees fouth 72 rod to Where it began. furvayed by Nathan Heywood and approved of by the Committee viz Jofiah Willard Nathan Heywood Edward Hartwell and Jonathan Willard . . . .

Recorded May the 7th annoque Domini. 1731.

℘ Edward Hartwell Clerk

Lunenburg November the 20th 1731.

ſeond Diviſion No -- 81

ſurvayed the ſecond Diviſion No 81 Ariſeing from houſe Lott No. 55 the Contents of which is 60 Acres Begining at a pillar of ſtones at the Northeaſt Corner and runing Weſt 11 degrees North 80 rod to a pillar of ſtones there making an angle and runing ſouth 7 degrees Weſt 125 rod to a pillar of ſtones there making an Angle and runing Eaſt 11 degrees ſouth 70 rod to a pillar of ſtones there making an Angle and runing North 12 deg Eaſt 123 rod to Where it began ſurvayed by Nathan Heywood and approved of by the Committee Viz Edward Hartwell Joſiah Willard Nathan Heywood and Jonathan Willard. Recorded may the 7th annoque Dommini. 1731

℔ Edward Hartwell Clerk

[4] Lunenburg January the 15th 1730 $\frac{31}{}$

Meadow Lott. No. 3

Survayed for hlb William Clark Esqr Claimer Meadow Lott. No. 3. in Cattaconamoug meadows Next to the Beaver Dam the Contents of which is. 6 acres.

Begining at Certain pine tree marked for the North Eaſt Corner and runing ſouth 12 degrees Eaſt on upland 16 rod to a ſtake there making an Angle and runing ſouth 2 degrees Eaſt on upland 14 rod to a heap of ſtones there making an Angle and runing Weſt 9 deg ſouth on Land of Eleazer Houghton 39 rod to a ſtake there making an Angle and runing North 25 Degrees Eaſt on a meadow Lott 44 rod to a pillar of ſtones on the upland there making an Angle and runing Eaſt 14 degrs ſouth on the upland 18 rod to Where it began Survayed by Nathan Heywood and approved of by the Committee to Edward Hartwell Joſiah Willard Nathan Heywood and Jonathan Willard

Recorded May the 18th annoque Domini. 1731

℔ Edward Hartwell Clerke

Lunenburg May ye 27th 1731.

Meadow. No 6. Survayed for William Clerke Esqr meadow Lott No: 6. beLow Cattaconamoug pond the Contents of Which is five acres. Begining at a Certain pine tree marked for the south Corner and Runing East 34 Degrees north on George Wheelers meadow Lott 47 rod there making an Angle and runing West 44 degrees north on Common Land 18 rod —— and a half. there making an Angle and Runing West thirty four Degrees south partly on Common but Chiefly on Land of John Heywood 38. rod there making an Angle and Runing south 31 degrees East on Common upland. 18 rod to Where it began survayed by Nathan Heywood and approved of by the Committee viz Josiah Willard Edwd Hartwell Jonathan Willard Nathan Heywood

Recorded September the 3^d Day anno Domini. 1731.—

Edward Hartwell Clerk

Lunenburg May the 29th 1731

Mead .6. in mulpus meadows No Survayed for William Clark Esqr Claimer. meadow Lott Nomber 6 in Lower mulpus meadow the Contents of Which is four acres and three quarters. Begining at a stake and heap of stones Erected for the north West Corner and runing south on the upland 6 rod and a halfe to a stake there making an angle and runing East 6. Degrees south on maddam Willards meadow Lot 85 rod to a stak there making an Angle and runing north 38 Degrees West by the Brook 18 rod to a stake there making an Angle and Runing West one Degree north on meadow Land 74 rod to where it Began. Survayed By Nathan Heywood and approved of by the Committee viz Josiah Willard Edward Hartwell Jonathan Willard and Nathan heywood — — —

Recorded Sept the 3^d anno Domini 1731.

Edward Hartwell Clerk

the other Lands of Mr William Clark Esqr are Recorded at page : 25 : & 26 forwards on

[5]   M̱ᴿ BENJAMIN PRESCOTT of Salem
Lunenburgh November 5th 1730

Laid out by the Committe appointed one hundred and fixty acres for two fourth Divifions to the Reverend Mṛ Benjamin prefcoott Claimer. arifeing from houfe Lotts Number ten and Number twenty three in the fouthwefterly part of faid townfhip begining at the norweft Corner of faid Prefcotts third divifion and runing fouth fifteen degrees weft on faid third Divifion 160 rod there making an angle and runing Eaſt 15 degrees weft on fd 3ᵈ Divifion fixty fix rod there makeing an Angle and runing fouth fifteen degrees Weft on Land Laid out to Major prefcotts right one hundred and fifty one rod there making an Angle and Runing Weſt fifteen degree north on Common Land one hundred and feventeen rod there making an Angle and runing North fifteen degrees Eaſt on Common Land three hundred and aleven rod there making an Angle and runing Eaſt fifteen degrees fouth on Common Land to where it began

furvayed by Nathan Heywood and approved of by the Committee viz Edward Hartwell Jonathan Willard and James Jewell

Recorded December the third Day in the year of our Lord one thoufand feven hundred and thirty
by me Edward Hartwell —— Clerk

Lunenburg June the 17th 1730

fecond
Divifion
No 36

Survayed for the Rnᵈ mṛ Benjamin Prefcott Claimer 2ᵈ Divifion No 36. the Contents of Which is 53 acres Begining at a Stake and heape of ftones Which is the Southerly Corner and runing Weft 31 Degrees 30 minits North 56 rod there making an Angle and runing North 30 Degrees Eaſt on Lott No. 35: 152 rod there making an Angle and runing Eaſt 31. Degrees 30 minits fouth on the North range of Lotts 56 rod there making an Angle and Runing South 30 Degrees Weft on Lott No 37. 152 rod to Where it Began furvayed by Nathan Heywood and approved of By the Committee viz Jofiah Willard Edward Hartwell Jonathan Willard and Nathan Heywood Recorded march yᵉ 7th 1733/4
℔ Edward Hartwell Clerk

[8] COLL? JOSIAH WILLARD
Lunenburg November the 14: 1734

Laid out by the Committee appointed fourty nine acres of Land to Col? Jofiah Willard it being part of the Hundred acres of Land he together with Edward Hartwell and Jonathan Willard had granted by faid proprietors of Lunenburg to Inable them to pay M^r famuell Jones what he demanded of the faid proprietors afore faid and alfo twenty four acres and an half to Jonathan Willard being part of the fame Grant and twenty four acres and an half Contained in this plan Laid to Edward Hartwell for the Damage Done to the third Divifion he bought of Walter beath by the Town ways going throught the fame and it begins at a Certain Black oak tree Marked for the Corner of faid Jonathan Willards two hundred acres and runs fouth 34: deg 30: minites Weft 200 rod to to a white oak tree then it runs Eaft two Degre north two hundred and fixty two rod to a with Hazel then it runs fouth thirty feven Degrees Eaft 54 rod then Weft 12 degree North 133. rod to a maple then north Eight degrees Eaft Eighty fix rod to where it began. furvayed

㊉ Nathan Heywood furvayer

approved of by the Committee   Edward Hartwell
                                       Nathan Heywood

Recorded November the 20th 1734
            Edward Hartwell proprietors Clark

[9]   CAP^T JOSIAH WILLARD of Lunenburgh – ——
Lunenburgh December 10th 1730

3d & 4th Divifion   Laid out by the Committee appointed feven hundred Acres of third and fourth Divifion Land to Capt Jofiah Willard Claimer and alfo fourty acres of Land to make up what is found Wanting in Coll° Taylers and Coll° Thaxters Lotts on flat hill Here is Contained in this Plan one third Divifion to houfe Lott Number fifty five and the fourth Divifions arifes from f^d Houfe Lott fifty five, and Houfe Lotts Eighty five Eighty fix fifty four fourty fix and thirteen and the above f^d

fourty acres maks up the afore ſd ſeven Hundred acres Begining at Certain maple tree marked for the Weſterly Corner and Runing north twenty nine deg Eaſt on Colonal Browns Land one hundred and Eighty nine rod to a pillar of ſtones there making an Angle and runing Eaſt twenty nine deg ſouth on Land of ſd Collº Brown and Land of John Hill three Hundred and ſeventy five rod to a ſtak and heap of ſtones in Wheelers and balls Line there making a Angle and Runing ſouth thirty two Degrees Weſt on ſaid Line ſeventy five rod to a Black Burch tree there making an Angle and runing ſouth twelve deg Weſt on Common Land three Hundred and twenty nine rod to a ſmall beach tree there making an Angle and Runing Weſt twelve Deg North on Common Land one Hundred and ninety rod to Collº Brows Land there making an Angle and Runing north twelve Degrees Eaſt nine rod on ſaid browns Land and three Hundred and twenty rod on Mr Clarks Land to a White aſh tree there making an Angle and Runing Weſt twelve Deg North on ſ^d Clarks Land two Hundred Rod to Where It began ſurvayed by Nathan Heywood and approved of by the Committee Joſiah Willard Edward Hartwell Jonathan Willard and Ephriam Pearce Recorded December the foreteen day in the year of our Lord one thouſand ſeven hundred and thirty

₱ Edward Hartwell Clerk

Lunenburg November ye 20th 1729.

ſeond Divi   ſurvayed for Capt Joſiah Willard ſecond
No — 79   Diviſion Number 79 the Contents of Which is
fifty five acres and a half ariſing from houſe Lott No 54 Begining at a ſtake and heap of ſtones Erected for the ſoweaſt Corner and runing Eaſt 11 deg ſouth 130 rod to a pillar of ſtones there Making an Angle and runing North 17 degrees Eaſt 65 rod to a pillar of ſtones there making an Angle and runing Weſt 11 deg North 141 rod to a pillar of ſtones there making an angle and runing ſouth 7 deg Weſt 65 rod to Where it began ſurvay^d by Nathan heywood and approved of by the Committee viz

Jofiah willard Jonathan willard Nathan heywood and Edwd Hartwell Recorded may the 7th anno Domini. 1731.

℔ Edward Hartwell Clerk

[10]　　　Lunenburg April the 23^d 1729. ——

4th divifion Land

Laid out to Capt Jofiah Willard Claimer by the Committee appointed fixty acres and fifty four rod of fourth divifion Land in Cludeing ten acres of meadow Land that was Laid out before. the Rights arifeing from Houfe Lotts Number fixty two and fifty fix. that is 20 acres out of fixty two. and thirty from fifty fix fituate in the northerly part of the Town. Begining at a pillar of ftones and Runing Weft thirty Eight rod to a pillar of ftones there making an Angle and Runing Weft thirty feven deg North fifty Six Rod to a pillar of Stones there making an Angle and Runing North twenty Six degres Eaft one hundred and twelve rod to a pillar of ftones there making an Angle and Runing Eaft thirty one Deg thirty minits fouth Eighty feven Rod to a pillar of Stones there making an Angle and Runing fouth twenty five deg Weft ninety fix Rod to Where It Began.　.　.　.　.　.　.　.　.

Survayed By Nathan Heywood and alowed by the Committee viz Edward Hartwell Benoni Boynton and Jofhua Hutchens

Recorded December the 29th annoque Domini: 1730.

℔ Edwd Hartwell Clerk

Lunenburgh June the 11th 1730.

4th Divifion

Laid out to Capt Josiah Willard Claimer by the Committee appointed fixty acres of fourth divifion Land to the Right Number fixty two begining at a ftake and heape of ftones which is mr William Clarks foutherly Corner of his fecond Divifion No: 9 and Runing North thirty feven deg Eaft on Mr Clarks Lott one hundred and fifty rod there making an Angle and Runing Eaft thirty one deg thirty minits fouth on the north Town Line fixty four rod there making an Angle and Runing south thirty seven deg West on Common Land one Hundred and fifty rod there making an Angle and Runing West thirty one Degs thirty minits North sixty four rod to Where It began survayed by Nathan Heywood and approved of by the Committee viz Edward Hartwell Jonathan Willard and Josiah Willard — — — —

Recorded December the twenty ninth Day in the year of our Lord one thousand seven Hundred and thirty
₱ Edward Hartwell Clerk

Lunenburg Novem^r 20th 1729

No survayd for cap^t Josiah Willard second Di-
2^d Divi 81 vision No 81 the Contents of which is 60 acres ariseing from house Lott 55 begining at a pillar of stones at the Northeast corner and runing West: 11: deg north 80 rod to a pillar of stones there making an Angle and runing south 7 deg West 125 rod to a pillar of stones there making an Angle and runing East: 11: degrees south 70 rod to a pillar of stones there making an angle and runing north 12 deg East 123 rod to Where it began survayed by Nathan Heywood and approved of by the Committee viz Josiah Willard Edward Hartwell Jonathan Willard and Nathan Heywood

Recorded May the 7th anno Domini. 1731
₱ Ed^{wd} Hartwell Clerk

[11] Lunenburgh August the 22^d 1729 ——

3d & 4th Laid out by the Committee appointed
Division Land three Hundred and one Acre and a half of third and fourth Division Land to Capt Josiah Willard Claimer belonging to the Rights N^o fourty two thirty seven taking out but fourteen acres out of N° 42 of the fourth Division. In Cluding fourty seven acres Laid out to Liv^t Hartwell. Begining at a pillar of stones and Runing East thirty five deg North two Hundred and twenty seven rod to a pillar of stones there making an Angle and runing north thirty five deg West fourty¶ rod to a pillar of stones there making an Angle and Runing East twenty

See page 69¶

degs north thirty feven rod to a pillar of ftones there making an Angle and runing north one hundred and ten rod to a pillar of ftones there making an Angle and Runing Weft one hundred and fixty rod to a pillar of ftones there making an Angle and runing fouth fourty three Deg Weft one hundred and twenty four rod to a pillar of ftones there making an Angle and runing fouth fourteen Degrees Eaft two hundred and twelve rod to Where it began. furvayd by Nathan Heywood and approved of by the Committee viz Jofiah Willard Edward Hartwell Nathan Heywood and Jonathan Willard Recorded December the twenty ninth Day in the year of our Lord one thoufand feven Hundred and thirty<——

℈ Edward Hartwell Clerk

Lunenburgh May the 12th 1729 ——

3d Divifion Land   Laid out by the Committee appointed four Hundred and Eighty Acres of third Divifion Land to Capt Jofiah Willard Claimer. Begining at a pillar of ftones and Runing fouth five Degs Weft two Hundred and fourty rod to a pillar of ftones there making an Angle and Runing Weft five Deg North three Hundred and twenty Rod to a pillar of ftones there making an Angle and Runing North five Degres Eaft two Hundred and fourty rod to a pillar of ftones there making an Angle and Runing Eaft five Degree fouth three Hundred and twenty rod to Where it began the Rights arifeing from Houfe Lotts Number fifty four Eighty five Eighty fix and fourty fix and is fcituate Weft of pearl hill and is Bounded all round on Common Land furvayed by Nathan Heywod and approved of by the Committee viz Jofiah Willard Edward Hartwell Nathan Heywood and Jonathan Willard Recorded December the twenty Ninth Day in the year of our Lord one thoufand feven hundred and thirty

℈ Edward Hartwell Clerk

[12]   Lunenburgh April the 21^t 1729 ————
3^d Divifion   Laid out to Capt Jofiah Willard by the Committee appointed three Hundred and feventy two Acres and fifty nine rod of third Divifion Land

Including ſixty Eight acres of firſt Diviſion Land. the Rights ariſeing from Houſe Lotts Number fifty ſeven ſixty and Seventy ſeven. Begining at a pillar of ſtones and Runing Eaſt thirty Eight deg ſouth one Hundred and ſeventy five Rod to a pillar of ſtones there making an Angle and Runing Eaſt ten Deg north one Hundred rod to a pillar of ſtones there making an Angle and Runing North ſixty five rod to a pillar of ſtones there making an Angle and Runing Weſt fourteen rod to a pillar of ſtones there making an Angle and Runing Weſt thirty five Deg North fifty ſix rod to a pillar of ſtones there making an Angle and Runing north thirty four rod to a pillar of ſtone there making an Angle and Runing Weſt thirty one rod to a pillar of ſtones there making an Angle and Runing north one hundred Ninety three rod to a pillar of ſtones there making an Angle and Runing Weſt two Hundred and fifty three rod to a pillar of ſtones there making an Angle and Runing ſouth one hundred and Eeven Rod to a pillar of ſtones there making an Angle and runing Eaſt nineteen deg North fourty four rod there making an an Angle and runing ſouth twenty Eight Degree Eaſt one Hundred and fourty ſeven rod to Where it Began —— ſurvayd by Nathan Heywood and approved of by the Committee viz Benoni Boynton Isaac Farnsworth and Jonathan Willard. Recorded December the twenty ninth Day in the year of our Lord one thouſand ſeven Hundred and thirty

p^r Edward Hartwell Clerk

Lunenburg February ye 26th 1728

By order of the Committee for the Laying out of the Lost Lotts in Lunenburg which was Laid out in the aditinial grant made to Lancaſter I have Laid out twenty three acres and three quarters for part of the Lott N° 60 which Lyeth north of Dorcheſter farm on the Weſt ſide of the Brook that runs in to the uper end of the ſaid farm it takes in to it part of an old Indain feild it is bounded round by undevided Land it begins at a red oak and runs eaſt thirty four degrees ſouth fifty one rod to a Limewood then north thirty four degrees Eaſt ſeventy five rod to a heep of ſtones then Weſt thirty four degrees north fifty one rod to a heep of ſtones then ſouth thirty four degrees weſt to where it Began Survaye ℔ Jonas Houghton and approved of By the Committee viz Edward Hartwell Jonathan Willard Joſiah Willard and Nathan Heywood

Recorded march the 4th anno Domini. 1731.

℔ Edward Hartwell Clerk

[13]   Lunenburgh May the 14th 1729 ——

Houſe Lott 77   Laid out to Capt Joſiah Willard by the Committee appointed by the proprietors for that porpurs fourty ſeven acres and ſeventeen rod of Land within the Townſhip of Lunenburg for an aquivelent for houſe Lott Number ſeventy ſeven which was taken away by Lancaſter new addinitial Grant. and the ſaid fourty ſeven acres was Laid out in two pieces. the first piece Contains fourty acres and twenty rod of Land and Lyeth ſouth from ſecond Diviſion No 70 and It bounds Westerly on the Land Laid to Benjamin Cory ſouth and Eaſt on Common Land North 02^d No 70 Begining at a pillar of ſtones and Runing ſouth five deg Eaſt one Hundred and ſeven Rod to a pillar of ſtones there making an Angle and runing Eaſt five Deg North ſixty rod to a pillar of ſtones there making an Angle and runing North five deg Weſt one Hundred and ſeven Rod there making an Angle and Runing Weſt five Deg ſouth ſixty rod to Where it began. ſurvayed by nathan Heywood and approved of by the Committee. Joſiah Willard Edward Hartwell Nathan Heywood and Jonathan Willard — — — —

Recorded December ye 31th annoque Domini. 1730 ——

℔ Edward Hartwell Clerk

Lunenburgh June ye 20th 1729 :

the other piece Lyeth partly ſoutheaſterly from uncachawalonk pond and Lyeth in between Lancaſter New Grant and Woborn farm. and is ſix acres and one Hundred fifty ſeven rod. Begining at a black oak tree at the Corner of the pond Called uncachewalunk Where the

Brook Runs out. and Runing ſouth thirty Degrees Eaſt ninty ſix rod Lancaſter Line there making an Angle and Runing Eaſt thirty two Deg north twenty rod there making an Angle and runing Weſt fourty four deg north twenty five rod on Woborn Line to a pillar of ſtones there making an Angle and runing north thirty five deg degr Weſt ſixty ſeven rod to a black oak tree there making an Angle and runing Weſt nine rod to where it began

ſurvayed by Nathan Heywood and approved of by the Committee viz Edward Hartwell Nathan Heywood and Jonathan Willard. Recorded December the thirty firſt day in the year of our Lord one thouſand ſeven hundred and thirty

₱ Edward Hartwell Clerk

[14] Lunenburg December the 26: 1729

ſurvayed for cap^t Joſiah Willard a piece of Land Between Woborn farm and the ends of ſeverel Houſe Lotts for part of his houſe Lott No. 60 which was taken in Lancaſter aditinal Grant. the Contents of the piece of Land here Laid out is twelve acres and three quarters Begining at a White oake tree marked for the Corner of Woborn farm and runing ſouth 16 degrees Eaſt 28 rod to a pine tree there making an Angle and runing Weſt 16 degrees South 40 rod and a half to a pillar of ſtones there making an Angle and runing Weſt 25 Degrees 30 minits South 45 rod there making an Angle and runing Weſt 15 degrees ſouth 60: rod to Woborn Line there making an Angle. and runing Eaſt 28 degrees North 152 rod to Where it Began ſurvayed by Nathan Heywood and approved of By the Committee viz Edward Hartwell Joſiah Willard and Jonathan Willard. Recorded march the 4th anno Domini. 1731

₱ Edward Hartwell Cler

Lunenburg Nov^m ye 29th 1731

4th Diviſion Laid out by the Committee appointed 120 acres of Land in ſaid townſhip to Joſiah Willard Esqr of ſd town for a fourth Diviſion be longing to the right of Walter Beath Right and to make up What is

Wanting in William Wallaſes ſecond Diviſion Cituate and Lying and being near the role ſtone hill Begining at a Certain poplar tree By the River and runing Weſt 27 Degree ſouth on Land of Benjamin Goodridge 140 rod to a pillar of ſtones there making an Angle and runing Weſt 13 degrees ſouth on Land of Collonal fitches 130 rod to a pillar of ſtones there making an Angle and runing north 40 Degrees Eaſt on Common Land :233: rod to the River and from thence runing down and Bounding on the river all the Way to Where it Began Excepting a few rods Where it bounds on m^r Fyffes Land ⅌ Nathan Heywood ſurvayer and approved of by the Committee viz Edward Hartwell Jonathan Willard and Joſiah Willard. Recorded March ye 7th anno Domini 1731/2

⅌ Edward Hartwell Clerk ——

Lunenburg March the 18th 1730/1

2^d Diviſion Survayed for Capt Joſiah Willard 2^d Divi-
No 70 ſion N^o: 70. in the ſoutheaſt part of ſaid townſhip the Contents of Which is .60. acres Begining at a ſtake and heap of ſtones which is the ſoutheaſt Corner of Said Lott and runing north .5. degrees Weſt on Land of 2^d Diviſion 160: rod to a ſtake there making an Angle and runing Weſt 5 degrees ſouth on Pearces Land 60. rod to a ſtake then runing South 5 degrees Eaſt on Land of Benj^a Cory :160: rod to a ſtake there making an Angle and runing Eaſt 5 deg North on Land of ſd Willard .60: rod to Where it began ſurvayed by Nathan Heywood and approved of By the Committee viz Joſiah Willard Edward Hartwell Nathan Heywood and Jonathan Willard

Recorded March the 7th 1731/2

⅌ Ed^{wd} Hartwell Clerk

[15] Lunenburg Apriel the 18th 1729

Laid out by the Committee appointed thirty ſix acres of Land in the ſoutheaſterly part of the townſhip to Capt Joſiah Willard Claimer to make up the meadow

Lott that is found Wanting to Coll? Taylers Right in Lunenburg. Begining a pillar of ftones and Runing fouth two Degrees Eaft 89 rod to a pillar of ftones there making an Angle and Runing Weft 8 Degrees 30 minits fouth 68 rod to a pillar of ftones there making an Angle and runing north 2. Degrees Weft 80 rod to a pillar of ftones there making an Angle and runing Eaft 15 Degrees fouth 70 rod to Where it Began furvayed by Nathan Heywood and approved of By the Committee viz Jofiah Willard Edward Hartwell and Jonathan Willard.

Recorded December the 4th anno. 1733.

₱ Edward Hartwell Clerk

Lunenburg may the 13th 1729.

Liet Jona
Capt Jofiah
Willard

Laid out By the Committee 26 acres and 72 rod of Land Including 15 acres more in this plan Laid out Before that was Laid out to Liv^t Jonathan Willard this twenty fix acres is Laid out to Capt Jofiah Willard Claimer on the Eafterly fide of his hom Lott and is in part to make up what is found wanting In Houfe Lott Number 43. Begining at a pitch pine tree and runing Eaft 9 Degrees fouth 103 rod to a pitch pine tree there making an Angle and runing fouth 9 Degrees Weft 26 rod to a pillar of ftones there making an Angle and runing fouth 90 rod to a pillar of ftones there making an Angle and runing North 31 Degrees weft 56 rod to a pillar of ftones there making an Angle and runing North 38 deg weft 48 rod to a pillar of ftones there making an Angle and runing weft 35 Degrees fouth 38 rod to a pillar of ftones there making an Angle and Runing north 37 degrees weft 14 rod to a pillar of ftones there making an Angle and runing north one Degree Weft 57 rod to Where it began

furvayed by Nathan Heywood. and approved of By the Committee Edward Hartwell Jonathan Willard and Isaac Farnsworth

Recorded January ye 4th 1733/4.

₱ Edward Hartwell Cler

[16]   Lunenburg February the 3ᵈ 1737.

3ᵈ & 4ᵗʰ Divifions   Laid out to Colᵒ Jofiah Willard Claimer 240 acres of Land for a third and fourth divifion arifing from Houfe Lott No 47 and to make up what is found wanting in Houfe Lott No 60: 77: and to make up the fourth divifions arifing from Houfe Lotts No 57: 56: and thirty two fcituat Lying and being in the norwefterly part of faid Townfhip Containing randizvous Lower meaddows Begining at a fmall Beach tree marked for the northeaft Corner of faid Land and runing Weft 32 degrees north on the town Line :278: rod to a ftake then runs fouth 12: degrees Weft on Land belonging to the Heirs of Collᵒ Brown .167. rod to a maple tree then Runs Eaft 32: degrees fouth :222: rod to a hemlock tree on Land belonging to the Hon.ᵃᵇˡᵉ Jofiah Willard of Bofton then runs north 32: degrees Eaft on on Land Laid out to Jonathan Ball :157: rod to where it began ℙ Nathan Heywood Suʳ and approved of By the Committee viz Edward Hartwell Nathan Heywood Jonathan Willard and Jofiah Willard.

Recorded December yᵉ 12ᵗʰ 1738

ℙ Edward Hartwell
Clark

Lunenburg June yᵉ 26ᵗʰ 1729

Laid out by the Committee appointed fix acres and ninty fix rod of Land to Jofiah Willard Claimer to make up what is wanting in Houfe Lott No: 43 Laid out at the old meeting Houfe place. begining at a heap of ftones fet up for Colborns Corner of His five acres by the Highway and runs north twenty Degrees Weft 51 rod there making an Angle and runing Weft one Degree north nine rod to a pillar of ftones there making an Angle and runing fouth three Degrees Weft 65 rod and half to appiller of ftones there making an Angle and runing Eaft 30 Degrees North 34 rod to where it began furvayed by me Nathan Heywood and allowed by the Committee Jofiah Willard Edward Hartwell and Jonathan Willard.

Recorded February the 19ᵗʰ 1749

ℙ Edward Hartwell Proprietors Clerk

Proprietors' Records. 215

[17] Lieu^t Edward Hartwell of Lunenburg
Lunenburg may the 9th 1730.

3^d Divifion Land — Laid out by the Committee appointed ninety acres of third Divifion Land to Lt Edward Hartwell Arifeing from the right No. 73. in the fouth Wefterly part of faid townfhip. begining at a Cartain ftake and heep of ftones Which is the Revd Mr Prefcotts NorEaft Corner of his third Divifions and runing Eaft 15 degrees fouth on Land of Nathan Heywood and Benj^a Prefcott Efqr one hundred and Eighty rod there making an Angle and Runing north 15 d degrees Eaft on Common Land Eighty rod there making an Angle and Runing Weft 15 degrees north on Common Land one hundred and Eighty rod there making an Angle and runing fouth 15 degree on Land of John Brewer Eighty rod to where it began furvayed by Nathan Heywood and approved of by the Committee viz Jofiah Willard Edward Hartwell and Nathan Haywood. Recorded February the twenty third day in the year of our Lord one thoufand feven hundred and thirty. thirty one —— ——

Edward Hartwell Clerk

3^d Divifion — Laid out to Lt Edward Hartwell thirty five acres and a quarter of Land on ye Eafterly fide of the apple tree hill twenty eight acres and 156 rod of which Land is third Divifion arifeing from Houfe Lott No 73. and fix acres and forty four rod is fourth Divifion Land arifing from houfe Lott No Eighty feven the Land above faid was Laid out by the Committee appointed by the proprietors of Lunenburgh and is Bounded Northerly on Common Land Eafterly on the Land of Rev^d mr prefcott foutherly on the Land of fam^{ll} page. Begining at a pillar of ftones made for a Corner and runing north twenty five Degrees Eaft one hundred and feventy rod there making an Angle and runing Weft 23 degrees North twenty five rod there making an angle and runing fouth twenty feven degrs Weft one hundred and Eighty one rod there making an angle and runing Eaft nine degrees fouth fourty one rod to where it began furvayed by Nathan Heywood and approved of by the Committee viz Jofiah Willard Edward Hartwell and Jonathan Willard.

Recorded February the twenty third Day in the year of our Lord one thoufand feven hundred and thirty thirty one

Edward Hartwell Clerk — —

Lunenburgh June the 25th 1729.

Laid out to Edward Hartwell by the Committee appointed by the proprietors for that purpors nine acres and 132 rod of Land arifeing from Houfe Lott No. 87. forth divifion begining at a pillar of ftones and runing Weft 37 deg fouth 66 rod to a pillar of ftones there making an angle and runing fouth 26 Degrees Eaft 19 rod and a half to a pillar of ftones there making an angle and runing Eaft 28 deg North 65 rod to a pillar of ftones there making an Angle and runing North 26 Degrees Weft 30 rod to Where it began furvayed by Nathan Heywood and approved of by the Committee Jofiah Willard Isaac Farnsworth and Edward Hartwell

Recorded fept ye 2d 1732

₱ Edward Hartwell Clerk

[18] Laid out to Edward Hartwell Esqr. Claimer by the Committee appointed ten acres of Land in Lunenburg neer the fouth Line on monoofnock Brook where it Coms out of Dea Jofiah Whites farm. for an equevilent for what the Town way takes and the Damage Done there by in the Houfe Lotts that formerly belonged to mr. Samuell Farnworth Late of Lunenburg Deceft. begining at a ftake on Lunenburg fouth line and runs Eaft 12 degrees fouth 41 rod then north 22 degrees Eaft 40 rod then Runs fouth 22 degrees Eaft 41. rod then fouth 26 degrs weft 40 rod to where it began

Survayed by Nathan Heywood

and approved of by the Committee viz Jonathan Willard Edward Hartwell and Jofiah Willard ————

Recorded November the 29th A. D. 1738

₱ Edward Hartwell Clerk

July ye 14
1783

Proprietors' Records.

Lunenburg December the 2ᵈ 1740.

Harkneſs
2ᵈ No 51
2ᵈ No 52
No. 50 2ᵈ Divi Tarble

Laid out by the Committee appointed ſixty acres of Land in the Common and undevided Land in the Townſhip of Lunenburg neer the ſouthweſt Corner thereof to Edward Hartwell Eſqʳ for an equevilent to make up what is found wanting in Thomas Harkeſſes tow Lotts. on flat hill viz ſecond Diviſion number fifty one and ſecond Diviſion number fifty tow and alſo what is found wanting in Eleazer Tarbells Lott on flat Hill which is ſecond Diviſion fifty: and alſo to make up what is found wanting to Jacob Goulds meadow Lott Number Eleven in mulpus meadows below the falls; and the ſaid ſixty acres is bounded northerly on the Land of the Revre'ᵈ mʳ Benjamin preſcott Eaſterly on the Land Laid out to John and Timothy poole ſoutherly on the Town line and Weſterly on Common Land: and it begins at a black oak tree and runs weſt forty degrees ſouth to a heap of ſtones one hundred rod then weſt fifteen degrees north to a heap of ſtones fifty ſix rod then ſouth to a ſtake one hundred and ſeventeen rod then Eaſt twelve degrees ſouth forty Eight rod to a ſtake and heap of ſtones then north twenty nine degrees Eaſt one hundred and ninety Eight rod to where it began. plan'ᵈ by Nathan Heywood ſurvayer allowed and approved of by the Committee viz Jonathan Willard Hilkiah Boynton and Edward Hartwell

Recorded December the 30ᵗʰ 1740

℞ Edward Hartwell proprietors Clerk

[19]　　EDWARD HARTWELL Eſqʳ

Hills 4ᵗʰ Divi

Laid out by the Committee appointed forty acres of Land to Edward Hartwell Eſqʳ in the ſouth weſterly part of the Townſhip of Lunenburg thirty acres of which Land is to make up what is found wanting in John hills forth Diviſion and ten acres is part of the twenty five acres Granted to the ſaid Edward Hartwell to enable him to pay to mʳ ſamuell Jones what was his part to pay him for what was owing to him the ſaid Jones from the ſaid proprietors. and it

Begins at a mark and runs Weſt fifteen Degrees north ſeventy two rods on the Lands of Mr. Benjamin Preſcott to a marke then Runs ſouth thirteen Deegrees Eaſt one hundred and thirty rod on Common Land to a maple tree then Runs Eaſt twelve Degrees ſouth forty two rods to a mark then runs north one hundred and ſixteen rod to where it began plan'd by Nathan Heywood ſurvayer and approved of By the Committee viz Jonathan Willard Ephraim Pearce and Edward Hartwell.

Recorded march the 16th 1740/1

₱ Edward Hartwell
proprietors Clerk

Lunenburg march the 15th 1744.

Laid out by the Committee appointed twenty ſeven acres within the Townſhip of Lunenburg to Edward Hartwell Eſqr. Claimer for an Equavelent in part of the 27 acres to the Damage done to Thomas Harkneſſ by Reaſon of the Town way goming through both his Lotts where he now Lives at flatt hill the ſaid way taking about three acres of his Good Land beſides other Damages 20 acres of 4 diviſion is part of the 27 acres this plan begins at a ſtake and runs ſouth ten Degrees Weſt Eighty five rod to a ſtake on the Land of David page then runing Eaſt ten Degrees north Eighty rod on the Land of the Heirs of John White thence north twenty five Degrees Eaſt ſixty one rod to a ſtake on the Land of Joſhua Farnworth thence runs weſt nine Degrees north ninety two rod on the Land of the Reverend Mr. Benjamin Preſcott to where it Began. planed by Nathan Heywood ſurvayer and approved of by the Committee viz Jonathan Willard Edward Hartwell

Recorded the 22d Day of april anno. 1745.

₱ Edward Hartwell proprietors Clerk

the twenty acres as mentioned as part of the twenty ſeven acres is forth diviſion ariſing from Houſe Lott No: 87

[20] Lunenburg march ye 8: 1748

Laid out by the Committee appointed feventeen acres of Land in the Eaft part of faid town to Edward Hartwell Efqr. Claimer and is in part to make up what is wanting in fecond Divifion Number thirty five.

it Begins at a heap of ftones in Groton which is the fouth Eaft of it and the north Eaft Corner of m^r James Gordons Land and from thence it runs north feventeen Degrees Eaft by Groton Line fixty rod to Jacob Warrens Land then it runs Weft thirty two Degrees north on faid Warrens Land 40 rod to a heap of ftones then it runs fouth thirty two Degrees Weft twenty rod on faid Warren and thirty nine on Nathaniel Harwoods Land to a heap of ftones then it runs Eaft thirty two Degrees fouth on faid Gordons Land fifty five rod to where it began furvayed by Nathan Heywood allowed and approved of by the Committee and ordered to be Recorded by

Edward Hartwell
Jonathan Willard

Recorded June ye 5th 1750:

℔ Edward Hartwell proprietors Clerk

Lunenburg march the 8. 1748.

Laid out by the Committee appointed five acres of Land to Edward Hartwell Esqr being in full with what has been allready Laid out for an Equevelant to make up what was found wanting in fecond Divifion Number thirty five

it begins at a heap of ftones and runs north thirty degrees Eaft Eighty rod on the Land of Mr James Gordon to a heap of ftones then Weft thirty degrees north ten rod on Land Laid out to Nathaniel Harwood to a heap of ftones then fouth thirty Degrees Weft Eighty rod to a heap of ftones then Eaft thirty Degrees north on Land Laid out to Ephraim Pearce ten rod to where it began furvayed by Nathan Heywood allowed by the Committee viz. Edward Hartwell and Jonathan Willard

Recorded January the 8th 1752

℔ Edward Hartwell proprietors Clerk

[21]   NATHAN HEYWOOD of Lunenburg —— ——
       Lunenburg May the 9th 1730. — —

3d Divifion   Laid out by the Committee appointed one hundred Acres of third Divifion Land to Nathan Heywood arifeing from Houfe Lott number 38 in the fouthwefterly part of the townfhip —— —— Begining at a Certain Chefnut tree marked for the foutheafterly Corner of the reverend m^r prefcootts Land and runing fouth feventeen Degrees Eaft on Common Land Eighty rod to a pillar of ftones there making an angle and Runing Eaft forty deg North on burbeens Land fixty Eight rod there making an Angle and runing weft fifteen deg north on Land of Live^t Edward Hartwell Eighty rod to the Reverend m^r prefcotts northeafterly Corner there making an Angle and and runing fouth fifteen deg Weft on fd prefcotts Line one hundred and fixty rod to where it began

furvayed by Nathan Heywood and approved of by the Committee viz Jofiah Willard Edwd Hartwell and Nathan Heywood

Recorded March the 17th anno domini —— 1730/31
            Edward Hartwell Clerk

Lunenburg March the 18th 1730/31

Laid by the Committee appointed a Certain piece of Land in the foutheafterly part of fd townfhip to Nathan Heywood for an Equevilent for What is Wanting in his 2^d Divifion and the Remainder of the Equivilent for the town Wayes going in fd 2^d Divifion and the Remainder of his 3^d Divifion the Contents of the of the Plan being 12 Acres and a half In Cluding fom part of a pond begining at a pillar of ftones Which is the Wefterly Corner of fd Land and runing Eaft on Capt Goulds Land 50 rod to a pillar of ftones there making an Angle and Runing fouth on Common Land 40 rod to a pillar of ftones there making an Angle and runing Weft on Common Land 50 rod there making an Angle and runing North on Common Land 40 rod to Where it began Survayed by Nathan Heywood and approved of by the Committee viz

Jofiah Willard Edward Hartwell Nathan Heywood and Jonathan Willard. Recorded april ye 20th annoque Domini. 1731

₱ Edward Hartwell Clerk

[23] JOHN FISK

Lunenburg april the 10th 1730.

2^d Divifion No. 3

Survayed for John Fifk fecond Divifion No. 3. Cituate and Lying in the Northeafterly part of faid townfhip. the Contents of Which is 57 ares and a half. . . . .

Begining at a Certain heap of ftones Erected for the most Northerly Corner and runing Eaft 31 degrees 30 minits fouth on the town Line 60 rod to a heap of ftones there making an Angle and runing fouth 33 degrees Weft on 2^d Divifion No. 2 160 rod to a heap of ftones there making an Angle and runing Weft 31 degrees 30 minits North on 2^d Divifions No. 43 & 44 55 rod to a heap of ftones there making an Angle and runing north 31 degr Eaft on the Colledge Land and other Land 160 rod to Where it Began furvayed by nathan Heywood and approved of By the Committee viz Jofiah Willard Jonathan Willard Edward Hartwell and Nathan Heywood Recorded June ye 18th annoque Domini. 1731.

₱ Edward Hartwell Clerk

Laid out to John Fifk by the Committee appointed two acres and three quarters of Land and pond hole. to make up What is found Wanting in his 2^d Divifion fcituate and adjoyning to faid fifks Land all ready Laid out. begining at a Certain Chefnut tree marked for Jonathan Whitneys Northerly Corner of his Houfe Lott. and runing fouth 28 degs Eaft on faid Whitneys Line 33 rod to a pillar of ftones there making an Angle and Runing Eaft 21 deg north on Common Land 6 rod to a pine tree there making an Angle and runing north one Degree Weft on Common Land 21 rod to a White pine tree there making an Angle and runing north 7 deg Eaft 16 rod to a White oak tree tree on Common Land there making an Angle and runing Weft 23 degrees North on Common

Land 2 rod to a poplar tree Which is the Corner of his other Land there making an Angle and runing fouth 39 Degrees 30 minits Weft on Land of faid fifk 22 rod there making an Angle and runing North 23 degrees Weft on Land of faid fifk 7 rod and a half to Where it began furvayed by Nathan Heywood and approved of by the Committee viz Jofiah Willard Jonathan Willard and Edward Hartwell. Recorded June the 18th 1731

℔ Edward Hartwell Clerk

[25] M.ʀ WILLIAM CLARK Esqʳ of Boston . . .
Lunenburg April the 26: 1731 . . . .

fourth Divifion

Laid out by the Committee appointed 165 ares of fourth Divifion Land to William Clark Esqʳ. arifeing from Houfe Lotts number : three and fixty five acres of the right No. one in the Wefterly part of faid townfhip and on the Wefterly fide of fd Clarks other Land. Begining at a Certain pillar of ftones in faid Clarks Line of his formar Divifions which is the Eaft Corner of this Land and the foutheaft Corner of Wheelers and Balls Land and runing fouth 38 degrees Weft on fd Clarks other Land 278. rod to a pillar of ftones there making an Angle and runing Weft 35 Degrees fouth on Common Land 42 rod to a ftake and heape of ftones Which is the Corner of Capᵗ Willards Land there making an Angle and runing north 12 degrees Eaft on fᵈ Willards Land 329 rod to a fmall black burch tree which is Wheelers and Balls fouthweft Corner there making an Angle and runing Eaft 32: degrees fouth on faid Wheelers and Balls Land :154: rod to Where it Began furvayed by Nathan Heywood and approved of by the Committee viz Jofiah Willard Edward Hartwell and Jonathan Willard Recorded December the 25ᵗʰ anno Domini: 1731

℔ Edward Hartwell Cler

Lunenburg July the 22ᵈ 1729.

3ᵈ Divifion Land

Laid out by the Committee appointed to the Right of William Clark one acre and one hundred and two rod of third divifion Land and it begins at a heap of ftones neer the Houfe and runs Weft nine degrees north twenty two rod to a heap of ſtones then Eaſt thirty Degrees north ſix rod to a tree then north one degree Eaſt twenty ſix rod to a heap of ſtones then ſouth twenty ſix degrees Eaſt thirty ſix rod to where it began at the heap of ſtone on the ſouth ſide of the Houſe by the highway ſurvayed by Nathan Heywood and approved of by the Committee Joſiah Willard Nathan Heywood and Edward Hartwell

Recorded November the 18th 1771.

at page 25. to make it more plain then the firſt record was

Edward Hartwell proprietors Clerk

[26] Lunenburg December 23 and 24: 1731. —

4th Diviſion Laid out by the Committee appointed three hundred and ſixty nine acres of fourth Diviſion Land by the Weſterly ſide of the pearl hills In ſaid town ſhip to William Clark Esqr ariſeing from houſe Lotts No: 48 84: 75: and ſixty nine acres of the right No: 19: Begining at a pillar of ſtones which is the moſt Northerly Corner and runing ſouth by ſaid Clarks one Land Which he had of Mr Gardner 95 rod there making an Angle and runing Weſt 23 Degrees ſouth on ſaid Land 210 rod there Making an Angle and Runing ſouth :5: degrees Eaſt on ſd Clarks own Land :175: rod to a black oak tree there making an Angle and Runing ſouth :5: Degree: Weſt on ſaid Clarks Land that he had of Joſiah Willard Esqr :160: rod there making an Angle and runing ſoutheaſt on Land of Jonathan Dows Esqr 46: rod to a pillar of ſtones there making an Angle and Runing Eaſt 40: degrees north 100 rod on Land of Ebenezer Wheeler and ten rod on Common Land to a pillar of ſtones there making an Angle and runing Weſt 32 degree North on Land Laid out to Colon Brown: 26 rod to a White pine tree there making an Angle and runing north 32 Degrees Eaſt on Land of ſaid Brown 224: rod there making an Angle and runing Weſt 31 deg 30 min north on Land of Joſiah Willard of Lunenburg Esqr 70 rod to a pillar of ſtones by a Cheſnut tree there making an Angle and runing north 31: degree 30 min Eaſt on ſaid Willards Land 70 rod to a beach tree there making an Angle and runing Weſt: 31: degree 30 mints north on Land of Hugh ſcot :10: rod there making an Angle and runing north 31 degree 30 minits Eaſt on ſaid ſcots Land 145: rod to the north on ſd town Line :71: rod to Where it began

ſurvayed By Nathan Heywood and approved of By the Committee viz Edward Hartwell

Recorded December the 27th anno Domini: 1731:

₱ Edward Hartwell Cler

[**29**]   EBENEZER WHEELER

Lunenburg May the 12th 1729 — — — —

3d Diviſion to the Right of John Haſtings

Laid out By the Committee appointed one hundred acres of Land for a third Diviſion on the Weſterly ſide of perl hill for Mr Ebenezer Wheeler Claimer the Right ariſeing from houſe Loott No. 63. Begining at a White pine tree and runing Eaſt forty Degrees north one hundred rods to a pillar of ſtones there making an Angle and runing North forty Degrees Weſt one hundred and ſixty rod to a pillar of ſtones there making an Angle and runing Weſt forty Degrees ſouth one hundred rod to a pillar of ſtones there making an Angle and runing ſouth forty Degrees Eaſt one hundred and ſixty rod to Where it began ſurvayed by Nathan Heywood and approved of by the Committee viz Joſiah Willard Edward Hartwell and Nathan Heywood. Recorded may the 9th 1729

₱ Edward Hartwell Cler

[**30**]   Lunenburg December the 8th 1732

3d Diviſion

Then Compleated the third Diviſion of Ebenezer Wheeler and Jonathan Ball Ariſeing from Houſe Lott No. 81: the Contents of Which is one hundred acres ſcituate ſoutheaſterly from apple tree hill Begining at a pillar of ſtones Erected for the moſt ſoutherly Corner and Runing Eaſt 10 degrees north on Common Land 30 rod to a white oak tree thence runing north 10. Degrees Weſt on Land of Ephraim pearce 96 rod to a pine tree thene runing Eaſt ten degrees north on Land of ſaid pearce one hundred rod to a pillar of ſtones thence runing north 10 degrees Weſt on Common Land 80 rod to a ſtake thence runing Weſt ten Degrees ſouth on Common Land. 127. rod to a ſtake thence runing ſouth 9 degees Weſt on Land of ſamuell Page 79 rod to a ſtake thence runing Weſt 9 degrees north on Land of ſaid page 60 rod to a pine tree thence ſouth 9 degrees on Common Land 42 rod to a maple tree by the River thence runing down by the River to Where it began — —

℔ Nathan Heywood ſurvayer

approved of by the Committee viz Edward Hartwell Joſiah Willard and Nathan Heywood

Recorded December yᵉ 18ᵗʰ 1732

℔ Edward Hartwell Clerk

[31] Lunenburg April the 30ᵗʰ 1729

3ᵈ Diviſion Land

Laid out to Ephraim pearce by the Committee appointed to the Right Number Eighty Eight one hundred and twenty acres of third Diviſion Land. Begining at a white oak and Runing Eaſt 11 degrees thirty minits North fifty three rod to a pine tree there making an Angle and Runing Eaſt 43 degrees ſouth 121 rod to an aſh tree there making an Angle and runing ſouth 20 degrees Weſt 109. rod to a pillar of ſtones there making an Angle and Runing Weſt 100. rod to a pillar of ſtones there making an Angle and runing north three Degrees thirty minits Weſt 37 rod rod to a pillar of ſtones there making an Angle and runing Eaſt 3 deg 30 minits north 7 rod to a pillar of ſtones there making an Angle and Runing north 36 deg 30 min Weſt 137 rod to Where it began approved of by the Committee viz Joſiah Willard Iſaac Farnſworth and Joſhua Hutchens

Recorded January the 9ᵗʰ 1732/3. ſurvayed by Nathan Heywood

℔ Edward Hartwell Clerk

Lunenburg November the 17ᵗʰ 1747.

Laid out twenty one acres by the Committee appointed to Deaꞓ: Ephraim pearce Claimer in part to make up what is wanting in fecond Divifion Number twenty three it Lyeth in the Eafterly part of faid Town and between a thirty fix acres Lott of faid pearces and Catoconomoug pond and ftream it begins at a pine tree marked for the moft Wefterly Corner of faid thirty fix acres and runs north forty five Degrees Eaft on faid thirty fix acres Eleven rod to a heap of ftones then it runs north forty Degrees Weft on Land of Mr James Gordon Eighteen rod to a heap of ftones then it runs fouth fixteen Degrees Weft on Land of faid Gordon twenty Eight rod to a pine tree then it runs fouth fifty Eight rod on meadow Land of faid Gordon to the brook by the ridge Hill then it runs by the pond and by the brook till it Comes to the moft foutherly Corner of faid thirty fix acres then it Runs north forty four Degrees Weft on faid thirty fix acres one hundred and twenty rod to where it firft began furvayed by Nathan Heywood and allowed of by the Committee viz Edward Hartwell Nathan Heywood and Jonathan Willard

Recorded February the 14th 1749.

₱ Edward Hartwell proprietors Clerk

[32]   EPHRAIM PEARCE

make up what is wanting 2^d Divifion No. 23

Laid out by the Committee appointed Eight acres of Land in the Eafterly part of Lunenburg to Deacon Ephraim Pearce Claimer it being in part to make up what is wanting in fecond Divifion Number twenty three it begins at a pine tree marked for the moft Eafterly Corner of thirty fix acres Lott all ready belonging to faid Pearce and from thence it runs fouth feventeen Degrees Weft forty four rod Bounding on faid thirty fix acres the Corner being a heap of ftones by Catoconamoug Brook then it runs Down by faid Brook thirty rod till it Comes to Groton Line then it runs north feventeen Degrees Eaft with Groton Line ninety four rod to a fpruce tree then it runs Weft thirty Degrees north on Land now belonging to Mr James Gordon fix rod to an other fpruce tree then it runs fouth thirty Degrees Weft on faid Gordons Land

Eighty rod to where it began furvayed by Nathan Heywood and allowed by the Committee viz Edward Hartwell Nathan Heywood and Jonathan Willard
Recorded february the 14th 1749
℔ Edward Hartwell proprietors Clerk

[33]   WILLIAM WALLIS

Wallis meadow Lott   furvayed for William Wallis his meadow Lott on Cataconamoug the Contents of Which is 13 acres Begining Near where the Brook runs into ye pond and runs by the upland while it comes to a pine tree then runs fouth twenty nine degrees Weft on Land Laid to faid Wallas fixty rod then runs north 43 degrees Weft on faid Wallafes Land 18 rod then runs north 35 Degrees Eaft on faid Wallas 38 rod then Runs as Exhibited by the plan to the Brook and and Down the Brook to Where it began
℔ Nathan Heywood fur.
and approved of by the Committee viz
Jofiah Willard Edward Hartwell
Nathan Heywood & Jonathan Willard
Recorded January the 31^{ft} 1734/5
Edward Hartwell pr^o Clerk

Lunenburg March the 9th 1733/4

Laid out by the Committee appointed feven acres and a half of Land in the foutheafterly part of faid townfhip four acres and a half of which Land was Laid to Edward Hartwell Esqr in part of the Land which he Bought of the proprietors and three acres to Jonathan Whitney to make up what was found wanting in his meadow Lott Begining at a Burch Bufh is which the Corner of Noah Dodges meadow Lott and runing Eeaft ten degree north 25 rod then runing fouth 32 degrees Eaft 24 rod then Eaft 11 degrees fouth. 22. rod then runing by afpruce fwampt till it Comes to Land of William Wallas then runing North 11 degrees Weft on faid Wallases Land 65 rod to Where it Began furvayed By
Nathan Heywood

and approved of by the Committee viz:
Jofiah Willard Jonathan Willard and Edward Hartwell.

Recorded January the 31^{ft} 1734/5

₱ Edward Hartwell Clerk

[35]   Lunenburg october the 26th 1736.

4th Divifion   Laid out by the Committee appointed by the proprietor fifty fix acres of fourth Divifion Land to the Right of John Calf fcituat and Lying on the Weft fide of the River adjoyning to his third Divifion begining at a Certain hem Lock tree marked for the fouthweft Corner of faid third Divifion then runs Eaft 19 deg north on fd 3^d Divifion 143 rod to a ftake then runs fouth 10 deg. Eaft on Eleazer Houghtons Land 51 rod then runs Weft 28 deg: fouth 110 rod to a ftake then runs north 43 degs Weft on Land beLonging to the Heirs of Colonel Fitch 70 rod to Where it began furvayed by Nathan Heywood and approved of by the Committee Edward Hartwell Jonathan Willard and Ephraim pearce

Recorded June the 18th 1737

₱ Edwd Hartwell Clerk

Lunenburg october the 26th 1736.

4th Divifion   Laid out by the Committee appointed 7 acres of fourth Divifion Land to the Right of John Calf Lying on the Weft fide of the River neer Role ftone hill Begining at a fmall White oak tree marked for the Norweft Corner and runs fouth 20 deg Eaft on Land Laid out to Colonel fitch 62 rod then runs Eaft 15 Deg North on Land of faid Calf 16 rod Then runs north 15 Deg^r Weft on land of John Heywood 62. rod then runs Weft 17 degs. fouth on Land Laid to Benjamin Goodridge 21 rod to Where it Began furvayed by Nathan Heywood and approved of by the Committee viz Edwd Hartwell Jonathan Willard and Ephraim pearce.

Recorded June the 17th 1737.

₱^{r} Edwd Hartwell Clerk

Lunenburg october ye 27th 1736

make up what is wanting 1ft & 2^d Divi

Laid out by the Committee appointed 50. acres of Land on the moonofufnock hill to Make up what is wanting In the firft and fecond Divifion of John Calf and to Compleat his fourth Divifion Begining at a Chefnut tree in the town Line Runing Eaft 17 degs and a half North on faid line 80 rod to a heap of ftones then Runs North 17 degrees and a half Weft on Common Land 101. rod to a fmall black oak then Runs Weft 17 degrees and a half fouth on Common Land Eighty rod to a hemlock tree by the Great Brook then Runs fouth .17. degrees and a half Eaft on Common Land to where it Began furvayed by Nathan Heywood and approved of by the Committee viz Edward Hartwell Jonathan Willard and Ephraim pearce

Recorded June the 17th 1737.

₱ Edward Hartwell Clerk

[36] Laid out to Alexander Forfter Claimer fourteen acres of Land in the fouthwefterly part of the Township of Lunenburg in ftead of that which was a Lotted to him which belonged to another man. Begining at a ftake fet up for the fouthweft Corner of faid Land and runs Eaft 12 degrees fouth on the Town Line 51 rods to a pillar of ftones which is the Angle of the Town Line then Runs on faid Town Line 16 rod then runs North 17 deg. Weft. on Land before Laid out to faid Forfter 60 rod to a ftake then runs South 44 deg. Weft. on Land Laid out to Capt Timothy pooll 72. rod to where it began ₱ Nathan Heywood furvayer and approved of by the Committee viz Edward Hartwell Ephraim Pearce and Jonathan Willard.

Recorded September the 27th A. D. 1738.

₱ Edward Hartwell proprietors Clark

[37] Lunenburg June the 10th 1740

Laid out to Mr Timothy Gibfon ten acres of Land in faid Townfhip for an Equevilent to what is wanting in his Houfe Lott and fecond Divifion Lying on the Eaftely fide of the pearl hill adjoyning to his own third Divifion

Begining at a pillar of ſtones Erected for the northeaſt Corner of Said Land and runs Weſt forty three Degrees thirty minuts north twenty ſix rod to a white aſh tree then runs ſouth thirty degrees Weſt on Common Land to a baſs wood tree twenty two rod then runs Weſt twenty nine Degrees ſouth on Common Land ſeventeen rod to a walnut tree then runs ſouth twenty two degrees Weſt on Common Land twenty two rod then runs ſouth Eight Degrees Weſt on Common Land forty one rod to the line of Said third Diviſion then runs north thirty nine Degrees Eaſt which is the line of ſaid third Diviſion ninety three rod to where it began ſurvayed by Nathan Heywood and allowed of by the Committee viz Edward Hartwell and Jonathan Willard

Recorded June the 21ſt 1740.

₱ Edward Hartwell Clerk

[39] JOHN GIBSON
ſeptember the 25th 1747

Laid out by the Committee three acres of Land on the Eaſterly ſide of the pearl Hill to John Gibſon for an a quivelent to the Land taken of of his home place for a town Road and begins a a pillar of ſtones which was Erected for the Northweſt Corner of Mr Timothy Gibſons 112 acres and Runs Eaſt 19. Degrees ſouth Chiefly on ſaid Gibſons Land but partly on Common Land 36 rod to a pillar of ſtones on a Ledge of Rocks then Runs North 17 degrees Eaſt on Common Land till it Comes to Colo Browns Land then Runs Weſt 20 Degrees ſouth 44 rod on ſaid Browns Land to where it began

ſurvayed by Nathan Heywood
allowed of by Jonathan Willard } Comttee
Edward Hartwell

Recorded November the 2d 1747.

₱ Edward Hartwell proprietors Clerk

Lunenburg may the 5th 1750

meadow Lott
ſurvayed for John Gibſon a meadow Lott number four in ſaid town ſcituate and Lying on the northerly ſide of maſhapoag pond. it Contains ſix

acres and fixty rods it begins by the Edge of the pond in Jofhua Goodridges Line and runs north twenty Eight Degrees Weft on faid Goodridges Land thirty one rod and an half to a heap of ftones then it runs Weft 28 Degrees fouth on Land of John Divoll twenty fix rod to an afh ftump and a ftak then it runs fouth fourteen Degrees Eaft partly on Land of faid Divoll and partly on that is not Land nor water but partly both thirty Eight rod to the pond then it runs by the pond thirty fix rod to where it began

    furvayed by Nathan Heywood ordered to be Recorded by the Committee viz Edward Hartwell Jonathan Willard Recorded June ye 5th 1750.

₱ Edward Hartwell proprietors Clerk

[41]   SAMUELL PAGE

            Lunenburg october the 26th 1747.

2^d Divifion   Survayed fecond Divifion Number 61.
No. 61   Arifing from Houfe Lott Number 52.

and is the moft foutherly Lott part of which Mofes Mitchel now poffeffeth and the other part in the poffeffion of Nathaniel Page Containing fixty five acres and twenty rod it begins at a Chefnutt tree marked for the moft foutherly Corner of faid Lott and runs north fixteen Degrees Eaft on Land Left for a highway fixty feven rod to a pillar of ftones then Runs Weft twenty nine d north on fecond Divifion Number 62 one hundred and fixty two rod to a pillar of ftones then it Runs fouth fixteen Degrees Weft on Land of Robert Clark fixty four rod to an old white oak tree bloon up then it runs Eaft thirty Degrees fouth on Land of faid page and Andrew Mitchel one hundred and fixty two rod to where it began. furvayed by Nathan Heywood and approved of in order to be Recorded by the Committee viz Nathan Heywood Edward Hartwell and

    Recorded December the 5th 1747.

                   Edward Hartwell
                       proprietors Clerk

[42]   Samuell Page
         Lunenburg December the 1ft 1747

meadow   furvayed for the Heirs of famuell page
Lott   Late of Lunenburg Deceafed two meadow
Lotts being number one and Number two in the meadow
Called Turkey Hill meadow the Contents of which are
ten acres begining at a Certain white pine bufh by the
Road at the end of the bever Damm which is the moft
foutherly Corner and runs Eaft twenty feven Degrees
north by the faid Bever Dam five rod then it runs north
fix Degrees Eaft on Land of Robert Clark twenty two
rod to a black oak tree then it runs north twenty four
Degrees Weft on Land of William Allexander thirty fix rod
then it runs Weft twenty feven Degrees thirty minites
fouth on Land belonging to the Heirs of Jonas Gilfon
Late of faid Town Deceafed forty three rod to a dead
tree then it runs fouth twelve Degrees thirty minites Weft
on faid Gilfons Land or by up land nine rod to a fump
then it runs fouth twenty three Degrees Weft on upland
twelve rod then it runs fouth twenty Degrees thirty minuts Eaft Eight rod then it runs Eaft twenty fix Degrees
north 12 rod to a white pine ftump then it runs north
thirteen Degrees Eaft fix rod then it runs Eaft thirty one
Degrees north ten rod and an half then Eaft twenty feven
Degrees fouth twelve rod then it runs fouth Eighteen
Degrees thirty minites Eaft Eleven rod then Eaft nine Degrees north twelve rod then fouth nine Degrees Eaft
twelve rod to where it began ℔ Nathan Heywood furvayer allowed of by the Committee viz Nathan Heywood
Edward Hartwell and Jonathan Willard.

Recorded December the 24th 1747
                    ℔ Edward Hartwell
                         proprietors Clerk.

[43]   Capt Jonathan Willard
         Lunenburg November the 30th 1747.

meadow   Survayed for Capt Jonathan Willard mead-
No. 4   ow Lott No: 4 in turkey hill meadow. Containing fix acres and thirty rod Begining at a Certain
white oak tree marked for the fouth Corner and runs
Eaft twenty feven Degrees thirty minuts north on meadow

belonging to the Heirs of Jonas Gilſon Late of Lunenburg Deceaſed thirty ſix rod to a ſtake then runs north twenty four Degrees Weſt on Land of Jacob Gould thirty four rod to a maple tree then it Runs Weſt twenty ſeven degrees thirty minuts ſouth on Common twenty rod and on ſecond Diviſion belonging to the to the Heirs of ſd Gilſon three rod and a half to a Black oak tree marked then it runs ſouth ſix degrees Eaſt on ſaid ſecond Diviſion thirty ſix rod to where it began

℔ Nathan Heywood ſurvayer
and approved of by the Committee viz
Nathan Heywood Edward Hartwell
and Jonathan Willard.
Recorded December yᵉ 25ᵗʰ 1747.

℔ Edward Hartwell
proprietors Clerk

Lunenburg February the 23ᵈ 1750.

Laid out by the Committee appointed to Capt Jonathan Willard Eight acres of Land in ſaid townſhip ſcituate and Lying ſoutherly from appletree hill it being in part for the Damage the Town way doth in going through his home Lotts it begins at a maple tree marked and is the ſouthweſterly Corner of Mr: Gordons Land and runs north nine Degrees Eaſt on ſaid Gordons Land fourty two rod to a pine tree marked thence it runs Weſt nine Degrees north on ſamuell Hunts Land twenty five rod to a Little black oak tree and heap of ſtones then it runs north nine Degrees Eaſt on ſaid Hunts Land. forty ſeven rod to a ſtake and heap of ſtones then it runs Weſt Eight Degrees north on Land of Mr Oliver forty rod to a black oak tree by punch Brook thence it runs down ſaid Brook aboute four rod till it Comes to to the River and thence Down the River to where it began

℔ Nathan Heywood ſurvayer
approved of by the Committee viz Edward Hartwell Nathan Heywood and Jonathan Willard.

in the above ſaid Land there is one acre allowed for the town ways going through the ſame.
Recorded march yᵉ 14ᵗʰ 1750.

℔ Edward Hartwell proprietors Cler

[44] Lunenburg September ye 7th 1748

Laid out by the Committee appointed to Edward Hartwell Esqr and Capt Jonathan Willard sixty one acres and ten rod of Land on the pearl Hill so Called in said Lunenburg to make up what is found wanting in the several Lotts here after mentioned viz House Lott Number one second Division Number fifty Eight second Division Number thirty one and 20 acres which was granted to me by the proprietors to pay M Jones granted to me Edward Hartwell above said.

and also Including a two rod road a Cross the southerly part of said Land It begins at a heap of stones by a black oak tree and runs West thirty two Degrees North on Land Laid out to Colo Brown one hundred and ninty one rod to a heap of stones then runs south thirty two Degrees West Eleven rod on Common Land then runs south forty Degrees East one hundred and sixty one rod on Land Laid out to Ebenezer Wheeler to a heap of stones then runs West forty Degrees south one hundred and four rod on Land Laid out to said Wheeler to a white pine tree then runs southeast forty Eight rod on Land Laid out to Jonathan Wheeler to a heap of stones then runs north forty Degrees East on Land Laid out to Timothy Gibson forty rod to a pillar of stones then runs north twelve Degrees East on said Gibsons Land sixty one rod to a heap of stones then runs East twenty nine Degrees north on said Gibsons Land seventeen rod to a heap of stones then runs North thirty Degrees twenty two rod on said Gibsons Land to a heap of stones then East thirty seven Degrees south on said Gibsons Land twenty six rod to a heap of stones then runs north forty Degrees on said Gibsons Land thirty Eight rod to where it began surveyed by Nathan Heywood and allowed by the Committee and ordered to be recorded. viz

      Josiah Willard ⎫
      Edward Hartwell ⎬ Committee
      Jonathan Willard ⎭

Recorded September 8th 1748.

        ℔ Edward Hartwell Clerk

Lunenburg march the 2ᵈ 1753.

wanting in 2ᵈ Divifion No 44 & 36

Laid out to Capᵗ Jonathan Willard Claimer by the Committee appointed Eighteen acres of Land in faid Lunenburg in part to mak up what is found wanting in fecond Divifion No. forty four and in fecond Divifion Number thirty fix Begining at a heap of ftones on the town Line and runs Eaft twenty Eight Degrees north on faid Town Line one Hundred rod to Deacon Whites Land then north twenty Eight Deegrees Weft thirty rod on faid Whites Land then weft twenty Eight Degrees fouth one Hundred rod on Land Laid out to the Heirs of phillip Goodridge Deceaft then then fouth twenty Eight Degrees Eaft thirty rod on Land belonging to the Heirs of Capᵗ Benjamin Bleaney Deceaft to where it began furvayed by Nathan Heywood and approved of by the Committee viz Edward Hartwell Jonathan Willard

Recorded march the 6ᵗʰ 1753.

℔ Edward Hartwell proprietors Clerk

[44²]   BENJAMIN BELLOWS Juʳ

Lunenburg feptember the 28ᵗʰ 1747

Laid out to Benjamin Bellows Juʳ twelve acres and thirty four rod of Land in Lunenburg at a place Called uper Mulpus meadows Bounded foutherly on two Houfe Lotts of Dea famuell Johnfon feventy four rods Eafterly on Land Laid out to Jofeph page northerly on Mulpus meadows Wefterly on Land Laid out to famuell Jones the above faid Land as it is Butted and bounded is Laid out by the Committee appointed to Benjamin Bellows Juʳ Claimer for an Equivalant in part for what Damage the town way dos in being Laid through His Houfe Lotts N̊ fix and Number forty and ordered to be Recorded to be Recorded by the Committee viz Edward Hartwell and Recorded January the 31ˢᵗ 1749

℔ Edward Hartwell proprietors Clerk

Lunenburg feptember the 28ᵗʰ 1747.

Laid out to Benjamin Bellows Juʳ Claimer three acres and fifty one rod of Land at a place Called mulpus

Bridge Bound foutherly on Land of Jofeph page Eafterly on Land or meadows of Cap.t Jofeph Gould Northerly on meadow of John Hill and meadows of faid Bellows Wefterly on meadow of faid Bellows allowance for a two rod Road in faid Land to go over the faid Bridge this Land was Laid out by the Committee appointed in part for an Equivalent for the Damages the town ways dos in going through faid Bellows Houfe Lotts No: 6: and No: 40: in faid Lunenburg ordered to be Recorded by the Committee viz Jonathan Willard and Edward Hartwell

  Recorded January the 31.ts 1749

    ℔ Edw.d Hartwell proprietors Clerk

[45]   JOSEPH WOOD
    Lunenburg may the 18th 1749

meadow Lott No. 1   furvayed for Jofeph Wood Claimer meadow Lott No: one: in pearl hill meadows fo Called in faid town the Contents of which is five acres and one hundred and forty rod it begins at a Certain pitch pine tree marked for the northweft Corner of faid Lott and runs fouth 22 degrees Weft on the Honourable Jofiah Willards Lott 22 rod to a heap of ftones then it runs Eaft 31: degree and an half fouth on Land of M.r Brown thirty rod to a white oak tree then it runs north ninteen Degrees Eaft on Land of M.r Allin twenty Eight rod to a Drye pine tree then weft 22 degres on Land of faid allin thirty fix rod to where it began by Nathan Heywood furvayer allowed to be Recorded by the Committee viz Jonathan Willard Edward Hartwell and Nathan Heywood

  Recorded may 23.d 1749:

    ℔ Edward Hartwell proprietors Clerk

[46]   M.R JAMES GORDON
    Lunenburg march the 8th 1748

make up what is wanting in 2.d Division No. 53.   Laid out by the Committee appointed thirty acres in faid Town to M.r James Gordon Claimer to make up what is wanting in fecond Divifion No: 43 which he the faid Gordon bought of Jonathan Whitney it begins at the moft foutherly Corner of faid Lott in Groton Line

and runs North feventeen Degrees Eaft bounding on faid Line feventy fix rod then it runs Weft thirty two Degrees North on Land Laid out to Efq.̇ Hartwell fifty five rod then runs fouth thirty two Degrees Weft on Harwoods feventy fix rod then it runs Eaft thirty Degrees fouth on faid Gordons own Land feventy five rod to where it began ℔ Nathan Heywood furvayer approved of and ordered to be Recorded. by the Committee viz. Edward Hartwell Nathan Heywood and
Recorded June the 10th 1749
℔ Edward Hartwell proprietors Clerk

[48]   Cap.̇ᵀ Goodridge
Lunenburg November yᵉ 5ᵗʰ 1730

4th Divifion   Laid out by the Committee appointed Eighty acres of fourth Divifion Land to Benjamin Goodridge arifing from the Right No: 67. in the foutherly part of faid Townfhip Begining at beach tree ftanding in Brews Line and runing fouth 15 degrees Weft on Land of faid Brewer 70 rod there making an angle and runing Eaft 15. degrees fouth on Land of L.̇ᵗ Hartwell 180 rod there making an angle and runing north 15 degrees Eaft on Land of Cap.̇ᵗ Jofiah Willard 72: rod there making an Angle and runing Weft 15. degrees. north on Land of faid Willard 178 rod there making an Angle and runing Weft 13 Degrees 30 minutes fouth two rod to where it began furvayed by Nathan Heywood

and approved of by yᵉ Committee viz Jofiah Willard and Edward Hartwell

Recorded December yᵉ 31.̇ᶠᵗ 1750
℔ Edward Hartwell proprietors Clerk

[50]   Phillip Goodridge
Lunenburg april the 1ᶠᵗ 1751

make up
2d Divifion   Laid out to phillip Goodridge Claimer nine acres of Land in faid Townfhip the Right arifing from Benjamin Goodridge in part to make up what is wanting in his own fecond Divifion it is fcituate and Lying adjoyning to faid Phillip Goodridges Houfe Lott where he now Dwells it begins at a Large white

oak tree marked for the moſt ſoutherly Corner of ſaid Land and runs Eaſt forty three Degrees north on thirſtin ſeventeen rod to a ſtake which is Ritters Corner of His meadow Lott then it runs north twenty nine Degrees Weſt on ſaid Ritters meadow Lott twenty two rod to a heap of ſtones then it runs ſouth one Degree Weſt on the end of the meadow Lotts twenty ſeven rod then it runs Weſt three Degrees north on Land Laid out to Walter Beath thirteen rod then it runs northerly Bounding on ſaid Beath fifty nine rod to a white oak tree then it runs ſouth thirty ſix Degrees Weſt ſix rod and an half on Land of John Fiſk to a pitch pine tree then it runs ſouth ſeven Degrees Weſt on ſaid fiſk twenty one rod to a popler tree then it runs Eaſt twenty two Degrees ſouth on ſaid Fiſk two rod to a white oak tree then it runs ſouth thirty nine rod to a heap of ſtones then it runs Weſt twenty degrees ſouth on Land of ſaid fiſk ſix rod to a heap of ſtones and Cheſnutt ſtump then it runs ſouth twenty Eight Degrees Weſt partly on Land of ſaid Phillip and partly on Land of ſaid thirſtin ſixty three rod to where it Began

₱ Nathan Heywood ſurvayer

allowed by the Committee viz Edward Hartwell and Jonathan Willard

Recorded the 30th day of November. 1751.

₱ Edward Hartwell Clerk

[51]   Lunenburg april ye 1ſt 1751.

Laid out to Phillip Goodridge Claimer one hundred and Eighty three rod of Land in ſaid Town and is ad-joyning to william Alexanders Houſe Lott and is part of the Land which was left for a road the Right ariſing in part to make up what is wanting in Benjamin Good-ridges ſecond Diviſion it begins at the north Corner of ſaid Alexanders Houſe Lott and runs north thirty ſix De-grees Eaſt on Land Laid out the ſame Day to Jacob Gould four rod and an half to a ſtake then runs ſouth twenty ſix degrees Eaſt on Land left for a road forty two rod to a ſtake then it runs ſouth twenty four degrees Eaſt on Land Left for a road twenty rod to a ſtake then it runs fouth thirty fix Degrees Weft two rod and an half to a ftake then it runs north twenty four Degrees Weft partly on Land of Ifaac Fofter and partly on Land of the faid Allexander fixty one rod to where it began

₱ Nathan Heywood furvayer

and approved of by the Committee viz Edward Hartwell and Jonathan Willard

Recorded November ye 30th 1751

₱ Edward Hartwell proprietors Clerk

Lunenburg January the 24th 1755.

Laid out to phillip Goodridge twenty two acres of Land in the northerly part of faid Townfhip being in part to make fatiffaction for a townway that is Laid out in faid Goodridges Land that formerly belonged to Mr Richard Thirstin and part in Lieu of what Leominfter Line takes of from Capt Benja Goodridges Land and purchefted by the faid phillip Goodridge there is to be a road allowed a Crofs faid Land it Begins at a ftake in a meadow Hole Eafterly from the Houfe belonging to the Heirs of Hezekiah Wetherbee and runs north twenty Degrees Eaft Bounding on faid Wetherbee Land thirty one rod to a heap of ftones then it runs Eaft thirty degrees fouth partly on faid Wetherbees Land and partly on the Colledge Land one Hundred and eighty fix rod to a heap of ftones then it runs fouth twenty two Degrees Eaft Eleven rod to Mr Daniel Auftins Corner then it runs Weft twenty three Degrees north on faid Auftins Land one hundred and ninety three rod to where it firft began

furvayed by Nathan Heywood

and allowed of and ordered to be Recorded by Edward Hartwell Jonathan Willard and Nathan Heywood

Recorded February the 17th 1755.

₱ Edward Hartwell proprietors Clerk

[52] EDWARD HARTWELL Efq^r.

Lunenburg November the 21^{ft} 1747

Laid out by the Committee appointed Eighty five acres and an half of Land to Edward Hartwell Efq^r thirty two acres of which Land is for a Equivalent for

Eight acres which ſaid Edward Hartwell bought of Capt Benjamin Goodridge the ſaid Eight acres being part of what was taken off from ſaid Benjamin Goodridges ſecond Diviſion by Lancaſter new Grant and alſo 32 acres in part to ſatiſſy the Damage for the town roads going through Houſe Lotts number Eight number forty and number ſix and alſo 7 acres in part of which Land iſ in part to make up the Damage done to meadow Lott number two in Lower mulpus the town way going through the ſame and alſo 15 acres of fourth diviſion ariſing from Houſe Lott No Eighty ſeven.

and the ſaid Eighty five acres and an half begins at maple tree which is the Corner of Mr Olivers Land and runs Weſt ſeventeen Degrees north one hundred and ninteen rod on ſaid olivers Land to a maple tree then ſouth fifteen Degrees Eaſt on Eliſha ſmiths Land one hundred and thirty Eight rod to a heap of ſtones then making an Angle and runing twenty rod on ſaid ſmiths Land then turning an Angle and runing on uptons Land ſixty rod then making an Angle and Runing on Common Land forty ſix rod to a hemlock tree then runing north ninteen Degrees Eaſt on Common Land fifty three rod to a beach tree then Eaſt five Degrees ſouth fourteen rod to a heap of ſtones then north five Degrees Eaſt on Common Land one hundred rod to where it began.

ſurvayed by Nathan Heywood
and allowed by the Committee viz Edward Hartwell Jonathan Willard. Ephraim Pearce
Recorded ſeptember the 27th 1751
℔ Edward Hartwell Proprietors Clerk

[53] Lunenburg may the 16th 1731.

Laid out to Edward Hartwell by the Committee appointed by the proprietors of the town of Lunenburg for that purpoſe twenty two acres and an half of Land in part for the Damage the town way doth to him by Reaſon of the ſaid way going through his Houſe Lotts where he now Lives in Lunenburg. begining at a ſtake and heap of ſtones and runs north thirty Eight rod on Land

Laid out to Ebenezer Richardson then north thirteen Degrees Weſt Eighteen rod on John Heywoods Land then north three Degrees and an half W on ſaid Heywood Land fourteen rod then north forty Degrees Eaſt twenty five rod on ſaid John Heywoods Land then weſt five Degrees ſouth fifty ſeven rod on Gibſons ſecond Diviſion then ſouth five Degrees Eaſt on Land Laid out to ſaid Richardſon ninty rod then Eaſt thirty nine rod on Common Land to where it began ſurvayed by Nathan Heywood allowed and approved of and ordered to be Recorded by the Committee viz Jonathan Willard Edward Hartwell and
   Recorded march the 6th 1753.
        ℔ Edward Hartwell proprietors Cerk

Lunenburg December the 14th 1756.

Laid out by the Committee appointed five acres and 64. rod to Edward Hartwell Esqr excluſive of the Highway and is in part to make up the Damage done in his Land by Reaſon of the Town road going through the ſame as it Leades to Leominſter by ſaid Lunenburg and it bounds Eaſterly on the Land of the ſaid Edward Hartwell northerly on Land of David Carlile and ſoutherly on Lancaſter Line it begins at a heap of ſtones in Lancaſter Line and runs Eaſt 24. degrees ſouth ſixty 8 rod to a ſtake and heap of ſtones then north five Degrees Weſt thirty two rod to a ſtake and heap of ſtones then Weſt five Degrees north ſixty rod to where it began this plan made by nathan Heywood ſurvayer. alled and ordered to be Recorded. by Committee Edward Hartwell and Jonathan Willard.
   Recorded auguſt the 18th 1757
        ℔ Edward Hartwell proprietors Clerk

[54]   Lunenburg may the 2^d 1766.

ſurvayed for Heirs of Col^o Downes and the Heirs of Capt Joſeph Fitch Claimers three hundred acres of Land in Fitchburg it begins at a white pine tree and runs north twelve degrees Eaſt forty ſix rod to a heap of ſtones thence Weſt fifteen degrees north one hundred and one rod to the river then two hundred and twenty five rod as the river runs to a heap of ftones then weft fifteen degrees fouth one hundred and thirty rod on Mr Olivers Land to his Corner then feventy rod on Common to a heap of ftones then fouth twelve degrees Weft two hundred and twenty rod on Common Land to a heap of ftones then Eaft twelve degrees fouth two hundred and fifty rod Bounding on Fullums Land to the firft mentioned white pine where it began: this furvay or plan Contains the three hundred acres of Land Lying in Fitchburg and is the Land Granted to Mr James Kibbey or his Heirs by the proprietors of Lunenburg for his the faid Kibbeys Farm inCluded in faid Townfhip of Lunenburg furvayed may the fecond Day 1766. by Nathan Heywood furvayer

Recorded the 5th day of may. 1766.

₱ Edward Hartwell proprietors Clerk

[56] July the 14th 1770

4th Divifion then Laid out by the Committee. appointed thirty two acres and an half of Land in Fitchburg in the County of Worcefter to Ifaac Gibfon Claimer being part of a fourth Divifion arifing from houfe Lott Number Eight it beging at a ftak and heap of ftones on the wefterly fide of the town road Leading from faid Gibfons to the meeting Houfe in faid town and is in the line of faid Gibfons own Land and runs from thence Weft one Degree fouth bounding on faid Gibfons Land forty three rod to a ftak and ftones at the Corner of faid Gibfons fence then it runs fouth thirty one Degrees Weft bounding on Land Called the fecretarys Land fixty Eight rod to a heap of ftones then it runs fouth twenty eight degrees Eaft bounding on Land of Zachariah Whitney eighty one rod to a heap of ftones by the a fore faid road thence North feventeen Degrees and an half Eaft bounding on faid Road one hundred and thirty five rod to where it began furvayed by Nathan Heywood and approved of by the Committee viz Edward Hartwell Nathan Heywood and Ephraim Pearce

Recorded Auguft the 29th 1770.

by me Edward Hartwell
proprietors Clerk

Auguſt the 11th 1770.

4th Diviſion then Laid out by the Committee appointed ſeventeen acres and an half of Land in Fitchburg in the County of Worceſter to Jonas Kendall Claimer it being part of a fourth Diviſion in full to make up that diviſion ariſing from Houſe Lott number eight it Begins at a heap of ſtones in the Line between Lunenburg and Leominſter and runs north thirty Degrees Weſt bounding partly on Land of ſaid Kendall and partly on Land of Mr. Wairs one hundred and eighteen rod to a heap of ſtones then it runs Weſt twelve Degrees north bounding on Common Land ſixteen rod to a white aſh tree then it runs Weſt thirty two degrees north on Common Land twenty rod to a maple tree then it runs Weſt twenty eight degrees ſouth on Common Land ten rod to a hemlock tree ſtanding on a Rock then ſouth forty rod to a heap of ſtones by a Large rock bounding on Common Land then it runs Eaſt fourteen degrees ſouth on Common Land ſixty one rod to a Large hemlock tree then it runs ſouth twenty four degrees Eaſt on Common Land ſixty nine rod to a heap of ſtones in the town line then Eaſt thirty Degrees north on ſaid town Line fifteen rod to where it began

ſurvayed by Nathan Heywood and approved of by the Committee viz Edward Hartwell Nathan Haywood and Ephraim Pearce

Recorded auguſt the 29th 1770.

by me Edward Hartwell proprietors Clerk

[57] Lunenburg June the 23d 1758

Houſe Lott No. 23 ſurvayed for John Buſs Claimer Houſe Lott Number twenty three the Contents of which is forty nine acres and ninty eight Rod. and it Bounds Eaſt one hundred and ſixty eight Rod on Houſe Lott Number twenty two which was docter Hales Lott to a heap of ſtones then it Bounds ſouth forty ſeven rod and an half on Land of John Wyman to a heap of ſtones.

then it Bounds Weſt one hundred and ſixty eight rod on Land of William ſnow and Jonathan Page to a heap of ſtones then it Bounds north forty ſeven rod on Land Left for a way to a heap of of ſtone to where it firſt began ſurvayed by ſtephen Hosmer ſurvayer I have Examined this plan and find it to be Correct and true Pr Nathan Heywood ſurvayer

ordered to by Recorded by the Committee.

Edward Hartwell
Nathan Heywood

Recorded Auguſt the 18th 1772.

By me Edward Hartwell proprietors
Clerk

[58]   February the 3^d 1772

make up what is wanting 2^d Diviſion No. 76

Laid out 70 acres of Land in Fitchburg ſome part to make up what is wanting in ſecond Diviſion No. 76 and ſome part of it to to ſatiſfy a Right that Capt Timothy Poole bought of Thomas Tayler and to ſatisfy a Right ſaid Pool bought of Burbeen it begins at a popler tree marked in the ſouth Line of the town and runs Weſt ten degrees north bounding on ſaid town Line 156. rod to a Cheſnutt tree marked then it runs north ten Degrees Eaſt 160. rod Bounding on the Committees farm ſo Called then it runs Eaſt 17 degrees ſouth 20. rod on Common Land to a heap of ſtones then it runs ſouth 15. Degrees Weſt Bounding 22 rod on Cobits Land and Eleven rod on Common Land to a heap of ſtones then it runs 189 rod to where it began Bounding on Common Land approved of by the Committee Edward Hartwell and Nathan Heywood

Recorded may 28. 1773

     pr me Edward Hartwell proprietors Clerk

[59]   December the 30th 1773.

4th Diviſion

Laid out by the Committee appointed one hundred acres of Land in Fitchburg for a fourth Diviſion to Phinehas Fullam Claimer ariſing from Houſe Lott Number forty which Belonged to Jeremiah Allen Eſq^r of Boſton Deceaſed. it Begins at a white pine

Proprietors' Records. 245

tree marked for the fouth weft Corner of it in Weftminfter Line and runs Eaft nine degrees fouth Bounding on Common Land one hundred rod to a maple tree marked then it runs North nine Degrees Eaft Bounding on Common Land on hundred and fixty rod to a Hemlock tree marked then it runs Weft nine degrees north bounding on Common Land one hundred rod to a Chefnut tree marked in Weftminfter Line thence it runs fouth nine Degrees Weft Bounding on faid Weftminfter Line one hundred and fixty rod to to where it began furvayed by Nathan Heywood and approved of by the Committee Edward Hartwell Nathan Heywood and Ephraim Pearce.

Recorded January the 5th 1774. By me
            Edward Hartwell Proprietors Clerk

[60]   Lunenburg may the 19th 1750.

to make up 2d Divi   Laid out to Phillip Goodridge Claimer Eight acres of Land in faid townfhip the rights arifing from Benjamin Goodridge in part to make up what is wanting in his own fecond Divifion it is Cituate and Lyeth adjoyning to faid phillips Houfe Lott where he now Dwells it begins at a Large white oak tree marked for the moft foutherly Corner of faid Land and runs eaft 43 degrees north on Land of Mr Thurftain 17. rod to a ftake in the Edge of the meadow then it runs north 22. degrees Weft on or near the head of the meadow Lotts 49. rod to a ftake then it runs Weft 3 degrees north on Land Laid out to walter Beath 13. rod to a ftake then it runs north Bounding on faid Beath 59 rod to a white oake tree then it runs fouth 36. Degrees Weft on Land of John Fifk 6 rod and an half to a pitch pine tree then it runs fouth 7 degrees Weft on faid Fifk 21 rod to a popler tree then it runs Eaft 22 degrees fouth 2 rod to a white oake tree then it runs fouth 29 rod to a heap of ftones then it runs Weft 20 degrees fouth on Land of faid Fifk 6 rod to a heap of ftones round a Chefnutt ftump then it runs fouth 28 degrees Eaft partly on Land of faid Phillip Goodridge and partly on Land of faid Thirftin 63 rod to where it began pr Nathan Haywood furvayer allowed and ordered to be Recorded by the Committee viz Edward Hartwell Jonathan Willard Nathan Heywood

Recorded march the 16th 1779.

Edward Hartwell Proprietors Clerk

[61] May the 15 1780

Surveyed for the Proprietors of the Town of Lunenburg By the Committe Chofen for that Purpofe Two hundred Forty seven acres of Land in the Town now called Fitchburg and is Bounded as follows viz^{tt} it Begins at a Rock maple Tree at the Northweft corner then Runs Eaft thirteen Degrees North Fifty Rods by Land of Phinehas Hartwell to a Stake and Stones there making an angle and Runs North Twenty Six Degres Eaft Twenty Six Rods to heap of Stones there making an angle and Runs Eaft Twenty three Rods by Land of one Froft to a heap of Stones then Runs South three Degrees Eaft Six Rods & a half to a heap of Stones then Runs Eaft three Degrees North one hundred and Two Rods by S^d Frofts Land to a heap of Stones then Runs North three Degrees weft Twenty three Rods to a heap of Stones then Runs Eaft three Degrees North Seventy Rods by Land of George Kimbal to a heap of Stones then Runs North three Degrees weft Fifty Six Rods to a heap of Stones by S^d Kimballs Land then Runs weft three Degrees South one hundred and Seventy Two Rods to a heap of Stones then Runs North three Degrees weft thirty three Rods by Land of Phinehas Hartwell to a heap of Stones then Runs Eaft three Degrees North one hundred and Seventy three Rods by Land of Thurftain to a heap of Stones then Runs Eaft Ten Degrees North Seventy Seven Rods by Land of one Brown to a heap of Stones then Runs Eaft three Degrees North one hundred Rods by Land of Nicholas Danforth to a heap of Stones then Runs South three Degrees weft Forty three Rods by Land of Macintire to a heap of Stones then Runs weft three Degrees South Fifty Two Rods to aheap of Stones then Runs South Forty three Degrees weft thirty Six Rods to a heap of Stones then

Runs weft Forty three Degrees North Forty Eight Rods by Land of Edward Scott to a Beach Tree then Runs South Forty three Degrees weft one hundred and Twenty Two Rods to a heap of Stones then Runs Eaft Forty three Degrees South Sixty Eight Rods to a heap of Stones then Runs North Forty three Degrees Eaft Twenty three Rods by Land of Edward Scot to a heap of Stones then Runs South Fifteen Degrees Eaft Seventy Six Rods by Land of Eben^r Bridge to a chefnut Tree then Runs weft thirty Seven Degrees North Sixteen Rods to a heap of Stones then Runs weft four Degrees North one hundred and thirty Eight Rods by Land of Perley to a heap of Stones then Runs by Land of one moor one hundred and Sixty three Rods to where it began

 Survayed by Thomas Cowdin Junr and approved of by the Committe Benjamin Goodridge Benjamin Redington and Eleazar Houghton Junr
 Recorded Decemb^r ye 6 1780
Pr Aaron Willard Cleark

November ye 24 1780

 Laid out by the Committe appointed Five acres of Land near Fitchburg meeting houfe for the Proprietors of the Town of Lunenburg and Bounded as follows Viz^{tt} it Begins at a Stake & Stones the Northeaft Corner Runs weft 10° North thirty Eight Rods to a Hazel Bufh by the River then down the River to a Stake and Stones where a creek Runs out of the River Toward the North eaft then Runs North 13° Eaft to where it began thirty four Rods alfo Two Islands in S^d River Containing Two acres and a Quarter the upper Island Laying partly oppofite to the above Peace of Land. & parly below it the other Island Laying Still further Down the River between the upper Island and the mill Dam Surveyed by Aaron Willard and approved of by Lut Phillip Goodridge Benjamin Goodridge and Aaron Willard Committe
 Recorded December 19. 1780
Aaron Willard Proprietors Clerk

[62]   September ye 30 1780

Surveyed for the Proprietors of Town of Lunenburg by the Committe appointed four acres and one hundred Rods of Land Laying by unachualem Pond and is Bounded Southerly on the Town Line by Land Thomas wilder and Northerly by uncachulem Pond, Surveyed by Aaron Willard approved of by the Committe Aaron Willard Benjamin Goodridge and Eleazar Houghton Junr
Recorded Decem^r ye 21 1780

Pr Aaron Willard Proprie^rs Clerk

September ye 30 1780

Surveyed for the Proprietors of the Town of Lunenburg by the Committe appointed one acre and one Hundred and Fifty Seven Rods of Land Laying near unachualem Pond it Begins at a hemlock Stump by Said pond in the Town Line then Runs South thirty nine Degrees Eaſt Seventy three Rods by Land of Thomas Wilder then South forty Two Degrees Eaſt by Land of Benjamin Goodridge Twenty Six Rods to a Stake then Runs Eaſt forty Two Degrees North four Rods & a half to a Stake then Runs weſt forty three Degrees north ninty Eight Rods to the firſt mentioned Corner Surveyed by Aaron Willard and approved of by Benjamin Goodridge Eleazar Houghton Junr and Aaron Willard Committe
Recorded Jany ye 10 1781

p^r Aaron Willard Prop^rs Clerk

Surveyed for the Proprietors of the Town of Lunenburg Twenty Seven acres and a half of Land and Bounded as follows Viz^tt it begins at the Northweſt Corner then Runs South Twenty Eight Degrees Eaſt one hundred and Sixty Rods by Land formerly belonging to Dea^n Joſiah White deceſed then Runs Eaſt Twenty Eight Degrees North Twenty Rods on the Town Line then Runs north Twenty Six Degrees weſt Seventy Six Rods by Lands of Edward Hartwell Eſq^r then Runs weſt to Dorcheſter Farm Line then Runs North Ten Degrees weſt Eighty Eight Rods on Said Dorcheſter Line then Runs Weſt thirty Degrees South by Land of Jacob Stiles Dceſed forty

Seven Rods to where it began Survayed by Nathan Hewood and appoved of by the Committe appointed Aaron Willard Benjamin Goodridge and Eleazar Houghton Junr
Recorded July ye 9 1781

p^r Aaron Willard Proprietors Clerk

November ye 24 1780

then Surveyed by the Committe appointed Six acres of Land near Fitchburg meeting houſe for Col^l Joſiah Willard Claimer to make up what is found wanting in Second Diviſion Number Eleven being five acres and one Quarter of an acre that is found wanting in meadow Lot N° 8 in uper mulpas it begins at a Stake & Stones Twelve Rods weſterly of a heap of Stones by punch Brook So called called Capt Cowdins Corner then Runs weſt Ten Degrees north thirty Rods to a Stake & Stones then South thirteen Degrees weſt thirty four Rods to the River then Runs down the River thirty Rods to a Stake then Runs North thirteen Degrees Eaſt thirty Rods by Land Laid out to   Brown to the firſt mentioned Bound Surveyed by Aaron Willard and approved by Phillip Goodridge Benjamin Goodridge & Aaron Willard Committe

Recorded Jany ye 10 1781

Pr Aaron Willard Prop^{rs} Clerk

[62^2]   October ye 21 1779

Surveyed by the Committe appointed Two hundred and Twlve acres of Land in the Southweſt part of Fitchburg for the Proprietors of the Town of Lunenburg begining at a Stake & Stones the South weſterly Corner in weſtminſter Town Line then Runs Eaſt 10° South 130 Rods by Land Laid out to gen^{ll} Courts Committe to a Stake & Stones then north 10° Eaſt 224 Rods by Downs Land to a Stake & Stones then Eaſt 15° north 70 Rod to a Stake & Stones then North 32° Eaſt 80 Rod to a Maple Tree then weſt thirteen Degrees North Two hundred Twenty Six Rods to a Stake & Stones then South Ten Degrees weſt Eighty Six Rods to a cheſnut Tree in weſtminſter Line then Eáſt Ten Degrees South one Hundred Rods to a hemlock Tree then South Ten Degrees weft one hundred and Sixty Rods to a maple Tree then Runs weft Ten Degrees North North one hundred Rods to a white pine Tree then Runs South Ten Degrees weft on the Town Line ninty Two Rods to the firft mentioned Corner Surveyed by James Boutell and approved by Benjamin Goodridge Benjamin Redington and Eleazar Houghton Junior Committe

Recorded January ye 12 1781

Pr Aaron Willard Proprietors Clerk

June ye 30 1780

then Surveyed by the Committe appointed for the Proprietors of the Town of Lunenburg one hundred and ninty five acres of Land at a place called Rolestone hill and is Bounded as follows viz^{tt} it Begins at a pich pine Tree on the River Bank

[63]   May the 7 1779

then Surveyed by the Committe appointed for the proprietors of the Town of Lunenburg Fifty one acres of Land Lying in the Southwefterly part of Fitchburg and Bounded as follows viz^{tt} South by the county Road Eaft by Lands of Capt Cowdin wilder & Fullam weft by Lands of Goodale Stratton Fullam and Downs North on Land that was Harrifes it begins at a chefnut Stand then Runs Eaft Twenty five Degres South Twenty Rods to white oak Stand then Runs North thirteen Degrees Eaft three hundred and Two Rods heap of Stones then Runs Twelve Degrees North thirty Seven Rods to white oak Stand then Runs South nine Degrees weft Two hundred ninty Eight Rods to where it began Surveyd by James Boutell and approved of by the Committe Benjamin Goodridge Eleazar Houghton Junr and

May the 3^d 1779

then Surveyed by the Committe appointed one hundred and Two acres of Land for the proprietors of Lunenburg Including in S^d Land Seventeen acres and ahalf of Land belonging to Jonas Kendall and the County Road goes through it it Lies on the South Line of Fitchburg it Begins at a white pine Tree in the Town Line. the South weſt Corner then Runs North Twenty one Degrees weſt one hundred Rods to a Red oak then Runs North Eight Degrees weſt forty Eight Rods to Stake & Stones then Runs North forty five Degrees Eaſt by Land of Sam[ll] Downs one hundred and Two Rods to a Stake & Stones then South fourteen Degrees Eaſt fifty Two Rods to a Stake & Stones then Runs South Twenty nine Degrees Eaſt one hundred & Twenty Two Rods to a Stake & Stones on Town Line then Runs by S[d] Town Line weſt Twenty nine Degrees South one hundred and Seventeen Rods to Where it began Surveyed by James Boutell and approved by the Committe Benjamin Goodridge Benjamin Redington and Epheraim Weatherbee Committe

Recorded January 25 1781

pr Aaron Willard Propri[rs] Cleark

Fitchburg may y[e] 29 1779

then Laid out by the Committe appointed Twenty acres of Land in Fitchburg for the Proprietors of Lunenburg and is Bounded as follows Viz[tt] it Begins at a Stake & Stones the Southeaſt corner then Runs weſt fifteen Degrees North ninty Six Rods by Land of william Thurlo to a Stake & Stones then Runs North three Degrees Eaſt Seventy Rods To a Black oak Tree then Runs South Eaſt one hundred and thirty Rods by Land of Capt william Thurlo to where it began there being an allowance for a highway through Said Land Surveyed by Thomas Cowden Jun[r] Surveyor and approved by the Committe Benj[a] Goodridge Benjamin Redington Eleazar Houghton Jun[r] Committe

Recorded February y[e] 6 1781

pr Aaron Willard Propri[ts] Clerk

[64] may y[e] 15 1779

then Laid out by the Committe appointed Forty Six acres of Land in Fitchburg for the Proprietors of Lunenburg and is Bounded as follows Viz[tt] it begins at the

moſt Southely corner then Runs North thirty Eight Degrees Eaſt Fifty Two Rods to a Stake and Stones then Runs North thirty one Degrees Eaſt Sixty Eight Rods to a Small Cheſnut Tree by Land of Isaac Gibson then Runs North Ten Degrees Eaſt by S^d Gibsons Land Forty four Rods to a Stake & Stones then Runs weſt three Degrees South by Land belonging to the Heirs of John Park ninty Six Rods to a Stake and Stones then Runs South Eight Degrees Eaſt by Land of Ebenezar Bridge one hundred and forty Rods to the firſt mentioned corner Surveyed by Thomas Cowdin Junr and approved by Benjamin Redington Benjamin Goodridg and Eleazar Houghton Junr Committe
 Recorded march 2^d 1781
    p^r Aaron Willard Prop^{rs} Cleark

    May ye 29 1779

then Laid out by the Committee appointed for that Purpoſe Six acres and three Quarters of Land in Fitchburg it Begins at the South Eaſt Corner a Stake & Stones a corner of Joſeph Lows Land then Runs weſt fifteen degrees North by Land of S^d Low one hundred and thirty Rods to a Stake & Stones then Runs weſt Forty four Degrees North by S^d Lows Land Twenty five Rods to a Stake and Stones then Runs Eaſt fifteen Degrees South by Land of Nicholas Danforth and Daniel Putnam one hundred and Twenty Eight Rods to a Stake & Stones then Runs Eaſt Twenty Two Degrees South by S^d Putnams Land Twenty Eight Rods to the firſt mentioned corner Surveyed by Thomas Cowdin Junr and approved by Eleazar Houghton Junr Benjamin Goodridge and Benjamin Redington Committe
 Record^d march ye 2^d 1781
    p^r Aaron Willard Prop^{rs} Cleark

[65]   June the 17th 1782.

Then Laid out by the Committee appointed one Hundred & Eighty Acres of Land in Fitchburg on Rolefton hill and all the Common Land Joyning there to and is

Bounded as follows Viz. Beginning at a maple tree the foutheaft Corner of pratts Land Running South 17 Degrees Eaft two Hundred & Sixteen rod on Pratts Land to aheap of Stones Pratts Corner then on orsbourns to a heap of Stones orsborns Corner then Eaft 10½ South 9. rods to a heap of Stones Foxes Souweft Corner then North 39 Degrees Eaft Ninty rods to a heap of Stones on Foxes Land to aheap of Stones Foxes Corner. then North 36 Degrees Eaft one Hundred & twenty Eight rods to the River to ahemlock tree. on Kimbals Land then North 35 Degrees Weft fourteen rod on the River then North 7 Degrees Weft twenty-Eight rods then North 47. Degrees Weft forty-Eight rod to a Elmn. then Weft 5 Degrees South Eighty Eight rods on Kimbals Land to a heap of Stones Kamps Corner then Weft 6 Degrees South Eighty-Six rods on Kamps Land to the River thence bounding on the River fourteen rod. then Eaft ten Degrees North twenty rod to where it began. Surveyed by Abraham Willard and approved by Samuel Johnfon. Benjamin Redington & Benjamin Goodridge Committee
Recorded June ye 4th 1792
Pr Joseph Hartwell proprietors Clark

[66]   MAJ^R JAMES RICHARDSON of Leominfter
This Being a Plan of a Certain Track of Land lying Fitchburg on flat Rock Hill now belonging to Maj^r James Richardson of Leominfter Lies as is Defcribed on the plan. beginning at a mapple tree the Soweft Corner of Said Land Eaft 24 Degrees South 170 rod to aheap of Stones on a Ledge. Moorfes Corner. then North 11 Degrees Eaft 111 rod to a heap of Stones Called Benj^a Frofts corner. then weft 3 Degrees South 102 Rod to the Soweft Corner of Mr Frofts Land there making an angle runing north Six rod there making an angle runing Weft 21 rod on the Highway there making an angle runing South 16 Degrees weft 26 rod ½ there making an angle runing weft 16 Degrees ½ South 50 rod to where it began this above Said plan Contains 67 acres and one Hundred & two rod Excluding the High way Leading to the Meeting Houfe

Survaid by Abraham Willard of Fitchburg Survaier of Land

october ye 31ft 1781   Abraham Willard
the above Plan Excepted and approved of by the Commettee appointed by the Proprietors of Lunenburg
Recorded ye 6th Day of may 1782
₱ Joseph Hartwell Proprietors Clerk

April ye 16th 1782.

then Survayed ten acres & Six rod of Common or undivided Land in the Noreafterly Part of Lunenburg. Bounded Eaft on Jonathan Adams Land Northerly on Colledge Land so Called and Wefterly on Jeremiah Belchers Land and Southerly, part on Auftens Land and part on Minifterial Land and part on Thuftens Land. it Begins at a heep of Stones the South Corner and Runs North 29 Degrees Eaft. 13. rod to a heep of Stones and then Weft 29. Degrees North 146 rod to a heep of Stones and then South 22 Degrees Eaft 15 rod to a heep of Stones and then Straight to the Corner firft mentioned 134 rod. and it is Laid out to Majr James Richardson by the Commettee appointted by the Proprietors
₱ James Boutell Survayer
Recorded ye 6th Day of may 1782.
₱ Joseph Hartwell Proprietors Clerk

April ye 17th 1782.

Then Survayed twenty four acres and Sixty four rod of Land in the Eaft part of Lunenburg it is Common or undivided Land Bounded Northeaft on Nathaniel Harreds Land and Southeaft on John Dunfmores Land and weft on Land unknown & part on Gordens meadow so Called it begins at a heep of Stones and a white oak Stand at the North Corner and Runs Eaft 43 Degrees South 76 rod to a heep of Stones and then Weft 42 Degrees South. 100. rod to a pitch pine tree Blowed Down or fell Down and then it Runs Straight to the Corner firft mentioned and it is Laid out to Majr James Richardson By the Commettee appointed by the Proprietors
₱ James Boutell Survayer
Recorded ye 6th Day of may 1782
₱ Joseph Hartwell Proprietors Clerk

[66²] April yᵉ 17ᵗʰ 1782.

Then Survayed two acres and 120. Rod of Common or undivided Land in the Eaſt part of Lunenburg Bounded weſt on a road and Noreaſt on John Richards Land and Southeaſt on Land unknown who owns it Begins at a heap of Stones. at the South Corner and Runs north one Degree Weſt 78 rod to Cheſtnut tree and then South 22 Degrees Eaſt 32 rod and a half to a heap of Stones and then Straight to the Corner firſt mentioned and it is Laid out for Majʳ James Richardson by the Committee appointed by the Proprietors philip Goodridge Samuel Johnſon

₱ James Boutell Survayer

Recorded the 3ᵈ Day of october 1782

₱ Joseph Hartwell Proprietors Clerk

Lunenburg June yᵉ 4ᵗʰ 1782

then Surveyed for Majʳ James Richardson 22 acres of Common or undivided Land Lying in the Northeaſt Part of Lunenburg by the Committee appointed for that purpoſe and it begins at a heap of Stones and Runs Eaſt 36 Degrees South 68 rod on Mʳ Thuſtins Land to a heep of Stones and then Weſt 18 Degrees North 62 rod on Thomas Harkneſs Land to a Cheſtnut tree and then Weſt 33 Degrees North 43 rod on Gordons Land to a white pine Stand and Stones and then North 22 Degrees Eaſt 65 rod on Leuᵗ Philip Goodridges Land to a heep of tones and then Eaſt 23 Degrees South 43 rod on Land Called Miniſterial Land and then it runs Southweſterly on Said Thuſtins Land Straight to the Corner firſt mentioned

₱ James Boutell Surveyer

Recorded the 3ᵈ Day of october 1782.

₱ Joſeph Hartwell Proprietors Clerk

Ashby November yᵉ 9ᵗʰ 1787

Laid out by the Committee appointed Eight acres and an half of Common Land for Majr. James Richardson Clamer and it lyeth in the South part of Aſhby. Beginning at a Corner of a Stonewall on the Southweſt Side of the road Leading from Fitchburg to ashby and runs northerly by the road two rod to a heep of Stones in the

Line of the Land laid out to Clark & Ball and then South 36 Degrees Weſt fifty-four rod. to a heep of Stones a Corner of Said Clarks and Balls Land. and then South five Degrees Weſt 49. rod on Weatherbees Land to a heep of Stones the Corner between Wetherbee and Fuller and then South two Degrees Eaſt 28 rod to a red-oak tree and then it runs northeaſterly on Land Straight to the Corner firſt mentioned

℔ James Boutell Surveyer

Philip Goodridge ⎫
Samuel Johnſon ⎬ Committee
Benjª Redington ⎭

Recorded yᵉ 10ᵗʰ of December 1793

℔ Joseph Hartwell Proprietors Clark.

[68] Know all men by theſe Preſents that we George Kimball Gent and Jedidiah Bailey Yeoman & Josiah Stearns Gent all of Lunenburg in the County of Worceſter and Common Wealth of Maſsachuſetts a Committee for and in behalf of Said Town have for and in conſideration of the Sum of Seventy three pounds two Shillings to us in hand paid before the enſealing hereof (for the uſe of the Town) by the proprietors of the TownShip of Lunenburg aforesaid have Bargined Sold and by theſe preſents do bergin Sell Convay Releaſe and forever Quitclaim unto them the Said Proprietors their Heirs and aſsigns all the Right title and priviledge that aforeſaid Town of Lunenburg has to Eighty nine acres of Land being the Remaining part of five hundred acres of Land that the Said Proprietors were Directed by the General Court to Lay out for the Support of a School and Miniſter within Said Town

And we the abovesaid George Jedidiah and Josiah for and in behalf of the Town of Lunenburg aforeſaid do Exonerate, acquit and for ever Diſcharge Them the Said Proprietors there Heirs and aſsigns from all and every part and parſel thereof . . . .

In witneſs whereof we have hereunto Set our hands and Seals this Firſt Day of January one thousand Seven

Hundred and Eighty three and in Seventh year of the Independince of America.

in prefence of   George Kimball (S L)
Thomas Harknefs   Jedidiah Bailey (S L)
Jofhua Martin Junr Josiah Stearns (S L)
Recorded the 2^d Day of January 1783
          per. Joseph Hartwell Proprietors Clerk

Know all men by thefe prefents that I James Richardson of Leomifter in the County of Worcefter and Commonwealth of Mafsachufetts Gen^t for and in Confideration of two pounds to me in hand paid by the proprietors of the Townfhip of Lunenburg in the County aforefaid. the Recept where of I do hereby acknowledge have Releafed Remifed and by thefe prefents Do for ever Quitclame unto them the Said proprietors all the Right title and Intereft which I have or may hereafter pretend to have to any of the Common Lands in Said Townfhip by Virtue of a purchafe made of them the faid proprietors at a Vandue may ye Seventh Seventeen Hundred & Eighty one which has not as yet been Surveyed to me by the Committee of Said proprietors and I do hereby fully and abfolutely acquit the Same unto them the Said proprietors forever in witnefs whereof I the Said James Richardfon have hereunto fet my hand and Seal this fourteenth Day of January one thoufand Seven Hundred & ninty four. Signed Sealed & Dilivered

in prefents of us   James Richardfon (S L)
Eleazer Houghton
Benj^a Goodridge
Recorded the 30th day of may 1794
          ℘ Joseph Hartwell Clark

[69]   Lunenburg Sep^t the 16th 1784.

then Laid out by the Proprietors Committee appointed, two acres and a quarter of Common Land lying in the Northeafterly part of Lunenburg Bounded South on Mr Goulds Land Weft on Daniel Chapmans Land. North on Co^{ll} Bellowsfes Land. and Eaft on Lieu^t Goodridges Land. and it begins at a pine Stump which is a

Corner of Said Goulds and Said Chapmans Land, and Runs North 35 Degrees Eaſt 42. rod to a Corner to be made and then North 11 Degrees Weſt 28 rod to a heep of Stones and then Weſt 42 Degrees South 11 rod to a heep of Stones and then South 30 Degrees Eaſt 15 rod to a heep of Stones and then Straight to the Corner firſt mentioned

℔ James Boutell Survayer

Recorded ye 25th of January 1785

℔ Joseph Hartwell Proprietors Clarke

December ye 27th 1794

Serveyed for the proprietors 17 acres and 115 rod of Land. by order of the proprietors Committee— Begining at the Southeaſt corner and runs North 25 Degrees Eaſt one hundred & 26 rod on Land Laid out to Harward then weſt 38 Degrees South one Hundred and Eight rod on Bridges Land and then Eaſt 56 Degrees South 53 rod to where it began

Surveyed by David Kilburn and approved of by the Committee viz. Benj^a Redington Benj^a Goodridge and Benj^a Johnſon

Recorded may ye 28th 1795

℔ Joseph Hartwell proprietors Clark

[70]   Leominſter may the forth 1789

To the Committee apointed by the Proprietors of Lunenburg to Lay out the Common Lands in Lunenburg Gen^t this is to Defire you to give Mr Neth^a Haiftings a deed of a peace of Land Joyning to Eleazer Houghton and Gordon and Kilborn after he has Satiffied you for your troble your Hum^{bl} Ser^t

James Richardſon

agreeable to the a bove the follow plan is by order of the above Said Committee.

Begining at the Southweſt corner and runs 27 Degrees north three rod & half then Eaſt 9 Degrees north Eight rod on Andrew mitchel then Notherly twenty rod on Gordon then weſt 29 Degrs South fifteen rod on Kilborn the

Same point three rod to Eleazer Houghtons Land then South 19 Degrees Eaſt fourteen rod and half on Houghtons to where it began this Common Land Survayed for the Proprietors Committee
April ye 30th 1789 and there is one acre and half & Eight rod
        David Kilburn Surveyer

Philip Goodridge ⎫
Benj^a Redington ⎬ Committee
Benj^a Goodridge ⎭
       ℔ Joseph Hartwell Clark

[71] this Track of Land Commonly Called Tophet Swamp

This is a plan of ninety-four acres of undevided Land lying in the South part of Fitchburg bounding South on the Town Line & Southweſt on Land Laid out to m^r pool & north on Capt Cowdens Land & Eaſt on Kendal Boutells Land begining at a maple tree the Southeaſt Corner runing Weſt 6 Degrees North 61 rod to a popler Stand there making an angle runing North 36 Degrees weſt 190 rod to Stake and Stones there making an angle & runing 11 rod to a hemlock tree there making an angle runing Eaſt 13 Degrees South 144 rod to Stake & Stones there making an angle runing South 11 Degrees Eaſt 140 rod to where it began. James Boutell Surveyer. by order of the Committee appointed. and approved of by Said Committee viz Benjamin Redington Benjamin Goodridge Ephraim Wetherbe
      ℔ Joseph Hartwell proprietors
          Clark

[72]   September the 20th 1793.

then Surveyed for Maj^r James Richardson ten acres & forty rod of Land lying in Fitchburg. it begins at a hemlock tree in David Pratts Line on the bank of the river and runs Weſt 12 Degrees 30 minits South 203 rod on Land of Said Pratt and on Land that was Laid out to Eleazer Houghton to a Stump on the bank of Said river and then it runs Down the river to the firſt mentioned hemlock approved of by the proprietors Committee viz. Phillip Goodridge Benjᵃ Goodridge Benjᵃ Redington Recorded December yᵉ 10ᵗʰ 1793.

David Kilburn Surveyer

℔ Joseph Hartwell proprietors Clark

Laid out by the Committee appoyented three acres and one Hundred and twelve rod of Land Lying in Aſhby for Majʳ James Richardson Clamer. it begins at the Northweſt Corner and runs South 28 Degrees 30 minits weſt 32 rod then Eaſt 29 Degrees South 18 rod then North 29 Degrees Eaſt 32 rod on Land Laid out to Wheler & boal then Weſt 29 Degrees North 19 rod on Said Wheler & Boal to where it began Serveyed by David Kilburn and approved of by the Committee viz Phillip Goodridge Benjᵃ Goodridge and Benjᵃ Redington.

Recorded the 10ᵗʰ December 1793

Joseph Hartwell proprietors Clark

Laid out by the Committee appointed one acre & half of Land Lying in Fitchburg for Majʳ James Richardson Clamer it begins at a white oak tree at the North Side of the river and runs Eaſt 2 Degrees 30 minits North 35 rod to Said river then up Said river 48 rod to where it began Serveyed by David Kilbourn and approved of by the Committee viz Philip Goodridge Benjᵃ Goodridge and Benjᵃ Redington

Recorded the 10ᵗʰ of December 1793

Joseph Hartwell proprietors
Clark

[73]   Fitchburg November yᵉ 15ᵗʰ 1794

Laid out by the Committee appointed twenty Seven acres and Seventy three rod Common Land for the proprietors of Lunenburg and it lyeth in Fitchburg Beginning at the northeaſt Corner of Said Land and runs South 17 Degrees Eaſt 82 rod then weſt 5 Degrees North 159 rod then Eaſt 74. rod then North 19 Degrees 30 minits Eaſt 61 rod on Land of Deaꞓ Thurſten then Eaſt 31 Degrees South 25 rod on Land of Edward Scot then North 41 Degrees Eaſt 27 rod on Land of Said Scot to where it began

David Kilburn Surveyer

Recorded the 26th of may 1803
by me Joseph Hartwell proprietors Clark

Benjamin Redington⎫
Benjamin Goodridge⎬ Proprietors Commitee
Benjamin Johnſon⎭

[78] At a Legal Meeting of the origanal Proproprietors of the Town of Lunenburg or their Legal Repreſentitives on the Seventh Day of April anno Domini 1780

article 3ᵈ Voted that the Said Proprietors will Sell the whole of the Common Lands that belong to Said Proprietors at Vendue in Lunenburg Fitchburg or Asby

article 4 Voted that Coˡˡ Aaron Willard Advertiſe the aforesaid Common Lands Laying in Lunenburg Fitchburg or aſhby for Publick Sale at Vendue to the higheſt Biders as the Law Derects

Coppy of Advert — Advertiſment To be Sold at Publick Vendue at the Houſe of Mʳ Jedediah Eſtebrooks Inholder in Lunenburg on wensday the 18th Day of October next at Publick Vendue to the higheſt Bider

200 acres of Land in the Southweſterly part of Fitchburg

200 do within a Quater of mile of the meeting houſe

100 in the South Part of Fitchburg

200 in the North part do

100 in the South Eaſterly Part of Fitchburg and Sundʸ other Peaces of Land in Fitchburg & Lunenburg Two many to be Enumerated the above Said Advertiſment was publiſhed in the Boston News Papers Six weeks before Sᵈ Sale on the 18 Day of october 1780

Pr Aaron Willard

account of the Sales of the Common Lands in Fitchburg & Lunenburg and who Conveyed to that were Sold on the 18th Day of october 1780 and the Sums Said Lands Sold according to the conditions of Sale

william Thulo 20 acres @ 27/ p^r acre ajoing to his own Land	27	″
Philip Goodridge 8 acres over mulpus @ 8/6 pr acre	3	8
Thomas Wilder 4½ acres by unachualem Pond @ 48/ pr acre	10	16
Benj^a Goodridge by his own Lands 1 acre & 157 rods @ 20/	2	0
David Prat 188 acres Rolestone hill @ 16/6 —	155.	2
Aaron Willard 88 acres by whitneys Land @ 17/	74 16	0
Joseph Paterson & others 48 acres by Hospital @ 18/	43	4
James Richardson Manosnet 85 accres @ 11/—	46	15
Jonathan wood 42½ acres @ 20/ — — — —	42	10
Josiah Willard 7¼ acres East Side of River and 2 Islands near Fitchburg meeting house deeded to Thos Cowden @ £3, 15, 0	27 3	9
Thadeus Cummings 27½ acres near weatherbes mills @ 8/	11	00
Benj^a Redington & others 51 acres @ 12/6 —	31 17	6
Eleazer Houghton Junr 50 acres at 8/0 pr acre	20 00	0
Leu^t Philip Goodridge 46 acres near Pearl hill @ 32/	73	12
Joshua martin Junr 42 acres at 20/0 pr acre —	42 00	0
Edward Scott 20 acres ajoining his own Land @ 12/	12	0
Benjamin Redington 55 acres fifty rod near E Scotts @ 5/4 —	14 15	0
James Richardson 67 acres 102 rod . . 4/ .	13 10	6
Eleazar Houghton Junr & others near the Hospital 74 acres @ 7/6	27	15
James Richardson all the Common Lands not Surveyed before the 7 Day of may 1781 that belong to the origanal Proprietors of Lunenburg Laying within the origanl Bounds of S^d Township is Sold to S^d Richardson his observing the conditions of Sale according to a Vote of S^d Propretors ye 7 Day of may 1781 for the Sum of £3, 3, 0	3	3

Meet on ajornment ye third Day of December, 1781

Bid off by Leu:t Philip Goodridge a Certain Track of Land Lying in Fitchburg between Joseph Lows and Daniel Putnams Lands at 27/0 per acre

per. Joseph Hartwell Proprietors Clark

[80] Worcefter fs

At the Requeft of a Sufficient Number of Proprietors of ᷉e Town of Lunenburg to me Derected in writing un᷉ r their hands Requefting I would Ifsue my worrent for calling a proprietors meeting to act on the Several articles hereafter mentioned viz^{tt}

{ feal } Thefe are therefore in the Name of the goverment and People of the State of the Mafsachufetts Bay to notifie and worn you the Said Proprietors to meet at the houfe of Mr Jedediah Eftebrook in Lunenburg on the Tenth Day Day of may next at one of the Clock in the afternoon then & there being met & Duly formed

1^{ly} To chufe a Moderator to govern Said Meeting

2^{ly} To hear the Report of the Committe appointed to Survey the Common Lands that belongs to the proprietors aforesaid

3^{ly} To See if the Proprietors will Sell the whole of their Common Lands or any part thereof or make Devifion of the Same

4^{ly} To See if the proprietors will chufe a Treafurer

5^{ly} To See if the Proprietors will chufe a committe to Settle accompts with thofe Perfons that have Done Service or that Shall hereafter Do Service for Said Proprietors and give orders on the Treafurer for the Payment of the Same

6^{ly} To See if the Proprietors will Raife money to pay thofe that that have Done Service for them or pay them in Land agreeable to a former Vote of the Said Proprietors and chufe any officers the Proprietors Shall think Necefsary

Given under my hand and Seal at Lunenburg this Seventeen Day of April Anoque Domini 1780

At a meeting Legally warned the Proprietors of the Common and undevided Lands in the Towns of Lunenburg & Fitchburg met at the houſe of Mr Jedediah Eftebrook in Lunenburg on Wensday the Tenth Day of may anno Domini 1780

1^{ly} Voted and choſe Aaron Willard Moderator to govern S^d meeting

2^d article not acted on

3^{ly} Voted to Sell the whole of the common and undevided Lands that belong to Said Proprietors Laying in Lunenburg Fitchburg or Ashby at Vendue

4^{ly} Voted & choſe Mr Benj^a Redington Treaſurer

5^{ly} Voted to chuſe a committe to Receive any accompts from any and Every perſon that have done Service or Shall do Service for Said Proprietors before the adjournment of this meeting and Lay them before the Proprietors at their next meeting for their acceptance Voted & choſe Maj^r James Richardson Capt Reuben Gibson and Mr Benj^a Goodridge Committe for the above purpoſe

6^{ly} Voted that Coll Aaron Willard Advertiſe the aforesaid Common Lands Laying in Lunenburg Fitchburg or Asby for Publick Sale at Vendue to the higheſt Bider as the Law Derects

Voted & choſe Benj^a Goodridge collecttor for Said Proprietors

Voted to Ajorn this meeting to the Laſt wensday in Auguſt next being the thirtyeth Day to meet at this place at nine of the clock Wensday

      Aaron Willard Moderator

Recorded Sep^t ye 11 1780

Wensday Auguſt ye 30 1780 being met according to AdJornment and Duly formed

Voted further to Adjorn this meeting to monday the ninth Day of october next nine o Clock to this Place

      Aaron Willard moderator

Recorded Sep^t 11 1780

monday october ninth 1780 met accorind to Ajornment

Voted that this meeting be disovled

Aaron Willard moderator

Recorded octo^r 17 1780

Edward Hartwell proprietors
Clerk

[81] Worcefter fs

At the Requeft of a Sufficient Number of the Proprietors of the Town of Lunenburg to me Derected in writing under their hands Requefting that I would Isue my Warrent for Calling a Proprietors meeting to act on the Several articles hereafter mentioned

(feal) Thefe are therefore in the Name of the goverment and People of Mafsachufetts Bay in New England to Notifie and worn you the Said Proprietors to meet at the houfe of m^r Jedediah Eftebrooks in Lunenburg on wensday the thirtyeth Day of this Inftant Auguft at one of the clock in the afternoon then and there being met & Duly formed

1^{ly} To chufe a moderator to govern Said meeting

2^{ly} To See if the Proprietors will chufe a Committe to make Sale of all the Common and undevided Lands that belong to the origanal Proprietors of the Town of Lunenburg their Heirs or Afsigns Laying and being in what is now Called Lunenburg Fitchburg or Ashby to be Sold at Publick Vendue So Soon as Said Proprietors Shall think fit or at Private Sale

3^{ly} To See if Said Proprietors aforesaid will Impower the aforesaid Committe when chofen to give warrentte deeds in behalf of Said Proprietors to and Every Perfon that Shall Said Lands or any part thereof also Receive the purchafe money arifeing by Said Sales and pay the Same to Each of Said Proprietors or their Legal Reprefentitives according to their Equal proportion and Intereft in Said Common Lands firft deducting out of Said monies arifeing by Said Sales So much as will pay the charges that have arifen on Said Common Lands and their Juft Proporton of Debts Due from Said Proprietors to any Perfon or Perfons that have Done Services for the aforesaid Proprietors and give Said Committe any further Inftructions with Regard to the Premifes they Shall think proper

4ly To chufe any other Committe or Committes officer or officers that the Proprietors Shall think Necefsary

given under my hand and Seal at Lunenburg this Tenth Day of Auguft anno Domini 1780

      Edward Hartwell proprietors Clerk

At a Meeting of the original Proprietors of Lunenburg or their Legal Reprefentatives Legally warned and to be holden at the houfe of Mr Jedediah Eftebrook in Lunenburg afores^d on wenfday the thirtyeth day of Auguft Anno Domini Seventeen hundred and Eighty being met and Duly formed

firft Voted and chofe Co^{ll} Aaron Willard moderator to govern S^d meeting

2d^{ly} Voted to chufe five men to be a Committe to make Sale of all the Common and undevided Lands that did originally belong to the Proprietors of Lunenburg and not already Devided Said Lands to be Sold at Publick Vendue to the highest Bider Except Such Pecess as the S^d Proprietors Shall order otherwife to be dispofed of

3d^{ly} Voted and chofe Co^{ll} Aaron Willard Mr Benjamin Redington Leu^t Philip Goodridge Capt Reuben Gibson & m^r Benjamin Goodridge to be a Committe to Sell all the Common and undevided Lands aforesaid at Publick Vendue to the Higheft Bider Except thofe peaces or parcles of Land that the Said Proprietors Shall order to be otherways Dispofed of

4^{ly} Voted that Coll Aaron Willard Advertife Said Lands to be Sold at Publick Vendue on the Eighteenth Day of october next at the houfe of Mr Jedediah Eftebrook at one oClock

5^{ly} Voted that the aforesaid Coll Aaron Willard Leut Philip Goodridge Benjamin Redington Capt Reuben Gibson and Benjamin Goodridge be a committe fully Authorized and impowered to Sell and Convey all and Every peace and parcel of the common Lands that are undevided that belong to the origin original Proprietors of Lunenburg their Heirs or Afsigns Laying and being in Lunenburg Fitchburg or Asby (Except thofe Peaces of Land that Said Proprietors Shall order to be otherways Sold or Difpofed of) and that the said Committe or any three of them be fully Impowered in Bhalf of Said Proprietors their Heirs or Afsigns to Sign Execute and Deliver good and Suffient Deeds of Sale and conveyance and worrentte to every Perfon or Persons that shall Purchafe any of the Lands afores^d and also to Receive the money arifing by S^d Sales and to pay the Same to the Proprietors or their Legal Reprefentatives in Equal Proportion according [82] according to their Intereft in Said common Lands after firft Deducting out of the monies arifeing by Said Sales So much as will pay the charges that have arifen on Said Lands and their Juft proportion of Debts Due to any Perfon or Perfons that have Done Service for Said Proprietors

Voted to Ajourn this meeting to monday october 9 1780 at one oClock afternoon to this Place

        Aaron Willard Moderator

Recorded Sep^t 20 1780

    Edward Hartwell proprietors Clerk

 october ninth 1780 met at the houfe of mr Jedediah Eftebrook in Lunenburg according to ajournment and being formed

firft Voted to give the Committe of Sales appointed to Sell the Common Lands belonging to the Proprietors of Lunenburg the following Inftructions Viz^{tt} that the Large Peaces of Land be Divided into fifty acres Lots as near as may be be Ecept Two Peaces called Rolestone hill & monofnet hill that Every purchaser pay one third part of the purchafe money that the Land he Buys is Sold for Down and the other Two third parts in one month after the S^d Eighteenth Day of october 1780 the time of Sale or forfeit & Loofe what money he payed Down and Every Person when he has Compleated the payment of his purchafe money in manner afores^d to Receive a good deed of worrentte the Lands aforesaid to be sold for Spainish milled Dollers at Six Shillings Each or gold Equelent

Voted to ajorn this meeting to the Eighteenth Day of october Inftant to this Place at Eight o Clock in Morning

Aaron Willard moderator

Recorded october 10 1780

october Eighteenth 1780 at Eight oClock in morning then met at the houfe of Mr Jedediah Eftebrook according to ajornment and being formed

firft Voted that Aaron Willard Benjamin Redington Philip Goodridge Reuben Gibson and Benjamin Goodridge the Committe for sale of the Common Lands belonging to the Proprietors of Lunenburg be further impowred to Sell all the Common Lands on Northfeild Road so called at private Sale and give warrentte Deeds of Said Lands in the same manner & form as they are impowered to give Deeds of the other Common Lands

2dly Voted further to impower the aforesaid Committe to profecute all Trefpafses on Said Proprietors Lands or to Settle the Same with any and Every perfon or perfons that have committed any Trefpafses or Trefpafs on Said Proprietors Lands and Receive Such Satisfaction as they Shall think fit also in the Name of the Said Proprietors and on their Behalf to Bring any action or actions in the Law that Shall be found Necefsary for the profecution of any Trefpafses or for Removeing any Incroachments or any unlawfull Entrys or Detainers of Said Proprietors Lands aforesaid

3dly Voted that the Committe of Sales be ordered to take Such Security of thofe perfons who Shall Bid of any of the Common Lands as they shall think fit in Liue or inftead of the Earneft money ordered in a former Vote to be paid Down also that the Lands aforesaid be sold for Spainifh milled Dollers at Six Shillings Each or Gold Equevalent or paper Continental Currency the Exchange to be Equal to Seventy Two paper Dollers for one Silver Doller

4^{ly} Voted & chofe Aaron Willard Proprietors Clerk

Proprietors' Records. 269

Recorded october ye 20 1780
                    Aaron Willard moderator
Voted to ajorn this meeting to 10 oClock in the morning october 19 1780
Recorded october ye 20 1780
                    Aaron Willard moderator

october nineteenth 1780 at Ten o Clock in the morning being met according to ajornment and Duly formed

Voted further to ajorn this meeting to November next the Twentyeth Day three o clock in the afternoon to this place

Recorded october ye 20 1780.
                    Aaron Willard moderator.

[83] November ye 20 1780 being met at the Houfe of Mr Jedediah Eftebrook Inholder in Lunenburg according to adjornment and being Duly Formed

Voted that there be one month allowed to thofe that have purchafed Lands of the Proprietors of the Town of Lunenburg at Publick Sale on the Eighteenth Day of october Laft to compleat and make out the whole of the purchafe money that Remains Due from Each Perfon Refpectively or make out to the Committe of Sales Such Security as they Shall Judge Sufficient or their Lands will be Expofed again to Sale in Such way and manner as the Said Proprietors Shall think proper

Voted further to adjorn this meeting to the Twentyeth Day of December next to the Houfe of Leu^t Philip Goodridge Inholder in Lunenburg at Ten oClock fore noon sales also ajorned
                    Aaron Willard moderator
Recorded Novr 22 1780
                    Edward Hartwell proprietors Clerk

Decem^r ye 20 1780 being. met at the Houfe of Leut Philip Goodridge Inholder in Lunenburg according to adjornment and being Duly formed

Voted that the sales of all the Common Lands not sold belonging to the Proprietors of the Town of Lunenburg be Advertifed by the Committe of Sales on the firft monday of marh next in the Towns of Lunenburg Fitchburg & Leominſter notifieing that the Lands aforesaid will be sold at Publick Vendue to the higheſt biders on monday the Seventh Day of may next at the houſe of Philip Goodridge Inholder in Lunenburg at Ten of the Clock

2dly Voted to adjorn this meeting to monday the Seventh Day of may next to the houſe of Leut Philip Goodridge Inholder in Lunenburg to Ten oClock before noon the sales also ajorned to the Time & place afores^d

Recorded Dcember 25 1780

p^r Aaron Willard Proprietors Cleark

may ye 7: 1781 being met and Duly Formed at the Houſe of Leut Phillip Goodridge Inholder in Lunenburg agreeable to the Laſt ajornment

Voted that the Commitee of Sales Sell all the Common & undevided Lands belonging to the Proprietors of Lunenburg this Day at Publick Vendue to the higheſt Bider Except thoſe Lands the said Proprietors shall otherwiſe order agreable to a former Vote of said Proprietors

2dly Voted that all the Common and undevided Lands that is not already Surveyed be Sold at Publick Vendue this Day to the higheſt Bider the Purchaſer or purchaſers of S^d Lands to be at the Expence of the Survey of Said Lands and in Surveying Said Lands he or they observe the Rules and orders of the Said Proprietors in their former Surveys of Common and undivided Lands belonging to Said Proprietors and when any of Said Surveys are compleated and properly Certified by the Committee & Surveyor who Surveyed the Same on Receiveing Such Certificate the Committe of Sales are ordered to give Sufficient Deeds of the Said Lands agreeable to a former vote of Said Proprietors for conviying their Common Lands Sold at Vendue

3dly Voted that the Committe of Sales are Derected to Sue all who have not Payed up their Securitys that bid of Lands belonging to Said Proprietors and was Sold on the Eighteenth Day of october Laſt or Complyed with the Conditions of Sale

4ly Voted that all Perſons who have this Day Purchaſed any of the Proprietors Lands of the Town of Lunenburg be allowed three months for the payment of their Purchaſe money they giveing proper Security for Said money to the Committe of Sales imediately

5ly Voted that the charge of this meeting be to the Proprietors of the Town of Lunenburg

6ly Voted to ajorn this meeting to Tuesday the 29 of this Inſtant may at one oClock A M to this Place Voted that the Sales be also ajorned to Time & place aforesᵈ

Record may 20 1781
      pʳ Aaron Willard Proprietors Clerk.

[84] May yᵉ 29 1781 being met and Formed at the houſe of Lut Philip Goodridge inholder in Lunenburg according to ajornment

1ly Voted that the committe that attended the Surveyers that Surveyed the Common Lands belonging to the Proprietors of the Town of Lunenburg Receive Six Shillings or a Spainiſh milled Doller Each for Each Day they were in Sᵈ Service and that Each Surveyor Receive nine Shillings Like money for Each Day they were in Said Service also that the Liquor neeſsary for Sᵈ Surveys be at the Expence of the Proprietors aforesᵈ

2ᵈˡʸ Voted that the Committe of Sales Receive and pass all accomts againſt Said Proprietors and Liquadate the Same for Payment and pay Sᵈ accomts So far as they Shall appear Juſt to them

3ly Voted that the Committe of Sales advertiſe the Common Lands belonging to the Proprietors of Lunenburg and unsold and not otherwiſe ordered to be Dispoſpoſed of to be Sold at the houſe of Capt Thomas Cowdin inholder in Fitchburg on monday June 25ᵗʰ next to the higheſt Bidder at Publick Vendue and that the Committe aforesaid Advertiſe Said Sale by Poſting the Same in the Towns of Lunenburg Fitchburg & Leominiſter

4ly Voted to ajorn this meeting to the 25ᵗʰ Day June next Two oClock A M To the Houſe of Capᵗ Thomas Cowdin Inholder in Fitchburg

Record June 27 1781
      pr Aaron Willard Proprietors Clark

June 25 178

being met & Duly formed at the houfe of Capt Thomas Cowdin Inholder in Fitchburg according to the Laft ajornment may 29 1781

1^{ly} Voted to Sell the Common Lands belonging to the Proprietors of according to the Vote of Said Proprietors at their Laft meeting may ye 29 1781 also proceded to Sell the following Peaces of Land in fichburg Viz^{tt} To Eleazar Houghton Junr & Reuben Smith 74 acres ajoining to the Hofpital Farm So Called @ 7/6 p^r acre 20 ares to Edward Scott ajoining to his own Land @ 12/ pr acre 64 acres to Benjamin Redington ajoining to S^d Scotts Land @ 5/6 pr acre also 73 acres of Land to James Richardson ajoining to the Laft mentioned Peace to James Richardfon @ 4/ pr acre

2^{ly} Voted that the charge of this meeting be paid by the Proprietors of Lunenburg

3^{ly} Voted to ajorn this meeting to monday the ninth Day of July next to the houfe of Leut Philip Goodridge in Lunenburg Inholder at 3 oclock P M the Sales are also ajorned to Time & place afores^d

Recorded June 27 1781

pr Aaron Willard Proprietors Clark

July ye 9th 1781. meet according to Adjornment

1.^{ly} Voted to Adjorn the Sale of the Common Land to the next meeting

2.^{ly} Voted that the Commettee of Sale be Directed to Settel with all thofe Persons that have Encroched upon the Northfield Road So Called and make Report at the adjoyrnment of this Meeting

3^{ly} Voted that the Expence of this meeting be at the Charge of the Proprietors

4^{ly} Voted to adjoyrn this meeting to the firft monday in Sep^t next at one o Clock in the after noon to the houfe of Leu^t Philip Goodridge in Lunenburg

Recorded october ye 2^d 1781

Pr Joseph Hartwell Proprietors Clark

September 3ᵈ 1781 meet at the houſe of Leuᵗ Philip Goodridge according to ajornment

Voted to ajorn this meeting to the firſt munday in october next alſo Voted to ajorn the Sale to the Same Day to meet at this Place at one Clock afternoon

Recorded 3ᵈ october 1781

      pr Joseph Hartwell Clark

[85] October yᵉ 1ſᵗ 1781 Being Meet at the Houſe of Leuᵗ Philip Goodridge Inholder in Lunenburg according to ajornment and being Duly formed Chooſe Leuᵗ Philip Goodridge Modirator

1ˡʸ Voted to alow Edward Hartwell Eſqʳ two pounds Eight Shillings on his account for Services Don for the Proprietors — — — — — —

2ˡʸ Voted and Chooſe Samuel Johnson Commettee man in the Rome of Colˡ Aaron Willard Deceaſed

3ˡʸ Voted to ajorn this meeting to the firſt Munday of December next at the houſe of Leuᵗ Philip Goodridge in Lunenburg at one Clock in the afternoon — — — —

4ˡʸ Voted to ajorn the Sale of the Common Land to the next meeting

5ˡʸ Voted the Charge of Said meeting be paid by the propriators

      Philip Goodridge modrator.

Recorded 2ᵈ Day of October 1781

   pr. Joseph Hartwell Propriators Clark

December the 3ᵈ 1781 Being Met according to ajornment at the Houſe of Leuᵗ Philip Goodridge Inholder in Lunenburg being Duly formed, Said meeting being opened

1ˡʸ Voted to pay Corlˡ Joseph Bellows forty Shillings Silver money for the Rent of that place Person Eaton Improved this preſent year, provided ſaid place appear to be ſaid Bellowses property by Lawfull Title. if not to Refund the ſaid money to the proprietors Commettee

2ˡʸ Voted an addition of ſix ſhillings and Eight pence to the above forty ſhillings of Rent for ſaid Place

3ˡʸ Voted to Except of a plan maid by Abraham

Willard of a feartain Lott of Land Sold to Major James Richardson by the proprietor of Lunenburg

4ly Voted the Coft of this Meeting be paid by the proprietors

5ly Voted to jorn this Meeting to the 2d Munday of February Next at the Houfe of Leut Philip Goodridge Inholder in Lunenburg at one a Clock afternoon

       Philip Goodridge Modirator

Recorded ye 4 Day of December 1781
   per Joseph Hartwell Proprietors Clark

February ye 11th 1782. Being met according to ajornment at the Houfe Leut Philip Goodridge Inholder in Lunenburg, being Duly formed Said meeting being opened.

1.ft Voted. after the Publick Rights are made – up that the Commettee by private Sale or Public Vendue Dispofe of the Lands un Sold as they think proper.

2.ly Voted that the Charge of this meeting be Paid by the proprietors

3ly Voted to ajorn this Meeting to firft Wednefday of June next at one a clock after-noon, at the Houfe of Leut Philip Goodridge Inholder in Lunenburg

       Philip Goodridge Modirator

Recorded ye 6th Day of march 1782
   per Joseph Hartwell Proprietors Clerk

June ye 5th 1782 Being Met according to adjornment at the Houfe of Leut Philip Goodridge Inholder in Lunenburg, being Duly formed faid meeting being opened

1.ft Voted and appointed Leut Philip Goodridge one of the Proprietors Commettee of fales of Common Lands to be the Receiver of all the moneys Due to the Said Proprietors arifeing from the Sales of there Common Lands that are already Sold or may hereafter be Sold and other moneys that are or may be hereafter Due to Said Proprietors he giveing his obligation to be Lodged with the Proprietors Clerk that he will pay and Difcharge himfelf of the Same agreeable to the orders of Said Propritors as he Shall Receive them from time to time

2ly Voted Choofe Joseph Hartwell to afseft the Commettee in making up their accounts of the Sale of the Common Lands of the proprietors of Lunenburg

3ly Voted the Expence of this meeting Shall be Charged on the proprietors

4ly Voted to adjorn this meeting to the nineteenth Day of Auguft next at one a Clock after noon at the Houfe of Leut Philip Goodridge in Lunenburg Inholder

Philip Goodridge Modirator

Recorded the 6th Day of May. 1782
per Joseph Hartwell proprietors Clerk

Auguft the 19th 1782. Being Met according to Adjornment at the Houfe of Leut Philip Goodridge in Lunenburg Inholder being duly formed faid meeting being opened

firft Voted. to Except Mr Benja Redingtons Plan of a Lott of Land Lying by Edward Scotts Land

2ly Voted to adjorn this Meeting to the firft Wednefday in october next at one a Clock after noon at this Place

Philip Goodridge Modirator

Recorded the 20th Day of auguft 1782.
per. Joseph Hartwell
Proprietors Clerk

October ye 2d 1782 Being Met according to Adjornment at the House of Leut Philip Goodridge in Lunenburg Inholder being Duly formed fd meeting opened.

Whereas Jofhua Martin Junr Bought of the Proprietors Committee of Sales a Scertain Track of Land & Gave his note for the Same to Coll Aaron Willard one of the Said Committee for the ufe of the Proprietors Said Willard Signing the Said note over to Doc John Taylor he the Said Taylor Sewing Said note Said Martin not Being able to attend Said Court the Action was Called out by Defolt

Therefore Voted the Committee of Sales Join with the abovefaid Jofhua Martin to Petition the Great and General Court that Said Martin have an hearing on Said action that Juftice may take place

2ly Voted if Said petition be anfwered Said Committee of Sales be and are hereby Impowered to Conftitute one or more of Said Committee to join with the Sd Jofhua martin to procicute the abovefaid action to final Judgment

3ly Voted to Except of Two plans made by James Boutell for Maj James Richardfon

4ly Voted allow Capt Benj^a Goodridge account of £7 " 14 " 7

[87] 5ly Voted the Expence of this Meeting be paid by the Proprietors

6ly Voted to adjorn this Meeting to the Sixth Day of November next at the Houfe of Mr James Patterson in Lunenburg Inholder at one a Clock after noon

Philip Goodridge Modirator

Recorded ye 3^d Day of october 1782

per Joseph Hartwell Proprietors Clerk

November ye 6th 1782 Being met according to adjornment at the Houfe of Mr James Pattersons in Lunenburg Inholder being Duly formed faid meeting being opened.

2ly Voted to make up the Difificency of the School Lott which is Eighty one acres in Securities Receved for the Common and undevided Lands Sold by the Proprietors Committee of Sales (in Lunenburg Fitchburg and Afhby) on an Equal Eaveridge per acre as Said Lands was Sold

3ly Voted the Expence of this meeting be paid by the Proprietors

4ly Voted to adjorn this Meeting to the firft Wednefday in January next at one a Clock after noon at this place

Philip Goodridge Modirator

Recorded ye 7th Day of November 1782

per Joseph Hartwell Proprietors Clerk

[88] January ye 1^{ft} 1783 Being met according to Adjornment at the Houfe of Mr James Patterson in Lunenburg Inholder. Being Duly formed Said meeting being opened.

1ft Voted to make up the Dificiency of the Minifterial Land which is Eight acres agreeable to a vote of the Proprietors at a meeting on the Sixth Day of November 1782 of making up the School Lott in Securities Receved for the Common and undivided Land Sold by the Proprietors Committee of Sales

2ly Voted to Chufe a Committee to Reckon with the Committee of Sales of the Proprietors of Lunenburg there Common and undevided Land and make Report at the adjornment of this meeting of there profeedings theron

3ly Voted to Chufe three for the abovesaid Committee

4ly Voted and Chofe Joseph Hartwell Thaddeus Commings and Eleazer Houghton Junr for Said Committee

5ly Voted Mr Benja Redington & Capt Jofhua Martin give Securities in Behalf of the Proprietors of Lunenburg the Sum of Seventy three pounds two Shillings to the Towns Committee for the Dificiencies of the School Lott and Minifterial Lott the Said Benja Redington and Jofhua Martin to Receve the Same Sum of Leut Philip Goodridge the Recever of the Proprietors Securities of the Sales of the Common and undevided Lands of Said proprietors they giving the Said Philip Goodridge a Recept for the Same

6ly. Voted the Expence of this meeting be paid by the Proprietors

7ly Voted to Adjorn this Meeting to the firft Wednefday in February next at one a Clock after noon at this place.

        Philip Goodridge Modirator
Recorded the 2d Day of January 1783.
    per Joseph Hartwell Proprietors Clerk

[89] February ye 5th 1783 Being meet according to adjornment at the Houfe of Mr James Patterson in Lunenburg Inholder Being Duly formed Said meeting being opened.

firft Voted and Chofe Capt Benjamin Goodridge Modirator per-temperary.

the Committee Chofen to Reckon with the Committee of Sales not haveing finifhed Said Reckoning therefore

2ly Voted the Said Committee finifh Said Reckoning and make Report at the Next adjornment of this Meeting

3ly Voted the Expence of this Meeting be paid by the Proprietors

4ly Voted adjorn this meeting to the firft Wednefday of March next at one a Clock after noon at this place

     Benjamin Goodridge Moderator

Recorded the third Day of March 1783 per temry

   ℔ Joseph Hartwell Proprietors Clerk

March ye 5th 1783 Being Meet according to adjornment at the Houfe of Mr James Patterson in Lunenburg Inholder Said meeting Being opened.

firft Voted the Committee to Reckon with the Committee of Sales make up their Settlement with Said Committee of Sales and make Report at the adjornment of this Meeting the Laft munday of April next

2ly Voted the Expence of this meeting be paid by the Proprietors

3ly Voted to adjorn this meeting to the Laft Munday of April next at the Houfe of Lieu^t Philip Goodridge in Lunenburg Inholder at one a Clock after noon

    Benj^a Goodridge Modirator

       per tempeary

Recorded the Sixth Day of March 1783

   P^{er} Joseph Hartwell Proprietors Clerk

[90] April the 28th 1783 Being met according to adjornment at the Houfe of Lieu^t Philip Goodridge in Lunenburg Inholder Said meeting being opened.

firft Voted to Chufe a man to Confer with the Widow Willard and her Lawyer Concerning a Convayence of a Scertain Track of Land bid off by Co^{ll} Aaron Willard Late of Lunenburg Deceaf^d and go to the Judge of Probate with them to Settle the Same

2ly. Voted and Choofe Mr Benj^a Redington for the above purpofe

3ly. Voted the Expence of this Meeting which is £0 = 3 = 7 = 1 be paid by the Proprietors

4ly Voted to adjorn this Meeting to the ninteenth Day of may next at this place at one a Clock after noon
Benja Goodridge Moderator
per temporary
Recorded the 29th Day of April 1783
Joseph Hartwell Proprietors Clerk

May the 19th 1783 Being met according to adjornment at the Houſe of Lieut Philip Goodridge in Lunenburg Inholder Said meeting being opened.

firſt Voted to Chuſe a Committee to Preſent an acount to the Commiſſioners on the Eſtate of Coll Aaron Willard Late of Lunenburg Deceaced of all the moneys the ſaid Willard Receivd of the Sales of the Common and undevided Lands belonging to the Proprietors

2ly. Voted and Choſe Mr Benja Redington and Capt Benja Goodridge for the aboveSaid Committee.

3ly Voted the Expence of this Meeting being three Shillings & four pence be paid by the Proprietors

4ly Voted to adjorn this meeting to the 18th Day of auguſt next at this place at one a Clock after noon
Philip Goodridge Modirator
Recorded the 20th Day of May 1783
Joseph Hartwell Proprietors Clerk

[91] Auguſt the 18th 1783 Being Met according to adjornment at the Houſe of Lieut Philip Goodridge in Lunenburg Inholder being Duly formed Said meeting being opned

firſt Voted to aloue to Joseph Hartwell an account of two pounds Eleven Shillings and Eight pence for Services don for the Proprietors

2ly. Voted to allow Thaddeus Commings an account of one pound four Shillings for Services don for the Proprietors

3ly Voted to allow to Eleazer Houghton Junr an account of fifteen Shillings for Services don for the Proprietors

4ly Voted to allow Capt Benja Goodridge an account of four pounds nine Shillings and one peney for Services don for the Proprietors

5ly Voted to petition the Honnourable Judge of Probate for the County of Worcefter for a new Miniftrator to be appointed to the Eftate of Aaron Willard Efq^r Late of Lunenburg Deceac^d

6ly. Voted Lieu^t Philip Goodridge Mr Benj^a Redington Shall prepare the above faid petition and one of them perfer the Same to the above Said Judge of probate

7ly Voted the Expence of this meeting be paid by the Proprietors which is one Shilling and Eight pence

8ly Voted to adjorn this Meeting to the twenty-forth Day of September next one a Clock after noon at this place

      Philip Goodridge Modirator

Recorded the 23 Day of auguft 1783
   Joseph Hartwell Proprietors Clerk

    Sep^t the 24th 1783

Being Met accorging to adjornment at the Houfe of Lieu^t Philip Goodridge in Lunenburg Inholder being Duly formed faid Meeting being opned.

firft Voted to alow Capt Benj^a Goodridge an account of Eight pounds one Shilling and five pence for Services don for the proprietors

2dly Whereas by a former Vote of the Proprietors of the Townfhip of Lunenburg the Committee of Sales to Sell off the Common and undevided Lands by Lotts and peaces as accomidated the Purcherfer of Said Lands. being lotted out and Sold, Some Lotts falling Short others over runing meafure. therefore Voted the Said Committee of Sails make up the Deficiency in Land or reduction of the Purches money of Said Lott or Lotts So falling Short fo much per acre as any perfon or perfons Gave per acre for Said Lott or Lotts and thofe Lotts that over run the Nomber of acres the Said purcherfer bought it for the S^d purcherfer paying the Same per acre for the over plufs as he gave for Said Lott then he or they to hold to the firft Survey and bounds

3ly Voted the Expence of this meeting be paid by the Proprietors which is two Shilling

           forthly

[92] 4ly Voted to adjorn this Meeting to the twenty-ninth Day of october next at one a Clock after noon at this place

                         Philip Goodridge Modirater

Recorded this firſt Day of october 1783.

                         Joseph Hartwell Proprietors Clerk

                 October ye 29th 1783

Being met according to adjornment at the Houſe of Lieut Philip Goodridge in Lunenburg Inholder being Duly formed Sd meeting being opened —

firſt Voted the Expence of this meeting be paid by the Proprietors which is ten Shillings

2ly Voted to adjorn this meeting to the Eighth Day of December next at one a Clock after noon at this place

                         Philip Goodridge Modirator

Recorded the 30 Day of october

                         Joseph Hartwell Proprietors Clerk

December the 8th 1783 Being met according to adjornment at the Houſe of Lieut Philip Goodridge in Lunenburg Inholder being Duly formed Said Meeting being opened

firſt Voted that the Committee Chooſe to Reckon with the Committe of Sales. Compleet their Settlement with Said Committee of Sale before the 29th Day of this Inſteant December that Every proprietor may have his proportion of moneys by the Sales made

2ly Voted the Expence of this meeting be paid by the proprietors the Sum of 7/4.

3ly. Voted to Adjorn this Meeting to the 14th Day of January next at one aclock after noon at this place

                     Benja Goodridge Modirator for this
                             Preſent Meeting

Recorded the 10th of December 1783.

                  ℈ Joseph Hartwell Proprietors Clerk

[93] January ye 14th 1784 being met according to adjornment at the Houſe of Lieut Philip Goodridge in Lunenburg Inholder being Duely formed Said meeting being opened

firſt Voted to petition the Grate and General Court that the Judge of Probate for the County of Worceſter be allowed the Lebirty of appointing a further time to his Commiſſioners on the Eſtate of Coll Aaron Willard Late of Lunenburg Deceaſd to Receive Examan and allow all Such Juſt Demands on Said Deceaſd Eſtate as has not ben Examand and allowed

2ly Voted Capt Benja Goodridge apply to Capt Josiah Stearns to Draw the above Said petition and preſent it to the Great and General Court and appear for Said proprietors to Carry on the Same to a thurrow hearing in Sd Court

3ly Voted the Expence of this meeting which is two Shillings be paid by the proprietors

4ly. Voted to adjorn this meeting to the twenty-Six Day of this Inſtant January at one aClock after noon at this place

       Philip Goodridge Modirator
Recorded the 17th Day of January 1784
       Joseph Hartwell proprietors Clerk

January ye 26th 1784 being met according to adjornment at the Houſe of Lieut Philip Goodridge in Lunenburg Inholder being Duly formed Said meeting being opened.

firſt Voted to allow Lieut Philip Goodridge nine pounds and two Shillings and Six pence for Services Don for the proprietors and Expences of proprietors meetings alſo for this preſent meeting nine Shillings and Sixpence

2ly Voted to adjorn this meeting to the third Day of February next at one a Clock after noon at this place
       Philip Goodridge Modirator
Recorded 27th Day of January 1784
       Joseph Hartwell proprietors
            Clerk

      February ye 3d 1784.

being met according to adjornment at the Houſe of Lieut Philip Goodridge in Lunenburg Inholder being Duly formed Said meeting opened.

firſt Voted and Choſe Capt Benj.^a Goodridge Modirator for this preſent meeting

2.^ly Voted the Expence of this meeting be paid by the Proprietors which is Seven Shillings

3.^ly Voted to adjorn this meeting to the Twenty third Day of February Inſtant at one o clock after noon at this place

      Benj.^a Goodridge Modirator for this
           preſent meeting

Recorded this forth Day of February 1784.
    Joseph Hartwell Proprietors Clerk

[94] February ye 23.^d 1784 being Met according to adjornment at the Houſe of Lieu.^t Philip Goodridge in Lunenburg Inholder being Duly formed Said meeting opened.

firſt Voted to Chuſe a Committee to See that thoſe that make Claim to any right or rights in the Proprietors Common and undivided Lands in the Townſhip of Lunenburg, have a good title thereto by Deed or Deeds or other ways to the Satiſfaction of Said Committee, alſo the Number of the Houſe Lott Said Right aroſe from that no perſon or perſons Shall make Clame to the Same number already granted to any person or persons for their Shair in the above Said Common and undevided Lands

2.^ly Voted and Chooſe Mr Samuel Johnson, Capt Benj.^a Goodridge, Mr Thaddeus Commings for the above Said Committee

3.^ly Voted the Expence of this Meeting be paid by the Proprietors which is Seven Shillings and ten penie.

4.^ly Voted to adjorn this Meeting to the Eleventh Day of march next at Eight a Clock in the morning at this place

       Philip Goodridge Modirator
Recorded ye 24.th Day of February 1784
    ℔ Joseph Hartwell Proprietors Clerk

March ye 11.th 1784 being met according to adjornment at the Houſe of Lieu.^t Philip Goodridge in Lunenburg Inholder being Duly formed S.^d meeting opened firſt Voted to allow Joſeph Hartwell an account of one pound Six Shillings and two pence for Services Don for the Proprietors

2ly Voted to allow James Boutle an account of one pound thirteen Shillings for Serveying for the proprietors

3ly Voted to allow Thaddeus Commings one pound one Shilling & four pence for Services Don for the Proprietors

4ly Voted to allow Samll Johnſon an account of one pound fourteen Shillings & Six pence for Services Don for the proprietors

5ly Voted to allow to Capt Benja Goodridge an account of one pound five ſhillings & Six pence for Services Don for the proprietors

6ly Voted to allow Lieut Philip Goodridge an account of twenty one pounds Seventeen Shillings and Six pence for Services Don for the proprietors and money paid for the proprietors

7ly Voted to allow Benja Redington an account of Seven pounds Eighteen Shillings for Services Don for the proprietors

8ly Voted to allow Benja Redington Six Shillings on his account as Intereſt

9ly Voted to allow Lieut Philip Goodridge three pounds for Serving as Treaſurer for the proprietors

10ly Voted the Expence of this meeting be paid by the proprietors which is 13/6

11ly Voted to adjorn this meeting to the Eighteenth of this Inſtant march one a Clock after noon at this place

Philip Goodridge Modirator

Recorded ye 12 of march 1784

Joseph Hartwell Clark

[95] March ye 18th 1784. Being met according to adjornment at the Houſe of Lieut Philip Goodridge in Lunenburg Inholder. being Duly formed Sd meeting opened.

firſt Voted to Except of the Reckoning of the Committee Chooſen to Reckon with the Committee of Sales of the Common and undivided Lands of the Townſhip of Lunenburg viz. as follows. We the Subſcribers being Chosen a Committee by the proprietors of the Township of Lunenburg to Reckon with thier Committee of Sales Viz. Coll Aaron Willard Benja Redington Lieut Philip Goodridge Capt Benja Goodridge, who ware Choosen for the purpose of Seling and Conveying all their Common and undivided Lands, by Examination we find the above Said Committee have Sold So much of the Said proprietors Lands as amounts to Six Hundred and Seventy pounds Ninteen Shillings and nine pence —— —— £670 19 9 0

We find Lieut Philip Goodridge Charges himself of having Recevd of the Proprietors money and Securities to the amount of four Hundred and Ninety pounds ninteen Shillings 0/3¾. 499 19 3 3

it appears to us that Coll Aaron Willard Did Recvd of the Proprietors money and Securities —— —— —— —— —— —— 134 14 10 1

that the abovesaid Goodridge Discharges himself by paying the Proprietors Debts, for which he produced proper Vouchers to the amount of one Hundred and Sixty Seven pounds two Shillings two pence two farthings —— —— —— —— —— 167 2 2 2

and that there Remains Due to the Proprietors from Said Goodridge three Hundred and thirty two pounds Seventeen Shillings one peney one farthing of moneys & Securities 332 17 1 1

it appears that Benja Redington Recevd three New Emition Dollers

and it appears that Josiah Willard purchest Land of the Proprietors for which he hath not given Security for, to the amount of —— —— —— —— —— —— £27 3 9

and that the above-Said Goodridge hath now in his hands of the property of the Proprietors in old Emition Continantal Currency 2073½ Dollars

Errors Excepted

Joseph Hartwell } Committee
Thads Commings

Dated January ye 17th 1784

2ly. Voted there be a Divifion made of three Hundred pounds for the firft Divifion of the Proprietors monies arifing from the Sales of their Common and undivided Lands

3ly. Voted to Chufe two men for a Committee Equally to Divide the above three Hundred pounds amongft the Said Proprietors

[96] 4ly. Voted and Choofe Thaddeus Commings and Benj<u>a</u> Redington for the above Said Committee

5ly. Voted to Chufe two men to prefent the order of Court to the Judge of Probate, that he order his Comiffioners on the Eftate of Co<u>ll</u> Aaron Willard Late of Lunenburg Deceaf<u>d</u> to Set according to Said order of Court alfo to wait on Said Comiffioners and Exebit the Clames of the Proprietors before them.

6ly. Voted the Expence of this meeting be paid by the Proprietors which is Eleven Shillings

7ly Voted to adjorn this meeting to the firft munday of June next at one Clock after noon at this place

Philip Goodridge Modirator

Recorded the 20th Day of march 1784.

₱ Joseph Hartwell Proprietors Clark

June ye 7th 1784 Being Met according to adjornment at the houfe of Lieu<u>t</u> Philip Goodridge in Lunenburg Inholder being Duly formed S<u>d</u> meeting opened.

firft Voted Lieu<u>t</u> Philip Goodridge Cap<u>t</u> Benj<u>a</u> Goodridge M<u>r</u> Benj<u>a</u> Redington be a Committee to wait on the Comiffoners and Exebit the Clames of the proprietors on the Eftate of Co<u>ll</u> Aaron Willard Late of Lunenburg Deceaf<u>d</u>

2ly Voted the Expence of this meeting be pay<u>d</u> by the proprietors which is 2^s/4

3ly Voted to adjorn this meeting to the Second munday of Auguft next at one a Clock after noon at this place

Philip Goodridge Modirator

Recorded the Eighth Day of June 1784

Joseph Hartwell proprietors Clark

Auguſt the 9th 1784 being met according to adjornmet at the Houſe of Lieu Philip Goodridge in Lunenburg inholder being Duly formed Sd meeting being opened.

not haveing a return from the Comiſſioners (on the Eſtate of Coll Aaron Willard Late of Lunenburg Deceaſd) of his writes in the Proprietors Common & undeveided Lands the Committee Chooſen to make a Diviſion of the moneys the aboveſaid Land was Sold for Could not proſcede thereon therefore Voted to adjourn this meeting to Second munday of Sept next at one a Clock afternoon at this place.

Philip Goodridge Modirator
Recorded by me Joseph Hartwell Clark

[97] September ye 13th 1784 Being Met according to Adjornment at the Houſe of Lieut Philip Goodridge in Lunenburg Inholder Being Duly formed Said meeting being opened.

firſt Voted to allow Samuel Billing an account of Eighteen Shillings for Services don for the Proprietors

2ly Voted the Expence of this Meeting be paid by the Proprietors Said Expence Eight Shillings

3ly Voted to adjorn this Meeting to the ninth Day of November next at one a Clock after noon at this place.

Philip Goodridge Modirator
Recorded by me Joſeph Hartwell Clark

November ye 9th 1784 Being Met according to Adjornment at the Houſe of Lieut Philip Goodridge in Lunenburg Inholder Being Duly formed Said meeting being opened.

by Reaſon of the Adminiſterators of the Eſtate of Coll Aaron Willard late of Lunenburg Deceaſd not being Ready to Settle with the Proprietors of the Townſhip of Lunenburg at this Meeting therefore. Voted to adjorn this meeting to the firſt tueſday of January next at one a Clock after noon at this place

Philip Goodridge Modirator

Recorded the 10th of November 1784.

℔ Joseph Hartwell Clark

January ye 4th 1785. being Meet according to adjormment at the Houſe of Lieu^t Philip Goodridge in Lunenburg Inholder being Duly formed S^d meeting being opened.

firſt Voted the Expence of this meeting be paid by the Proprietor.

2^ly· Voted to adjorn this Meeting to the third Tueſday of March next at one a Clock after noon at this place

Philip Goodridge Modirator

Recorded 25th of January 1785

₱ Joseph Hartwell Clark

[98] March ye 15th 1785. Being met according to adjornment at the Houſe of Lieu^t Philip Goodridge in Lunenburg Inholder being Duly formed Said meeting opened.

firſt Voted to allow Joseph Hartwell an account of Six Shillings & Six pence for Recording one plan & proceidings of Six meetings

2^ly· Voted to Chuſe a man to Confer with the Adminiſtrators of the Eſtate of Co^ll Aaron Willard Late of Lunenburg Deceaſ^d and procure the Deeds which S^d Willard had of a Number of Rights of Land in S^d Lunenburg for which Said Willard did Receive his full pay in his life time of Said Proprietors. and procure a Diſcharge for Said proprietors for the Same: from S^d Adminiſtrators.

3^ly· Voted and Chooſe Mr Thaddeus Commings for the above porpoſe

4^ly· Voted the Expence of this Meeting be paid by the proprietors 2^s·/₀

5^ly· Voted this meeting be adjorned to the firſt wedneſday of may next at one a Clock after noon at this place

Philip Goodridge Modirator

Recorded ye 16th Day of march 1785.

₱ Joseph Hartwell Proprietors Clark

May ye 4th 1785

Being meet according to Adjornment at the Houſe of Lieu^t Philip Goodridge in Lunenburg Inholder being Duly formed Said meeting opened.

Some maters on the Eftate of Co¹ Aaron Willard Deceaſᵈ not being Settled with the Proprietors therefore

Voted to adjorn this meeting to the twenty Second Day of June next at three a Clock after noon at this place

      Philip Goodridge Modarater

Recorded yᵉ 12 Day of may 1785

    ℔ Joseph Hartwell Clark

June yᵉ 22ᵈ 1785 being met accordind to adjorment at the Houſe of Lievᵗ Philip Goodridge in Lunenburg Inholder being Duly formed Said meeting being opened

Voted to alowed Mʳ Thomas Harkneſs Six Shilling for Sitting on the new Commiſion on the Eſtate of Coˡˡ Aaron Willard Deceaſᵈ

Voted to Send a letter to Doc Lee one of the Adminiſtrators of the Eſtate of Coˡˡ Aaron Willard of Lunenburg Deceaſᵈ to Call on him to make a ſpeedy Settlement with the proprietors of Lunenburg

Expence be paid by the Proprietors 10/11

Voted to adjorn this Meeting to the firſt munday of Sepᵗ next at one a Clock after noon at this place

      Philip Goodridge Modirator

Recorded by me Joseph Hartwell Proprietors Clark

[99] September yᵉ 5ᵗʰ 1785.

Being met according to Adjornment at the Houſe of Lieuᵗ Philip Goodridge in Lunenburg Inholder. Being Duly formed Sᵈ meeting opened

1. Voted to allow Phinehas Hartwell an acount of Eight Shillings for Services Don for the proprietors.

2ˡʸ· Voted that the proprietors Committee of Sales be directed to Deſire the Judge to Call the Adminiſtrators on the Eſtate of Coˡˡ Aaron Willard Deceaſᵈ to a Speedy Settlement of their accounts they have againſt Said Eſtate. and Sᵈ Committee or any three of them be impowered to Settle all matters of Diſpute Subſiſting between Sᵈ proprietors and the adminiſtrators on the aboveſaid Eſtate and make their Report at the adjornment of this meeting

3ly. Voted the Expence of this meeting be paid by the proprietors which is 2/0

4ly. Voted to adjorn this meeting to the firft munday of December next at one o,Clock after noon at this place

Philip Goodridge Modirator

Recorded by me Joseph Hartwell Proprietors Clark

December ye 5th 1785. Being met according to adjornment at the Houfe of Lieu^t Philip Goodridge in Lunenburg Inholder being Duly formed Said meeting opened.

the Proprietors Committee of Sales made their Report according to a Vote of Said proprietors at a meeting on the 5th Day of September Laft as follows.

there was a Deed Given in behalf of S^d proprietors of a Scartain track of Land to Co^{ll} Aaron Willard Deceaf^d in which there was a mifstake in the Boundaries there of and that the adminiftrators of the S^d Eftate have agreed with the Said Committee and by Confent of the Judge of probate have given a Deed of aquitance of all the Lands Comprehended by the firft mentioned Deed.

Voted to Except of the profcedings of the above Said Committee of Sales

2ly Voted the Expence of this meeting be paid by the proprietors which is 7/0

3ly Voted to adjorn this meeting to the Second munday of march next at one o,Clock after noon at this place.

Philip Goodridge Modirator

Recorded by me Joseph Hartwell proprietors Clark

[**100**] March ye 13th 1786. Being meet according to adjornment at the Houfe of Lieu^t Philip Goodridge in Lunenburg Inholder being Duly formed Said meeting opened.

firft Voted to Chufe a Committee to Reckon with the proprietors Receiver of monies arifing from the Sales of there Common Lands and make Report at the adjornment of this meeting

2ly Voted to Cheufe three men for Said Committee

3ly Voted and Choofe Mr Samuel Johnson Capt Benj^a Goodridge Mr Thaddeus Commings for the above Said Committee

4ly Voted the Expence of this meeting be paid by the proprietors which is 8ˢ/0

5ly Voted to adjorn this meeting to the Second munday of april next at one o,Clock after noon at this place

Phillip Goodridge Modirator

Recorded by me Joseph Hartwell proprietors Clark

April yᵉ 10ᵗʰ 1786 being met according adjornment at the Houſe of Lieut Philip Goodridge of Lunenburg Inholder being Duly formed Sᵈ meeting opened

firſt Voted to allow Mʳ Samuel Johnſon an account of one pound & ſeven pence for Services Don for the proprietors

2ly Voted to allow Joseph Hartwell an account of Six Shilling and Eight pence for Recording meeting & Copping of plans

3ly where as Lieu Philip Goodridge Received of the proprietors monies ariſing from the Sales of their Common & undevided Lands Did Lend to Coll Aaron Willard one of the Committee of Sales of Sᵈ proprietors Lands 8361 Continintal paper Dollers as the Eſtate of Sᵈ Willard was Rendered Enſolvent therefore

Voted the Sᵈ Goodridge be acountable to the Sᵈ proprietors two thirds of the above 8361 paper Dollers at 75 for one in Silver Doller which is £22 = 6–0 Silver money

4ly Voted the Expence of this meeting be paid by the proprietors is 7ˢ/0

5ly Voted to adjorn this meeting to the Seventeenth day of this Inſtent April one a,Clock after noon at this place

Philip Goodridge Modirator

Recorded by me Joseph Hartwell proprietors Clark

[101] April yᵉ 17ᵗʰ 1786 Being met according to Adjornment at the Houſe of Lieut Philip Goodridge in Lunenburg Inholder being Duly formed Said meeting opened

firſt Voted to Except the Reckoning of the Committee Choſen to Reckon with the Receveir of the Proprietors monies arifing from the Sales of their Common and undevided Lands Viz. We the Subfcribers being appointed a committee to Reckon with the Proprietors Receiver of monies arifing from the Sales of their Common Land Viz. Lieu^t Philip Goodridge have attended Said bufinefs and find Due from S^d Receiver three Hundred and twenty four pounds four Shillings three farthings, and alfo twenty-Seven pounds three Shillings and nine pence which is Due to the Proprietors from Co^{ll} Josiah Willard for Land he Bought of Said Proprietors, for which Sum he hath given no fecurity for

Lunenburg April ye 17th 1786

Errors Excepted   Samuel Johnfon   ⎫
                      Benj^a Goodridge   ⎬ Committee
                      Thadeus Commings ⎭

                           Philip Goodridge} Receiver

2^{ly} Voted to Divide 300 pounds and Divide two thoufen Sixty Eight one half Doller paper Continantal Currency (now in the Recever hand) among the Proprietors. and hear the Report of the Committee Chofen to make a Divifion of moneis arifing from the Sales of their Common and undivided Lands, at the Adjornment of this meeting.

3^{ly} Voted the Expence of this meeting be paid by the proprietors which is Six Shillings and five pence

4^{ly} Voted to Adjorn this meeting to the third munday of may next at one o,Clock after noon at this place

Philip Goodridge Modirator

Recorded by me Joseph Hartwell proprietors
                                                       Clark

[102] May the 15th 1786. Being met according to Adjornment at the Houfe of Lieu^t Philip Goodridge in Lunenburg Inholder being Duly formed Said meeting opened

firft Voted to accept the Report of the Committee Chofen to Divide three Hundred pounds Silver money. and two thoufends and Sixty Eight and a half Dollers of Continantal paper Currency among the Porprietors. viz.

we the Subſcribers being appointed by a vote of the proprietors of the town of Lunenburg to Divide three Hundred pounds of Silver money and two thouſands and Sixty Eight & ½ Continantal paper Dollars Equially amongſt Seventy five proprietors (co[ll] Aaron Willard having Rec[d] the full pay for ten Rights in his Lifetime and the Miniſteral and miniſter School and Collage Rights being Excluded from any Share in the money ariſeing from the Sale of their Common Land) do find that Each of the above Said Seventy-five proprietors have a right to Receive four pounds Silver money and twenty Seven Continantal paper Dollers. Each perſon Claiming a Shair in the moneys above mentioned are to make out Sufficient titals therefor unto Miſ[ers] Sam[l]. Johnſon Benj[a] Goodridge & Thaddeus Commings who are a Committee appointed to give orders for the payment of the Same to be Drawn on Philip Goodridge Receiver of the proprietors money

Lunenburg may 15th 1786

Benj[a] Redington } Committee
Thaddeus Comming }

2[ly] Voted the Expence of this meeting be paid by the proprietors which is Seven Shillings and four pence

3[ly] Voted to Adjorn this meeting to the third munday of July next one o,Clock after noon at this place

Philip Goodridge Modirator
Recorded by me ℔ Joseph Hartwell Clark

[103] July y[e] 17th 1786 being met according to Adjornment at the Houſe of Lieu[t] Philip Goodridge in Lunenburg Inholder being formed S[d] meeting opened

firſt Voted to allow to Cap[t] Benj[a] Goodridge an account of one pound Six[s] Shillings and Eight pence for Services Don for the proprietors

2[ly]. Voted to allow Thaddeus Commings an account of one pound one ſhilling for Services Don for the proprietors

3[ly]. Voted to allow Benj[a] Redington an account of one pound Eight Shillings and Eight pence for Services Don for the proprietors

4ly Voted the Expence of this meeting be paid by the proprietors which is 8/2

5ly Voted to Adjorn this meeting the firft munday of October next at one o,Clock after noon at this place

      Philip Goodridge Modirator
  Recorded by me ℔ Joseph Hartwell Clark

october ye 2d 1786 being met according to adjornment at the Houfe of Lieut Philip Goodridge in Lunenburg Inholder being Duly formed Said meeting opened.

firft Voted to allow Eleazer Houghton Junr an account of Six Shillings and nine pence for Services don for the Proprietors

2ly Voted to allow Joseph Hartwell Eighteen pence per meeting for his attending as proprietors Clark. and two Shillings for one quire of paper

That where as a Smole Number of the Proprietors of the Townfhip of Lunenburg have attended the bufinefs in the Settlement of the proprietors Common and undivided Lands we think it Highly Reafonable that they be allowed for their attendance on Said meetings

3ly Voted to allow Each proprietor so attending Eighteen pence for every meeting he Shall make appear he attended

4ly Voted the Expence of this meeting be paid by the proprietors which is Eight Shillings

5ly Voted to Adjorn this meeting to the firft munday of January next one o'clock after noon at this place

      Philip Goodridge Modirator
  Recorded by me ℔ Joseph Hartwell Proprietors Clark

January ye 1ft 1787 met according to Adjornment at the Houfe of Lieut Philip Goodridge in Lunenburg Inholder and Adjorned this meeting to the Eighth Day of this Inftant January at one o,Clock after noon at this place

      Philip Goodridge Modirator
  Recorded by me ℔ Joseph Hartwell Clark.

[104] January ye 8th 1787: Being met according to Adjornment at the Houſe of Lieu^t Philip Goodridge in Lunenburg Inholder being Duly formed Said meeting opened.

Firſt Voted to allow Samuel Johnson three pounds fourteen Shillings for Services Don for the proprietors and for attending Sundry proprietors meetings £3 : 14 : 0

2^ly. Voted to allow Lieu^t Philip Goodridge ten pounds three Shillings and four pence for Expences of meetings to this Day and Services Don for the Proprietors to this time 10 : 3 : 4

3^ly Voted to allow Eleazer Houghton Ju^r two pounds Six Shillings and Six pence for attending Sundry proprietors meetings 2 : 6 : 6

4^ly Voted to allow Capt Benj^a Goodridge four pounds three Shillings and Six pence for Services Don for the proprietors and for attending Sundry proprietors meetings 4 : 3 : 6

5^ly Voted to allow Thaddeus Commings two pounds Seventeen Shillings for Services Don for the proprietors and for attending ſundry proprietors meetings 2 : 17 : 0

6^ly Voted to allow Benj^a Redington three pounds ten Shillings and Six pence for attending ſundry proprietors meeting 3 : 10 : 6

7^ly Voted to adjorn this meeting to ye firſt munday of may next at one o'Clock after noon at this place

      Philip Goodridge Modirator
Recorded this 9th Day of January 1787
    Joseph Hartwell proprietors Clark

May ye 7th 1787 Being met according to Adjornment at the houſe of Lieu^t Philip Goodridge in Lunenburg Inholder being Duly formed Voted to adjorn this meeting to the twenty-Eighth day of this Inſtant may at two o'clock after noon at this place
      Philip Goodridge Modirator
Recorded this 8th day of may 1787
    Joseph Hartwell proprietors Clark

may the 28th 1787 Being met according to adjornment at the Houſe of Lieut Philip Goodridge in Lunenburg being Duly formed Said meeting opened.

firſt Voted Sel a Track of Land lying in Fitchburg adjoyning to Thomas Cowdrin Junr. Land about forty acres alſo a nother Track or lott of land in Sd Fitchburg Containing about twenty acres lying South of Edward Scott's Houſe which Said Scott bid off and has not fulfilled the Condiſions of the Sale thereof

2ly Voted to adjorn this meeting to the firſt mon-day of october next at one o'clock after noon at this place

Philip Goodridge Modirator
Recorded by me Joseph Hartwell proprietors Clerk

[105] october ye 1ſt 1787 Being met according to Adjornment at the Houſe of Leiut Philip Goodridge in Lunenburg.

Being Duly formed Said meeting opened

firſt Voted to allow Joseph Hartwell twelve Shillings and Eight pence for Recording Eight meetings and attending four meetings

2ly Voted to Adjorn this meeting to the firſt Day of January next at one o,Clock after noon at this place

Philip Goodridge Modirator
Recorded by me Joseph Hartwell Proprietors Clark.

January ye 1ſt 1788. Being met according to Adjornment at the Houſe of Leiut Philip Goodridge in Lunenburg. being Duly formed Said meeting opened

firſt Voted Mr Samuel Johnſon be Directed to Receive of Dr Joseph Lee of Concord (Adminiſterator on the Eſtate of Coll Aaron Willard Late of Lunenburg Deceaſ'd) Eighteen pounds Sixteen Shillings (agreable to the Decree of the Judge of probate for the County of Worceſter) which is Due to the proprietors of Lunenburg from the Said Coll Aaron Willard Eſtate; and that Said Johnſon be Impowered to give a Diſcharge for the Same Sum. and be acountable to the proprietors for the Same

2ly Voted the Committee of Sales be Directed to poſt and Sell at Publick Vandue the two peaces of Land in

Fitchburg (as before ordered to Sell) on the Second tuefday of April next. if not Sold before at privet Sale.

3ly Voted the Expences of this meeting be paid by the proprietors which is nine Shillings

4ly Voted to adjorn this meeting to the Second tuefday of April next at the Houfe of Thomas Cowdin Efq^r inholder in Fitchburg at one o'Clock after noon

Philip Goodridge Modirator

Recorded this Second day of January 1788

Joseph Hartwell proprietors Clark

April ye 8th 1788 being met according to Adjornment at the Houfe of Thomas Cowdons in Fitchburg Efq^r Inholder being Duly formed f^d meeting opened.

firft Voted to Choofe a modirator for this prefent meeting

2.ly. Voted and Choofe Mr Samuel Johnfon Modirator for this prifent meeting

Voted the Expence of this meeting be paid by the Proprietors

Voted to Adjorn this Meeting to the firft Munday in June next at Mr Samuel Johnfons in Lunenburg Inholder at one o'clock after noon and the Sale of the twenty acres of Land lying by Edward Scoots to the Adjornment of this meeting

Samuel Johnson Modirator

Recorded by me ℔ Joseph Hartwell Proprietors Clark

[107] June ye 2^d 1788. being met according to Adjornment at the houfe of Mr Samuel Johnfon in Lunenburg Inholder being Duly formed S^d meeting opened

firft Voted that Edward Scoot Donot Settle with the Proprietors for the twenty acres of Land he bought of them at Vandue that the Commettee of Sales is hereby Directed to Sell the Same within one week Either at publick Vandue or at private Sale as they Shall think beft

2ly Voted the Expence of this meeting be paid by the proprietors being nine Shillings

3ly Voted to Adjorn this meeting to the Second mun-

day in September next at the houfe of Lieu^t Philip Goodridge in Lunenburg at one o'clock after noon
Philip Goodridge Modirator
Recorded this third Day of June 1788
℔ Joseph Hartwell proprietor Clark

September ye 8th 1788 being met according to Adjornment at the Houfe of Lieu^t Philip Goodridge in Lunenburg being Duly formed Said meeting opened

firft Voted the proprietors Treafurer Difcharge all the taxes affefed on the proprietors Lands un fold

2^{ly} Voted to Adjorn this meeting to the firft munday of February next at one o'clock afternoon at this place
Philip Goodridge Modirator
Recorded by me ℔ Joseph Hartwell Clark

February ye 2^d 1789 being met according to Adjornment at the Houfe of Lieu^t Philip Gooridge in Lunenburg being Duly formed faid meeting opened

firft Voted that Lieu^t Philip Goodridge call on Edward Scott to Settle his note he gave to the proprietors and alfo his promife if faid Scott Refufes to Settle the Same to put it in Suit Inediately in behalf of the proprietors

2^{ly} Voted to allow Jonas Kindall an account of Eight Shillings for Services Don for the proprietors

3^{ly} Voted the Committee appointed to give out orders (upon Lieu^t Philip Goodridge Receiver of the proprietors monies) to thofe that Clame Rite in the undivided Lands of Said proprietors of Lunenburg Townfhip Said Committee be Diricted to publifh in one of the Bofton papers that all those that have rites or Clames to the Said undivided Lands bring in there Clames to Said Committee to Receive orders for payment

4^{ly} Voted the Expence of this meeting be paid by the proprietors being Eight Shillings

5^{ly} Voted to adjorn this meeting to monday ye 23 Day of march next at one o'Clock after noon at this place
Philip Goodridge Modirator
Recorded ye 3^d day of march 1789
Joseph Hartwell Clark

[108] March ye 23^d 1789 Being met according to Adjornment at the Houfe of Lieu^t Philip Goodridge in Lunenburg being Duly formed S^d meeting opened

firft Voted that Mr Benj^a Redington one of the Proprietors Committee be directed to Inquire of and advife with Lawyer Gill Refpecting Scootts affairs with the Proprietors and Likewife with Scoott if he thinks it nefsiary. and Repoort to the Committee on what tearms Settlement may be had and Receive their farther Direction

2.^ly Voted the Expence of this meeting be paid by the Proprieter being four Shillings

3^ly Votd to adjorn this meeting to the Second munday in June next at one o'clock after noon at this place

      Philip Goodridge Modirator
   Recorded by me Joseph Hartwell Clark

June ye 8th 1789 being met according to Adjornment at the houfe of Lieu^t Philip Goodridge in Lunenburg being Duly formed S^d meeting opened.

first Voted to allow Edward Scoot Six-teen Shillings & Sixpence for his attending Eleven meetings as a proprietor alfo Six Shillings for Services Don for the proprietors in Showing the Common & undevided Lands alfo nine Shillings for three Days in affifting in Serveying common Lands total £1: 11: 6:

2^ly Voted the Expence of this meeting be paid by the proprietors being 5/0

3^ly Voted to Adjorn this meeting to the Second munday of Sep^t next at one o'clock after noon at this place

      Philip Goodridge Modirator
 Recorded by me ⅏ Joseph Hartwell proprietors Clark

Sep^t ye 14th 1789. Being met according to Adjornment at the Houfe of Lieu^t Philip Goodridge in Lunenburg being Duly formed Said meeting opened a number of the propietors not prefent at S^d meeting thougt fit to adjorn to Sum futer Day

Voted the Expence of this meeting be paid by the proprietors being 3/0

Voted to Adjorn this meeting to the firſt munday of November next at this place at one o,Clock after noon
Philip Goodridge Modirater
Recorded by me ⅏ Joseph Hartwell proprietors Clark

November yᵉ 2ᵈ 1789 being met according to Adjornment at the Houſe of Lieuᵗ philip Goodridge in Lunenburg being Duly formed Said meeting opened. firſt Voted the Expence of this meeting be paid by the proprietors being Seven Shillings and Six pence

Voted to adjorn this meeting to the Second munday of January next at nine a o'clock in the morning at this place
Philip Goodridge Modirator
Recorded by me ⅏ Joseph Hartwell Proprietors Clark

[109] January yᵉ 11ᵗʰ 1790. being met according Adjornment at the Houſe of Lieuᵗ Philip Goodridge in Lunenburg being Duly formed Said meeting opened.

firſt Voted to allow Joseph Hartwell an account of —— —— —— —— —— —— —— £1　5　10

2ˡʸ Voted to allow Eleazer Houghton an account of —— —— —— —— —— ——　　　　0　9　0
for attending Sundry meeting

3ˡʸ Voted to Adjorn this meeting to morrow at one aClock afternoon at this place *(being met according to Janury 12ᵗʰ* adjornment at the Houſe of Lieuᵗ Philip Goodridge in Lunenburg Said meeting opened.)

firſt Voted to allow Benjᵃ Redington an account of —— —— —— —— —— —— —— 2　10　8
for Services don for the proprietors & attending Sundry meetings

2ˡʸ· Voted to allow Bejᵃ Goodridge an account of —— —— —— —— —— —— —— 2　6　1
for Services don for the proprietors and attending Sundry meetings

3ˡʸ· Voted to allow Thaddeas Commings an account of —— —— —— —— —— —— —— 1　9　6
for Services don for the proprietors and attending Sundry meetings

4ly. Voted to allow Samuel Johnson an account
of ⸺ ⸺ ⸺ ⸺ ⸺ ⸺ ⸺ ⸺ 3 13 10
for Services don for the proprietors and attending Sundry meetings

5ly. Voted the Expence of this meeting be paid
by ye proprietors it being ⸺ ⸺ ⸺ ⸺ 1 3 0

6ly Voted to Adjorn this meeting to the Second munday of February next at one a'Clock after noon at this place

      Philip Goodridge Modirator

Recorded the 13 Day of January 1790 by me
    Joseph Hartwell proprietors Clark

February ye 8th 1790 being met according to adjornment at the House of Lieut Philip Goodridge in Lunenburg Being Duly formed Said meeting opened

first Voted to allow Lieut Philip Goodridge
an account of   5 11 0

2ly Voted to Chuse a Committee to Reckon with the proprietors treasurer

3ly Voted and Choose Thaddeus Commings & Capt Benja Goodridge for Said Committee

4ly Voted the Expence of this meeting be
paid by the proprietors being ⸺ ⸺ ⸺ 0 6 0

Voted to Adjorn this meeting to the first munday of June next one o'Clock after noon at this place

      Philip Goodridge Modirator

Recorded the ninth Day of June 1790 by me
    Joseph Hartwell proprietors Clark

[110] June the 7th 1790. being met according to adjornment at the House of Lieut Philip Goodridge in Lunenburg being Duly formed Sd meeting opened

Voted to adjorn this meeting to the Last munday of this Instant June at two o'clock after noon at this place

      Philip Goodridge Modirator

Recorded by me ℔ Joseph Hartwell proprietors Clark

June the 28th 1790. Being met according to Adjornment at the House of Lieut Philip Goodridge in Lunenburg being Duly formed Said meeting opened firſt Voted to alow Philip Goodridge an account of four pounds Seventeen Shillings £4 17 - 0 for Expences of meetings and Serveing Treaſurer for the proprietors (and other Services don for the S.ᵈ proprietors) to this time

the Report of the Committee Choſen (February the 8ᵗʰ 1790.) to Reckon with the proprietors Treaſurer is as follows. viz. we the Subſcribers being Choſen a Committee to Reckon with Philip Goodridge Treaſurer or Recever of the Proprietors moneis of the Town of Lunenburg ariſing from from the Sale of the Common Lands have attended the buſineſs and find that there is Due from Said Goodridge to the above Said Proprietors one hundred and Seventy pounds fifteen Shillings and one peney one farthing £170 15 s. 1 d. 1 far

June the 28ᵗʰ 1790   Thadˢ· Commings ⎫ Committee
                              Benjᵃ Goodridge ⎭

                          Philip Goodridge ⎫ Receiver

Voted to Adjorn this meeting to the firſt munday of September next at one o'Clock after noon at this place
                    Philip Goodridge Modirator

Recorded this 29ᵗʰ day of June 1790
               by me Joseph Hartwell Clark

September the 6ᵗʰ 1790 Being met according to adjornment at the Houſe of Lieuᵗ Philip Goodridge in Lunenburg being Duly formed S.ᵈ meeting opened

an order called a general order Supoſeing to Contain Several particuler orders (being in the Treaſurers hand) not to be found Could not profeed to buſineſs therefore thought beſt to adjorn for a ſhort time

firſt Voted the Expence of this meeting be paid by the proprietors being 3/0

2ˡʸ Voted to Adjorn this meeting to munday the twentieth day of this Inſtent Sepᵗ· at one o'Clock after noon at this place
                  Philip Goodridge Modirator

Recorded this Seventh day of Sepᵗ· 1790
               ℔ me Joseph Hartwell Clark

[112] September the 20th 1790 Being met according to Adjornment at the Houfe of Lieut Philip Goodridge in Lunenburg being Duly formed Sd meeting opened

firft Voted to Chufe a Treafurer in the Roome of Lieut Philip Goodridge.

2ly. Voted and Choofe Eleazer Houghton Treafurer

3ly. Voted to adjorn this meeting to, to morrow at four a Clock after noon at this at this place

Philip Goodridge Modirator

Sept ye 21th 1790 being met according to adjornment Sd meeting opened

firft Voted to Except of a Settlement made this Day with Philip Goodridge Receiver of the proprietors moneis, by the Commette Choofen for that purpofe viz. the Said Goodridge Difschargefes himfelf from the Ballance Due to the Proprietors. acording to a Reckoning on the 28th of June 1790 of —— —— —— —— —— —— £170 $^{s.}_{15}$ $^{d.}_{1}$ $^{f.}_{1}$

by Dilivering up to Said Proprietors Sundry Notes of hand and obligations which he had in his hands belonging to Sd proprietors to the amount of —— —— —— —— £161 $^{s}_{8}$ 7 3

and by giving his note of hand for —— —— 9 7 6 2

which Settlement is hereby Excepted and the Said Goodridge is Difcharged from any further Demands from the proprietors as a Receiver of their monies

2ly. Voted to allow an account to Jofeph Hartwell of —— —— —— —— —— —— £0 13 2

3ly. Voted the Expence of the above meetings be paid by the proprietors being —— —— 0 6 0

4ly Vted to Adjorn this meeting to to the firft munday of December next at one o'clock after noon at this place

Philip Goodridge Modirator

Recorded this 22d Day of Sept 1790

℔ Joseph Hartwell Clark

[113] December the 6th 1790 Being met according to Adjornment at the Houfe of Lieut Philip Goodridge in Lunenburg being Duly formed Said meeting opened.

firft Voted to allow Benj^a Goodridge an account of —— —— —— —— —— —— £1 8 2
for Services don for the Proprietors

2$^{ly.}$ Voted to allow Thaddeus Commings an account of —— —— —— —— —— —— 1 2 0
for Services don for the Proprietors

3$^{ly.}$ Voted to Chufe a man to lay the Cafe of this Propriety before Some Sutable perfon that may direct him how to petifion the great & General Court that they pafs an act or Refolve for the finial Settlement of the Proprietorfhip of the Town of Lunenburg.

4$^{ly.}$ Voted and Choofe Mr Benj^a Redington for the above Service

5$^{ly.}$ Voted the Expence of this meeting be paid by the proprietors being 4/0

6^{ly} Voted to Adjorn this meeting to the Second munday of march next at the Houfe of Capt Benj^a Goodridge in Lunenburg at one o'Clock after noon

      Philip Goodridge Modirator

Recorded this 22^d Day of December. 1790.

    ₱ Joseph Hartwell proprietors Clark

March the 14th 1791. Being met according to Adjornment at the Houfe of Capt Benj^a Goodridge in Lunenburg being Duly formed S^d meeting opened.

firft Voted to Chufe a Modirator for this prefent meeting

2^{ly} Voted and Choofe Mr Samuel Johnson modirator for S^d meeting

3^{ly} Voted to allow Joseph Hartwell an account of —— —— —— —— —— —— £1 1 10

4^{ly} Voted to allow Edward Scoot an account of —— —— —— —— —— —— 0 12 00

5^{ly} Voted the Expence of this meeting be paid by the proprietors being ten Shillings

6^{ly} Voted to Adjorn this meeting to munday ye 13th day of June next at one o'clock after noon at this place

      Samuel Johnfon Modirator

Recorded this 13th day of march 1791

    ₱ Joseph Hartwell proprietors Clark

[**114**] June ye 13th 1791 Being met according to adjornment at the Houſe of Capt Benjamin Goodridge in Lunenburg being Duly formed Said meeting opined.

Firſt Voted and Chooſe Mr Samuel Johnſon Modirator for this preſent meeting

2ly. Voted to allow Benja Redington an account of — — — — — — £1 11 7 for Services don for the proprietors and attanding Sundry meetings

3ly

4ly. Voted the Expence of this meeting be payed by the proprietors being four Shillings

5ly. Voted to adjorn this meeting to munday the Seventh Day of November next at one o'Clock after noon at this place

Samuel Johnſon Modirator

Recorded this 14th of June 1791

℘ Joseph Hartwell Clark

November ye 7th 1791 Being met according to Adjornment at the Houſe of Capt Benjamin Goodridge in Lunenburg being Duly formed Said meeting opened.

firſt Voted and Choſe Capt Benja Goodridge Modirator for this preſent meeting

2ly. Voted to Adjorn this Meeting to munday the Second day of January next at one o'Clock afternoon at this place

Benjamin Goodridge Modirator

Recorded ℘ me Joſeph Hartwell proprietors Clark

January ye 2d 1792. Being met according to Adjornment at the Houſe of Capt Benja Goodridge in Lunenburg being Duly formed Said meeting opened.

firſt Voted and Choſe Capt Benjamin Goodridge Madirator for this preſent meeting

2ly Voted to allow Joseph Hartwell an account of £0 7 0

3ly Voted Eleazer Houghton proprietors Treaſurer by a Vote of Said proprietors is Directed to Call on the Adminiſtrators on the Eſtate of Aaron Willard late of

Lunenburg Deceased for emmediate payment of the Devidand Due to S^d proprietors of Lunenburg as will appear by the Decree of the Judge of probate for the County of Worcester.

4^{ly} Voted the Expence of this be paid by the proprietors being 0–10–4

5^{ly} Voted to adjorn this meeting to the first munday of June next at one o'Clock after noon at this place

Benj^a Goodridge Modirator
Recorded ℞ me Joseph Hartwell
Proprietors Clark

[115] June ye 4.th 1792. being met according to adjornment at the House of Capt Benjamin Goodridge in Lunenburg being Duly formed Said meeting opened

first Voted and Chose Mr Samuel Johnson Modirator for this present meeting

2^{ly} Voted to adjorn this meeting to munday the third Day of September next at one o'Clock after noon at this place

Samuel Johnson Modirator

Recorded this 4th Day of June 1792.

℞^{r} Joseph Hartwell proprietors Clark

September ye 3.^{d} 1792 being met according to adjornment at the House of Capt Benjamin Goodridge in Lunenburg Said meeting opened

first Voted and Chose Capt Benjamin Goodridge Modirator —— —— —— —— —— —— —— —— ——

2^{ly} Voted to adjorn this meeting to munday the fifth day of November next at one o'clock after noon at this place

Benjamin Goodridge
Modirator

Recorded this 3th day of Sep^t 1792

℞ Joseph Hartwell Clark

November ye 5th 1792 being met according to adjornment at the House of Capt Benjamin Goodridge in Lunenburg Inholder Said meeting opened.

first Voted the Expence of this meeting and the two

former meetings June ye 4.th Sep^t ye 3^d 1792 be paid by the proprietors being ten Shilling & Eight pence

2^{ly} Voted to adjorn this meeting to thurſ day the fifteenth Day of this Inſtant at one o'Clock after noon at this place

the proprietor Committee are Directed by S^d proprietors to Rectify a miſſtake in Laying-out Common Land on Land before Laid out, and make Return at the adjornment of this meeting

Recorded this Six Day of November 1792

Benjamin Goodridge Modirator
℘ Joseph Hartwell
proprietors Clark

November ye 15th 1792 being met according to Adjornment at the Houſe of Capt Benjamin Goodridge Inholder in Lunenburg Said meeting opened

firſt Voted Mr Benj^a Redington Receive the proprietors book of Records into his hand and Return it Safe at the adjornment of this meeting

2^{ly} Voted to adjorn this meeting to munday the twenty-Sixth Day this Inſtant November at one o'Clock after noon at this place

Benj^a Goodridge Modirater

Recorded this twenty-ſixth Day of November 1792
℘ Joseph Hartwell Clark

[116] November ye 26th 1792 being met according to Adjornment at the Houſe of Capt Benjamin Goodridge in Lunenburg Inholder Said meeting opened.

firſt the Committee of the proprietors haveing deeded to Phinehas Dunsmore a Track of Land clamed by Mr Jacob Welch as his propity

therefore Voted to Chueſe a Committee of three men in behalf of Said proprietors to Submit all the matters of damages which accrue to Said Welch by reaſon of Said Dunsmores Treſpaſsing upon his Land as alledged in the writ brought by Said Welch aganſt said Dunſmore

Voted and Chooſe Capt Benjamin Goodridge Benjamin Redington and Thaddeus Commings for the above Said

Committee the Said Committee or any two of them to act on behalf of the Said proprietors on the above Said Damages or any other Damages that may appear by miſstakes in Laing out Common Lands

Voted to allow Joseph Hartwell an account of 13/8

Voted the Expence of this meeting be paid by the proprietors being

Voted to Adjorn this meeting to the Laſt munday of march next one o'Clock after noon at this place

Benj^a Goodridge Modirator

Recorded this 27th Day of November 1792

℔ Joſeph Hartwell Clark

March ye 25th 1793. Being met according to Adjornment at the Houſe of Capt Benj^a Goodridge Inholder in Lunenburg. Said meeting opened.

after Settleing the Diviſion money Due to the heirs of Phinehas Parker of Groton Deceaſed ariſing from the Sale of the Common Lands of the proprietors of Lunenburg

Voted to Adjorn this meeting to thurſ Day ye 28th day of this Inſtant march at one o'Clock after noon at this place

Benjamin Goodridge
Modirator

Recorded this 27th day of march 1793

℔ Joseph Hartwell Clarck

[117] March ye 28th 1793 Being met according to Adjornment at the Houſe of Capt Benjamin Goodridge in Lunenburg Inholder Said meeting opened.

Voted that the proprietors Treaſurer Viz. Eleazer Houghton be hereby Directed to pay to the Committee that was Choſen by the S^d proprietors Viz. Benj^a Redington Benj^a Goodridge and Thaddeus Commings to Defend or Settle the action brought by Jacob Welch againſt Phinehas Dunſmore Such Sums of money as they Shall Expend in Defending or Settleing the above Said Cauſe and there Recept Shall be allowed to the S^d Treaſurer by ye S^d proprietors

2^{ly} Voted to allow Samuel Johnſton an ac-

count of — — — — — — — £1 5 6
for attending meetings
3ly Voted to allow Benj^a Goodridge an account of — — — — — — —   6 7 8
for Services don for the proprietors & Expences & attending meetings
4ly Voted to allow Thaddeus Commings an account of — — — — — — —   1 6 6
for attend meetings & Services don for the proprietors
5ly Voted to allow Eleazer Houghton an account of — — — — — — —   1 4
for attending meetings & Services don for the proprietors
6ly. Voted to allow Benj^a Redington an account of — — — — — — —   3 18 6
for attending meetings & Services don for the proprietors

7ly Voted Chufe a Committee of two to Reckon with the propretors Treafurer

8ly Voted and Chofe Thaddeus Commings & Jofeph Hartwell for S^d Committee

9ly Voted the Expences of this meeting and munday meeting be paid by the proprietors being —

1ly Voted to adjorn this meeting to nonday the third day of June next one o'Clock after noon at this place

      Benj^a Goodridge Modirater
Recorded this 29th day of march 1793
      ℟ Joseph Hartwell Clark

[**118**] June ye 3^d 1793 being met according to Adjornment at the Houfe of Capt Benjamin Goodridge in Lunenburg Inholder S^d meetting opened

 firft Voted to Except the Reckoning of the Committee Chofen to Reckon with Eleazer Houghton Treafurer for the proprietors of the Town of Lunenburg as followeth; we the Subfcribers Being Chofen a Committee to Reckon with the above Said Treafurer have attended S^d Reckoning and find in Said Houghtons hands of the proprietors Securityes and moneys arifing from the Sales of thier Common Lands to the amount of — — £260 $^s_{14}$ $^p_3$ $^Q_3$

two Hundred and Sixty pounds fourteen Shillings and three pence three farthings alſo one thouſand Continantal paper — Dllers 1000

Dollers, the above Said Houghton Diſcharges himſelf by paying the proprietors Debts to the amount of — 66 13 1

Sixty-Six pounds thirteen Shillings one peney, for which he produced proper vouchers, and alſo paid out — Dolers 563½

five hundred and Sixty three & ½ Continantal paper Dollers. and there Remains Due to the S^d proprietors from Said Houghton one Hundred ninty-four pounds one Shilling two pence three farthings. —— —— —— —— —— —— 194 1 2 3

and four hundred. thirty-Six. & ½ Continantal paper Dollers

Lunenburg April ye 2^d 1793

Thad^s Cummings } Committee
Joseph Hartwell

Eleazer Houghton } Treaſurer

2^{ly}. Voted to allow Eleazer Houghton for Serving Treaſurer from Sep^t 1790 to June the Second 1793. one pound — 1 00 00

3^{ly}. Voted to allow Benj^a Redington an account of —— —— —— —— —— 1 10 9

4^{ly}. Voted the Expence of this meeting be paid by the proprietors being Seven Shillings —— —— —— —— —— 0 7 0

5^{ly} Voted to Adjorn this meeting to munday the ninth day of September next one o'clock after noon at this place

Benjamin Goodridge Modirator

Recorded this 4th Day of June 1793

₱. Joseph Hartwell Clark

September the 9th 1793 being met according to Adjornment at the Houſe of Capt Benj^a Goodridge in Lunenburg Inholder S^d meeting opened.

Voted to Adjorn this meeting to munday the forth Day of November next at one o'Clock after noon at this place
Benj^a Goodridge Modirator
Recorded this 10th Day of Sep^t 1793
℗ Joseph Hartwell Clark

[**119**] November ye 4th 1793 being met according to Adjornment at the Houfe of Capt Benjamin Goodridge in Lunenburg Said meeting opened

firft Voted to Except four plans in feavour of Maj^r James Richardfon in order to be recorded

2^{ly}· Voted the Expence of this meeting be paid by the proprietors 14/0

3^{ly}· Voted to Adjorn this meeting to monday the ninth day of December next one o'Clock after noon at the Houfe of Leu^t Philip Goodridge in Lunenburg.
Benjamin Goodridge Modirator
Recorded this fift day of November 1793
Joseph Hartwell Clark

December ye 9th 1793 being met according to Adjornment at the Houfe of Leu^t Phillip Goodridge in Lunenburg Said meeting opned

firft Voted to Chufe a Committee to meet with Mr Thurstain to See the Lines run between Said Thurftains Land and the proprietors Lands

2^{ly} Voted and Chofe Mr Benj^a Redington Capt Benj^a Goodridge for Said Committee

3^{ly} Voted to allow David Kilburn an account of one pound Seven Shillings — — — — — — — — £1-7-0

4^{ly}· Voted to allow Joseph Hartwell an account of ninteen Shillings & Six pence — — — — — 0:19.6

5^{ly} Voted the Expence of this meeting be paid by the proprietors being 2/0 — — — — — — — 0:2:0

6^{ly} Voted to Adjorn this meeting to monday the thirteenth day of January next at one o'Clock after noon at the Houfe of Mr Samuel Johnfon in Lunenburg
Benjamin Goodridge Modirator
Recorded this tenth day of December 1793
Joseph Hartwell Clark

January ye 13th 1794. being met according to adjornment at the Houfe of Mr Samuel Johnfon in Lunenburg S^d meeting opened.

firft Voted to Receive the minifterael 2^d Divifion Lott of Doc Abraham Hafkel as bid off at the Vandue and Settle with the Town for the Same

whereas Maj^r James Richardson bought of the proprietors of Lunenburg all the Common land at vandue that had not ben Surveyed and whereas the Committee appointed by the proprietors to Survey the abovefaid Common Lands for Said Richardfon and as the Committee aforef^d returned a plan of two peces of Land Containing about 32 acres to the proprietors as common Land which S^d Richardfon Sold to phinehas Denfmore and Jonathan Adams Ju^r but it now appears that the abovefaid Lands was not Common Land and the purcherfsers Call Damage. therefore.

Voted that if the above Said Richardson will pay to the proprietors the full of what he owes them and likewife the one half of the money that the above Said Danfmore and Adams gave for the abovefaid Land and Likewife give the proprietors a relefe or a Deed of acquittence from any further Demands for any Common Lands bought of the proprietors as aforefaid in Confidration of the S^d Richardfon Receiveing two pounds of S^d proprietors that the abovefaid proprietors do hereby Engage to Settle the Damage that the above S^d Dunfmore or Adams Could have had againft Said Richardfon

Voted the Expence of this meeting be paid by the proprietors being 9/4

Voted to Adjorn this meeting to wedenfday the 28th Day of may next at the Houfe of Capt Benj^a Goodridge in Lunenburg one o'Clock after noon

Benjamin Goodridge Modirator
Recorded by me Joseph Hartwell Clark

[120] May ye 28th 1794 being met according to Adjornment at the Houfe of Capt Benj^a Goodridge in Lunenburg Said meeting opened

firſt Voted to Chuſe a Committee man in the Rome of Mr Samuel Johnſon Deceaſed

2ly Voted and Choſe Mr Benja Johnſon in the Rome of the Said Samuel Johnſon

3ly Voted that the proprietors purchaſe of Benja Goodridge the miniſteral Second Diviſion Lott Lying in the Northeaſt part of Lunenburg Townſhip which Said Goodridge bought of Said Town of Lunenburg at Vandue and when Said Goodridge Shall Give a Deed of acquittence of the aboveſaid Lott of Land to the proprietors aforeſaid of the Same tennor and form of the Deed he had of the Town of Lunenburg afore ſaid that then the proprietors Committee Namely. Benja Goodridge Benja Redington and Benja Johnſon, be directed to take up the Security that the aboveſaid, Benja Goodridge gave the Town for Said Land by giveing their Security in behalf of the proprietors aforeſaid.

4ly Voted that the Committee of Sales be Directed to make Sale of all the Common Lands and all Lands they Shall find belonging to the proprietors of Lunenburg as Sone as they can with convenencey and in that way they Shall Think beſt, and that they tranſact all matters Reſpecting Said Lands as they Shall think beſt for Sd proprietors

5ly Voted the Expence of this meeting be paid by the proprietors being 9/3

6ly Voted to Adjorn this meeting to munday the 5th day of January next one o'Clock after noon at this place

Benjamin Goodridge Modirator

Recorded this 29th day of may 1794.

℔ Joseph Hartwell Clark

January the 5th 1795. being met according to adjornment at the Houſe of Capt Benja Goodridge in Lunenburg Said meeting opened

firſt Voted to allow an acount to David Kilborn of — — — — — — — — — — — £1- 7 0

2.ly. Voted to Except a plan of Seventeen acres & 115 rod lying in Fitchburg bounding on Eſqr Putnoms & Lows Lands

3ly. Voted to allow Stephen Whitney an account of — — — — — — — — — 0- 7 6
4ly. Voted to allow Capt Benja Goodridge an account of — — — — — — — — — £6-11 5
5ly. Voted to allow Joseph Hartwell an account of — — — — — — — — — — — 0- 7-6
6ly. Voted the Expence of this meeting be paid by the proprietors being Sixteen Shillings and four pence — — — — — — — — 0-16 4
7ly. Voted to Adjorn this meeting to wednesday the 27th day of may next one o'Clock after noon at this place

Benjamin Goodridge Modirator

recorded this 12th day of January 1795

Joseph Hartwell Clark

[121] May ye 27th 1795 being met according to Adjornment at the House of Capt Benjamin Goodridge in Lunenburg Said meeting opened.

first Voted to allow James Richardson an account of — — — — — — — — — £1 7 0 meetings attended

2ly Voted to Chuse a committee to Reckon with the proprietors Treasuer

3ly Voted and Chose Joseph Hartwell & Thadeus Commings for the above Said committee

4ly Voted the Expence of this meeting be paid by the proprietors being fifteen Shillings — — — — 0 15 0

5ly Voted to Adjorn this meeting to monday the forteenth day of September next one o'Clock afternoon at this place

Benjamin Goodridge Modirator

recorded this 28th day of may 1795

Joseph Hartwell proprietors Clark

Sept ye 14th 1795 being met according to Adjornment at the House of Capt Benja Goodridge in Lunenburg Said meeting opened.

first Voted to allow Benja Redington an account of two pounds Seventeen Shillings and Eight pence — — — — — — — — — — — 2 17 8 for Services don for the proprietors & attending nine meeting

2ly. Voted the Expence of this meeting be paid by the proprietors being

3ly Voted to Adjorn this meeting munday the Eleventh day of January next at one o'Clock after noon at this place

      Benjamin Goodridge Modirator
Recorded this 15th day of Sept 1795
     Joseph Hartwell proprietors Clark

January ye 11th 1796 being met according to adjornment at the Houfe of Capt Benja Goodridge in Lunenburg Said meeting opened

firft Voted to Except the Reckoning of the Committee Chofen to Reckon with Eleazer Houghton proprietors Treafurer for the proprietors of Lunenburg as follows we the Subfcribers being Chofen a Committee to Reckon with the proprietors Treafurer: viz. Eleazer Houghton have attended Said Reckoning and find in Said Houghtons hands of the proprietors moneys arifing from the Sales of their Common Lands to the amount of two Hundred and Sixty-Seven pounds Eighteen Shillings Seven pence two farthings. — — — — — — — — — £267 18 7 2

 the above Said Houghton Difcharges himfelf by paying the proprietors Debts for which he produces proper vouchers to the amount of Eighty-four pounds Six Shillings Eight pence three farthings.   84 6 8 3
and there remains Due to the proprietors from Said Houghton one hundred Eighty three pounds Eleven Shillings ten pence three farthings — — — — —   183 11 10 3
alfo in his hands one thoufand Continantal paper Dollers paid out five five Hundred twenty one there remains four hundred & ninty paper Dollers
January ye 2d 1796. (Errors Excepted)
    Joseph Hartwell ⎫
    Thadeus Commings ⎭ Committee

    Eleazer Houghton ⎱ Treafurer

2ly. Voted to allow an account of one pound two Shillings & Six pence to Edward Scott for attending fifteen meetings — — — — — — — — — — 1 2 6

3ly Voted to allow Joseph Hartwell an account of twelve Shillings and nine pence for Services don for the proprietors and attending meetings — — — — — — 0 12 9

torn over

[122] 4ly Voted to allow an account of three pounds ten Shillings & two pence to Capt Benja Goodridge for Services don for the proprietors and attending meetings — — — — 3 10 2

5ly Voted to allow an account of one pound five Shillins to Thadeus Commings for Services don for the proprietors and attending meetings — 1 5 0

6ly Voted to allow an account of Eight Dollers for Services don for the proprietors and attending meetings to Eleazer Houghton all that is due to him to this time — — — — — 2 8

7ly Voted to adjorn this meeting to wednefday the 25th day of may next at one oClock after noon at this place

     Benjamin Goodridge Modirator
recorded this 12th day of January
     Joseph Hartwell Clark

May. ye 25th 1796 being met according to Adjornment at the Houfe of Capt Benjamin Goodridge in Lunenburg Said meeting opned

firft Voted to allow Stephen Whitney an account of Six Shillings for attending four meetings 0 6 0

2ly Voted the Expence of this meeting be paid by the proprietors

3ly. Voted to Adjorn this meeting to monday ye 26th day of December next at one oClock after noon at this place

     Benja Goodridge Modirator
Recorded this 26th day of may 1796
     ℔ Joseph Hartwell Clarck

December ye 26th 1796 being met according to adjornment at the Houfe of Capt Benjamin Goodridge in Lunenburg Said meeting oped

firft Voted the proprietors Treafurer is Diricted to Call upon Leu^t Philip Goodridge for the money Due to the proprietors by puting the note or notes in Sute that are againft S^d Goodridge —— —— —— —— ——

2^{ly}. Voted the Expence of this meeting be payed by the proprietors being

3^{ly} Voted to adjorn this meeting to Wednefday the 31^{ft} day of may next at one o,Clock after noon at this place

      Benjamin Goodridge modirator

Recorded this 27th day of December 1796.

      ℔ Joseph Hartwell Clark

[123] May ye 31^{ft} 1797 being met according to Adjornment at the Houfe of Capt Benjamin Goodridge in Lunenburg Said meeting opned.

firft Voted that the vote pafsed on the 26th of Laft December by the proprietors (viz. that the proprietours Treafurer Call upon Lea^t Philip Goodridge by puting the notes in Sute, Due to the proprietors,) Shall not be put in Sute till further orders from the proprietors Committy.

Voted to allowe Joseph Hartwell an account of Six Shillings & nine pence for attending three meetings and recording Said meetings   £.0 6 9

Voted the Expence of this meeting be paid by the proprietors —— —— ——

Voted to Adjorn this meeting to Election day in the year 1798 at one o'Clock after-noon at this place

      Benjamin Goodridge
        Modirator

Recorded this firft day of June 1797

      ℔ Joseph Hartwell Clark

May ye 30th 1798 being met according to Adjornment at the Houfe of Capt Benjamin Goodridge in Lunenburg, Said meeting opned.

firſt Voted and Choſe Stephen Whitney in the Rome of Benjamin Redington and Thadeus Commings in the Rome of Leat Phillip Goodridge to Serve as a Committee with the other Committee men in Laying out the Common land making Sale of any that is to be Sold according to former Votes of the proprietors of S^d Lunenburg

Voted the Expence of this meeting be paid by the proprietors

Voted to Adjorn this meeting to the tenth Day of December next at one o,Clock after-noon at this place

Benj^a Goodridge Modirator

Recorded the 31^{ſt} Day of may 1798

₱. Joseph Hartwell Clark

December ye 10th 1798 being met according to Adjornment at the Houſe of Capt Benjamin Goodridge in Lunenburg Said meeting opned through the Deepneſs of the Snow, the proprietors Did not attend in in geniral, So it was though Beſt to adjorn the meeting

Voted to adjorn this meeting to the 29th day of may next at one o'Clock after noon at this place.

Benjamin Goodridge Modirator

Recorded the 13th Day of December 1798

₱ Joseph Hartwell Clark

May ye 29th 1799. being met according to Adjornment at the Houſe of Capt Benjamin Goodridge in Lunenburg Said meeting opned

Voted to allow Joseph Hartwell an account of Six Shillings & nine pence. — — — — —   s d / 6 9
for attending three meetings and recording Said meetings

Voted to allow Benj, Goodridge an account of three pounds ſeventeen Shillings & Eight pence for Expences of S^d meetings & attendance on Said meeting

Voted to adjorn this meeting to Election Day in the year 1800.

turn over

[124] the 28th of may at this place one o'Clock after noon

     Benjamin Goodridge Modirator
Recorded the 30th Day of may 1799
     ℘ Joseph Hartwell Clark

May yᵉ 28th 1800. being met according to Adjornment at the Houſe of Capt Benjamin Goodridge in Lunenburg Said meeting opned

Voted the Expence of this meeting be paid by the proprietors

Voted to Adjorn this meeting to the Laſt wedneſday in May 1801 at one oclock after noon at this place
     Benjamin Goodridge Modirator
Recorded the Laſt day of may 1800.
     ℘ Joseph Hartwell Clerk

May yᵉ 27th 1801 being met according to Adjornment at the Houſe of Capt Benjamin Goodridge in Lunenburg Said meeting opned

         dol cts
Voted to alow an ancount of David Kilburns of — 1—25
Voted to alow an account of Joseph Hartwells of 0—75

Voted the Expence of this meeting be paid by the proprietors

Voted to Adjorn this meeting to the laſt wedneſday in may 1802 at this place at one o.clock afternoon at this place
     Benjamin Goodridge modirator
Recorded the 28th Day of May 1801
     ℘ Joseph Hartwell Hartwell Clerk

May yᵉ 26th 1802 being met according to Adjornment at the Houſe of Capt Benjamin Goodridge in Lunenburg Said meeting opned

firſt Voted to allow Capt Benjamin Goodridge an account of Six Dollers thirty four Sent for Expences & attend meetings   Dol. Cts
              6 34

2ly Voted to Chuſe a commity to conſult an a torney Reſpecting the Northfield road So Called.

3ly Voted and Chofe Capt Benjamin Goodridge for Said committy man

4ly Voted to chufe a Committee to Recon with the propriertors treafuer

5ly Voted and Chofe Capt Benjamin Goodridge & Thadeus Commings for Said Committee

6ly Voted the Exfpence of this meetting be paid by the proprietors

7ly Voted to adjorn this meetting to the laft wednefday in may next 1803 at one o clock after noon at this place

      Benjamin Goodridge Modirator
Recorded the 27th Day of may 1802
      ℀ Joseph Hartwell Clerk

[125] May ye 25th 1803 being met according to Adjornment at the Houfe of Capt Benjamin Goodridge in Lunenburg Said meeting opened.

firft Voted to receive the Committee reckoning with the proprietors Treafurer. &c: we the Subfcribers being chofen a Committee to reckon with the proprietors Treafurer of the Townfhip of Lunenburg. viz., Eleazer Houghton have attended Said reckoning and find due from Said Houghton to Said proprietors two Hundred and twenty two pounds fourteen Shillings and nine pence two farthings —— —— —— —— —— —— —— l. s p. fr
                 222 14 9 2
alfo in his hands four hundred & ninty paper Dollers —— —— —— —— —— 490 0-0-0 0 0

June ye 2d 1802 Errors Excepted

    Benja Goodridge } Committee
    Thadeus Commins

    Eleazer Houghton } Treafurer

Voted that Josiah Stearns Efqr is admitted to act as the legal Reprefentative of Edward Emerfon Efqr by virtue of a power of attorney from Jonathan Bowman Efqr.

Voted to Chufe a Commettee to attend the Committee Choufen by the town to afcertain the bounds of Northfield road.

Voted and Chofe Capt Benja Goodridge Eleazer Houghton Stephen Whitney for the abovefaid Committee which

May ye 25th 1803 being met according to adjournment at the House of
Capt. Benjamin Goodridge in Lunenburg said meeting opened.

first voted to receive the Committee reckoning with the proprietors Treasurer &c.

We the Subscribers being chosen a Committee To reckon with the proprietors
Treasurer of the Township of Lunenburg Viz: Eleazer Houghton
have attended said reckoning and find due from said Houghton to said
proprietors Two Hundred and twenty two pounds fourteen shillings and
nine pence two farthings — — — — — — — — — — £222..14..9¼
also in his hands four hundred & ninety paper Dollars 490..—..—

June ye 2d 1803 — — — — — — — — Benj.a Goodridge } Committee
                                  Thadeus [Osgood?] }

Eleazer Houghton } Treasurer

Voted that Josiah Stearns Esqr. is admitted to act as the legal Representative
       of Edward Emerson Esqr. by virtue of a power of attorney from Jonathan
Voted Bowman Esqr.
       to Chose a Committee to attend the Committee Chosen by the
       town to ascertain the bounds of Northfield road. Stephen Whitney 2d
Voted and Chose Capt. Benja. Goodridge Eleazer Houghton Stephen Whitney 2d
       the abovesaid Committee which Committee are authorized & empower-
       ed by the town or to make any Settlement which may be thought
       parsons that the said Committee may think most for the
       Interest of the proprietors
Voted to allow an account of Stephen Whitney's of two Dollars Eighty three Cents
Voted to allow an account of Eleazer Houghton's Sixteen Dollars twenty five Cents
Voted to allow an account of Benja. Goodridges of three Dollars Eighty three Cents
Voted the Expence of this meeting bepaid by the proprietors
Voted to adjorn this meeting to the Last Wednesday of may next at this place
       at one a Clock after noon.   Benjamin Goodridge Moderator

Recorded 26th day of may 1803 ⅌ Joseph Hartwell Clerk

May ye 30th 1804 being met according to Adjornment at the
House of Capt. Benjamin Goodridge in Lunenburg said meeting open-
ed to allow an account of Joseph Hartwell's of one Dollar & 25 cents
Voted the Expence of this meeting be paid by the proprietors
Voted to adjorn this meeting to the first day of January 1805 next at one
a Clock after noon at this place.   Benjamin Goodridge Moderator
Recorded the 31st day may 1804 ⅌ Joseph Hartwell Clerk

Committee are authorized & empowered to make Sale of any part or parts of Said road which may be relinquſhed by the town or to make any Settlement with any perſon or parſons that the Said Committee may think moſt for the Intereſt of the proprietors

Voted to allow an account of Stephen Whitneys of two Dollers Eighty three Cents

Voted to allow an account of Eleazer Houghtons Sixteen Dollers twenty five Cents

Voted to allow an account of Benjᵃ Goodridges of three Dollers & Eighty three cents

Voted the Expence of this meeting be paid by the proprietors

Voted to adjorn this meeting to the Laſt wedneſday of may next at this place at one o.Clock after noon.

Benjamin Goodridge Modirator

Recorded 26ᵗʰ Day of may 1803
℔ Joseph Hartwell Clerk

May yᵉ 30ᵗʰ 1804. being met accerding to Adjornment at the Houſe of Capᵗ Benjamin Goodridge in Lunenburg Said meeting opened

firſt Voted to allow an account of Joseph Hartwells of one Doller & 25 cents

Voted the Expence of this meeting be paid by the propritors

Voted to Adjorn this meeting to the firſt day of January 1805 next at one o,Clock after noon at this place
Benjamin Goodridge Modirator

Recorded the 31ſᵗ Day may 1804
℔ Joseph Hartwell Clerk

[126] January yᵉ 1ſᵗ 1805 being met according to Adjornment at the Houſe of Capᵗ Benjamin Goodridge in Lunenburg Said meeting opened

firſt Voted that all contracts Sales & conveyances are estableſhed agreeable to there preſent bounds

2ˡʸ Voted that the proprietors will contract with Such perſon or perſons (to Settle with & pay to the Several proprietors or their legal representatives Such Sums of money as they are legally intitled to from Said propriety) as will undertake to Settle with the Several proprietors for the leaft Sum, provided Such person or persons Shall give land Security to the Satiffaction of the Said proprietors for the performance of Such contract.

3ly Voted that the money Saved by the aforesaid contract Shall be distrebuted amongft the proprietors eaqually and to be paid out by the perfon, or perfons who may be contracted with agreeable to the aforesaid vote.

4,ly Voted to Chufe a committy to Reckon with the Treafurer

Voted & chofe for Said Committy Meffrs. Josiah Stearns Thaddeus Commings & Benjamin Goodridge

5.ly Votd that the expence of this meeting be paid by the proprietors

6,ly Voted to adjorn this meeting to monday the 14 day of January Instent at ten o.clock in the forenoon at this place

Benjamin Goodridge Modirator

Recorded ye 2d Day of January 1805

℔ Joseph Hartwell Clerk

[127] January ye 14th 1805 being met according to Adjornment at the Houfe of Capt Benjamin Goodridge in Lunenburg Said meeting opened

The Committee appointed to Reckon with Mr Eleazer Houghton proprietors Treafurer find that there is in the hands of the Treafurer the Sum of eight hundred and twenty four dollors after deducting Eight Dollers & ninty five cents which is his due

January ye 17th. 1805 accepted and ordered to be recorded

Josiah Stearns } Committee
Thadeus Commings

Eleazer Houghton } treasurer

2ly Voted that the Sum of ninteen Dollers be paid to the Legal Representives of the original proprietors of twenty five Rights which have not Receved their Dividend of four pounds which will be in full of the legal Shears on thofe rights

3ly Voted that the proprietors accept of the proposals of Meffrs, Eleazer Houghton Benj$\underline{a}$ Goodridge Benj$\underline{a}$ Johnfon & Josiah Stearns for undertaking to pay all thofe of the aforefaid twenty five Shears that Shall be legally Demanded for the Sum of one hundred and Sixty Six Dollers & Sixty Seven cents. provided that they Shall give Sufficient Security for the preformance of that truft

4ly Voted to accept the Securety of Eleazer Houghton Benjamin Goodridge & Josiah Stearns for the fullfelment of the aforesaid truft; and order the Treasurer to pay them the aforefaid Sum of money accordingly

5ly Voted that the owners of Lots Number 28: & 74: & 81: with two thirds of Lot number 70: excluded from receiving any part of this dividend untill the principle & intereft of two notes given by Phillip Goodridge to the proprietors Shall be fully paid. alfo that the owner of lot Number two Shall be excluded from receiving any part of this dividend untill the principle & intereft of a note of hand given to the proprietors by James Richardson Shall be fully paid. Likewife that the owner of lot number 20: and of one half of lot 32: Shall be excluded from receiving any part of this dividend untill a note of hand given by Edward Scott to the proprietors Shall be fully paid. whereas Col, Aaron Willard at the time of his deceafe owed to the proprietors a Sum of money which is now Equal to more than one thousand dollers by which means the propriety have been much Injured therefore

6ly Voted that the Eftate of the Said Aaron Willard be forever excluded from receiving any part of the money which has or Shall be divided amongft the Said proprietors Since his deth

7ly Voted that M$\underline{r}$ Eleazer Houghton the proprietors Treasurer be & he hereby is authorized & empowered forthwith to collect all the money that the proprietors have due to them, with power of inftituting Suets at law (if neceffary) and to plead prosecute & perfue the Same to final Judgement, and Execution, with power of Substitution, and when the faid money is received to pay to the Several persons to whom the money is due the Several Sums which are their due and the remainder to pay to the proprietors or owners of Such rights as are to receive the Same agreable to the vots of the proprietors at the rate of fifteen Dollers & eighteen cents to each right.

8¹ʸ Voted to adjorn this meeting to the firft Day of January 1806 at one o clock at this place

Benjamin Goodridge Modirator

Recorded yᵉ 18ᵗʰ of January 1805

℞ Joseph Hartwell Clark

[128] 1806

January 1ᶠᵗ The proprietors being met according to adjournment at the house of capt Benjamin Goodridge in Lunenburg, the said meeting was opened, and voted to adjourn this meeting to the sixth day of this Instant at one o clock in the after noon to this place

January 6 the proprietors being meet according to adjournment

Voted that the proprietors Treasurer deduct such sum from the intereft of each shear of fifteen dollers and eighteen cents, as will make the shear owned by Mʳ Simon Goodridge (being number twenty eight) equal to the other shears, and pay out the same accordingly — — — —

Voted to excuse Mʳ Joseph Hartwell from serving clerk for the proprietors any longer — — — —

Voted and choose Josiah Stearns clerk of the aforesaid proprietors — — — — — —

Voted that the propriety pay the expence of this meeting — — — — —

Voted that this meeting be adjourned to Monday the twenty eighth day of April next at two o clock in the after noon to meet at the house of Mʳ Benjamin Johnson in Lunenburg

Benjamin Goodridge Moderator

attest — — Josiah Stearns proprietors clerk

*Worcester fs. January 7ᵗʰ 1806. personally appeared the Honˡᵉ Josiah Stearns Esqʳ and made solemn oath

---

*This is a slip affixed to the page by a seal.

that he would be faithfull to the trust reposed in him as Clerk to the proprietors of the Township of Lunenburg. Before me
    William Cunningham Justice Peace.

1806

April 28 The proprietors of the original township of Lunenburg met agreeable to adjournment at two of the clock in the after noon at the House of Mr Benjamin Johnson in said Lunenburg — Voted & choose Mr Eleazer Houghton moderator protem in the room of Decon Benj^a Goodridge who is absent — —

Voted to allow Mr Eleazer Houghton fourteen dollers & thirty six cents which sum he was charged with in the last settlement as being due from Jon^a Adams as compound Interest on his note to the proprietors & which sum he refuses to pay — voted to deduct so much of the interest which has arisen on the shears as will reimburst to Mr Houghton the aforesaid sum of fourteen dollers & thirty six cents

[129] Voted that the treasurer do not pay any of the proprietors their shears untill the administrators of the estate of Leut Phillip Goodridge deceased is settled with — — —

Voted that the expence of this meetng by paid by the proprietors

Voted to adjourn this meeting to the last wednesday in May next at three of the clock in the after noon to the house of Mr Benj^a Johnson in Lunenburg

    Eleazer Houghton Moderator protem
 attest — — — Josiah Stearns proprietors clerk

1806

May 28 The proprietors of the original township of Lunenburg met according to adjournment at the house of Mr Benj^a Johnson in said Lunenburg — — — — —

Voted that the treasurer pay Mr Samuel Kimball administrator of the Estate of Lieut Phillip Goodridge two dollers & sixty one cents which is the ballance due to said Goodridges Estate on two rights and two thirds of one right — — — — —

Voted to allow the following persons the several sums affixed to their names amounting to thirteen dollers & Eighty Eight cents in the whole viz to Mr Joseph Hartwell for attending two meeting — — — — $0 50
to Decon Benj^a Goodridge for the expence of one meeting at his house & for attending three meetings — 2 41
Mr Benj^a Johnson for the expence of this meeting & for attending four meetings 3 62
Mr Eleazer Houghton for serving treasurer to this time & for the attendance of four meetings — — 3 25
Mr Stephen Whitney for attending this meeting — — 25
Mr Thaddeus Cummings for attending two meetings 50
Mr Simon Goodridge for attending 4 meetings — 1
Mr Samuel Kimball for attending 3 meeting 75
Josiah Stearns for attending 4 meetings $1— paying Esqr Cunningham,, 20— recording the votes of 3 meeting 1 60 $13,,88

Voted that the treasurer pay Interest on the shears of fifteen dollers & Eighteen cents each; after this day untill paid; unlefs ordered otherwise by the proprietors

Voted to adjourn this meeting to the first Monday in January next at one of the clock in the after noon to meet at the house of Mr Benj^a Johnson

      Benj^a Goodridge Moderator
  attest Josiah Stearns proprietors clerk

[130] 1807

January 5 The proprietors met according to adjournment at the house of Mr Benj^a Johnson — — — — —

Voted & Josiah Stearns one of the committee to look up & make sale of the common land in addition to the Committee — — —

Voted to adjourn this meeting to the last wednesday

in May next at two of the clock in the after noon to the house of Mr Benj^a Johnson — — —
Benj^a Goodridge Moderator
attest — — — Josiah Stearns proprietors Clerk

May 27 1807 the proprietors met according to adjournment —

Voted that the treasurer do not pay any Interest on the shares of fifteen dollers & eighteen cents each untill further order from the proprietors — — — — —

Voted that the committee for laying out the proprietors land employ a surveyor & chain men for the purpose of making such surveys as the committee shall think proper, and that one or more of said committee attend such surveys, and in case they find any land which they can recover & dispose of, that the committee proceed to lay out & sell such land and pafs deed or deeds of the same, in behalf of the proprietors — —

Voted to allow Mr Benj^a Johnson three dollers for the expence of providing for this meeting & two dollers & fifty cents for the meeting in January last — — $5 50

Voted To adjourn this meeting to the 22^d of June next at two of the clock in the after noon to meet at the house of Mr Benj^a Johnson
Benj^a Goodridge Moderator
attest — — — Josiah Stearns proprietors Clerk

June 22 The proprietors met according to adjournment at the house of Mr Benj^a Johnson — — —

Voted to choose two agents to make a settlement with the persons who are here after named that have any of Common land in their pofsefsion—Said agents Empowed to submit to Reference all matters of dispute which may arise respecting said proprietors land, that may be in the pofsefsion of Jacob Jaquith, Aaron Wheeler, Samuel Phelps or David Whitemore, and in the said proprietors behalf to enter into any agreeament, or contract for that purpose as fully & absolutely as said proprietors could do if they were all personally present

[131] Voted and choose Josiah Stearns & Mr Samuel Kimball for said agents — — — — — — — —

Voted that the proprietors Treasurer furnish the agents with a sum of money, not exceeding twenty dollars for the purpose of transacting the aforesaid buisnefs

Voted that the proprietors treasurer pay the expence of this meeting — — — — — — —

Voted to adjourn this meting untill the tenth of august next at 3 oclock in the after noone, to the house of Mr Benj^a Johnson

      Benj^a Goodridge Moderator
attest   Josiah Stearns proprietors clerk

1807
Aug 10—The proprietors met according to adjournment at the house of Mr Benj^a Johnson —

Voted that Josiah Stearns & Samuel Kimball the agents choosen at the last meeting be directed to procure a copy of Josiah Williards deed (of the three hundred & one acre & a half lot, which was laid out to him on the 22 day of august 1729—) to John Bridge; or the person to whome it was given; also the copy of the deed to Benj^a Danforth of a part of said lot if the said copies can be obtained; and afterwards to make a statement of the whole matter respecting said lot & the adjoining lands to some able attorny for his consideration & advice

Voted that the expence of this meeting be paid by the proprietors Treasurer — — — — — —

Voted to adjourn this meeting to monday the second day of November next at two o clock in the afternoon to meet at this place

      Benj^a Goodridge moderator
  attest Josiah Stearns proprietors Clerk

1807
November 2 the proprietors met at the house of Mr Benjamin Johnson agreeable to adjournment

Voted to allow the following sums to the persons to whose names they are affixed viz — — — — — —

Proprietors' Records.

To Josiah Stearns for going to Fitchburg nine times & to mulpus & Cllollege land 6 times equal to 9 days in the whole	9 0
Aug 4 for half a Journy to Worcester viz 1 day 1— cash expended 1,,9— half a horse 0.50	2 59
Sept 3 to horse to Worcester 1— cash expended in Worcester 1,,84 — —	2 84
for examining books & making plans &c —	8 0
for recording the votes of five meetings and attending do —	1 82

To Benj^a Goodridge for three & a half days Carrying chain &c	3 50
for attending four meetings	1

[132] Brought forward

To Eleazer Houghton for one day 1— & for attending 5 meetings	2 25
To Stephen Whitney for one day 1— for attending 3 meetings 0,,75	1 75
To Samuel Kimball for two days 2— attending 5 meetings 1.25	3 25
To Simon Goodridge for attending 4 meetings 1 —	1 0
To Thaddeus Cummings for one meeting,, 25 —	25
To John Hartwell for attending two meetings,, 50 —	50
To David Kilburn for surveying 3 — — — — —	3
To Zabdiel B. Adams Esqr for his advice 2 — —	2
To Zacharah Whitney for going to Fitchburg,, 50 —	50
To Benj^a Johnson for providing for 5 meetings & to attending 5 meetings, carrying chain three days & for other expences in full Including this time — — — — — —	16 40

Voted to pay the expence of this meeting

Voted to sell a piece of land lying west of nepesegaset pond adjoining to Israel Gibsons land containing about three acres 100 rods

Voted to adjourn this meeting to the last wednesday in May next at 2 o clock after noon to this place —

Benj^a Goodridge Moderator

Attest Josiah Stearns proprietors —— Clerk

Wednesday May 25th 1808 the proprietors met according to adjournment at the house of Mr Benja Johnson in Lunenburg

Voted & chose Mr Samuel Kimball Moderator pro tem to act as Moderator of this meeting — — —

Voted that the expence of this meeting be paid by the proprietors

Voted to adjourn this meeting to the twentieth day of June next at two o clock in the after-noon to the house of Mr Benja Johnson in Lunenburg

     Samuel Kimball Moderator pro tem
 attest Josiah Stearns proprietors clerk — — — —

1808
June 20 The proprietors met according to adjourment at the house of Mr Benja Johnson in Lunenburg — — — —

Voted to adjourn this meeting to the last wednesday in May next at one o clock in the after noon to meet at the house of Mr Benja Johnson in Lunenburg —

     Benja Goodridge moderator
 attest Josiah Stearns proprietors clerk

Common Land laid out

[133] May 31ft 1809—The proprietors of the township of Lunenburg met at the house of Mr Benja Johnson agreeable to adjournment

Voted that the clerk make a record of a peice of land as laid out by the Committee containing about two and a half acres bounded as follows viz Begining at a heep of stones east of the road, and north of bridge which is over cateconemoug brook Begining at the most Westerly corner thence runing north two degrees west eleven rods & twenty links by land of David Kilburns to a stake & stones the corner of Clarks land, thence east nine degrees north sixty eight rods by Clarks land to a heep of stones, thence west eighteen degrees south, about sixty nine rods by land of Nathan Tyler to the bound first mentioned

Voted that the expences of this meeting be paid by the proprietors — — — — — —

Voted to adjourn this meeting to the last wednesday in May next at one Oclock in the after noon to the house of Mr Benja Johnson in Lunenburg

     Benja Goodridge
 attest Josiah Stearns proprietors clark

1810

May 30—The proprietors of the township of Lunenburg met at the house of Mr Benj^a Johnson agreeable to adjournment

Voted to adjourn this meeting to the third monday in Sept next at two of the clock in the afternoon to the house of Mr Johnson in Lunenburg

Benj^a Goodridge

attest   Josiah Stearns proprietors clerk

1810

Sept 17   The proprietors of the township of Lunenburg met according to adjournment — — — —

Voted and chose Mr Samuel Kimball moderator pro tem

Voted to allow the following accounts, and order the treasurer to pay the same to the several persons to whom due viz

To Benj^a Johnson for providing for five meetings and attending the same and for going to Harris Tylers &c 3 times to lay out land — — — $5 50

to Benj^a Goodridge for attending 3 meeting & for going to Harris; Tylers &c 3 times to lay out land — — —   1 75

to Stephen Whitney for attending 5 meetings & going to Harris' once to lay out land — — —   1 58

To Eleazer Houghton for attending four meeting and for his service as treasure up to this time —   7 00

turn two leaves for the remainder

[134] Know all men by these presents that we Eleazer Houghton, yeomen Benjamin Goodridge Gentleman & Josiah Stearns Esqr all of Lunenburg in the county of Worcester & Common wealth of Massachusetts — Are holden & stand firmly bound & obliged unto the proprietors of the original township of Lunenburg in the full & Just sum of five hundred dollers to the which payment well & truly to be made we bind ourselves our heirs Executors & administrators firmly by these presents, sealed with our seals dated this seventeenth day of January in the year of our Lord one thousand Eight hundred & five

The conditions of this present obligation is such that whereas the above bounden Eleazer Houghton, Benjamin Goodridge & Josiah Stearns in consideration of one hundred & sixty six dollers & sixty six cents have undertaken to pay the sum of ninteen dollers to the legal owners of each of the following rights in the original township of Lunenburg viz numbers seventy nine, sixty five, seventy one, Eighty nine, Eighty Eight, Eighty five, fourteen, nine, seventy five, Eight, three, ten, forty, thirty, sixty six fifty, thirty five, twenty six, fifty nine, ninteen Eighty, sixty one, seventy six, fifteen, & twenty one

Now therefore if the said Eleazer, Benjamin or Josiah, their heirs Executors or administrators shall well and truly pay or cause to be paid the sum of ninteen dollers to the legal representative of any one or more of the aforsaid twenty five Rights before mentioned, when legally demaned with lawful Interst for the same after it is legally demanded, then this obligation to be void otherwise to remain in full force & virtue in witnefs whereof we have hereunto set our hands & seals this seventeenth day of January 1805—in presence of

Thad^s Cummings	Eleazer Houghton	[Seal]
Benj^a Johnson	Benjamin Goodridge	[Seal]
	Josiah Stearns	[Seal]

The words when legally Demanded was interlined before signing sealing

[135] Know all men by these presents that we Eleazer Houghton & Benjamin Johnson yeoman, Benjamin Goodridge Gentleman & Josiah Stearns Esqr all of Lunenburg in the county of Worcester and Commonwealth of Mafsachusetts —— Are holden & Stand firmly bound & obliged unto the proprietors of the original township of Lunenburg in the full & Just sum of five hundred dollers to the which payment well & truly to be made we bind ourselves our heirs Executors & administrators firmly by these presents in witnefs whereof we have here unto set our hands & seals this seventeenth day of January in the year of our Lord one thousand eight hundred & five ——

The conditions of this present obligation is such that whereas the above bounden Eleazer Houghton Benjamin Johnson, Benjamin Goodridge & Josiah Stearns have in consideration of one hundred & sixty six dollers & sixty six cents, undertaken to pay the sum of ninteen dollers to the legal owners of each of the following rights in the original township of Lunenburg Viz numbers, Seven, fifty Eight, fifty three, eighteen, thirty four, Eleven, thirty three, Seventy two, thirty eight, forty one, forty five, sixty Eight, twenty nine, thirty six,

Sept

[136] brought forward 2 leaves

To John Hartwell for attending four meeting	$1 00
to Simon Goodridge for attending 2 meetings	50
to David Kilburn for surveying ——	1 0
to Samuel Kimball for attending 5 meeting ——	1 25
to Thaddeus Cummings for attending 2 meetings	50
to Josiah Stearns for attending 5 meetings & for Recording 5 do — and for going to lay out land 3 times	2 87

Voted to adjourn this meeting to the last wednsday in May next at two O clock in the after noon to meet at the dwelling house of Mr Benj^a Johnson in Lunenburg

Samuel Kimball Moderator Pro tem

attest Josiah Stearns proprietors clerk

1811

May 29 The proprietors met according to adjournment

voted that the committee for making sale of the proprietors lands are directed to examin the evidence Respecting a peice of land lying between the land laid out to William Wallis and the land laid out to Moses Mitchell & Nathaniel Page and if it shall appear that said land belongs to the proprietors, to cause the same to be laid out and sold — — also any other peice or peices of land that the committee may be informed of, which belongs to said propritors and make Report at the next — ing — — —

voted that the proprietors adjourn this meeting to the last Wednesday in May next at two oclock in the after noon to meet at the dwelling house of Mr Benj^a Johnson in Lunenburg

Benj^a Goodridge moderator
attest Josiah Stearns proprietors clerk ——

1812

May 27 The proprietors met according to adjournment at the Dwelling House of Mr Benjamin Johnson in Lunenburg — ——

Voted & choose Mr Samuel Kimball & Josiah Stearns a Committee to Reckon with Mr Eleazer Houghton proprietors treasurer & report at the next meeting

voted to allow to the several persons hereafter named the sum affixed to their name

[137] To Benj^a Goodridge for attending two meetings $0 50

To Eleazer Houghton for attending two meetings & for his service as treasurer to this time — — —   2 50

to Benj^a Johnson for providing for two meetings & for his attendance at two meetings in full to this time — — — —   2 08

to Stephen Whitney for his attending at two meetings   50

to Samuel Kimball for his attending at two meetings   50

to Simon Goodridge for attending one meeting   25

to Josiah Stearns for attending, & Recording two meetings   75

voted to adjourn this meeting to the last Wednesday in May next at two Oclock in the after noon, to meet at the dwelling House of Mr Benj^a Johnson in Lunenburg —

Benj^a Goodridge Moderator
attest — — — Josiah Stearns proprietors clerk

1813

May 26 The proprietors met according to adjornment at the House Mr Benj^a Johnson in Lunenburg — — — —

voted to accept the Report of the Committee for Reckoning with Mr Eleazer Houghton their treasurer which is as follows viz —— The committee appointed by the proprietors to Reckon with Mr Eleazer Houhgton their treasurer have attended that buisnefs, and find that the treasurer has now in his hands notes to the amount of five hundred & thirty dollers and eighty six cents including the Interest to the twenty sixth day of October last which is due from the persons hereafter named — — —

John Patterson & John Billings — — —	43 87
James Richardson — — —	16 88
Edward Scott — — — — —	25 54
Thomas Gould & Samson Gould — — —	49 12
Asa Johnson — — — — — —	82 15
Kendall Bouttell — — — —	33 70
John & John Goodridges — — —	35 90
M Chase — — —	16 52
Caleb Lealand & Eben^r Lealand — — — —	186 58
Jacob Gibson — — — — —	40 60

we also find that there is due to said treasurer the sum of three dollers & thirty four cents

May 26 1813 — Samuel Kimball } Committee
Josiah Stearns

turn ove

[138] Meeting on the 26 day of May 1813 Brought fordard — — —

Voted that the Proprietors treasurer call on all persons that owe the proprietors either pay the money or to Renew their notes with good security — — —

voted to allow Samuel Kimball & Josiah Stearns one doller & fifty cents each for Reckoning with the treasurer — — — — —	3 00
Voted to allow Benj^a Johnson ninety eight cents for providing for this meeting & twenty five cents for attending said meeting	1 23
voted to Benj^a Goodridge twenty five cents for attending this meeting	25
to allow Eleazer Houghton five dollers for his service as treasurer up to this time & twenty five cents for attending this meeting	5 25
to allow Stephen Whitney twenty five cents for attending	25
to allow John Hartwell twenty five cents for attending	25

to allow Samuel Kimball twenty five cents for attending 25
to allow Josiah Stearns twenty five cents for atting this meeting & twelve cents for recording } 37

Voted to adjourn this meeting to monday the 31st day of May Instant at four oclock in the after noon to meet at the dwelling house of Mr Benj^a Johnson in Lunenburg

Benj^a Goodridge Moderator

attest — — Josiah Stearns Proprietors clerk

1813

May 31 The proprietors met according to adjournment

Voted to Excuse Mr Eleazer Houghton from serveing Treasurer — — —

Voted & choose Mr John Hartwell Treasurer for the proprietors to serve untill another Treasurer is choosen in his Room — — (and said Hartwell was duly sworn at the same time)

Voted to allow the expence of this meeting as usual and that the clerk enter the same —

to allow Benj^a Johnson for providing for this meeting 58
  and for attending said meeting — — 25
to allow Benj^a Goodridge for attending this meeting 25
to allow Eleazer Houghton for ditto 25
to allow Stephen Whitney for do — — 25
to allow Samuel Kimball for do — — 25
to allow John Hartwell for do 25
to allow Josiah Stearns for do & for Recording — 38

Voted to adjourn this meeting to the last wednesday of May next to two o clock in the after noon to meet at the dwelling house of Mr Benj^a Johnson in Lunenburg

Benj^a Goodridge Moderator

attest — — — Josiah Stearns proprietors clerk

[139] 1814

May 25 The proprietors met at the house of Mr Benj^a Johnson in Lunenburg agreeable to adjournment

voted that the treasurer pay one doller & fifty cents on the grant made on the 27th May 1812 — —

voted to allow each of the proprietors fifty cents for attend this, and all future meeting that they shall attend

voted to allow Mr Benj^a Johnson one doller for providing for this meeting — — —	1 00
voted that the expence of this meeting be paid by the proprietors—viz to Benj^a Goodridge for attending this meeting	50
to Eleazer Houghton for do — — —	50
to Stephen Whitney — — —	50
to Samuel Kimball — — —	50
to John Hartwell — —	50
to Josiah Stearns for recording and attending — —	62
voted to allow Benj^a Goodridge for going to the east part of the town to look for common land in June last — —	1 00
voted to allow Benj^a Johnson for the like service	1 00
voted to allow Josiah Stearns for do & for serveying — —	1 50

voted to adjourn this meeting to the first Monday in Octr next at one Oclock in the after noon to meet at the house of Decon Benj^a Goodridge in Lunenburg

        Benj^a Goodridge Moderator
  attest Josiah Stearns proprietors clerk ——

1814
Octr 3^d The propritors met at the house of Decon Benj^a Goodridge in Lunenburg agreeable to adjournment — —

 Voted and choose a committee to examin into the last settlement with Mr Eleazer Houghton treasurer and to asertain whether he was allowed fourteen dollers & thirty six cents which was granted him for what he was charged with in the settlement preceeding the last, as being due on a note which Jonathan Adams owed the proprietors & was found not to be due on said note —— for said committee choose Josiah Stearns & Mr Saml. Kimball ——

 Voted to Excuse Mr Stephen Whitney from serving as one of the committee for looking up & selling proprietors land —— and choose Mr John Hartwell one of said committee ——

Voted to allow Decon Benj^a Goodridge three dollers & fifty cents for providing for this meeting — —	$3 50
and fifty cents for attending said meeting — —	50
to allow Mr Eleazer Houghton for attending	50

[140] 1814

Octr 3^d Voted to allow Mr Benj^a Johnson for attending this meeting $0 50
to allow Mr Samuel Kimball for do — — —   50
to allow Mr Stephen Whitney for do — — —   50
to allow Mr Simon Goodridge for do — — — —   50
to allow Mr John Hartwell for do — — — —   50
to allow Josiah Stearns for do & for recording   63

Voted to adjourn this meeting to the last Wednesday in May next at two o clok in the after noon to meet at the Houfe of Mr Benj^a Johnson in Lunenburg

Benj^a Goodridge Moderator
attest Josiah Stearns proprietors clerk

1815

May 31 The proprietors met at the house of Mr Benjamin Johnson in Lunenburg agreeable to adjournment

Voted that the treasurer pay to Mr Eleazer Houghton (the late treasure) fourteen dollers & thirty six cents which was allowed him on the twenty Eighth day of April 1806 -- with interest for said sum from that date, his not haveing been allowed that sum in the last Reckoning — — —

Voted that the mortgage deeds from Benj^a Goodridge Eleazer Houghton & Josiah Stearns be lodged in the office of the proprietors treasurer — — —

Voted to choose a committee to Reckon with the proprietors treasurer, and choose Josiah Stearns & Mr Samuel Kimball for said committee

Voted to allow Decon Benj^a Goodridge for attending this meeting   50
to allow Mr Eleazer Houghton for do — —   50
to allow Mr Stephen Whitney for do — — — —   50
to allow Mr Samuel Kimball for do — — —   50
to allow Mr Simon Goodridge for do — — —   50
to allow Mr John Hartwell for do — — —   50
to allow Mr Benj^a Johnson for attending & providing for this meeting — —   3 50

to allow Josiah Stearns for attending, and recording this meeting — — 62

Voted To adjourn this meeting to Monday the second day of October next at one oclock in the after noon to meet at the House of Mr Benj^a Johnson in Lunenburg —

Benj^a Goodridge Moderator
attest Josiah Stearns proprietors clerk

1815 Octo 2^d

The proprietors met at the House of Mr Benj^a Johnson agreeable to adjournment — —

Voted that after deducting from the money that shall be collected the amout of all sums that shall be due from Individuals, other than for shares, that we will make a new dividend on the number of shares that have not [141] Received their dividend of fifteen dollers & eighteen cents, and pay out the same to the owners of such shares, or to their legal Representatives as soon as may be convenient

Voted To choose a committee to asertain all sums of money due from the proprietors to individuals, other than for dividends on shares; and also the number of shares that have Rec^d their dividend of four pounds, that have not Rec^d their dividend of fifteen dollers & Eighteen cents each

Voted and choose Josiah Stearns Decon Benj^a Goodridg & Mr Samuel Kimball for said committee — —

Voted To allow Mr Benj^a Johnson for providing for this meeting and for attending said meeting — —	3 50
To allow Decon Benj^a Goodridge for attending said meeting	50
To allow Mr Eleazer Houghton for do — — —	50
To allow Mr Stephen Whitney for do — — — —	50
To allow Mr Samuel Kimball for do — — —	50
To allow Mr Simon Goodridge for do — — —	50
To allow Mr John Hartwell for do — —	50
To allow Josiah Stearns for do & for recording — —	62
To allow Mr John Hartwell for his service as treasurer in full to this time — — — — —	13 75

Voted To adjourn this meeting to Monday the 30 day of october Instant at one O clock in the after noon to meet at the House of Mr Benj^a Johnson in Lunenburg —

Benj^a Goodridge Moderator

attest — — Josiah Stearns proprietors clerk —

1815 octo 30

The proprietors met according to adjournment at the House of Mr Benj^a Johnson

Voted To allow Mr Benj^a Johnson for providing for this meeting and for attending said meeting — —	1 30
to allow Decon Benj^a Goodridge for attending this meeting —	50
and for attending on a committee appointed at the last meeting —	50
to allow Mr Eleazer Houghton for attending this meeting	50
to allow Mr Stephen Whitney — — —	50
to allow Mr Samuel Kimball for do — — —	50
to do for Reckoning with the treasurer and for his service as one of a committee appointed at the last meeting — — —	1 00
to allow Mr John Hartwell for attending said meeting	50
to allow Josiah Stearns for attending & Recording this meeting	75
& for his service in Reckoing with treasurer and for his attendance on a committee appointed at the last meeting —	1 00

Voted to accept the Report of the committee appointed to Reckon with their Treasurer which Report is in the following words We the subscribers appointed by the proprietors to Reckon with Mr John Hartwell their treasurer have attended their service — and find the treasure charges himself with haveing Rec^d the proprietors money as follows viz

on Caleb Lealands & Eben^r Lealands note	$6 95
[142] Brought over — — — —	6 95
on Mary Chases note — — — — —	16 36

Proprietors' Records.

on John Goodridges & John Goodride Juns note	6 00
on Kendall Bouttells note — — — — —	37 05
on Asa Johnsons note — — — — —	91 81
on Jacob Gibsons note — — — — —	40 00
Interest on money whilest in his hands	4 50
Whole amount —	$202 67
The treasurer accounts for the money so Received as follows viz By paying on the several grants made by the proprietors up to this date — —	80 57
To paying Mr Eleazer Houghton — — —	3 34
To paying Abijah Bigelow Esqr on two bills of cost	27 50
to paying Abel Carter for going to Dorchester	2 00
by money on hand — — — — —	89 26
	$202 67

The committee also finds that there are in the treasurers hands notes against the following persons for the sums affixed to their names viz Jacob

Gibson — — —	7 50
John Billings — — — — —	51 76
Thomas Gould & Samson Gould — — —	57 96

Also notes against the following persons that are doubtfull viz Caleb Lealand & Eben^r Lealand now in Execution

John Goodridge & John Goodridge Junr — —	36 67
Edward Scott — — —	30 13
James Richardson — — —	19 91

Interest on the above notes is cast up to the 26 day of October 1815 — — all which is submitted by
October 30—1815   Josiah Stearns \} Committee
Samuel Kimball

Voted To adjourn this meeting to Monday the first day of January 1816 at one oclock in the after noon to meet at the house of Decon Benjamin Goodridge in Lunenburg — — — — —

Benj^a Goodridge Moderator
attest   Josiah Stearns proprietors clerk

1816–

Jan.ʸ 1ˢᵗ—The proprietors met at the Dwelling house of Decon Benjᵃ Goodridge agreeable to adjournment —
Voted To allow Mʳ John Hartwell their treasurer
    the sum of seven dollers and sixty three cents
    for paying the amount of their grants made on
    the 3 day of October 1814 — that was not al-
    lowed him in the last Reckoning — — —   7 63

*first judgment	$196,,33 debt
Cost — — — — —	16,,93
	213,,26
Second judgᵗ — — — — —	226,,04 debt
	9, 25 Cost
	25. Exon.
Officers fees for selling equity of Redemption	17, 00
for recording deed —	1, 00 —
Cost of first suit —	$16,,93
of second suit —	9, 50
Officers fees —	17, 00
recording deed	1, 00
	$44,,43

[143] 1816

Janʸ 1 Brought up

Voted To adjourn this meeting to Monday the fifth day of Febrary next at one Oclock in the afternoon to meet at the dwelling house of Mʳ Benjᵃ Johnson in Lunenburg —

                    Bejᵃ Goodridge Moderator
attest — — — Josiah Stearns proprietors clerk

1816

Feb.ʸ 5 The proprietors met according to adjournment at the House of Mʳ Benjᵃ Johnson in Lunenburg

Voted to allow Decon Benjᵃ Goodridge for provid-
    ing for the meeting on the first day of Jan,ʸ last $2 90

---

*This is a slip affixed to the top of page 143.

to do for attending the last and the present meeting & for two & a half days time in looking up common land — — — 3 50
to allow Mr Benj^a Johnson for attending two meetings and for two & a half days in looking up common land, and for providing for this meeting the sum of — 4 31
to allow Mr Stephen Whitney for attending two meetings — — — 1
to allow Mr Samuel Kimball for attending two meetings 1
to allow Mr Simon Goodridge for attending two Meetings 1
to allow Mr John Hartwell for attending two meeting and for paying capt Harris, Leut Peirce & Mr Amos Peirce one doller & thirty seven cents, & for cash paid for expences when looking up Common land, and for his time in doing that buisnefs — 5 41
to allow Josiah Stearns for attending & recording two meetings and for two & a half days surveying common & other land 3 75

 Voted to adjourn this meeting to the last wednsday in May next at one o clock in the after-noon, to meet at the House of Decon Benj^a Goodridge in Lunenburg — —
Benj^a Goodridge Moderator
 attest Josiah Stearns proprietors clerk —

1816
May 29 The proprietors met at the house of Decon Benjamin Goodridge agreeable to adjonment
 Voted that the committee for laying out Common land Examine the land on the north easterly side of the meadow lots laid out to John Heywood, William Clark & George Wheeler below Cataconemug pond, and ascertain Whether there is any Common land between those lots and the ministeril lot that was laid out on the east side of those lots
 Voted to allow Capt Joshua Walker of Rinde seven dollers for the Expence that he has been at in

asetaining the lines of the land that he bought of Henry — — —	7 00
Voted to allow Decon Benjamin Goodridge for afsisting in laying out land near Cataconymug pond,, 50, for providing for, and attending this meeting 2,,83 — — —	3 33
to allow Mr Eleazer Houghton for attending this meeting	50
to allow Mr Stephen Whitney for do — — —	50
to allow Mr Samuel Kimball for do — — —	50

[144] 1816
Brought over —

Voted to allow Mr Benjamin Johnson for afsisting in laying out land near Cataconemug pond & for attending this meeting — — —	1 00
to allow Mr John Hartwell for money paid out for the use of the proprietors, for afsisting in laying out Common land, and for attending this meeting — — —	2 25
to allow Josiah Stearns for surveying Common land and for making plans &c, and for attending & Recording this meeting	1 62

Voted to adjourn this meeting to Monday the tenth day of June next to meet at two o clock in the afternoon at the house of Mr Benjamin Johnson in Lunenburg — —

Benj^a Goodride Moderator
attest Josiah Stearns proprietors clerk — —

1816
June 10 The proprietors met according to adjournment at the house of Mr Benj^a Johnson in Lunenburg — — —

Voted to direct the committee for laying out Common land, to make further examination Respecting any Common land below Cataconamug pond, adjoining the brook

Voted to adjourn this meeting to the first Monday in Octr next to meet at the dwelling House of Mr Benj^a Johnson in Lunenburg at one o clock in the after noon

Benj^a Goodridge Moderator
attest Josiah Stearns Proprietors clerk

1816

Oct[r] 7 The proprietors met at the House of M[r] Benj[a] Johnson agreeable to adjournment —

this land laid out a new
Voted to accept the following report of the Committee for laing out Common land viz September 28th 1816 laid out for the proprietors of the original Township of Lunenburg a piece of land on the southerly side of Cataconamug pond & brook containg about fifteen acres Begining on the south side of the brook 26 rods from Shirley line, thence North 35 west 50 rods by ministeral land to the Edge of the swamp, thence north 83 west 24 rods to the north East corner of meadow lot N[o] 6 laid out to William Clark Esqr, thence north 49° west by said meadow 18½ rods to the corner of meadow lot N[o] 5 laid out to John Heywood thence north 39 west by said meadow N[o] 5—16 rods thence south 39° west by said meadow 38 rods to a heep of stones on the side of the Ridge hill, thence South 39° East on up land 7½ rods to the south west corner of meadow lot N[o] 6, thence south 34° East, to the corner of land laid out to Ephraim

[145] 1816
Oct[r] 7

Peirce, thence south 87 west by land laid out to Joshua Goodridge, twenty five rods to land laid out to Nathaniel Page, thence North 6° west 75 rods to a heep of stones on the ridge hill near the pond, thence, south 87 west by Pages lot 12 to land laid out to Edward Hartwell Esqr thence North 39 west 4 rods thence North 15 west 12 rods to the brook, thence down the brook to the pond, thence on the westerly & southerly sides of the pond untill it comes to the brook below the pond, thence down the brook, to where it began — —

Serveyed by Josiah Stearns

approved by the Committee viz Benj[a] Goodridge Benj[a] Johnson & John Hartwell — —

Voted that M[r] John Hartwell the proprietors treasurer use all proper means for recovering the debt due from Caleb & Ebenezer Lealands, by attending to it himself, or by appointing some other person or persons for that purpose, and to give any deed, or acquitance in behalf of the proprietors that may be necefsary & proper in case the Right of Redemtion should be sold —

Voted to allow Decon Benj^a Goodridge for two days looking up common land, and for attending this & the last meeting — —	$3 00
to allow Mr Benj^a Johnson for looking up Common land and for attending this & providing for this and the last meeting — — —	3 92
to allow Mr John Hartwell for attending this & the last meeting & for two days looking up common land and for going to Wm Kilburns & cash paid out —	3 50
to allow Mr Stephen Whitney for attending this & the last meetings	1 00
to allow Mr Saml Kimball for attending this & the last meetings — — —	1 00
to allow Mr Eleazer Houghton for attending this meeting	0 50
to allow Josiah Stearns for surveying &c and for attending and recording this and the last meetings — —	3 75

Voted to adjourn this meeting to the first monday in February next at one o clock in the after noon to meet at the Houfe of Mr Benj^a Johnson in Lunenburg

      Benj^a Goodridge Moderator
 attest Josiah Stearns proprietors clerk —

1817
February 3^d The proprietors met at the house of Mr Benja. Johnson agreeably to adjournment —

Voted that Mr Eleazer Houghton is hereby requested to raise a sum of money sufficient to pay two mortgages on the Estate of Ebenezer Lealand of Roxbury and that if the estate does not sell for enough to pay him

1817
 Febr^y 3
The proprietors will make good to him the deficiency and reasonable pay for his trouble —

Voted that Josiah Stearns make application to Mr Houghton to perform the aforegoing service for the proprietors

Voted to adjourn this meeting to monday the 10 Instant at one O clock in the after noon to meet at the House of Mr Benj^a Johnson in Lunenburg — — —

    attest   Josiah Stearns proprietors clerk

Feby 10 The proprietors met according to adjournment at the House of Mr Benj^a Johnson in Lunenburg

Voted to allow Decon Benj^a Goodridge for attending two meetings, and for going to Leominster to see Esqr Bigelow & Esqr Laurence respecting Ebene^r Lealands Estate and for going to Fitchburg to look up a peice of Common land	1 50
to allow Mr Benj^a Johnson for attending two meetings & for providing for two meetings and for his horse to Mr Houghtons	3 62
to allow Mr Stephen Whitney for attending two meetings — — —	1
to allow Mr Samuel Kimball for do —	1
to allow Mr John Hartwell for do — —	1
to allow Josiah Stearns for attending two meetings and for recording, and for going to M^r E Houghton	1 50

Voted to adjourn this meeting to Wednesday the 28 day of May next to meet at two o clock in the afternoon at the House Mr Benj^a Johnson in Lunenburg

                      Benj^a Goodridge Moderator

    attest — — Josiah Stearns proprietors clerk

1817

May 28 The Proprietors met at the House of Mr Benj^a Johnson according to adjournment — — —

Voted and choose Josiah Stearns an agent to confer with the owners of land adjoining the land that the proprietors have lately laid out on the southerly side of Cataconemug pond & brook, and request them to show the bounds of their lands

                                      carried up

[**147**] 1817
May 28 Voted to allow Decon Benjamin Goodridge
for attending this meeting 0 50
to allow Mr Eleazer Houghton for attending this
meeting — 50
to allow Mr Stephen Whitney for attending this
meeting 50
to allow Mr Benj^a Johnson for attending, and providing for this meeting — — — 2 80
to allow Mr Samuel Kimball for attending this
meeting 50
to allow Mr John Hartwell for attending this
meeting 50
to allow Josiah Stearns for attending & recording
this meeting 63

Voted to adjourn this meeting to Monday the 6th day of October next, at one o clock in the after noon, to meet at Mr Benj^a Johnson in Lunenburg

      Benj^a Goodridge Moderator
 attest Josiah Stearns Proprietors clerk

October 6 The proprietors met according to adjournent —

Voted that the proprietors Committee for making Sale of Common land, are directed to make, or Renew all the necefsary bounds of the land lately laid out by Cataconeymug pond and brook; or in any other place where it is necefsary — — —

Voted to choose a committee to Reckon with the Executor or administrator of the Estate of Mr John Hartwell deceased (the late treasurer) and to Receive the money or obligations that belong to the proprietors and to Settle, and Receipt for the same —

Voted and choose Josiah Stearns, Mr Samuel Kimball & Mr Simon Goodridge for said Committee — —

Voted and choose Mr Simon Goodridge for one of the Committee for looking up, and making sale of Common land in the Room of Mr John Hartwell deceased — — —

Voted to adjourn this meeting to Monday the fifth

day of January next to meet at the House of Mr Benjamin Johnson at one o clock in the after noon —
      Benj^a Goodridge Moderator
  attest Josiah Stearns proprietors clerk

1818
Jany 5 The proprietors met according to adjournment at the house of Mr Benj^a Johnson in Lunenburg

Voted and choose Mr Samuel Kimball moderator pro tem

Voted to accept the Report of the committee appointed to Reckon with the administratrix of the Estate of Mr John Hartwell their late treasurer which is as follows viz

[148] 1818

January 5 Brought forward — — We the subscribers appointed by the original proprietors of the township of Lunenburg to Reckon with the administratrix of the Estate of Mr John Hartwell late of Lunenburg deceased, their late treasurer have attended that service; find that

he had Rec^d the following sums — of John Billings	58 49
of Thomas Gould — — —	38 99
money in his hands on the last Reckoning — —	89 26
interest on the last sum — — —	11 60
	198 34

It appeared that the treasurer had paid out the following sums viz to Abijah Bilelow Esqr	10
on the bill granted February 1816 — —	21 87
on two bills for May & Octo 1816 — — —	33 37
also a bill allowed to Mr Hartwell — —	7 63
interest on the money paid out — — —	6 23
allow for said Hartwells attending three meeting as p^r book	1 50
Rec^d in money — —	17 74
Rec^d Miss Hartwells note — —	100
	198 34

The committee finds notes against the following persons viz Jacob Gibson — interest now due from the last Settlement   7 50

350   *Proprietors' Records.*

Thomas Gould Jur — — —   26 11
Edward Scott — — —   30 13
James Richardson — — —   19 91
due on the debt of Caleb Lealand & Eber Lealand
   supposed not Recoverable — — —   253 54
   Dec 29—1817—all which is submitted by
                Samuel Kimball } Committee
                Simon Goodridge }

   Voted to accept the laying out of the following peice of land that was laid out by the committee on the 8 day of octo 1817

   Begining at three maple trees on the southerly side of the brook below Cataconemug pond—thence South 54° west thirteen rods by land of Ezra Cowdry thence north 49 west 18½ rods by land of E Warren Jur thence South 54° west Eight rods to a Juniper tree marked thence north 39° west sixteen rods by land of said Cowdry— thence South 39° west thirty eight rods—thence south 39° East Seven and a half rods—thence north 54° East three rods to Warrens South west corner—thence south 34 East Eighteen rods to the heep of stones where the pine tree stod that was the ancient corner of Wm Clarks, George Wheelers & Ephm Peirces meadow lots thence South 87° west twenty five rods over the Ridge hill to the line of the land lately owned by Henrys—thence north 6° west by said Henrys land to a pilliar of stons on the Ridge hill being about 75 rods—thence south 87 west twelve rods to capt Harrises land, thence n 39 E four rods thence north 15 W twelve rods by Harrises land to the brook thence down the brook to the pond, thence on the West and Southerly side of the pond to the brook below the pond thence down the brook to where it began

[149]
   January 5 1818 brought fordard —
   Voted and choose Mr Simon Goodridge Treasurer— Sworn at the same time
   Voted that the present treasurer pay Mr Simon Goodridge one doller that is his due one the

Proprietors' Records.

grant of Febr^y 5—1816 that sum not having been paid to him by the late treasurer — —	1
Voted to allow Decon Benj^a Goodridge for attending this meeting, and for one day laying out Common land —	1 50
to allow Mr Eleazer Houghton for attending this and the last meetings	1
to allow Mr Stephen Whitney for attending the last meeting — —	50
to allow Mr Benj^a Johnson for attending and providing for two meetings — and for one day lay out common land	3 62
to allow Mr Samuel Kimball for attending two meetings and for Reckoning with the administratrix of the late treasurer — —	2
to allow Mr Simon Goodridge for attending this and the last meetings and for one day laying out Common land — and for Reckoning With the treasurer — —	3 50
to allow Josiah Stearns for going to Shirly, to notify Mr Ames — for going to Alexanders, Warrens & Cowdrys, and Surveying almost most two days, and for making plans, for paying Mr David Kilburn 75 cents; and for attending and recording two meetings	6 32

Voted to adjourn this meeting to the last wednesday in May next to meet at the house of Mr Benj^a Johnson in Lunenburg at one O clock in the after noon

       Samuel Kimball Moderator pro tem
  attest Josiah Stearns proprietors clerk

1818
May 27 the Proprietors met accoring to adjornment at the houſe of Mr Benj^a Johnſon in Lunenburg —

 Voted and Chose Saml. Kimball Clark Pro Tem:

 Voted to adjorn this meeting to monday the fifth Day of October Next at one of O clock in the after noon at the houſe of Mr Benj^a Johnson in Lunenburg — —

       Benj^a Goodridge Moderator
  attest Saml. Kimball Proprietors Clerk Pro Tem:

Worcester fs May 27—1818 personally appeared Mr Samuel Kimball and made solemn oath that as clerk Pro tem of the proprietors of the original township of Lunenburg that he would act faithfully and impartially according to the best of his abilities

Josiah Stearns Just peace

[150] 1818

October 5 The Proprietors Met according to adjornment at the houfe of Mr Benj^a Johnfon in Lunenburg

Voted to allow Mr Benj^a Johnson for attending and providing for two meetings — —	$5 35
and also for going to Shirley & m^r Kilborns	1 50
Voted allow Dec^n Benj^a Goodridge for attending two meetings — —	1 00
Voted to allow Mr Eleaz^r Houghton for Ditto —	1 00
Voted to allow Mr Stephen Whitney for Ditto —	1 00
Voted to allow Mr Simon Goodridge for attending two meetings and for going to Shirley and to Mr Kilborns — —	2 00
Voted to allow Saml Kimball for attending two meeting and for recording the same	1 25

Voted to adjorn this meeting to Last Wednesday in may Next to meet at the houfe of Mr Benj^a Johnfon in Lunenburg at one O Clock in the afternoon —

Ben^ja Goodridge modertor
attest Saml Kimball Clark Pro tem

May 26 1819

the Proprietors met at the houfe of Mr Benj^a Johnsons according to adjornment — —

the committee for the sale of Common Land Report that they have sold a piece of Common land near Catacolamug Brook & pond to Mr Mofes Carleton for sixty four Dollars and Rec^d S^d Carltons Note Dated october 26 1819 for the same payable to the Treasurer to him or his succefer in S^d office for the ufe of the Propietors of the township of Lunenburg

Benj^a Johnson } Comittee
Simon Goodridge }

Proprietors' Records. 353

Voted to accept the above Report and order the Same to be Recorded — —

Voted to allow Mr Benjᵃ Johnson for attending and providing for this meeting and Eighty seven Cents not allowed the Last meeting	$3 9
Voted to allow Decⁿ Benjᵃ Goodridge for attending this meeting — — —	0 50
Voted to allow Mr Elezʳ Hougton for Ditto — —	0 50
Voted to allow Mr Simon Goodridge for attending this meeting and seventy five Cents money advanced — —	1 25

[151] 1819

May 26 Brought forward

Voted to allow Samˡ Kimball for attending this meeting and Recording the same	$00 62

Voted to adjorn this meeting to the Last wednesday in may Next to meet at the houſe of Decⁿ Benjᵃ Goodridge in Lunenburg at one O: Clock in the after noon

Benjᵃ Goodridge Moderator

attest Samˡ Kimball Proprietors Clerk pro tempʸ

1820

May 31ſt the propieters of the original township of Lunenburg met according to adjornment at the houſe of Decⁿ Benjᵃ Goodridges in Lunenburg

Voted to allow Decⁿ Benjᵃ Goodridg for attending and providing for this meeting — — —	3. 08
Voted to all Mr Eleazar Houghto for attending this meeting — — —	0 50
Voted to allow Mr Benjᵃ Johnſon for Ditto — —	0 50
Voted to allow Mr Simon Goodridge for Ditto —	0 50
Voted to allow Samˡ Kimball for attending this meeting and Recording the Same —	00 63

Voted to adjorn this meeting to monday the Second Day of october Next to meet at the houſe of Decⁿ Benjᵃ Goodridges in Lunenburg two O Clock in the after noon —

Moderator

Attest Samˡ Kimball Clark Pro Tem

1820

October 2ᵈ the Proprietor met at the houſe of Decⁿ Benjᵃ Goodridges agreeable to adjornment and Voted the Treasurer Call on Mʳ Moſes Carlton to pay his Note Given to Sᵈ Treaſurer Renew it with a good bondsman

Voted to allow Decⁿ Benjᵃ Goodridge for attending this meeting — — —	$0 50
to allow Mʳ Eleazʳ Houghton for Ditto — —	0 50
to allow Mʳ Benjᵃ Johnſon for Ditto —	0 50
to allow Mʳ Simon Goodridge for Ditto —	0 50
to allow Samˡ Kimball for Ditto & Recording —	0 62

Voted to Chooſe a Committee to recon with the Treaſurer and Choſe Mʳ Eleazʳ Houghton and Samˡ Kimball

Voted to adjorn this meeting to the thurſday after the Last wenday in may Next at one O clock P. m. to meet at the houſe Mʳ Simon goodridges in Lunenburg

     Benjᵃ Goodridge Moderator
    attest Samˡ Kimball Cark P T

[152] May 31ᵈ 1821 the Proprietors Mett att the houſe of Mʳ Simon Goodridge according to adjornment

Voted to accept the Report of the Committee for Reconing with the treaſurer and to have the Same Recorded

we the subscribers appointed a Committee by the Propretors of the township of Lunenburg to Recon with their treaſurer have attended that Sevice and find that he has Recᵈ of the proprietors money the following Sums.

viz of Mrs. Hartweell — — —	$17 72
of Thoˢ Gould — — —	27 28
of Jacob Gibson — —	9 45
of Mrs Hartwell — — —	104 00
intereſt on the same to this Date	15 46
Mʳ Moſes Carlton — — —	64 00
intereſt on the Same to this Date — —	9 49
	247 40
	60 39
	187 01

Proprietors' Records.

it appears the treaſurer has paid out on Sundry bill to the amount of. — —	60 39

and that the Notes against Sundy persons	
viz — Calvin Eaton — — —	67 20
intereſt on the Same to this Date — —	1 92
Colo Cuſhing — — —	30
intereſt to this Date — —	4 46
Colo Edmon Cuſhing — — —	72 00
intereſt to this Date — —	2 53
Cash on hand — — —	8 90
	187 01

Note Desperate. Edward scott — — —	30 18
James Richardson — — —	19 91
Lealands Debt —	253 44
all which we Submit	

Eleazr Houghton ⎫
Saml Kimball ⎬ comittee

Voted to allow Mr Elezr Houghton for Reconing with treasurer — — —	0 75
and Saml Kimball for the Same Sevice	75
and Mr Simon Goodridge for his attendance on that Sevice — — —	75
Voted to allow Simon Goodridge for his Sevice as treaſurer and Going to Shirley Leominster & Fitchburg for his Sevice to this Date — —	9 00
Voted to allow Decn. Benja Goodridge for attending this meeting — — —	0 50
to allow Mr Elezr. Houghton for Ditto —	0 50
to allow Mr Stephen Whitney for Ditto — —	0 50
to allow Mr Benja Johnſon for Ditto — —	0 50
to allow Mr Simon Goodridge for Ditto — —	0 50
to allow Mr Simon Goodridge for providing for this meeting — — —	2 85

carried up

[**153**] 1821 May 31 Voted to allow Sam!. Kimball
for attending this meeting — — —   0 .50
and for Recording the meeting and Reconing with
treafurer — —   0 25

Voted to adjorn this meeting to thurfday after the Last wednesday in may Next at one oclock after noon to meet at the houfe of M!. Simon Goodridges in Lunenburge
Benj^a Goodridge moderator
attest Sam!. Kimball Clerk Pro tem

May 30 1822 the Proprietors met at the house of M!. Simon Goodridges according to adjornment

Voted to allow Elez^r Houghton for attending this
meeting   0 50
to Dec^n Benj^a Goodridge for Ditto —   0 50
to Mr Simon Goodridge for attending this meeting
and Providing for the same —   1 49
to Saml Kimball for attending this meeting and
Recording and paying Esqr Stearns — —   0 92

Voted to allow the abov
Voted to adjorn this meeting to thurfday after the the Laft wednefday in may Next to meet at the houfe of M!. Simon Goodridges in Lunenburg one o Clock after noon
Benj Goodrige Modrator
Saml Kimball Clark Pro Tem

May 29 1823

the Propieters met according to adjornment at the houfe of M!. Simon Goodridges in Lunenburg and agree^d that Doc^t Aaron Beard and Mr Sam!. Johnfon be admited to act on the Rights of Mr Benj^a Johnfon, Dec^t Voted and Chofe Mr Simon Goodridge Moderator Pro Tem

Voted — and Chofe Sam!. Kimball as agent for the proprietors to afertain what money has ben paid by the Treafurer as Devidens and for other purposes — — —

Voted to allow Simon Goodridge two Dollars forty
  Eigt Cents for providing for this meeting fifty
  Cents for attending s^d meeting   2 98
Voted to allow Doc^r Aaron Bard fifty Cent for at-
  tending this meeting   0 50

Voted to allow Sam¹ Johnſon fifty cents for attend
   this meeting — —   0 50
Voted to allow Sam¹. Kimall Seventy five Cents for
   Recoding and attending this meeting   0 75

Voted to adjorn this meeting to thursday the twenty Sixth Day of June Next to meet at the houſe of Simon Goodridge in Lunenburg at two of the Clock in the after Noon

Simon Goodridge Mod^r Pro Tem
atteſt   Sam¹ Kimball Clerk P T

[154] 1823 June 26 the proprietors of the township of Lunenburg met at the houſe of M^r. Simon Goodridges according to adjornment

Voted to Chuſe an agent to enqure and aſertain if the proprietors Common Land be ever out lawed and to furnish s^d agent with money to Defray the Neſary Expence of the same

Voted and Chose Doc^r. Aaron Bard for s^d agent

Voted to allow Mr Simon Goodridge for providing
   and attending meeting   2 92
Voted to allow Decⁿ Benj^a. Goodridge for attend-
   ing this meeting   0 50
Voted to allow M^r. Ele^r. Houghton for Ditto — —   0 50
Voted to allow Doc^t. Aaron Bard for Ditto — —   0 50
Voted to allow Sam¹ Kimball for services and at-
   tending this meeting   2 25

Voted to adjorn this meeting to the firſt monday in Sepr. Next at one O clock in the after noon to meet at the houſe M^r. Simon Goodridges —

Benj^a Goodridge Moderato
attest   Sam¹ Kimball Clerk Pro Tem

1823 Sepr. 1^{ſt}. the proprietors of the Township of Lunenburg met at the houſe of M^r. Simon Goodridges according to adjornment

   1 Voted and Choſe M^r. Elea^r. Houghton Moderator Pro Tem

2 Voted that Mr. Eleazr. Hougton be annexed to the Comittee to Search for common Land belonging to the proprietors of Lunenburg

3 Voted that the aforesaid Committee Search and Look up all the Common Land and and employ a Survayor to Lay out all the their Land

4 Voted to allow the following account —

to Mr. Simon Goodridge for providing & attending this meting	$2 79
to Mr. Eleazr. Houghton for attending this meeting	0 50
to Docr. Aaron Bard for Ditto Ditto	0 50
to Saml. Kimball for attending & Recording this meett	0 75

5 Voted to adjorn this meeting to monday the thirteeth Day of October Next one of the Clock after noon to meet at this place

Eleazer Houghton Moderator P m
atteft Saml Kimball Clerk Pro Tem

1823 Octr. 13

the Proprietors of the Townſhip of Lunenburg met according to adjornment at the houſe of Mr. Simon Goodridges in sd. Lunenburg —

Voted 1ft. and Choſe Mr. Simon goodridge moderator Pro Tem

2d to allow Mr. Simon Goodridge for Providing and attending this meeting and other Services	$3 0
3d to allow Docr. Aaron Bard 25c for Cash paid and for attinding this meeting .50 — — —	0 75
4th to allow Mr Saml. Johſon for Attending this meeting	0 50
5th to allow Saml. Kimball for attending this meeting and other Services — —	1 50

Voted 6 to adjorn this meeting to the Laſt thursday in may next to meet at this place at one oclock after noon

Simon Goodridge Moderator, P T
atteft Saml Kimball Clerk Pro Tem

[155] 1824 May 27 the Proprietors met according to adjornment at the houſe of Mr. Simon Goodridge in Lunenburg

Voted and Choſe Simon Goodridge Moderator P Tem and Voted to allow the following Sums to the Several perſon here after mentioned

to Mr. David Kilborn for Survaying — —	$3.00
Mr. Simon Goodridge for Proiding & Services and attending — —	"8.30
Mr. Eleazr Houghton for Services & attending	3 50
Docr. Aaron Bard for attending — — —	0 50
Mr. Saml. Johnſon for attending — — —	0 50
Saml. Kimball for services and attending —	5 00

Voted the Treaſurer Pay out the Same
Voted to Chuſe a New Clerk
Voted and Choſe Doct. Aron Bard Clerk
Voted to adjorn this meeting to the Last thurſday in may 1825 to meet at this place at one oClock in the after Noon

       Saml. Kimball Clerk P T

Worcester ſs. May 27th 1824. Personally appeared Doct Aaron Bard and made solemn oath that as Clerk of the proprietors of the original Township of Lunenburg he would act faithfully and impartially according to the best of his abilities before
    Esek Whiting Justice of the Peace

1825
May 26th The Proprietors of the town of Lunenburg met according to adjournment at the house of Simon Goodridge in Lunenburg

Voted to allow Simon Goodridge for providing for this meeting — —	1 78
Voted to allow Simon Goodridge for attending this meeting — — —	1 00
Voted to allow Samuel Kimball for attending this meeting —	1 00
Voted to allow Aron Bard for attending this meeting —	1 00
Voted to allow Aron Bard for recording the proceeding of the Proprietors	0 25

Voted to adjourn this meeting until the Thursday next after the last Wednesday in May AD 1826 at two of the clock in the afternoon then to meet at Simon Goodridge in Lunenburg

attest Aron Bard Proprietors Clerk

1826

June 1st The Propritors of the town of Lunenburg met at the house of Simon Goodridge in said town according to adjournment and choose Simon Goodridge Moderator of the meeting

Voted to accept of Artimas Goodridge as a proprietor of said town Benjamin Goodridge having resigned being a member of the committee to look up and sell proprietors land

Voted and choose Artemas Goodridge in the stead of said Goodridge to look up and sell the common and undivid land not yet disposed of belonging to the propietors

[156] Voted to dismiss Eleazar Houghton from serving as committee Man to look up and sell proprietors Land

Voted and choose Aron Bard for one of the committee to look up and sell the common and undivided lands belongin to the proprietors

Voted That the Proprietors who have attended this meeting be allowed to receive one dollar each for his attendance this day.

Voted To pay a bill for attendance of the Proprietors at this meeting Samuel Kimball for selling land in Fitchburg to Jeremiah Kinsman to Aron Bard for box for proprietors book to Simon Goodridge for refreshment amounting to $11.09

Voted and chose Aron Bard a committee man to recon with the treasurer

Voted and choose Artemas Goodridg a committee man to recon with the treasurer

Voted to adjourn this meeting untill the Thursday next succeeding the last Wednesday in May at two of the clock in the after noon at the House of Simon Goodridge

Attest Aron Bard Proprietors Clerk

1827

May 31 The Proprietors committee appointd to recon with there Treasurer make the following report

That they find due to the proprietors the sum of   242 85

and that the Charge of their Treasurer for his Services as Treasurer and attending meeting Paying the Members for attending providing for Meetings and looking up Common Lands for the space of Six years amounts to the sum of $129 60

Including the following Bill

To Simon Goodridge serving treasurer 6 years	18	
To Simon Goodridge going to Fitchburg after Land	1 12	
Providing for and attending this meeting Simon Goodrid	3 04	
Samuel Kimball attending the last meeting	1 00	
Aaron Bard going to Fitchburg and attending meeting	2 75	
Samuel Johnson attending this meeting	1 00	
Artemas Goodridge going to Fitchburg attending	2 36	
	29 27	129 60

Leaving a Ballance Due the 31st May 1827 of   113 25

        Aron Bard
        Artemas Goodridge

Voted to adjourn this Meeting until the 29th Day of May 1828 at two of the clock in the afternoon at the Dwelling house of Aron Bard

        attest   Aron Bard Clerk

1828 May 29th The Proprietors of the the Town of Lunenburg met at the Dwelling House of Aron Bard according to adjournment and chose Simon Goodridge Moderator of the Meeting

Voted to pay the Proprietors who atted this meeting the sum of one dollar each Viz

To Simon Goodridge the sum of one Dollar —	1 "
To Samuel Kimball the sum of one Dollar	1 "
To Aron Bard for attending one Dollar recording twenty five Cts.	1 25
To Samuel Johnson the sum of one Dollar —	1 "
To Artemas Goodridge the sum of one Dollar	1 "
To Aron Bard for providing	2 05

[157] 1828
    amounting to the sum of seven Dollars thirty five cents $7 35

Voted That the above sum be paid out of the Treasury

Voted To adjourn this Meeting until Thursday the twenty eight day of May AD 1829 to the Dwelling House of Simon Goodridg in said Lunenburg at three of the Clock in the after noon

    Attest   Aron Bard: Proprietors Clerk

1829
May 28 The Proprietors of the Town of Lunenburgh met at the Dwelling-House of Simon Goodridge in Lunenburg agreeable to adjournment and chose Simon Goodridge Moderator Pro Tem

Voted To pay those who attend this Meeting one Dollar each

	D. cts	D cts
Voted To allow Simon Goodridge for attending this meeting the sum of one Dollar	1 00	
Voted To allow Simon Goodridge for examinging Warrens and Cowdry,s lines the sum of one Dollar	1 00	
Voted To allow Artemas Goodridg for attending this meeting the sum of one Dollar —	1 00	
Voted To allow Artemas Goodridge for examinging Warren,s and Cowdry,s lines the sum of one Dollar	1 00	
Voted To allow Samuel Kimball for attending this meeting the sum of one Dollar —	1 00	

Proprietors' Records.

Voted To allow Aron Bard for attending this meeting and recording the sum of one Dollar twenty five cent	1 25
Voted To allow Samuel Johnson for attending this meeting the sum of one Dollar	1 00
Voted To allow Simon Goodridge for providing for this meeting the sum of fifty five cents	0 55
	7 80

Voted That the above sum of seven Dollars and eighty cents be paid out of the Treasury

Voted To adjourn this meeting until Thursday the twenty seventh day of May next at three of the Clock in the afternoon at the Dwelling House of Aron Bard in Lunenburg

  attest   Aron Bard } proprietors
                 Clerk

[158] 1831 The Proprietors of the Town of Lunenburg met at the dwelling house of Aron Bard in Lunenburg agreeable to adjournment and chose Simon Goodridge Moderator

Voted To allow Simon Goodridge as Treasurer	7 00
" To allow Aron Bard for attending meeting and rcording —	1 25
" To allow Simon Goodridge for attending	1 00
" To allow Artemas Goodridge for attending	1 00
" To allow Samuel Johnson for attending	1 00
" To allow Samuel Johnson for providing	33
	11 58

Voted That the above sum of eleven dollars and fifty eight cents be paid out of the Treasury

Voted To adjourn this meeting until Thursday the twenty sixth day of May AD 1831 at the dwelling house of Simon Goodridge in Lunenburg at three of the Clock afternoon

  attest   Aron Bard Proprietors
                 clerk

[159] 1833

May 28. The Proprietors met at the Dwelling-house of Aron Bard

    Choose Samuel Johnson Moderator Pro tem
    Choose Aron Bard Treasurer

The Proprietors having recconed with the former Treasurer find due from him the sum of one hundred and nine dollars thirty four cents — — —   109 34

Voted to pay Aron Bard Simon Goodridge Artemas Goodridge Samuel Johnson for attending two meetings each two dollars   8 00

Voted to pay Artemas Goodridge Samuel Johnson Aron Bard for attending one meeting each one dollar — —   3 00

Voted to adjourn this meeting until May 29th 834 at the Dwelling house of Aron Bard at four of the Clock in the afternoon

---

[The remainder of the book is blank, with the exception of the last leaf, on the first page of which is the following "Sum of Accounts," and on the reverse the single line relating to interest.]

Sum of accounts Due from the Propriaty of Lunenburg July ye 9th 1781

	Eleazer Houghton — — in Silver	£2	00	0
	Ben^a Redington — — —	3	17	9
	Philip Goodridge — — —	3	7	6
	Aaron Willard — — —	13	4	10
	Thomas Cowdin — — —	1	4	0
	Ephraim Weatherbee — — —	0	6	0
	Philip Goodridge Store — — —	0	19	0
May 7th 1781	Phenehas Hartwell — — —	0	6	0
	Edward Hartwell — — —	2	8	0

this account taken of one of the papers on file and Recorded the 2^d Day of october 1781 by order of the propriators of Lunenburg

              pr Joseph Hartwell Propriators Clark

Feby 22 1810 — paid Interest & one doller & ten cents

INDEX.

INDEX.

The references of the more prominent proprietors have been classified, the first series containing only those relating to lands.

ADAMS, Francis, 181–184.
——, Jonathan, 254, 325, 337.
——, ——, Jr., 312.
——, Zabdiel B., 329.
Advertisement of Common Land, copy of, 261.
—— of Dividends ordered, 298.
Alexander, 351.
——, Francis, 86, 87.
——, William, 23, 86, 87, 94, 232, 238, 239.
Allen, Hon. Jeremiah, 2, 12, 42, 73–76, 157, 236, 244.
Ames, 351.
Apple Tree Hill, 18, 22, 43, 54, 84, 100, 102, 116, 131, 139, 151, 215, 224, 233.
Ashby, 255, 260, 264, 265, 267, 276.
Attendance on meetings to be paid for, 294.
Austin, Daniel, 16, 17, 20, 21, 40, 74, 76, 79, 83, 118, 239, 254.
——, Samuel, 144.

BAILEY, Jedidiah, 256, 257.
——, Josiah, 29, 30.
Ball, Jonathan, 138–141, 214, 224, 256. (See Wheeler and Ball.)
Bard, Dr. Aron, 356–364.
Beard, see Bard.
Beaver Dam, 94, 201, 232.
—— Pond Meadows, 102.
Beath, Walter, 3, 38, 88–91, 101, 170, 204, 211, 238, 245.
Beeth, see Beath.
Belcher, Jeremiah, 254.
Bellows, Benjamin, Jr., 61, 235, 236.
Bellows, Col. Joseph, 257, 273.
Bennet, Samuel, 117.
Bigelow, Abijah, 341, 347, 349.
Billing, Samuel, 287.
Billings, John, 335, 341, 349.
——, Joshua, Jr., 32.

Billings, Reuben, 32.
Bird, Benjamin, 45, 53, 160.
Bleaney, Capt. Benjamin, 235.
Blunt, William, 79.
Borman, 70, 105–107, 110, 111, 118, 125.
Boston, Residents of, see Allen, Jeremiah, Clark, William, Fitch, Zachariah, Hill, John, Willard, Madam Hannah, Willard, Hon. Josiah.
Bounds, Present, established, 321.
Boutell, James, 250, 251, 254–256, 258, 259, 276, 284.
——, Kendall, 259, 335, 341.
Bowman, Jonathan, 320.
Boynton, Benoni, 99, 104, 138, 145; 9, 15, 21, 23, 57, 90, 96, 125, 143, 171, 173, 175, 177, 209.
——, Eleazer, 82.
——, Hilkiah, 2, 146; 15, 18, 21, 24, 68, 78, 79, 96, 100, 119, 122, 124, 125, 143, 151, 170, 171, 173, 175, 177, 217.
Brandon, Joseph, 65.
Brewer, John, 10, 27, 53–55, 116, 120, 122, 132, 134, 158, 161, 166, 215, 237.
Bridge, Ebenezer, 247, 252, 258.
——, John, 328.
Brown, 236, 246, 249.
——, Aaron, 22, 93.
——, Col., Hon. Samuel, 33, 34, 37, 42, 109, 132, 137, 156–159, 163, 199, 205, 214, 223, 230, 234.
——, William, 75.
Burbeen, James, 8, 11–13, 17, 74, 76, 141, 162, 163, 220, 244.
Burying Place, 172, 174, 178.
Buss, John, 243.

CALF, John, 30, 34, 35, 228, 229.
Carleton, see Carlton.
Carlile, David, 241.
Carlton, Moses, 352, 354.

Carter, Abel, 341.
Cataconamoug*, 6, 39, 70–73, 111, 118, 121, 127, 150–152, 198, 202, 226, 227, 330, 343–345, 347, 348, 350, 352.
Chapman, Daniel, 257, 258.
Charlestown, see Dowse, Jonathan.
Chase, Mary, 335, 340.
Clark, Jonas, 34, 36, 37, 45, 160.
——, Robert, 22, 23, 87, 93, 108, 231, 232.
——, William, 13, 25, 38, 42, 66, 88, 90, 140, 152, 156, 157, 197–202, 205, 206, 222–224, 256, 330, 343, 345, 350.
Clay Pit Meadows, 12, 20, 40, 79, 80, 83.
Cobit, 244.
Colbern, James, 7–9, 24, 142, 175, 214.
Colbourn, see Colbern.
College Land, 155, 221, 239, 254, 293, 329.
Comin, see Commings.
Commings, Robert, 41, 45, 109, 132, 159, 160.
——, Thaddeus, 262, 277, 279, 283–286, 288, 290, 292, 293, 295, 300–302, 304, 308–310, 314–316, 318, 320, 322, 326, 329, 332, 333.
Concord, see Commings, Robert, Lee, Dr. Joseph, Prescott, Jonathan.
Cory, Benjamin, 5, 7, 63, 66–68, 124, 170, 210, 212.
County Road, 250.
Cowdin, Capt. Thomas, Jr., 247, 249–252, 259, 262, 271, 272, 296, 297, 364.
Cowdry, Ezra, 350, 351, 362.
Cunningham, William, 325, 326.
Cushing, Col. Edmon, 355.

DANFORTH, Benjamin, 328.
——, Nicholas, 246, 252.
Davies, Samuel, 24.
Densmore, see Dunsmore.
Divoll, John, 115, 231.
Dodge, Noah, 178, 227.
Dorchester, 341; see Tailer, Col. Wm.
—— Farm, 46, 98, 113, 114, 124, 130, 133, 209, 248.
Downes, Col. Samuel, 241, 249–251.
Dowse, Jonathan, 3, 28, 47, 48, 223.
Dunsmore, John, 254.
——, Phinehas, 307, 308, 312.

EATON, Calvin, 355.
——, Person, 273.

Eighty acres laid out, 185.
Emerson, Edward, 130–132, 134, 158, 160, 320.
Estebrook, Jedediah, 261, 263–269.
Evans, Thomas, 32.

FARNSWORTH, 62, 110, 114, 120.
——, Isaac, 71, 141–143; 23, 25, 32, 49, 77, 97, 116, 165, 169, 175, 177, 178, 180, 209, 213, 216, 225.
——, Joshua, 218.
——, Samuel, 113, 114, 216.
Ffyfe, see Fyffe.
Fisk, John, 16, 20, 77–83, 155, 170, 221, 222, 238, 245.
Fitch, Capt. Joseph, 241.
——, Col. Thomas, 122, 159, 212, 228.
——, Zachariah, 181, 182, 184.
Fitchburg, 10, 28, 196, 241–244, 246, 247, 251–253, 255, 259–265, 267, 270–272, 276, 296, 297, 313, 329, 347, 355, 360, 361.
—— Meeting House, 242, 247, 249, 253, 262.
Flagg, Maj. Eleizer, 9.
Flat Hill, 8, 21, 57, 58, 65, 75, 86, 87, 101, 142, 146–148, 204, 217, 218.
—— Rock Hill, 253.
Forster, Alexander, 162, 229.
Foster, Isaac, 239.
Fox, 253.
Frost, 246.
——, Benjamin, 28, 253.
Fullam, Col. Francis, 164, 165, 180.
——, Phinehas, 244.
——, see Fullum,
Fuller, 256.
Fullum, 242, 250.
——, see Fullam.
Fyffe, Robert, 17–19, 44, 60, 212.

GARDNER, Rev. Andrew, 1, 38–40, 43, 46, 83, 88, 89, 144–146, 223.
General Court, Petitions to, 275, 282, 304.
—— Court's Committee's Farm, 129, 164, 165, 179–181, 187, 188, 244, 249.
Gibson, Arrington, 53, 59.
——, Isaac, 242, 252.
——, Israel, 32, 329.
——, Jacob, 335, 341, 349, 354.
——, Capt. John, 109, 230.
——, Jonas [error, see Gilson].
——, Capt. Reuben, 109, 264, 266, 268.

---

*The spelling here followed is the one most frequently used of the thirteen forms which appear on the records.

Index. 369

Gibson, Timothy, 6, 46, 61–64, 68, 110, 112, 114, 149, 150, 157, 229, 230, 234, 241.
Gill, Lawyer, 299.
Gilson, Jonas, 22, 80, 86, 87, 93–95, 232, 233.
Goodale, 250.
Goodridge, Artemas, 360-364.
——, Capt. Benjamin, 5, 36, 62, 109, 113–117, 120, 125, 149, 153, 154, 178, 184, 212, 228, 237–240, 245.
——, Capt., Dea. Benjamin, 248, 262, 313; 192, 195, 247–253, 257–262, 264, 266, 268, 276–286, 290, 292, 293, 295, 300–302, 304–349, 351–357, 360.
——, David, 192.
——, John, 52.
——, John and John, Jr., 335, 341.
——, Joshua, 109, 112, 115, 120, 121, 231, 345.
——, Lieut. Philip (d. 1729), 115, 120, 122–124, 235.
——, Lieut. Philip, 237–239, 245, 255, 257, 262, 263; 191–193, 195, 196, 247, 249, 256, 259, 260, 266, 268–275, 277–304, 311, 317, 318, 323, 325, 326, 364; his store, 364.
——, Simon, 324, 326, 329, 333, 334, 338, 339, 343, 348, 350-364.
Gordon, James, 108, 219, 226, 233, 236, 254, 255, 258.
Gould, 257, 258.
——, David, 66.
——, Jacob, 80, 85, 87, 137, 172, 217, 233, 238.
——, Capt. Joseph, 6, 15, 16, 27, 28, 49–51, 68, 72, 73, 76, 110, 112, 121, 152, 167, 220, 236.
——, Moses, 85, 86.
——, Samson, 335, 341.
——, Thomas, 335, 341, 349, 354.
——, Thomas, Jr., 350.
Great Brook, 229.
Groton, see Parker, Phineas.
—— Line, 8, 11, 17, 60, 72, 74, 102, 136, 146–148, 167, 219, 226, 236, 237.
—— Meeting at, 180, 181.
—— Road which goeth to, 90.
—— Southwest Corner, 72.
Grout, John, 39, 143, 144.

Haistings, John, 108, 169, 224.
——, Nathaniel, 258.
Hale, Dr., 243.
——, Thomas, 26, 34, 36–38, 89, 163.
Harkness, Thomas, 217, 218, 255, 257, 289.

Harrington, Ebenezer, 10.
Harris, 250.
——, Capt., 331, 343, 350.
——, Nathaniel, 55–60, 112, 120, 134, 154.
Hartwell, Lieut. Edward, 5, 43, 44, 67, 69, 99, 110-112, 121, 123–127, 152, 162, 168, 169, 175, 189, 190, 204, 207, 215–220, 227, 234, 237, 239–241, 248, 345; 1–75, 77–88, 90–117, 119–185, 187–246, 265–267, 273, 364.
——, John, 329, 333, 335-349.
——, Joseph, 192, 253–261, 263, 272-322, 324, 364.
——, Miss, 349.
——, Mrs., 354.
——Phinehas, 10, 246, 289, 364.
Harvard College, see College Land.
Harward, 258.
Harwood, Nathaniel, 74, 75, 90, 101–103, 113, 219, 237, 254.
——, Peter, 100.
Haskel, Dr. Abraham, 312.
Hastings, 107, 153, see Haistings.
Heal, see Hale.
Henry, 354, 350.
Heywood, John, 4–7, 36, 63, 67–69, 73, 124, 137, 166, 170, 178, 202, 228, 241, 343, 345.
——, Nathan, 5, 7, 68–72, 105, 112, 124, 215, 220; 1–60, 62–75, 77–88, 90–117, 119–129, 131–169, 173, 175, 180, 192, 197-246, 249.
Highways, 4, 6, 7, 9–11, 13, 16, 22–24, 28, 30, 34, 41, 43–46, 56, 58, 59, 62, 64, 65, 67, 68, 70, 74–78, 80, 86–88, 90, 93, 95, 101, 113, 119, 125, 130, 132, 138, 139, 141, 143, 145–148, 151, 164, 166, 177, 179, 204, 214, 216, 218, 220, 223, 230, 231, 233–236, 238–242, 244, 250, 251, 253, 255, 319–321, 330.
Hill, John, 7, 8, 24, 25, 29-34, 142, 192, 205, 217, 236.
——, Thomas, 24, 25.
——, Zaccheus, 24-26, 137, 163.
Hingham, see Thaxter, Samuel.
Horsemeat Meadows, 9, 142.
Hosmer, Stephen, 244.
Hospital Farm, 262, 272.
Houghton, Eleazer, 36, 39, 43, 106, 110, 118-120, 122, 149, 154, 198, 201, 228, 258, 259.
——, Eleazer, Jr., 262, 272; 28, 192, 247-252, 257, 277, 279, 294, 295, 300, 303, 305, 308-310, 315, 316, 320-323, 325, 326, 329, 331-341, 344, 346-348, 351-360, 364.
——, Jonas, 113, 125, 131, 178, 210.

370 Index.

Houghton, Jonathan, 178.
House Lots:
  1—1, 38, 88, 89, 145, 200, 222, 234.
  2—2, 3, 153, 154.
  3—2, 4, 13, 89, 197, 222, 332.
  4—2, 4, 161, 162.
  5—4, 28, 199.
  6—4, 5, 7, 235, 236, 240.
  7—7, 8, 156, 157, 333.
  8—9-11, 240, 242, 332.
  9—11, 12, 332.
  10—11, 13, 84, 203, 332.
  11—14-16, 156, 333.
  12—15-19, 143.
  13—20, 21, 204.
  14—3, 40, 167, 332.
  15—24, 25, 332.
  16—3, 26, 199.
  17—198, 199.
  18—29, 156, 157, 333.
  19—13, 29, 89, 197, 223, 332.
  20—30-32, 34, 51.
  21—34, 36, 332.
  22—36, 37, 145, 243.
  23—144, 145, 203, 243.
  24—40-42, 145.
  25—41, 159.
  26—44, 46, 332.
  27—47, 48.
  28—49, 51.
  29—52, 53, 156, 333.
  30—53-56, 332.
  31—53, 55-57, 134.
  32—56, 59-61, 214.
  33—61-64, 158, 333.
  34—62, 64, 65, 156, 157, 333.
  35—45, 46, 64, 65, 332.
  36—2, 45, 65-67, 153, 156, 157, 333.
  37—45, 66, 67, 69, 207.
  38—46, 67, 69, 70, 158, 220, 333.
  39—
  40—73, 235, 236, 240, 244, 332.
  41—76, 77, 156, 158, 333.
  42—77, 79, 170, 171, 207.
  43—81, 159, 213, 214.
  44—72, 81-83, 85.
  45—72, 80, 156, 158, 333.
  46—43, 72, 84, 89, 204, 208.
  47—86, 214.
  48—88, 197, 198, 223.
  49—89.
  50—91, 92, 332.
  51—22, 23, 159.
  52—22, 152, 159, 231.
  53—43, 93, 94, 146, 147, 156, 157, 333.
  54—89, 148, 164, 200, 204, 205, 208.

House Lots—*Concluded:*
  55—148, 201, 204, 207.
  56—95, 96, 98, 206, 214.
  57—44, 96, 97, 209, 214.
  58—8, 99, 156, 333.
  59—100-103, 140, 332.
  60—44, 209, 214.
  61—54, 55, 332.
  62—105-107, 206.
  63—140, 224.
  64—
  65—109, 332.
  66—113, 332.
  67—114, 116, 117, 237.
  68—149, 151, 158, 333.
  69—117-119.
  70—120.
  71—57, 134, 332.
  72—61, 63, 158, 333.
  73—43, 123, 124, 127, 215.
  74—127-129, 165, 166.
  75—13, 89, 130, 197, 223, 332.
  76—133, 134, 332.
  77—209, 210, 214.
  78—130-132.
  79—135-137, 170, 171, 332.
  80—104, 332.
  81—138-140, 224.
  82—141, 143, 159.
  83—54, 55, 141, 143, 144.
  84—38, 39, 89, 143, 144, 223.
  85—43, 89, 204, 208, 332.
  86—43, 89, 204, 208.
  87—44, 123, 125-127, 138, 168, 169, 215, 216, 218, 240.
  88—110-112, 150, 332.
  89—135, 136, 163, 332.
Hubbard, Jonathan, Jr., 24, 165, 187, 188, 190.
Hunt, Samuel, 233.
Hutchens, Benjamin, 3.
Hutchings, Lieut. Phinehas, 191.
Hutchins, Joshua, 13-16, 75, 89, 170, 173, 175, 177; 3, 17, 53, 54, 56, 57, 91, 108, 112, 124, 125, 127, 134, 143, 173, 175, 225.

INDIAN Field, 209.
Islands, 247.

JAQUITH, Jacob, 327.
Jewell, James, 2, 109, 122, 153-155; 93, 135, 165, 178, 180, 187, 203.
Johnson, Asa, 335, 341.
——, Benjamin, 258, 313, 323-340, 342-349, 351-356.
——, Dea. Samuel, 4, 172, 235.
——, Samuel, 253, 256, 273, 283, 284, 290-293, 295-297, 301, 304-306, 308, 311-313.

Index. 371

Johnson, Samuel, 356-359, 361-364.
Jones, Elnathan, 127, 128.
——, Lieut. Josiah, 62, 64.
——, Samuel, 101, 124, 130, 179, 181, 187-190, 204, 217, 234, 235.
——, William, 53, 59, 172.

KAMP, 253.
Kendall, Asa, 32.
——, Jonas, 243, 250, 298.
Kibby, James, Heirs of, 184, 242.
Kilborn, 258, 352.
Kilburn, David, 258-261, 311, 313, 319, 329, 330, 333, 351, 359.
——, William, 346.
Kimball, 253.
——, George, 28, 246, 256, 257.
——, Samuel, 325, 326, 328-331, 333-341, 343, 344, 346-362.
——, Thomas, 26.
Kinsman, Jeremiah, 360.

LANCASTER, see Wheeler, Jonathan.
——, Line, 7, 57, 68, 69, 72, 112, 115, 117, 153, 155, 211, 241.
——, New Grant, 69, 96, 99, 105, 125, 130, 131, 170, 171, 209-211, 240.
——, North River, North Branch of, 126.
Laurence, Esq., 347.
Lawrance, William, 14-16.
Lealand, Caleb, 335, 340, 341, 345, 350.
——, Ebenezer, 335, 340, 341, 345-347, 350, 355.
Lee, Dr. Joseph, 289, 296.
Leominster, 270, 271, 347, 355.
—— Line, 239, 243, 248. See South Line.
—— Road leading to, 241.
Little Pond, 112.
Low, 313.
——, Joseph, 252, 263.

MACFEDRICH, Macfedris, Mackfeddrich, Mackfadrich, Macpheadris, Archibald, 21, 59-61.
MacIntire, 246.
Manoosnock, 12, 59, 162, 216, 229, 262, 267.
Manosnet, see Manoosnock.
Martin, Joshua, Jr., 257, 262, 275-277.
Mashapoag, Mashapooge, see Massapog.
Massapog, 39, 115, 117, 121, 125, 230.

Meadow Lots:
  Beaver Pond, 1, 102.
  Cataconamoug, 1, 39, 198; 2, 39, 198; 3, 201; 5, 6, 202, 345; 6, 345.
  Clay Pit, 1, 83; 2, 80; 3, 79; 4, 20; 6, 12; 7, 12.
  Horsemeat, 2, 9; 3, 142.
  Massapog, 4, 230.
  Mulpus, 1, 38; 5, 66; 11, 217; 14, 47. Lower, 1, 161; 2, 2, 160, 240; 3, 35, 160; 4, 18; 6, 202; 7, 4; 8, 3; 9, 3. Upper, 1, 49; 2, 32; 3, 15, 29, 33; 4, 15, 29; 5, 15, 104; 6, 129; 7, 96, 100; 8, 96, 100, 249; 9, 52.
  Pearl Hill, 1, 236; 3, 1; also 14, 41, 75.
  Perham's, 27, 48.
  Turkey Hill, 1, 232; 2, 232; 3, 94; 4, 232.
Meeting House, 176, 214.
—— —— in Fitchburg, Road leading to, 242, 253.
—— —— Land, 7.
Menoosnock, see Manoosnock.
Mills, 118, 119, 170, 172, 247, 262.
Ministerial Land, 1, 9, 24, 71, 72, 91, 141, 142, 145, 196, 200, 254-256, 277, 293, 312, 313, 345.
Mitchel, Andrew, 108, 231, 258.
——, Moses, 23, 87, 231, 233.
Moffet, Joseph, 87.
——, William, 87.
Monoosnock, Monosnet, Moonosusnock, Moonussnouck, see Manoosnock.
Moor, 247, 253.
——, Jonathan, 166.
Mulpus, 2, 3, 14, 15, 18, 21, 29, 32, 35, 38, 47, 49, 66, 79, 89, 96, 100, 104, 129, 147, 160, 170, 172, 202, 217, 235, 236, 249, 329.

NEESEPEGESUCK Ponds, 38, 89, 140, 141, 329.
Nepesegaset, see Neesepegesuck.
Newbury, see Poor, Jonathan.
Norcross, Jeremiah, 172.
North Range of Lots, 28, 31, 37, 40, 41, 54, 56, 62, 203.
—— Town Line, 3, 11, 14, 27, 30, 35, 42, 48, 50, 75, 97, 99, 106, 128, 131, 134, 140, 141, 155, 156, 161, 206, 214, 221, 224.
Northeast Corner, 11.
Northfield Road, 24, 30, 34, 41, 44, 56, 69, 130, 145, 268, 272, 319-321.

Northwest Corner, 156, 158.
OLIVER, Hon. Andrew, 2, 166, 233, 240, 242.
Orsborn, 253.
PAGE, 40, 79.
——, David, 218.
——, Jonathan, 152, 243.
——, Joseph, 13, 17, 20, 50, 73, 74, 76-78, 235, 236.
——, Nathaniel, 23, 73, 87, 111, 121, 152, 231, 333, 345.
——, Samuel, 18, 22, 23, 39, 93-95, 107, 170, 177, 215, 225, 231, 232.
Park, John, 252.
Parker, Phineas, 17, 18, 308.
Paterson, Joseph, 262.
Patterson, James, 276-278.
——, John, 335.
Paul, Robert, 40.
Pearce, 121, 212.
——, David, 63, 68, 109-112, 120, 124, 152.
——, Dea. Ephraim, 62, 73, 110, 112, 114, 119, 121, 124, 132, 139, 149-151, 178, 219, 224-227, 345, 350; 11, 28, 61, 129, 156-158, 160, 162, 166, 180, 184, 187, 189, 192, 199, 205, 218, 228, 229, 240, 242, 243, 245.
——, see Peirce.
Pearl Hill, 32, 42, 63, 102, 108, 126, 131, 157, 208, 223, 224, 229, 230, 234, 262.
—— —— Brook, 143.
—— —— Meadows, 1, 14, 41, 75, 236.
Peirce, Amos, 343.
——, Ephraim, Jr., 117.
——, Lieut., 343.
——, see Pearce.
Perham's Meadow, 27, 48.
Perley, 247.
Phelps, Samuel, 327.
Platts, Abel, 24.
Pool, Poole, 7, 71, 104, 141, 142, 259.
——, Eleazer Flagg, 16.
——, John, 10, 161, 162, 217.
——, Jonathan, 9, 10, 129,
——, Justice, 158, 161.
——, Capt. Timothy, 10, 161-163, 217, 229, 244.
Poor, Jonathan, 164.
Pratt, David, 253, 259, 262.
Prescott, 37, 41, 55, 81, 103.
——, Justice Benjamin, 158, 159, 215.
——, Rev. Benjamin, 81-85, 129, 135, 168, 203, 215, 217, 218, 220.
——, Maj. Jonathan, 167, 168, 203.
Present Bounds Established, 321.
Probate Court, 278, 280, 282, 286, 290, 296, 306.

Proprietors' Debts, 116, 176.
—— Meetings, 169-196, 261, 364.
—— ——, Attendants to be paid, 294.
Puffer, Jacob, 32.
Punch Brook, 233, 249.
Putnam, Daniel, 252, 263.
——, Esquire, 313.

REDINGTON, Benjamin, 262, 272, 275; 192, 195, 247, 250-253, 256, 258-261, 264, 266, 268, 277-280, 284-286, 293, 295, 299, 300, 304, 305, 307-311, 313, 314, 318, 364.
Rendezvous Lower Meadows, 214.
Richards, John, 108, 255.
Richardson, Ebenezer, 110, 112, 166, 167, 241.
——, Maj. James, 253-260, 262, 264, 272, 274, 276, 311, 312, 314, 323, 335, 341, 350, 355.
——, Thomas, 123.
Rindge, see Walker, Capt. Joshua.
Ritter, 238.
River, 5, 18, 19, 36, 116, 120, 132, 134, 135, 139, 212, 225, 228, 233, 241, 242, 247, 249, 250, 253, 259, 260, 262.
Rollstone Hill, 19, 115, 119, 122, 212, 228, 250, 252, 262, 267.
Roxbury, see Lealand, Ebenezer.
Russell, William, 61.

SALEM, see Brown, Samuel, and Prescott, Rev. Benjamin.
Sanderson, 128.
Sawmill at Mulpus Falls, 170, 172.
——, Capt. Willard's, 118, 149.
School Lot, 108, 109, 196, 256, 277, 293.
Scott, 154.
——, Edward, 247, 261, 262, 272, 275, 296-299, 304, 316, 323, 335, 341, 350, 355.
——, Hugh, 33, 41, 42, 224.
——, John, 59, 60, 62, 170.
Second Divisions:
    1—11.
    2—12, 221.
    3—221.
    4—10.
    5—43.
    6—43.
    7—135.
    8—135.
    9—97, 197, 206.
    10—97.
    11—97, 99, 249.
    14—128.
    15—3.
    16—153.
    18—48.
    20—131.

Index. 373

Second Divisions—*Continued:*
21—131, 132, 234.
22—30, 134.
23—26, 30, 226.
24—26, 30, 106.
25—50, 27, 106.
26—35, 50.
27—35, 50, 161.
28—35, 161.
29—14, 161.
30—41.
31—40, 41, 153.
32—40, 25, 31.
33—62, 31.
34—62, 31.
35—62, 203, 219.
36—56, 203, 235.
37—37, 56, 203.
38—37, 54, 56.
39—37, 54.
40—27, 28.
41—17.
43—221, 236 (see No. 53).
44—82, 221, 235.
46—91.
47—92.
49—60.
50—21, 142, 217.
51—21, 86, 142, 217.
52—86, 142, 217.
53—147, 236 (see No. 43).
54—147.
55—148.
56—74, 148.
57—74, 75.
58—74, 146, 234.
59—8, 146.
60—8, 167.
61—23, 231.
62—23, 231.
63—87.
65—58, 101.
66—58, 101.
67—57, 65.
68—58, 65.
69—63.
70—210, 212.
71—67.
72—5.
73—69.
76—52, 244.
77—45, 160.
78—160.
79—200, 205.
80—1, 38, 80, 200.
81—200, 201, 207.
82—28.
83—138.
84—138.
85—121.
86—111, 149, 150.

Second Divisions—*Concluded:*
87—149.
89—123.
90—115.
93—123.
97—94.
Second Part, The, 197.
Secretary's Land, 34, 242. See Willard, Hon. Josiah.
Sheple, Capt. John, 164, 180. See General Court's Committee.
Shirley, 351, 352, 355.
—— Line, 345. See Groton and Stow.
Smith, Elisha, 104, 137, 158, 159, 240.
——, Reuben, 272.
Snow, William, 243.
South Line, 162-164, 216, 217, 229, 235, 244, 248, 251, 259. See Leominster Line and Lancaster Line.
—— —— Angle of, 229.
Southeast Corner, 71, 72.
Southwest Corner, 85, 129, 164, 165, 180, 217.
Speer, Robert, 24.
Sprage, Ebenezer, 2, 3.
Stearns, Col. Abijah, 192-195.
——, David, 190.
——, Capt. Josiah, 256, 257, 282, 320, 322-349, 351, 352, 356.
Stiles, 76.
——, Jacob, 95-100, 248.
Stow Line, 52, 72.
Stratton, 250.
Strobridge, Capt. William, 165.
Swan, John, 87.

TARBELL, Eleazer, 217.
Tayler, Thomas, 244.
——, Col. William, 146-148, 164, 180, 204, 213. See General Court's Committee.
Taylor, Dr. John, 275.
Thaxter, Col. Samuel, 147, 148, 164, 180, 204. See General Court's Committee.
Thayer, Col., 144.
Third Division laid out, 174, 175.
Thirstin, Richard, 239.
——, see Thurstin.
Thurlo, Capt. William, 251, 262.
Thurstin, Thurstain, 19, 38, 81, 89, 238, 245, 246, 254, 255, 311.
——, Daniel, 44, 91-93, 166.
——, Dea., 261.
Tophet Swamp, 196, 259.
Town of Lunenburg, 312, 313.
Town's Committee, 277, 320.
Towns, Nathan, 51.
Trespasses, 195, 268.

Turkey Hill Meadows, 94, 232.
Tyler, Nathan, 330, 331.

UNACHUALEM, Uncachawalonk, Uncachewalunk, Uncachulem, 210, 248, 262.
Upton, 166, 240.

WAIR, 243.
Waite, David, 26, 37, 137, 163.
Walker, Capt. Joshua, 343.
——, Nathaniel, 181, 182, 184.
Wallis, William, 70, 105-108, 118, 137, 170, 212, 227, 333.
Warren, E., Jr., 350, 351, 362.
——, Jacob, 219.
——, Samuel, 29.
Welch, Jacob, 307, 308.
Wendell, Jacob, Esq., 65.
West Line, 132, 156-160, 165, 199. See Westminster Line.
Westminster Line, 245, 249, 250. See West and South Lines.
Weston, see Jones, Lieut. Josiah.
Wetherbee, 256.
——, Ensign Ephraim, 13-16, 20, 74, 76, 141; 165, 177, 180, 189.
——, Ephraim, 192, 251, 364.
——, Hezekiah, 239.
——, Paul, 192.
Wetherbee's Mills, 262.
Wheeler, Aaron, 327.
—— and Ball, 205, 222, 224, 260.
——, Ebenezer, 138-141, 223, 224, 234. See Wheeler and Ball.
——, George, 86, 150, 202, 343, 350.
——, Jonathan, 3, 28, 128, 129, 165, 234.
——, William, 86, 88.
White, Charles, 192.
——, John, 28, 128, 132, 192, 218.
——, Dea. Josiah, 123, 216, 235, 248.
Whiting, Esek, 359.
Whitney, 102, 262.
——, Abraham, 45, 52.
——, John, 100, 120, 131, 133, 134.
——, Jonathan, 78, 80, 81, 83, 85, 170, 171, 221, 227, 236.
——, Jonathan, Jr., 85.
——, Stephen, 314, 316, 318, 321, 326, 329, 331, 334-340, 343, 344, 346-348, 351, 352, 355.

Whitney, Zachariah, 242, 329.
Whittemore, Benjamin, 164, 181.
——, David, 327.
Wilder, 250.
——, Ebenezer, 178.
——, Joseph, 170, 178.
——, Thomas, 248, 262.
Willard, Col. Aaron, 195, 247-252, 261, 262, 264-273, 275, 278-280, 282, 285-291, 293, 296, 305, 323, 364.
——, Mrs. Aaron, 278.
——, Abraham, 253, 254, 274.
——, Capt., 25, 63, 67, 149.
——, Madam Hannah, 46, 65, 66, 202.
——, Lieut., Ensign, Capt. Jonathan, 22, 25, 39, 43, 93-95, 103, 116, 135-137, 151, 163, 166, 170-172, 174, 189, 190, 204, 213, 232-235; 1-6, 8-10, 12, 13, 15-21, 24-53, 55, 56, 58, 60-74, 77-84, 86-88, 90-95, 97-108, 110-115, 117, 119-121, 123-133, 135-140, 142-175, 177-180, 187, 189, 197-203, 205-214, 216-222, 226-236, 238-241, 246.
——, Capt., Col. Josiah, 28, 31, 32, 34, 37, 42-44, 46, 63, 67, 68, 89, 96, 106, 113, 115, 118, 149, 156, 164, 199, 204-214, 222, 223, 237, 249, 292, 328; 1, 3-10, 12-21, 23, 25-31, 33-47, 49-58, 60, 62-75, 77-86, 88, 91, 92, 96-106, 108, 110-116, 119-152, 154-165, 167-190, 197-203, 205-208, 210-216, 221-225, 227, 228, 234.
——, Hon. Josiah, 44-46, 53, 109, 130, 160, 214, 236. See Secretary's Land.
——, Josiah, 262, 285.
Woburn Farm, 29, 30, 34, 37, 39, 41, 43, 71, 109, 130, 135, 141, 143, 145, 153, 154, 210, 211.
—— ——, Gore of Land by, 109.
Wood, John, 44, 46, 130.
——, Jonathan, 262.
——, Joseph, 160, 236.
Woodman, Capt. Jonathan, 27, 28, 54, 118, 128.
Woods, Nathaniel, 96, 98-100, 124.
Worcester, 329.
Wyman, John, 243.

PLATES.

Presentation, ... frontispiece
Folio 64, first page, ... opp. 123
Page 125 of Second Part, ... opp. 320

www.ingramcontent.com/pod-product-compliance
Lightning Source LLC
Chambersburg PA
CBHW060938230426
43665CB00015B/1986